Lecture Notes of the Inst for Computer Sciences, S and Telecommunications

4

Stephen Hailes   Sabrina Sicari
George Roussos (Eds.)

Sensor Systems and Software

First International ICST Conference, S-CUBE 2009
Pisa, Italy, September 7-9, 2009
Revised Selected Papers

 Springer

Volume Editors

Stephen Hailes
University College London
Department of Computer Science
London, WC1E 6BT, United Kingkom
E-mail: s.hailes@cs.ucl.ac.uk

Sabrina Sicari
University of Insubria
Dipartimento di Informatica e Comunicazione
21100 Varese, Italy
E-mail: sabrina.sicari@uninsubria.it

George Roussos
University of London
School of Computer Science and Information Systems
London WC1E 7HX, United Kingdom
E-mail: g.roussos@bbk.ac.uk

Library of Congress Control Number: 2009942541

CR Subject Classification (1998): C.2, J.3, K.4.2, K.6, C.2.1, C.3

ISSN   1867-8211
ISBN-10   3-642-11527-6 Springer Berlin Heidelberg New York
ISBN-13   978-3-642-11527-1 Springer Berlin Heidelberg New York

springer.com

© ICST Institute for Computer Sciences, Social-Informatics and Telecommunications Engineering 2010
Printed in Germany

Typesetting: Camera-ready by author, data conversion by Scientific Publishing Services, Chennai, India
Printed on acid-free paper   SPIN: 12830282   06/3180   5 4 3 2 1 0

Preface

The First International ICST Conference on Sensor Systems and Software (S-cube 2009) was held during 7–8 September in Pisa, Italy. This new international conference was dedicated to addressing the research challenges facing system development and software support for systems based on wireless sensor networks (WSNs) that have the potential to impact society in many ways. Currently, wireless sensor networks introduce innovative and interesting application scenarios that may support a large amount of different applications including environmental monitoring, disaster prevention, building automation, object tracking, nuclear reactor control, fire detection, agriculture, healthcare, and traffic monitoring. The widespread acceptance of these new services can be improved by the definition of frameworks and architectures that have the potential to radically simplify software development for wireless sensor network-based applications. The aim of these new architectures is to support flexible, scalable programming of applications based on adaptive middleware. As a consequence, WSNs require novel programming paradigms and technologies. Moreover, the design of new complex systems, characterized by the interaction of different and heterogeneous resources, will allow the development of innovative applications that meet high-performance goals. Hence, WSNs require contributions from many fields such as embedded systems, distributed systems, data management, system security and applications. The conference places emphasis on layers well above the traditional MAC and routing and transport layer protocols. The aim of the conference is to create a forum in which researchers from academia and industry, practitioners, business leaders, intellectual property experts and venture capitalists may work together in order to compare and debate different innovative solutions.

The technical program of S-cube 2009 well reflected the current priorities in wireless sensor networks. Several papers addressed modeling and performance evaluation; several contributions were related to support sensor programming paradigms and infrastructure properties, such as middleware architectures and security. In addition, a considerable part of the technical program was devoted to consolidated and emerging application areas for wireless sensor network services, such as e-health applications and home applications.

The conference program started with a keynote speech followed by seven technical sessions distributed over a period of two days. There were around 50 registrants for the conference.

The conference received around 45 submissions from different countries. After a thorough review process, 16 papers were accepted from an open call and 3 distinguished researchers were invited to contribute 3 invited papers. The overall paper acceptance rate is around 35%. The keynote speech titled "From Sensor Networks to the Web of Things" was delivered by Kay Römer from the University of Luebeck, Germany.

The social program included a tour of the city and a social dinner held on the first day of the conference. It provided a good opportunity for networking among the attendees.

S-CUBE 2010 is under organization. In addition to the technical sessions, S-CUBE 2010 is also soliciting tutorials and workshop proposals.

Organization

Steering Committee Chair

Imrich Chlamtac   Create-Net, Italy

Conference General Co-chairs

Sabrina Sicari   Universitá degli studi dell'Insubria, Italy
Stephen Hailes   University College of London, UK

Technical Program Chair

George Roussos   Birkbeck College, University of London, UK

Local Chair

Gianluca Dini   Universitá di Pisa, Italy

Publications Chair

Luca Mottola   Swedish Institute of Computer Science, Sweden

Publicity Co-chairs

Matteo Cesana   Politecnico di Milano, Italy
Houda Labiod   Telecom Paris, France

Web Chair

Pietro Colombo   Universitá degli studi dell'Insubria, Italy

Conference Coordinator

Barbara Török   ICST

Technical Program Committee

Marco Benini   Universitá dell'Insubria, Italy
Jan Beutel   ETH Zurich, Switzerland
Alberto Coen Porisini   Universitá dell'Insubria, Italy
Christine Julien   The University of Texas at Austin, USA

Sponsored by ICST

Technically Co-Sponsored by Create-Net, ACM SIGBED, UKRI IEEE, University of Pisa

Table of Contents

Applying Complex Event Processing and Extending Sensor Web Enablement to a Health Care Sensor Network Architecture

Gavin E. Churcher and Jeff Foley

BT Research Adastral Park,
Martlesham Heath, Ipswich IP5 3RE
{gavin.churcher,jeff.foley}@bt.com

Abstract. The limited reuse of middleware components for wireless sensor networking projects has driven interest in emerging standards from the Sensor Web Enablement Working Group which offers methods to virtualize sensor data into a common, self-describing format, using access mechanisms based on HTTP. Using these standards, applications are able to discover and access different sensor offerings, automatically understand the data format used and even specify conditions in the sensor data. This paper examines how an existing sensor network platform in the health care domain can make use of these standards and examines the possibility of extending the Sensor Alert Service with a richer set of functions. Concepts taken from Complex Event Processing engines are explored in the context of this particular health care platform, where it is shown that there are clear advantages to extending the standard.

Keywords: Complex Event Processing, Health Care, Sensor Web Enablement.

1 Introduction

The Sensor Network Group in BT Research has had a long interest in wireless sensor networking based projects and has participated in a number of collaborations covering a wide range of domains from health care and assisted living through to environmental monitoring, and traffic management. Typically, these projects have required bespoke solutions where middleware reuse has been minimal. Our interest in emerging standards to address this issue has led us to investigate the use of Sensor Web Enablement (SWE) from the Open Geospatial Consortium (OGC) [1] as a possible approach for the virtualization of sensors. This would form part of our strategy for building a more generic sensor network architecture with components that could be reused in a diverse range of sensor network projects. We feel that the use of standardized middleware will help drive the acceptance of sensor network solutions as we move away from costly, bespoke solutions; a problem particularly relevant to our approach given the broad range of application areas.

We have investigated the SWE standards for the Sensor Observation Service (SOS) [2] and Sensor Alert Service (SAS) and how they may be applied to one of our existing sensor network projects, SAPHE (Smart and Aware Pervasive Healthcare Environment) [3]. SAPHE is one of a number of growing industrial and academic

S. Hailes, S. Sicari, and G. Roussos (Eds.): S-Cube 2009, LNICST 24, pp. 1–10, 2009.

wireless sensor network projects in the health care domain. The most notable being Intel IrisNet [4], Hitachi Collectlo [5], and A Remote Health Care System Based on Wireless Sensor Networks [6].

This paper reviews the previously published findings where we applied SWE to SAPHE [7] and highlights the possibilities of extending the SAS service with more advanced filtering mechanisms, such as those found in Complex Event Processing (CEP). An example CEP engine, Esper [9] was investigated with the view that the application of CEP to the SAS service may result in a number of benefits to sensor network architectures and to SAPHE in particular. CEP is particularly relevant to SAS as it offers the ability to aggregate and correlate large volumes of events through the real-time processing of continuous queries. It is possible to apply pattern matching to asynchronous events through the use of logical and temporal event correlation, and defined 'window' views of the event streams. Current standards for defining which events are relevant to an application using SAS are severely limited to a simple definition of a property of a single event. It is not possible to correlate multiple events, a capability that has the potential to reduce bandwidth and processing overheads of edge network applications.

2 Sensor Web Enablement

The concept of Sensor Webs was coined in the 1990's: millions of connected on-line sensors monitoring the physical world, the sensor capabilities being described using metadata so they can be published and understood by anyone with web access and appropriate authentication. This model is similar in concept to the World Wide Web where a standard web browser can access this vast information space due to the adoption of key standards such as HTTP, HTML and XML. In 2001, a data modeling language for sensors, SensorML [10], was introduced into the OGC which led to the SWE working group. The group was tasked to produce a framework of open standards for Web connected sensors and all types of sensor systems. The SWE standards draw from a number of existing OGC standards from SensorML to Observations & Measurements [11] and propose a number of services that use the HTTP protocol for access. The services are able to self-describe the data they represent and the access mechanisms they provide.

Version 1.0 of the Sensor Observation Service (SOS) was published as an OGC OpenGIS Implementation Standard in October 2007 [2]. Of particular interest to SAPHE are the proposed standards for SOS and SAS. Together they provide the ability to store data that can be accessed and queried by an external application and to detect simple conditions that can then generate an alert, published to the external network and various application subscribers.

The role of the SOS is to translate incoming sensor data into a data model that represents the sensor and the data as a series of observations of a particular feature of interest. This translated representation is then archived until an external client makes a request for data, providing a number of parameters that act as filters. The parameters for the SOS include the ability to specify a time constraint, for example, between two time periods, or after a time point, and the identification of the particular sensor cluster. In the case of multiple sets of data from a sensor cluster, the observed property (phenomenon) can be specified along with the features of interest. Once the request for data has been made, the application client receives a set of Observations and Measurements which encapsulate the sensor data in the data model. Sensor data can also be streamed into an SAS where a similar transformation occurs. An external application is able to specify conditions for data as it arrives at the SAS. When the data meets those conditions an event is sent to the application using the publisher/subscriber methodology. The conditions that can be applied in the current proposal for the SAS are limited to specifying whether a sensor data value is less than (or equal to), greater than (or equal to), equal to, not equal to a value, or between two values. For example, an application could specify that an alert should be sent when a PIR sensor detects movement, or when a temperature sensor reports a value over 40°C which could be critical for certain medicines.

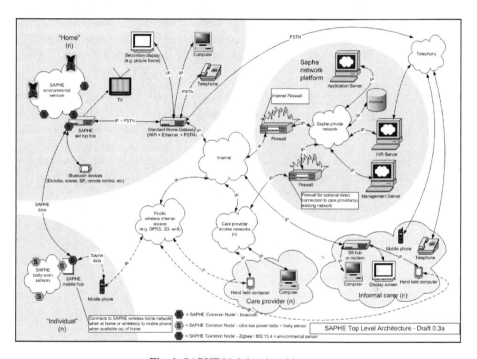

Fig. 1. SAPHE high level architecture

3 Key Challenges in SAPHE

SAPHE is a collaborative research project co-funded by the UK's Technology Strategy Board, involving Imperial College, BT, Philips UK, University of Dundee, Cardionetics and Docobo. It aims to develop a holistic monitoring solution to support the care and self-care of people with long-term health conditions with the placement of a number of sensors around the home and on the patient that monitor both the immediate environment in the home along with physiological traits. SAPHE targets patients who typically receive a specialist service provided by community matrons and multidisciplinary teams. The desire is to support these users, providing a new tool for professional care, encouraging greater patient self-care and to monitor the patient in order to detect early indications that a patient's wellbeing is changing and preventative care is required. Independent monitoring of the patient and their environment can lead to early detection of worsening conditions that may either not be reported by the patient nor detected by the health care professional and help prevent escalation of a patient's conditions and their ability for self-care. For example, changes in sleeping patterns, mobility around and outside of the home, and eating habits can be early indicators of a worsening of a patient's condition.

The present SAPHE system architecture is shown in Fig. 1. Within the home environment there are a number of sensors that use either ZigBee or Bluetooth to communicate to the SAPHE set-top box which has the task of managing the communication from the sensors and reformatting the sensor data into a common format based on BinX [12]. The canonized data is then sent securely to the SAPHE network platform via the Internet, using the BT Home Hub as a gateway. Within this network the data is analyzed for significant events and other factors that can lead to an assessment of the patient's wellbeing. This information is then sent on to health care professionals. For example, patient data is visualized in real-time on the secure SAPHE health care monitoring portal as a series of histograms or line graphs using Dundas Chart, which the authors helped to develop and is shown in Fig. 2.

The patient also wears a number of sensors in the form of a single device worn on the ear. This device reports back blood oxygen levels, heart rate and an activity index derived from a 3D accelerometer when within range of the set-top box within the home. When outside the home environment, the patient wears a mobile device that stores the body-worn sensor data until it is in range of the set-top box at which point it uploads all cached data. The mobile device is also able to communicate directly with the SAPHE network platform in the case of an emergency via a Bluetooth connection to the patient's mobile phone and GPRS connection.

The SAPHE environmental and physiological sensors and the observations they report are listed in Table 1, below.

Table 1. SAPHE Sensors

Sensor	Reports	Comms	Message Frequency
PIR room sensors	Detection of movement within range of sensor	ZigBee	Up to 10,000 per 24h period
Entry/exit door sensors	door open/close event	ZigBee	Varies according to patient
Fridge door sensor	door open/close event	ZigBee	Varies according to patient
Activity sensor	activity index, SpO2 and bpm	Proprietary low-power radio	Aggregate 1 per second
Weighing scales	weight when used	Bluetooth	2 per day
Blood pressure monitor	blood pressure when used	Bluetooth	2 per day
Bed sensor	number of bed exits, first time in bed, last time out of bed	Bluetooth	Every 30 seconds

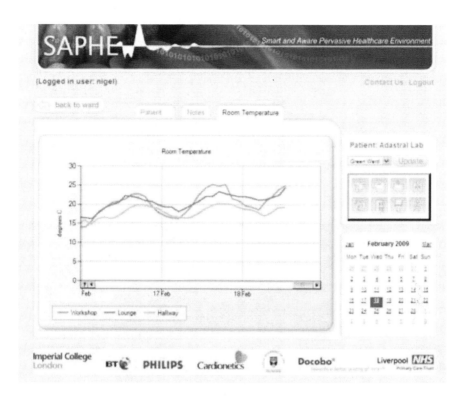

Fig. 2. SAPHE monitoring portal showing room temperature sensor data

4   Lessons Learned

In the current proposed SAPHE architecture, all sensor data from each patient and home environment is sent to the external, back-end servers in the SAPHE platform network which archive and check for patterns and trends in the data that are indicators of deteriorating health in the patient. The frequency of sensor communication and the overhead of BinX sent externally would indicate large volumes of bandwidth usage growing as the patient user base expands.

Creating SWE services offers a number of generic advantages and some specific to this type of application where local processing could prove advantageous. SWE offers a standardized protocol for discovering and accessing sensor data which enables data to be reused in potentially new and novel ways. An application could simply repurpose sensor data for another domain, or fuse together data from several services to provide radically different applications. Standardizing on the access mechanism and the data model for the sensor data conveys advantages to the application developers as there are a growing number of 3rd party tools that facilitate access, analysis and visualization of data, reducing the time to develop new applications and facilitating innovation [13].

SWE services can exist anywhere in the architecture between the sensors and the applications that utilize their data. Specific to SAPHE and similar sensor network architectures, placing the SWE services at the local level could reduce real-time bandwidth requirements. An SOS archives sensor data in a common data format allowing applications to query and retrieve data as appropriate. An SAS would be able to offer basic analysis of sensor data, publishing an alert or data fragment to subscribing applications. An application could then use the SOS to access relevant data when appropriate rather than receiving data in real-time for analysis.

The architecture and protocols were already established for the SAPHE system, making use of proprietary data formats and protocols. The SWE services were created in parallel to the existing framework, an approach not untypical for sensor network platforms where such services can readily be developed as an adjunct to an existing platform; in effect, applications can be retro-fitted to provide SWE services. Our previous research [7] shows how an SOS service could be retro-fitted to the existing framework. The exercise was a valuable one and clearly showed that there was quite a high overhead in creating a standards-based service. The cost in doing so would hopefully, with time, be mitigated through the reuse of that service by new applications, although it remains to be seen whether the cost would be simply too high for closed solutions.

The process of creating an SOS service began with the definition of the data models that represented the sensor data in terms of 'observations' of 'features of interest' that were presented in the form of 'offerings'. There were two initial types of offering: sensor data from the ambient sensors around the house, and body-worn physiological sensor data, neatly mapping on to two features of interest being the house and the patient. Sensors and sensor clusters are known as 'procedures' under SWE terminology. A simple example of how the data model would look for a set of single sensor observations follows:

Table 2. SAPHE Data Model

Offering:	Physiological observations
Feature of Interest:	Patient
Phenomenon:	Heart rate
Procedure:	Cardionetics ECG Sensor
Unit:	Beats per minute

The process of creating an SAS overlaps with that of creating the SOS since the definition of the data models and the transformation from raw sensor data to these models is the same. The SWE standards do not stipulate how the services should be implemented and so an SOS and SAS can exist on the same extended platform, receiving the same sensor data and even sharing the data transformation overhead. The SAS provides a service where an external application can specify the sensor data conditions which would lead to an alert being generated and published to that subscribing application. The contents of that alert could be simple message or actual sensor data. In this discussion we consider the arrival of sensor data at a service to be an event.

The role of an SAS as defined in the current proposed specification would be of limited benefit to the SAPHE platform because of the narrow range of conditions that can be tested for in the filter schema. The SAPHE system relies on the detection of patterns in the sensor data often over differing periods of time. One main limitation of the current filter specification is the inability to aggregate sensor readings over time. The data collected from both body-worn and ambient house sensors provide a rich picture of a patient's activity and wellbeing. The notion of wellbeing depends on the context of the individual and their own patterns of behaviour. Detecting deviation from the norm in certain behaviours, for example increased activity in the night indicative of a deteriorating sleep pattern or a drop in consumption of food and water, requires specialist applications that perform statistical analysis on large volumes of data.

An SAS functioning at the local level could still be of benefit to SAPHE if it could be extended to handle more sophisticated conditions on the sensor data. The ability to examine sensor data for patterns of behaviour and create appropriate abstract events that can be published to applications could lead to the advantages of SWE being realized in SAPHE and reduce the bandwidth needed for real-time communication of sensor data to applications.

Complex Event Processing (CEP) is an event processing concept that takes asynchronous, real-time, high-volume data event streams and provides a mechanism for application developers to specify correlations, aggregations and other forms of event pattern matching. The approach taken by CEP turns the traditional, database-led approach of application development upside-down. Rather than an application repeatedly compiling a query, submitting it to a database and waiting for a result, applications using CEP submit a query once. This is compiled by the engine and as data events arrive they are passed through this query. When conditions are met, the resulting data is published to the subscribing application. CEP provides a publish/subscribe view of event streams that supports complex analysis of the data stream and negates the need for an application to repeatedly poll a database.

Typically an application registers one or more queries that are similar in style to SQL but have been extended to support the correlation and pattern matching of asynchronous events. Pattern matching for instance, supports the occurrence of sequences of events meeting certain criteria, and even detect the non-occurrence of events. The versatility of CEP to specify correlations and analysis of data streams, makes it potentially a very useful component to use in the analysis of sensor data and applicable to a wide range of wireless sensor networking applications.

From the small number of CEP engines available we chose Esper [9], a Java and .NET based framework because of its extensive documentation, online community support and open source licensing. Esper supports many of the critical functions needed by CEP applications that require low-latency analysis of real-time data. Esper supports the following key methods of analysis in CEP:

- windows on events: sliding windows (time, length, sorted, time-ordered); tumbling windows (time, length, multi-policy, first-event)
- grouping, aggregation, sorting, filtering and merging of event streams
- output rate limiting and stabilizing
- access to a wide range of data formats using a standardized interface language
- logical and temporal event correlation

One of the basic, yet powerful ways of using a CEP engine is to define a pattern. These examples are taken from [9] and use the EPL language to define rules. Programmatic handlers can detect when a pattern has a match and report back to the CEP container/application. The following is an example of a time-based pattern where after event 'A' arrives it will wait 10 seconds before reporting:

```
A -> timer:interval(10 seconds)
```

More sophisticated patterns using sequences and time windows can be easily expressed, for example the following detects event 'A' followed by event 'B'. Once 'B' is found then reset the pattern:

```
every ( A -> B )
```

Patterns can be combined with SQL-style SELECT statements to create increasingly sophisticated rules, for example the following taken from [9] will look for the occurrence of three temperature sensor events that report a temperature of more than 50 degrees within 90 seconds of the first event, with no events reporting a reading below that threshold. This pattern is inserted into another internal stream upon which other rules can be based. Chaining of rules can lead to sophisticated pattern matching.

```
insert into TemperatureWarning
select * from pattern
[every sample=Sample(temp > 50) ->
((Sample(sensor=sample.sensor, temp > 50) and not Sam-
ple(sensor=sample.sensor, temp <= 50))
->
(Sample(sensor=sample.sensor, temp > 50) and not Sam-
ple(sensor=sample.sensor, temp <= 50))
) where timer:within(90 seconds))]
```

There are a number of design patterns for applications that analyze asynchronous, real-time, high-volume event streams.

Within SAPHE there is the need for applications to abstract away from the raw sensor data and look for patterns which could indicate certain events have occurred. These events could then form the basis for further statistical analysis, contributing to a broad picture of a patient's wellbeing and the detection of early symptoms of a deteriorating situation. One factor of a patient's wellbeing relates to how sociable the patient is, for example, how often they leave their house, or whether they have visitors on a regular basis. A good example of this is automatically detecting when there is more than one person in the patient's house which can then form the basis for more sophisticated analysis. The PIR sensors in each room send data whenever movement is detected, potentially up to 10,000 events per 24 hour period per sensor. Providing the logic to look for meaningful events such as multiple occupancy or an empty house from this at a local level would negate the need to transmit the raw sensor data to the back-end applications. The logic to detect multiple occupancy could be represented as follows:

if a PIR sensor (PIR_A) reports movement and a different PIR sensor (PIR_B) reports movement within 5 seconds of the first, then report multiple occupancy

This simple example can be extended much further where sensors in non-adjacent rooms are triggered within a specified time-frame, or combined with other sensors such as the bed activity sensor and the front-door. The ability to specify a window of time from which to look for patterns in the data is essential to detect these higher-level, application specific events. CEP is adeptly suited to detect these types of events from the real-time data. CEP engines such as Esper also provide statistical analysis of patterns of events.

An SAS based on the current proposed standard could readily be implemented using a CEP engine, however it would be unable to take advantage of the level of sophistication possible in CEP, particularly the ability to analyze across a number of sensor data readings. The SAPHE platform needs to perform high-level correlations and analysis of sensor data in order to calculate critical factors for a patient. Some of this correlation and analysis could be performed 'in-network' using CEP as opposed to at the 'edge'. Exposing the rich functionality of a CEP engine through an SAS would convey the advantages of both – expressiveness in pattern matching alongside access to data and its derivatives through a standard protocol. The ability to process this data in-network also has a tangible benefit to the network bandwidth and processing overhead of the edge SAPHE applications. As the application domain scales up the number of sensors and patients, placing processing close to the data source will lead to lower overheads and a more rapid response from a system that is critical to the welfare of its patients.

5 Conclusions and Future Work

This paper has reviewed how Sensor Web Enablement services can be retro-fitted to an existing sensor network platform and has highlighted what the potential benefits are in doing so. SWE enables sensor data to be virtualized, providing a common, self-describing data format and access protocol. The number of domain-agnostic toolkits becoming available indicates that the rather large overhead in creating new applications based on accessing these services can be mitigated by the re-use of data, the use of third-party analysis engines and the reductions in bandwidth and processing overhead to edge applications. The ability to access a diverse range of real-time data has the potential to lead to exciting and radically different applications including health care.

Considering the range and growing number of sensors monitoring each patient and his or her environment, there is a recognized need to optimize the processing of sensor data in order to make informed inferences on the well-being of each patient. Support for data fusion using components from the SWE framework (e.g. SAS) extended through concepts such as CEP may prove to be a valid approach to meeting this growing volume and complexity of data whilst providing a standard method for accessing this data.

Technologies such as Complex Event Processing are designed to process high-volumes of sensor data with minimal latency. They provide a potential solution to the growing world of sensor data that is becoming available. Our experiences with Esper highlights that CEP is ideal for this critical and dynamic environment in contrast to a traditional database approach, where real-time processing of large volumes of data is critical. With respect to the SAPHE project, we have shown that in this and previous research, it is possible to retrofit existing wireless sensor network projects with SWE services.

Recent events have seen the publication of two OGC discussion papers proposing the adoption of Event Pattern Markup Language (EML) [14] and OpenGIS Sensor Event Service Interface Specification [15] for SWE services and in particular SAS. These approaches continue the discussion on the need for a more flexible and extensible method of defining which events and sequences of events are of interest to edge applications. The exercise of applying SWE to SAPHE has added to that discussion and the potential benefits of using a CEP-style aggregation/correlation engine made clear.

Acknowledgements

This research was supported by British Telecommunications Plc., University College London and the EPSRC. Our thanks to J. Echterhoff (iGSI) for SAS developments, T. Mizutani (BT) for SAPHE sensor capabilities, and Dr. Yang (UCL) for suggested revisions.

References

1. Botts, M., Percivall, G., Reed, C., Davidson, J.: OGC Sensor Web Enablement: Overview and High Level Architecture. OGC Inc. 06-050r2 (2006)
2. Na, A., Priest, M.: Sensor Observation Service. OGC Inc. 06-009r6 (2007)
3. Barnes, N., Mizutani, T., et al.: SAPHE Architecture Overview (2008), http://ubimon.doc.ic.ac.uk/saphe/m338.html
4. Gibbons, P.B., Carp, B., Ke, Y., Nath, S., Seshan, S.: IrisNet: An Architecture for a Worldwide Sensor Web. In: Pervasive Computing. IEEE, Los Alamitos (2003)
5. Ando, N.: Sensor Information Web Service for Healthcare Management at Home Powered by Collectlo. Hitachi (2008)
6. Zhang, P., Chen, M.: A Remote Health Care System Based on Wireless Sensor Networks. IEEE Xplore (2008)
7. Churcher, G., Foley, J., Bilchev, G., et al.: Experiences Applying Sensor Web Enablement to a Practical Telecare Application. In: ISWPC, Greece (2008)
8. Foley, J., Churcher, G.: Recent Developments in the Design of Sensor Network Architectures. In: 2nd European Conference on Smart Sensing and Context, England (2007)
9. EsperTech: Esper Reference Documentation, Version 2.2.0, http://esper.codehaus.org/
10. Botts, M.: Sensor Model Language for In-situ and Remote Sensors. OGC Inc. 02-026r4 (2002)
11. Cox, S.: Observations and Measurements. OGC Inc. 05-087r4 (2006)
12. Binary XML Description Language, http://www.edikt.org/binx
13. 52North OX-Framework, http://52north.org/
14. Everding, T., Echterhoff, J.: Event Pattern Markup Language 08-132 (2008)
15. Echterhoff, J., Everding, T.: OpenGIS Sensor Event Service Interface Specification 08-133 (2008)

Turn-Based Gesture Interaction in Mobile Devices

Sanna Kallio[1], Panu Korpipää[1], Jukka Linjama[2], and Juha Kela[1]

[1] Finwe Ltd, Elektroniikkatie 8, 90570 Oulu, Finland
[2] Senseg, Valimotie 27, 00380 Helsinki, Finland
{sanna.kallio,juha.kela,panu.korpipaa}@finwe.fi,
jukka.linjama@senseg.com

Abstract. When properly designed, gesture interaction can bring usability benefits to mobile device users. This article introduces a new accelerometer-enabled method of mobile device gesture control, namely the turn-based interaction. Turning is a commonly understood concept in interaction with tangible objects. Applied in mobile devices as an abstracted virtual key command, it extends the variety of potentially useful gesture control use cases. This article compactly explains the essential factors of designing a successful sensor-enabled gesture interface for mobile devices. In the light of these design factors, two example use cases of turn-based interaction with a prototype are presented. The reliability of recognizing a turn gesture is verified quantitatively to confirm that the introduced method is technically feasible.

Keywords: Gesture interface, acceleration sensors, turn, gesture interaction, haptic interaction, feedback.

1 Introduction

Advances in the research of sensor technologies in the last decade have led to their deployment in variety of application domains. As mobile devices are used in a diverse and dynamic context, development of new sensor-enabled applications and, especially, interaction methods has lately been a subject of great interest. As a result, the mobile computing community has recently witnessed large-scale deployment of smartphones applying sensor-enabled gesture control as a complementary user interaction modality [1].

1.1 Gesture Input

Generally, movement-based interaction can bring several advantages to the user of a mobile device in use cases where traditional modalities are insufficient [2], [3], [4]. Gesture control is eyes-free, button-free, and silent. The user is not required to see the keyboard or display to interact. The modality is "keypad lock"-free, which is a specifically beneficial property in mobile phones. The user does not have to look at the phone, open the keypad lock, and press buttons to navigate and perform a control action. Moreover, gestures can be performed while wearing gloves.

S. Hailes, S. Sicari, and G. Roussos (Eds.): S-Cube 2009, LNICST 24, pp. 11–19, 2009.

Traditionally, many gesture recognition systems have been based on visual recognition. Although more and more mobile phones are equipped with camera, this approach has limited potential in mobile context. Another emerging approach is to use position and/or acceleration sensors embedded into mobile devices themselves. Acceleration sensors indicate the motion of the device in one to three dimensions. Thus, user can move the device and perform some controls by gestures [5]. Acceleration sensors measure both dynamic and static acceleration and can thus also be used to implement, e.g., tilt control.

1.2 Related Work

Common examples of small to medium-scale types of gestures, captured using acceleration sensors, include shaking the device [6], and swinging it from side to side [7]. However, both of these interaction methods can be considered quite noticeable to other people, regardless of scale. Tapping control, in turn, stands for a minimalist extreme in hand gestures for interacting with mobile devices [8], [9]. Simple accelerometer-based tilting and orientation controls have been discussed in the literature in many studies over the years [10], but also more recently, e.g. combining tilting with vibrotactile feedback [11], and switching between landscape and portrait display orientations [12], a use case that has gained a lot of commercial popularity lately. Tilting and orientation are unobtrusive, and very simple to implement movement-based interaction types applicable to well-selected use cases in mobile computing. Tilting combined with a set of free form gesture commands can also be used to control external entities such as a 3D design studio [4]. However, as far as is known, the literature to date has not addressed simple turning movement as a separate type of method for gesture interaction.

1.3 Aims

This study addresses the relevant factors in designing successful sensor-enabled gesture input and, on this basis, introduces new gesture interaction modality, namely, turn-based interaction. The most important design factors are the user effort in performing gestures, reliability of recognition, clarity of function, social acceptability [8], feedback during interaction, multimodality, and well-selected use cases that match the metaphors behind the interaction. Based on the addressed design factors, turn-based interaction is introduced and two use cases are presented. Method for detecting turn-gestures using acceleration sensor is contemplated and discussed in the light of experience. The emphasis is on the user-friendly timing of acceleration sequence as well as on the feedback design. To validate that the gesture detection method is feasible in practice, the reliability of the method is quantitatively evaluated based on collected user data. Finally, a video demonstration is given to illustrate the application of turn gestures with example use cases [13].

2   Guidelines of Gesture Interaction Design

Complementary to the commonly applied usability criteria [14], gesture interaction has specific characteristics that affect the flavor of design parameters. Experience of movement-based interaction design has indicated that at least the following guidelines need to be considered in order to reach a properly balanced outcome.

1. User effort: the user task should become more effortless to perform than before, and the user experience should improve.
2. Multimodality: the gesture should be provided in addition to the traditional modality, if any, to perform the same task.
3. Reliability: it should not be possible to perform the gesture command by accident when not intending to do it, and when intending to perform the gesture, it should be consistently recognized correctly.
4. Feedback: it should be clearly, but not too obtrusively, indicated to the user whether the gesture was performed successfully.
5. Clarity of function: if there are multiple different gestures available in a device, their function should be clearly distinguishable from each other and clearly communicated to the user (e.g. by providing different feedback content).
6. Social acceptability: gestures should be as unnoticeable as possible, i.e. small in spatial scale [3].
7. Use case: the use of the new modality for a selected task should bring benefit to the user in terms of usability or joy of use.

3 Turn-Based Interaction

Turning an object is a commonly understood concept in interaction with tangible objects and is familiar to most people. The main contribution of this paper is in describing and evaluating a type of mobile device gesture interaction that is based on turning the device with regard to gravity.

Turn-based interaction is different from the common tilting and orientation-based interaction described in the literature [10], [11], [12]. The main difference is that an abstracted turn gesture is applied as a single discrete command instead of controlling an application with events from tilt angles or related orientation states. A single abstracted turn gesture command consists of a sequence of turn movements and orientations. It is important to handle a turn-based gesture as a single abstracted entity since this facilitates using turn gestures in a mobile device as virtual key-press commands that can be easily connected to perform various actions, in addition to the existing input methods. Moreover, as a separate abstraction, turn gestures can potentially be applied together with, and additionally to, other types of gestures. Table 1 presents a categorization of mobile device movement interaction types to clarify the main differences of the methods.

The suitability of movement interaction to a selected use case strongly depends on the type of gesture applied. Increased variety in the types of available common gestures enables mobile device usage to benefit from the new modality potentially more widely than before.

As a type of gesture, compared to the others in Table 1, turning has the primary advantage of being very effortless for a user to perform. It does not require accurate aimed motion from the user, nor excess concentration and attention focus. From a technical perspective, turn gestures can be recognized with a low event-based sampling rate, thus facilitating low power operation, which is essential in mobile devices containing limited battery resources.

Table 1. Categorization of movement interaction types applied in mobile devices

Gesture type	Control type	Movement characteristics	Movement scale
Tilting	Stream of angles	Aimed angle	Small
Orientation	Discrete state	Keep/change state	Small
Free-form trainable	Discrete event	Match form	Small to large
Tapping / knocking	Discrete event	Aimed event	Tiny
Shaking / Swinging	Stream or discrete	Coarse match form	Medium to large
Turning	Discrete event	Coarse match form	Small

4 Turn Gestures with Example Use Cases

Following the addressed design guidelines, two use cases were selected to demonstrate the use of the interaction method. Two gestures that utilize a turning movement of the device are applied for the selected tasks. Turn gestures function as virtual keys, which are named *TurnDown* and *DoubleTurn*, Figures 1 and 2 respectively. Virtual keys can be connected to any action in the mobile device, similarly to tapping commands in the Nokia 5500 phone [1]. Use cases 1 and 2 illustrate the use of turn gestures to control two different common tasks of a mobile phone user.

4.1 Use Case 1

In use case 1, *TurnDown* is applied to mute the ringing of the phone. The procedure of the scenario for *TurnDown* in Figure 1 is the following:

1. The phone is "ringing".
2. The user turns the phone display up, then display down and holds it still - sound and vibra feedback notify the recognized *TurnDown* gesture.
3. Ringing tone is muted.

 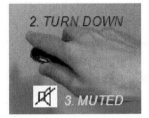

Fig. 1. Use case 1: *TurnDown* gesture use. Turn the phone display down to mute ringing.

4.2 Use Case 2

In use case 2, *DoubleTurn* is used to switch the screen lights on. The procedure of the scenario for *DoubleTurn* in Figure 2 is the following:

1. The user starts the gesture from display up and then turns the display down.
2. The user turns the display back up - sound and vibra feedback notify recognized *DoubleTurn* gesture.
3. Device wakes up and turns the display light on.

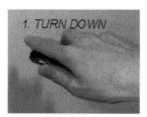 

Fig. 2. Use case 2: DoubleTurn gesture use. Turn the phone display down and then up to switch the screen light on.

5 Input Methods

Two specific turn gestures, *TurnDown* and *DoubleTurn*, are used for controlling the device. The turn gestures are detected using accelerometer built inside the mobile device (STMicroelectronics, type LIS302DL) and Nokia sensor API is utilized to get data from the embedded sensors.

The algorithm designed is simply based on applying a threshold to the acceleration value within a time interval window. Performance optimization and tuning is done case-by-case. Basically, the *TurnDown* is a simple common movement pattern that could easily occur also in other than intended situations. However, in this case, the gesture detection needs to be active only when the phone is ringing. Binding the gesture to the controlled situation restricts misrecognitions. As a result, observing a single threshold crossing within a certain time interval window provides a reliable recognition in the use case 1.

In the use case 2, the detection must always be active. This increases the likelihood of false positives resulting from other daily user activities similar to the *DoubleTurn* gesture pattern. To develop, improve and optimize *DoubleTurn* algorithm, an extensive dataset was collected and analyzed.

6 Algorithm Optimization and Evaluation

The importance of reliability depends on a use case. When a gesture is used for a function that should never occur by accident, e.g. opening a keypad lock or calling, the corresponding gesture detection must have very high reliability. In practice, this is such a demanding requirement that these kinds of critical actions should not be selected to be controlled with gestures at all.

In the example use cases, false positives are not critical. In the use case 1, detecting the *TurnDown* gesture is only active while the phone is ringing. This narrows the application scope so that misrecognitions are only inconvenient. In the use case 2, the possible misrecognitions wake up the phone and turn the screen light on, which is inconvenient at most. However, should there be too frequent false positives, the battery consumption increases and the unintentional display light activations may become unwanted. More importantly, the gesture should be detected correctly when the user, any user, does intend to perform it (true positive), even if the user is simultaneously performing another movement activity, such as walking.

6.1 Data Collection

To address the reliability, user data was collected by logging the acceleration stream with phone logger application. The collected data was analyzed and the results were used to optimize and confirm the reliability of *DoubleTurn*. Turn gesture data was collected from 10 users, 6 female and 4 male. The gestures were performed while standing still and walking. The dataset contained 200 gesture repetitions in total. To analyze the occurrence of false positives, data containing movement activities (walking, climbing stairs, jogging, roller-skating) was collected from 8 users, in total 96 minutes. Figure 3 presents samples of 3-axis turn gesture data.

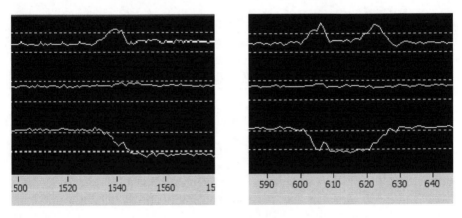

Fig. 3. An example of a *TurnDown* (left) and *DoubleTurn* (right) acceleration (X,Y,Z) signal trace performed in a stationary situation, applied to recognize the gestures

6.2 Algorithm Optimization

To minimize false positives during activity and eliminate the impact of user variation to *DoubleTurn* gesture, the algorithm was optimized based on the collected dataset. Firstly, to capture the variation on how users tend to perform the *DoubleTurn* gesture, the timing profile of the gesture was calculated from the dataset. Timing information was used to analyze how fast people generally perform the turn gestures. The recognition algorithm was then optimized accordingly so that the gesture is recognized independent of the user. Secondly, the acceleration data from activity dataset was carefully analyzed so that the type of the movements causing false positives could be identified. To further examine and validate the algorithm against these false positives, a new data set consisting of false positive data was collected. Finally, an additional maximum threshold limit was implemented to decrease the false positives during activities.

6.3 Recognition Results

Table 2 shows recognition results for basic dataset consisting of *DoubleTurn* gestures performed while standing still and walking. When standing still, a user-independent recognition accuracy is 100% and when walking and performing the *DoubleTurn* gesture concurrently, the recognition accuracy is 96%. The total recognition accuracy is 98%. The occurrence of false positives was calculated from the activity dataset. During 96 minutes, only 8 false positive occurred. Most of the false positives occurred during jogging and roller-skating.

Table 2. Recognition accuracy of *DoubleTurn* gesture

Situation of performing *DoubleTurn*	User-independent average true positive %
Standing still	100
Walking	96
Total	98

7 Feedback Design

In gesture interaction it is important to deliver information on the result of the performed control action to the user; otherwise, the user does not know whether the gesture was detected and may repeat it. Because the gestures are captured by acceleration sensor, they can also be performed eyes-free. As a concequence, a visual feedback may not be the best option.

The interaction feedback in the example use cases was designed to examine whether multiple feedback elements add value to the interaction. In addition to the feedback from the phone function performed as a result of a successful gesture, tactile (vibration) and sound feedback was applied to enforce the message.

The aim in the feedback indicator content design was minimalism. Subtle short vibration pulses were applied with rhythm as a parameter. The key benefit with this approach is that with proper content design, the same rhythm can be rendered with multiple modalities (touch, hearing, vision). Thus, in different contexts, when one particular modality is not available, the intended feedback metaphor can still be perceived.

8 Discussion

The results of the experiences are qualitatively discussed in this section. A formal usability study is beyond the scope of this study. Thus, for factors other than reliability, the discussion is based on the experiences gathered informally from the development team during the interaction design process, and on the prior experience of the authors.

8.1 Use Cases

Gestures can only be used for a restricted set of carefully selected control tasks, and the type of gesture should be selected to fit and benefit the task. Failure in matching the gesture type and the target task will lead to user confusion and disturbance, at the least. The selected example use cases demonstrated how turn gestures benefit the user by relieving the attention focus through button-free interaction. Multimodal operation allows using the gestures alternatively to the traditional way of performing the tasks.

8.2 Reliability

The reliability evaluation confirmed that the *DoubleTurn* gesture can be recognized user independently with a high accuracy, even when the user is on the move. False positives occurred infrequently enough, having an insignificant effect on power consumption and on the user experience.

8.3 Feedback Indicators

During the feedback development process, four users experimented with vibration pulses in various phases of interaction. The sound pulses were then added, experimenting with different pitch and character. An essential goal of the feedback content design was that it is not disturbing, but still clearly noticeable. To help the user distinguish the two gestures, a different number and rhythm of feedback pulses was provided for each gesture.

It was found that when sound and vibration are in synchrony, they enhance each other. The actual vibration pulse details are not important, as sound, when perceivable, grabs the attention. Vibration, on the other hand, adds to the perception of the sound as being more distinct and clear, compared to having just subtle sound without vibration.

9   Conclusion

Turn-based interaction was presented as a new type of method for gesture interaction with mobile devices. The accelerometer-enabled method was introduced and evaluated through example use cases and related user experiences. An essential element in the design was providing feedback indicators during interaction. The reliability of recognizing a turn-based gesture was verified quantitatively with user data. Turn-based interaction can benefit the mobile device user by extending the variety of usable gesture control use cases, potentially enhancing the user experience.

References

1. Nokia Corporation. 5500 phone (2006), http://europe.nokia.com/5500
2. Pirhonen, A., Brewster, S., Holguin, C.: Gestural and Audio Metaphors as a Means of Control for Mobile Devices. In: Proc. CHI 2002, pp. 291–298. ACM Press, New York (2002)

3. Brewster, S., Lumsden, J., Bell, M., Hall, M., Tasker, S.: Multimodal 'eyes-free' interaction techniques for wearable devices. In: Proc. SIGCHI conference on human factors in computing systems, pp. 473–480. ACM Press, New York (2003)

4. Kela, J., Korpipää, P., Mäntyjärvi, J., Kallio, S., Savino, G., Jozzo, L., Di Marca, S.: Accelerometer based gesture control for a design environment. Personal and Ubiquitous Computing, 1–15 (2006); Online First Springer

5. Linjama, J., Häkkilä, J., Ronkainen, S.: Gesture Interfaces for Mobile Devices – Minimalist Approach for Haptic Interaction. Position paper in CHI 2005 Workshop Hands on Haptics, Portland, Oregon, April 3-4 (2005)

6. Levin, G., Yarin, P.: Bringing sketching tools to keychain computers with an acceleration-based interface. In: Proc. CHI 1999, pp. 268–269. ACM Press, New York (1999)

7. Sawada, H., Uta, S., Hashimoto, S.: Gesture recognition for human-friendly interface in designer - consumer cooperate design system. In: Proc. IEEE International Workshop on Robot and Human Interaction, pp. 400–405 (1999)

8. Linjama, J., Kaaresoja, T.: Novel, minimalist haptic gesture interaction for mobile devices. In: Proc. NordicCHI 2004, pp. 457–458 (2004)

9. Ronkainen, S., Häkkilä, J., Kaleva, S., Colley, A., Linjama, J.: Tap input as an embedded interaction method for mobile devices. In: Proc. TEI 2007, pp. 263–270. ACM Press, New York (2007)

10. Rekimoto, J.: Tilting operations for small screen interfaces. In: Proc. ACM Symposium on User Interface Software and Technology, pp. 167–168 (1996)

11. Oakley, I., Ängeslevä, J., Hughes, S., O'Modhrain, S.: Tilt and Feel: Scrolling with Vibrotactile Display. In: Proc. Eurohaptics, pp. 316–323 (2004)

12. Hinckley, K., Pierce, J., Horvitz, E., Sinclair, M.: Foreground and background interaction with sensor-enhanced mobile devices. ACM Transactions on Computer-Human Interaction 12(1), 31–52 (2005)

13. Video available, http://www.finwe.fi/video

14. Shneiderman, B., Plaisant, C.: Designing the User Interface: Strategies for Effective Human-Computer Interaction, 4th edn., p. 672. Addison-Wesley, Reading (2005)

A Large-Scale Wireless Network Approach for Intelligent and Automated Meter Reading of Residential Electricity

Victor Custodio, Jose Ignacio Moreno, and Juan Pablo Viñuela

Telematic Engineering, Carlos III University of Madrid,
Av. Universidad, 30, E. Torres Quevedo. E-28911 Leganés (Madrid), España
{victor.custodio,joseignacio.moreno,juanpablo.vinuela}@uc3m.es

Abstract. Control of electrical energy consumption is a critical aspect when electric companies try to establish the correct balance between the supply and demand of energy. Current solutions are based on experience, historical demand behavior and global control of the electrical grid, but they lack of detailed information about users consumption behavior. In the future, electric companies will need to know, almost in real time, user needs on energy to avoid extra costs of an over provisioning infrastructure or a lack of service during peak times. In this paper we address network topology, capacity planning and security issues of an IT platform, based on wireless sensor networks, to meet the new market requirements. The resulting automated control system will be able to provide real-time control of user demands, as well as to open the market to future services in this area: differential billing schemes, remote control and others.

Keywords: Electricity Metering Platform, AMR, Security, ZigBee, WSN.

1 Introduction

Electricity meter reading is a common task that must be accomplished by every single electric company in the market. Why? This is a standard way they have to measure the effective amount of energy a certain user consumes over a period of time.

Until now, traditional methods for residential meter reading, involves the physical presence of companies' personnel at the user premises every one or two months to visually read the corresponding meters for every user or client of the service, a number big enough to reach hundreds of thousands or even millions of devices to be read. Although, many solutions have been developed to improve the time required to get manual readings from the meters through the use of wireless equipment, just a few of them, if any, introduces the possibility to do it remotely and automatically. Another big problem that electric companies have is that they face an uneven consumption curve during the day, forcing them to provision enough network infrastructure and operations to support periods of peak demand. This difference between the supply and demand of energy, introduces high operational costs and complex grid management.

Naturally, the described process leads to very high operational costs for the electric companies and also, complex logistics and management problems. But even more

S. Hailes, S. Sicari, and G. Roussos (Eds.): S-Cube 2009, LNICST 24, pp. 20–32, 2009.
© Institute for Computer Sciences, Social-Informatics and Telecommunications Engineering 2009

important, this old-fashioned method does not allow these companies to be major players, and actively participate in one of today's world-most significant challenge which is energy efficiency, as stated by the European Union as one of the top important subjects in energy field for the next coming years [1].

In this work we present an IT platform to perform remote electricity-meter readings, which will enable companies to automate the process without the need of in-premises personnel, reducing operational expenditures and opening an unprecedented way for real-time energy metering, and consequently, the possibility of energy efficiency, not only saving money for electric companies and end-users, but also making big savings to the environment and the world. Moreover, companies will have the possibility to offer new services related to energy consumption. The proposed IT platform will make use of different communication technologies depending on the requirements and restrictions of each network segment of the design.

With the evolution of technology in recent years, new communications systems are coming into the markets. Wireless networks are no exception of this phenomenon, and these kinds of technologies are even more present in people's today's life, having outstanding advantages for a meter-reading platform such the one presented here. In the access network, there will be no need to deploy costly wired infrastructure around user premises, where wireless sensor networks (WSN) will be a good solutions due to its low cost and low power consumption. In the other hand, for a long range path, WSN won't provide the necessary range and processing power, where a different technology, wireless or not, will be more suitable (GPRS, WiMAX, ADSL, etc).

The main objective of this paper is to present an IT platform capable of reading every meter from the electric-service users at previously designated time-intervals of the day, or even on demand, and then send this information to the central servers of the electric company. This will enable them to develop differential billing schemes based on the energy demand during the day and the real-time knowledge of energy consumption, as well as to reduce the operational costs associated with the reading of the meters. It is important to mention that even thou this work have been done in an electricity meter context, it can also be applied to any other utility application.

The rest of this paper is organized as follows: Section 2 focuses on the analysis of requirements and the architecture for the meter reading platform. Section 3 explains the core aspects of network deployment and security for the platform. Section 4 shows a sample deployment and network dimensioning using typical values for an average electric company. Finally, we present some conclusions and future work.

2   Requirements and Architecture for Electricity Meter Reading

Until now, traditional methods of residential electricity metering has consisted in electric companies having to send dedicated employees to client premises (houses, buildings, etc) every one or two months to visually read the customer meter, and take note of the readings. Based on the reading made by the employee, the company is able to charge the user for the amount of energy consumed over the period of time being measured. Unfortunately, such method requires a big effort in terms of the number of employees needed to perform the task and many times involves having to get into users home to reach a meter, which could also represent a problem.

The purpose of Automated Meter Reading (AMR) technology is to enable electric companies to perform meter readings remotely, without sending employees to users home. Many technologies exist today for the automation of the process, but they generally involve sending an employee to the neighborhood or to a point of close vicinity of a group of users, or deploying wired infrastructures at user's premises.

With the introduction of WSN's, we can develop a distributed and automated process to perform the readings, where the edge is that we can avoid costly and/or complex situations such as the ones mentioned above. In this sense, the results obtained will turn into great improvements for electrical companies and end-users:

- Billing Schemes: Encourages energy use during low demand periods.
- Operational Expenditures Reduction: There is no longer need to send huge number of employees to customers' premises to perform readings.
- New Services: Companies can offer new services to their customers.

Automating the process through the use of WSN's, involves taking into account several aspects related to features, requirements and the specific scenario and architecture of applications, all of which we will describe in the rest of this section.

2.1 Features and Requirements

The proposed IT platform is based in a group of features and requirements for the technology to be used, as well as a series of features related to the specific applications to be implemented. Depending on these parameters, the proposed methodology tries to accommodate and solve the majority of the different scenarios.

2.1.1 Application Requirements

Nodes Identification. The EndPoints (devices attached to meters) have to be uniquely identifiable in the network and correctly associated to a specific customer.

Node Mobility. This is a very important feature of general WSN's, but in this case is not very relevant. Most of the time there will be no movement of the EndPoints.

Energy Consumption and Battery Lifetime. This is a very restrictive parameter for WSN's, especially if units are battery powered. For electricity meters, endpoints are expected to draw power from the corresponding electricity meter they are attached to.

Scalability. In the future, new endpoints will be joining the network. The design should consider the possibility of automatic growth of the network, without the need to perform specific and/or technical modifications to the design.

Reliability. This is one of the most important requirements for an AMR platform. Information cannot get lost, even considering that there could be connection dropouts in the network. Readings must be taken in a secure and timely manner.

2.1.2 Requirements Imposed by the Technology

Identification of Devices. Wireless endpoints will be based on ZigBee technology. There are two possibilities of addresses for the devices: 64 bits pre-encoded MAC addresses and 16 bits network addresses. The first of them are globally unique and usually used when a device is about to join a ZigBee network. The second of these two, is a much shorter address used for routing purposes inside the network.

Network Size. The size of a ZigBee network is theoretically determined by the limitation of the 16 bits addresses. Nevertheless, because of physical limitations, the maximum number of devices is 100 per ZigBee network, a much smaller amount.

Type of Sensors. Sensors connect to electricity meters through serial interfaces, so the wireless device will be inside the meter, thus reducing the range for the devices.

Maximum Number of Coordinators. There is a limit, by design, of 4 coordinators that can be directly attached to the interfaces of the concentrator.

2.2 Scenario Description

A typical scenario consists of a group of houses or buildings in dense urban areas, where the different buildings are in proximity one from another. We will find other situations too (small towns or isolated houses) but this scenario is a good start.

Every house has an electricity meter to be read. The location of the meter will depend on the type of edification: in houses, most of the time it will be just outside of the house; in buildings, it could be just outside of the apartment or sometimes in a special designated area to group a number of them. The meters connect through a wireless interface to a special device called concentrator, which aggregates all the readings of the meters in close proximity. The concentrator is responsible for sending all the information back to the management servers of the electric company, which in most cases will be several miles away from the customer's premises.

As we can see in Fig. 1, the scenario comprises a series of important elements, each of them having different roles. The combination of these elements in a network, make possible the automated meter reading process.

EndPoint. Network element integrated into the meter. It implements a physical and logical interface so it can interact with the meter to obtain the readings and manage the device.

Coordinator. Device responsible for the coordination of a ZigBee network. It allows nodes to join the network and assigns them network addresses, and it is in charge of routing, outside the network, the information from all the meters.

Concentrator. It's the network element responsible for collecting and aggregating all the information generated by a group of endpoints. It implements the logical interfaces to communicate with endpoints and the middleware platform

Management Servers. They represent the middleware platform that is responsible of making requests to nodes and storing the information of the readings from meters.

It is possible to identify two different network segments in the path that information has to travel from an endpoint all the way to the management servers: A *short range* which we will call "last mile" and correspond to the segment that goes from the endpoints to the concentrator; and a *long range* segment composed by the portion between the concentrators and the management servers.

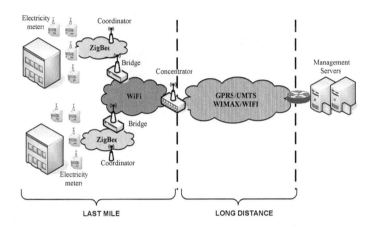

Fig. 1. Typical scenario for the meter reading platform

In order to make fast and economic deployments, which are a very important requirement in today's applications, we take advantage of wireless technologies as a base infrastructure for the network. The reading platform will sit on top of this infrastructure, regardless of the specific technologies used in each segment.

The last mile segment usually corresponds to one or several ZigBee networks, connected to a Concentrator directly through a serial connection or via a Wi-Fi Bridge. The Concentrator collects all the readings from the meters it serves in its area and is responsible of sending the information back to the management servers through the long range segment of the network. ZigBee is a low-cost and low-power wireless technology that perfectly suits the requirements for this part of the network, due to geographical disposition of meters and low traffic generated by them. Wi-Fi connections are needed when Concentrators are far away from the ZigBee networks.

The long range is used to connect the Concentrator to the middleware platform, and usually will be composed by one or a combination of GPRS/UMTS or Wi-Fi/WiMAX technologies. These technologies provide the necessary infrastructure to make possible for the aggregated meter information to reach the management servers.

It is important to mention that currently there are some alternatives to the one presented here, such as using PLC instead of ZigBee for the last-mile segment, or even using GPRS connections directly attached to each endpoint. Using GPRS directly on endpoints results in a very costly solutions, especially when it comes to get readings from million units. In the other hand, we use ZigBee instead of PLC because has some bandwidth limitations (depending on the place of deployment) and also it is not as flexible as ZigBee. In the future, this platform could be used for other utilities, like gas or water, where a PLC connection could not be fully guaranteed.

3 Network Deployment Analysis

The main objective of the deployment analysis is to correctly identify problems and solutions related to the deployment of the network, to be able to successfully obtain the readings of all the electricity meters, subject to a series of constraints, such as reliability, costs, scalability and others. From this point of view, we have stated three fundamental tasks in the deployment activity: Sensor Identification, Network Security and Capacity Planning. The first one specifies how to univocally identify each and every node of the network, letting the management servers, or any other network element, to communicate with a specific endpoint; Network Security section explains the mechanisms to obtain authentication, data confidentiality and integrity, and high availability of the service; The third part, analyzes the different data size related to the meter, and uses this information to plan the capacity, in terms of needed bandwidth, to be supported in every section of the network.

3.1 Sensor Identification, Addressing and Naming Convention

Devices identification is one of the important and challenging parts of the deployment of the solution. As stated before, the number of meters for an electric company can easily reach hundreds of thousands or million units. Having a way to univocally identify them, involves the association of the meter with a specific customer.

Even if it was possible to use all the 16 bits addressing space given by ZigBee technology, it wouldn't be enough. Besides the number of addresses problem, there is a problem related to persistency. A ZigBee coordinator assigns networks addresses to devices dynamically, thus, the address of a specific device can change in time. This means that we cannot use only network addresses as a way to identify nodes. In a situation like this, it is convenient to use the long 64 bits MAC addresses as a way to uniquely identifying the nodes, although its use is not meant for routing purposes.

Now, provided that we are going to use 64 bits MAC addresses for identification, there is still a need to associate these addresses with specific customers. Taking into account that the meters will be grouped under concentrator devices, which will be operating on an IP network in the long-range segment, we will have the following tuple of information that has to be recorded into the management servers:

customer_id	node_mac_address	concentrator_id

The *customer_id* corresponds to a company-assigned identification for its customers, *node_mac_address* is the unique 64 bits addresses for ZigBee devices, and *concentrator_id* corresponds to an identifier for the concentrators of the network.

Using a scheme like this requires additional considerations and could introduce some potential problems. The row has to be repeated for each and every customer of the service, which can grow to a very large number and could lead to data-access efficiency problems. Each time the management middleware has to contact a customer meter, it first has to consult the database to obtain the MAC address of the corresponding device, as well as the information regarding to the identification of the concentrator under which the meter operates. This way, the platform knows which concentrator to send a request to, in order to communicate with a certain meter. Once a concentrator receives a request, it passes the request, along with the MAC address to the coordinators it has attached to its interfaces, and the coordinators in turn, using the MAC address, search for the corresponding device inside the ZigBee network. Under a situation like this one, there is no chance for a good organization or hierarchy of the network, thus increasing complexity of the process.

As a workaround of the problems mentioned above, we propose the use of virtual networks and addresses. The main idea behind this is to build a complete IP-based network on top of the heterogeneous infrastructure of the different network technologies used. We have seen in the scenario description, that there will be an IP portion in the design, primarily corresponding to the long distance segment and maybe some portion in the short range part. The last mile, which considers the endpoints (electricity meter nodes), is based on ZigBee technology. The virtual network will sit just on top of this infrastructure.

ZigBee technology does not support the TCP/IP stack, mainly because of its size, but it is possible to implement a network address translation between IP and ZigBee addresses [2], without having to use the whole TCP/IP stack. This method is intended to be used for naming and addressing purposes but not for routing purposes. This means that the ZigBee network remains intact from the network-inside point of view. For the addresses translation to work, it is needed to add a gateway at the edge of the ZigBee network, which will be in charge of the translations. This way, from the outside, it will be possible to address endpoints through an IP address, simplifying the whole process of communicating with an endpoint. The main advantages will be:

- No need to send long MAC addresses through the network (end-to-end). Just the gateways need to know them.
- Network Hierarchy. It is possible to subdivide the network into subnets.
- The whole meter-reading process becomes more transparent to middleware.

Finally, to implement a solution like this one, it is needed to know what will be the size of the network, in terms of how many endpoints and concentrators there will be. This will lead to a correct address or naming convention and how to structure the network. The important things to take into account in this section are:

- Estimated number of endpoints
- Estimated number of concentrators
- Network planning: IP addresses to use and number of subnets

3.2 Network and Data Security

The AMR communication platform presented here is mainly based on wireless networks. These types of networks are generally exposed to a number of vulnerabilities that wired networks do not have, starting with the fact that possible attackers have direct access to the network media. This way, anyone being in range and knowing the frequency of transmission could have access to the network, almost like any other device does. Among the most common and important types of attacks we have:

- Denial of Service: causing interference, taking advantage of the vulnerability of the CSMA-CA protocol. This is used in ZigBee and Wi-Fi.[3]
- Attack to the Confidentiality of the Data
- Replay Attacks
- Supplanting of endpoints

In the context of automated meter reading, the supplanting of endpoints will be the most likely attack to occur, therefore, authentication is one of the most important aspects to take into account, without leaving behind confidentiality and integrity of the data, and the availability of the service, which are of extreme importance too.

Now we describe possible solutions to provide security mechanisms for, at least, each of the five characteristics mentioned above, considering last mile and long-range segments.

3.2.1 Last Mile Segment
The communications in the last mile correspond to ZigBee and Wi-Fi networks.

The ZigBee Pro standards [4][5] provides two types of security: Standard Security and High Security. The standard mode is focused to avoid the access of external devices to the network, and it is based on a trust center that authenticates and distributes a network key that is used to encrypt all messages that flow through the network.

The high security mode is thought for networks where the security control is critical, and in order to satisfy the requirements of the system, it adds two more keys, master and link keys, besides the secure key exchange (handshake). In this mode all the messages are encrypted from point-to-point with a *link* key that is generated from a master key, after a handshake between both points. This way, the high security of ZigBee also avoids insider attacks. Because of its strength, this is the security standard that we are going to use for the meter reading platform.

In order to provide for the minimum security needed for the Wi-Fi network, we can make use of Wi-Fi security standard 802.11i (WPA/WPA2) with 802.1x authentication (EAP), which currently is considered to be safe. To strengthen its security even more, there are several mechanisms to consider:

- IPSEC (VPN tunnels): The information travels encrypted through the tunnel from the client to the VPN server.
- MAC Filtering: Only authorized devices are allowed access to the network.
- Hiding Access Point: Hiding the access point is possible (if available)

Given that we are working with mesh networks, hiding the access point is not supported, and the management of MAC filtering tables becomes very costly for large deployments. That's why both of these are not to be used.

On the other hand, due to high sensitivity of information against attacks and future potential vulnerabilities of the 802.11i standard, we introduce an extra level of security through the use of IPSec VPN tunneling.

3.2.2 Long Distance Segment

The communications in this segment consider any or a combination of GPRS/UMTS and/or Wi-Fi/WiMAX. In the latter case, the same safety mechanisms considered in the last mile apply here, because they are considered to be safe enough for now. The standards to be used consider 802.11i (WPA2) and 802.1x (EAP) authentication for Wi-Fi networks, 802.16g with EAP and PKMv2 for authentication in WiMAX networks [6]. Like in the last mile, we also increase security by using VPN tunneling based on IPSec.

Table 1. Security Mechanisms

Network	Link level	Network level	Application level
ZigBee	High Security		
Wifi	WPA2	VPN based in IPsec	-
GPRS	Security offered by telecomm operator		AES Encryption + PKI-based Authentication and key exchange
WIMAX	802.16g security with EAP and PKMv2	VPN based in IPsec	-

In situations where the information through the long range segment is sent over GPRS/UMTS, the telecomm operator that offers the service will be responsible for ensuring authentication, confidentiality, integrity, and service availability, in an end-to-end basis. As a safety measure, we again provide an extra level of security. In this case, all messages are encrypted using application-level AES. The exchange of symmetric keys for AES encryption and a second authentication is performed using a system public key (PKI). This information is summarized in Table 1.

3.3 Network Capacity Planning

Capacity planning is about estimating and knowing what are going to be the limitations and restrictions with respect to the different technologies involved in the design, making it possible to address and provision the necessary equipment for the system to work in optimal conditions, based on a set of requirements. This will lead to an estimation of the number of the different equipment needed for deployment and the bandwidth requirements over the different networks segments, among others.

The most important requirements and capacities limits for the design are:

- Number of Nodes
- Number of ZigBee Coordinators
- Number of Concentrators
- Size of summarized meter readings and firmware in each network segment.

To calculate the above restrictions, it is needed the following list of parameters:

- Number of customers to obtain energy consumption information from.
- Maximum number of nodes per ZigBee network
- Maximum number of coordinators supported per Concentrator
- Size of an electricity-meter reading
- Time interval between each reading.

These kind of considerations are well suited for a general purpose scenario, but in a real case deployment, it is necessary to take into account other parameters such as the types and level of isolation of buildings involved, communications technology availability and coverage in the specific area of deployment, among others.

The next section will show an example of a deployment and how the above information is useful to obtain gross estimations for infrastructure requirements.

4   Practical-Case Application of the Deployment

In this section we present an application of the deployment methodology presented in the previous section, covering the most relevant aspects of identification and capacity planning. Security parameters correspond to the ones presented in previous sections.

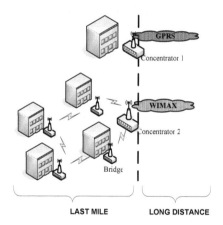

Fig. 2. Sample scenario for the application of the deployment methodology

The example is based on Fig. 2, where we assume the values presented in Table 2 for the different parameters involved the scenario. There are 5 buildings in the scenario. Four of them will connect to one concentrator through Wi-Fi bridges, and the fifth one will connect to another concentrator through its serial interface, because it is not close to the rest of the buildings. It has been stated that the reading of a meter consumes at most 60 bytes, including headers and security redundancy.

Table 2. Parameters for the example of the applications of the deployment methodology

Parameter	Value
Number of Buildings	5
Number of Floors per Building	8
Number of Apartments per Floor	6
Distance Between Buildings	< 30 mt
Distance from the Buildings To Management Servers	5 km
Maximum number of nodes per ZigBee network	50
Number of ZigBee interfaces per Concentrator	4
Size of an electricity-meter reading (including headers)	60 bytes
Size of a Firmware Update of a Meter	60 Kb
Meter-Reading Interval	15 min

Based on information from Table 2, it's possible to estimate the requirements on equipment and devices to be used for the solution. This is presented in Table 3.

Table 3. Estimation of number of needed devices based on parameters of the scenario

Parameter	Value
Number of Electricity-Meters/EndPoints	240
Number of Coordinators (ZigBee networks)	5
Number of Bridges (one per coordinator not connected directly)	4
Number of Concentrators	2

4.1 Identification and Addressing

In this scenario, we need to be able to uniquely identify 240 nodes, each of them corresponding to a customer. This is a very small number, so if we consider the use of Virtual IP, a Class C IPv4-network would be enough. Scalability is one of the requirements for the solution, so we have to consider the possibility of future growth of the network as new EndPoints are added under the management of an existing concentrator. Here is where we make use of the advantages of IP hierarchy characteristics, so we can assign a different Class C network to each of the concentrators. Table 4 shows the addressing scheme. For this purpose, we make use of private addresses. There is plenty of space for adding new endpoints.

Table 4. EndPoint identification and addressing scheme

Network Parameters	Concentrator 1	Concentrator 2
Network	192.168.1.0	192.168.2.0
IP Address	192.168.1.1	192.168.2.1
IP Range for Bridges	192.168.1.10-192.168.1.20	N/A
IP Range for End-Points	192.168.1.128-192.168.1.254	192.168.2.128-192.168.2.254

For Virtual IP to work, a special gateway is needed which is going to be in charge to do the translation between IP addresses and ZigBee address. That way, the coordinator will receive a request in a protocol it can understand. One gateway is needed per concentrator. Now, when the middleware platform makes a request to one of the EndPoints, it only need to know the IP address of the node, and the request automatically will arrive to the corresponding concentrator, where the gateway will make the address translation and then send it to the appropriate coordinator.

4.2 Capacity Planning

We already calculated, in Table 2, the requirements about number of nodes (endpoints), number of ZigBee coordinators and the number of needed concentrators. Now we are going to calculate what are going to be the amount of information to be handled by each device and, consequently, the capacity requirements on the communications links. This is calculated for meter readings and firmware updates.

Table 5. Total traffic to be managed by each element of the network

Network Element	Energy Reading	Firmware Update
Node (endpoint)	60 bytes	60 Kb
Coordinator	3 Kb	3 Mb
Bridge	3 Kb	60 Kb
Concentrator 1	2.88 Kb	60 Kb
Concentrator 2	11.5 Kb	240 Kb
Management Server	14.38 Kb	120 Kb

We assume mean values for coordinators and bridges, that is, they handle about the same amount of information regardless if they are alone or grouped under a concentrator. On the other hand, this design corresponds to a distributed network, so firmware updates only needs to be sent once to each concentrator, and this device is in charge to send the necessary copies to each endpoint.

The requirements on the amount of information are not so big, and this mainly reflects the fact that this is a small example. If we consider a complete deployment for a modern mid-size city, we can end up having about 2 millions electricity meters. For such condition, it would be needed around 10.000 concentrators, each having to manage 12 Kb. This implies a total of 120 Mb on the management server. Special care has to be taken, because some connections between a concentrator and the core could be over a GPRS connection, which has important restriction of bandwidth.

5   Conclusions and Future Work

Throughout this article we have presented an IT platform for remote management of electricity meters, covering deployment and security of the platform.

The implantation of this platform will enable electric companies to develop sophisticated billing schemes, helping to mange smartly and more efficiently the great differences that companies have to face between supply and demand of electric energy during a day. This energetic efficiency will make big savings for the companies, end-users and with no doubt, for energy resources in the world. The key of the solution is the ability to do real-time and on demand electricity consumption readings. Another great advantage, besides the energy efficiency, is that electric companies will have the opportunity to offer new services, like differential billing, on-line service management and promotional offers with minimal operational costs.

ZigBee is a low-cost and low-power wireless technology that perfectly suits the requirements for the last mile segment, which are related to the geographical disposition of the meters and low traffic generated by them. Moreover, if we combine ZigBee with better-cover wireless technology such as Wi-Fi, WiMax, GPRS and/or UMTS, we obtain a complete solution for the remote AMR system. There is no need for expensive deployments of wired networks.

Unlike the standard and well-know data networks mentioned above which have better range, ZigBee does not support the TCP/IP stack, which generates problems for addressing and identification of the endpoints. Fortunately, these problems are resolved by the use of virtual IP addresses, which provide network hierarchy and transparency to middleware.

This platform could be extended for the use of other utilities companies, like gas and water. It is also possible to do remote readings of water or gas meters, as long as they can be integrated with sensor networks technologies. The communications system has been designed to be flexible and to be able to support the integration of other meter equipment. Nevertheless, it is quite important to take into account that these other purposes, most probably will have special requirements. Just to mention one, water or gas meters cannot draw electric power from the very service supply like electricity meters do, thus introducing new challenges worth a specific analysis before adopting this platform to the new scenario.

Acknowledgements

The presented work was mainly done within the research project IRIDIUM [7], which was partly funded by the Spanish Ministry of Industry, Tourism and Trade under the contract TSI-020400-2008-152. The authors would like to thank all the members of the project that contribute with fruitful discussion.

References

1. European Parliament: Action Plan for Energy Efficiency: Realising the Potential (2007/2106(INI))
2. Transmission of IPv6 Packets over IEEE 802.15.4 Networks. RFC4944, IETF
3. Raymond, D.R., Midkiff, S.F.: Virginia Tech:Denial-of-Service in Wireless sensor Networks: Attacks and Defenses (January-March 2008), http://www.ieee.org
4. ZigBee Alliance: ZigBee Specification (January 2008), http://www.zigbee.org
5. ZigBee-PRO Stack Profile: Platform restrictions for compliant platform testing and interoperability (January 2008), http://www.zigbee.org
6. 802.16g-2007 IEEE Standards for Local and metropolitan area networks, http://standards.ieee.org/getieee802/download/ 802.16g-2007.pdf
7. Project IRIDIUM, http://www.amr-iridium.com/

Weak Process Models for Attack Detection in a Clustered Sensor Network Using Mobile Agents

Marco Pugliese[1], Annarita Giani[2], and Fortunato Santucci[1]

[1] Center of Excellence DEWS, University of L'Aquila, L'Aquila, Italy
marco.pugliese@ieee.org, santucci@ing.univaq.it
[2] Department of Electrical Engineering and Computer Sciences,
University of California at Berkeley, Berkeley, CA, USA
agiani@eecs.berkeley.edu

Abstract. This paper proposes a methodology for detecting network-layer anomalies in wireless sensor networks using weak process models (WPM). Weak process models are a non-parametric version of Hidden Markov models (HMM), wherein state transition probabilities are reduced to rules of reachability. Specifically, we present an intrusion detection system based on anomaly detection logic. It identifies any observable event correlated to a threat by applying a set of anomaly rules to the incoming traffic. Attacks are classified into low and high potential attacks according to its final state. Alarms are issued as soon as one or more high potential attacks are detected.

We model hello flooding, sinkhole and wormhole. We introduced single threat models and aggregated models and study how effective they are to detect each attack.

We present the design approach for the proposed WPM-based detection technique using mobile agents. Early implementations of the agent based secure platform have already been implemented.

Keywords: Weak Process Models, Anomaly Detection, Threat Identification, Alarm Generation.

1 Introduction

Sensor networks permit data collection and computation to be deeply embedded in the physical environment. Sensor nodes are often left unattended so that they are susceptible to security attacks. Typical threats affecting wireless sensor networks (WSNs) are reported in [1]. An intrusion detection system (IDS) is a defense system, which detects hostile network activities. It recognizes patterns of known attacks (signature based) [19,18], or identifies network activities that differ from historical norms (anomaly based) [2].

This work considers an IDS based on anomaly detection logic (ADL). Threats are correlated to any sequences of observable events by applying a set of anomaly rules to the incoming traffic. Computer networks are typically provided with mechanisms to identify changes in system parameters or anomalous exchange of

S. Hailes, S. Sicari, and G. Roussos (Eds.): S-Cube 2009, LNICST 24, pp. 33–50, 2009.
© Institute for Computer Sciences, Social-Informatics and Telecommunications Engineering 2009

information. Such data can be used as relevant observations to predict the hidden state of the system and infer if it is under attack. A HMM is a doubly stochastic finite state machine with an underlying stochastic process that represents the real state of the system. The real state of the system is hidden but indirectly observable through another stochastic process that produce a sequence of observable events [5,15]. The relationships between hidden states and observable data are stochastic as well as the transitions between states. HMMs [5,15] have been widely used in network-based IDS for wired systems [9,10,11,12,22,23] as well as for modeling Internet traffic [21]. The Baum-Welch algorithm as likelihood criterion and parameter estimation is extensively used [5].

Silva et al. [13] have proposed a decentralized IDS that fits demands and restrictions of WSNs. The network behavior is obtained from the analysis of events detected by a monitor node. A set of rules are compared with the information gathered from the network traffic. In general, application of traditional IDSs to sensor networks is challenging. In fact they require intense computation capability [20] and they are too limited to a restricted number of threats [7]. Some conventional intrusion detection systems perform cross-correlation and aggregation of data. For example, they analyze fluctuation in sensor readings [6], or detect abnormal traffic patterns [26].

Implementing an effective IDS on a wireless sensor network leads to the problem of finding a trade-off between the capability of identifying threats (i.e. with a bounded false alarm rate), the complexity of the algorithms and memory usage [8]. Doumit and Agrawal [7] proposed a novel approach for applying a lightweight, yet robust IDS designed for wireless sensor networks based on self-organized criticality and HMM. They model the natural dynamic of the system so that unusual activity can be identified. We propose here an intrusion detection system which replaces HMMs with WPMs. WPMs are a non-parametric version of HMMs wherein state transition probabilities are reduced to rules of reachability.

Very low state transition probabilities are reduced to zero which increases false negatives. This means that some sequences are classified as not possible when instead in a probabilistic model would be achievable. The number of false negatives decreases if we add states [4] but the drawback is a larger memory requirement. The matrices that describe the models are sparse and can be compacted for faster computation.

The estimation of a threat in the case of weak processes is greatly simplified and less demanding for resources. The *most probable* state sequence generated by the Viterbi algorithm [3] for HMM becomes the *possible* state sequence. The intensity of the attack is evaluated by introducing a threat score, a likelihood criterion based on weighting states and transitions [4]. Intrusions and violations are classified into low potential attacks (LPA) and high potential attacks (HPA) depending on their distance from the state corresponding to a successful attack. When at least one HPA occurs, an alarm is issued.

We assume that a secure routing protocol [14,24] is running on the network and that routing messages are ciphered and authenticated through an underlying cryptographic scheme. We analyze hello flooding, sinkhole and wormhole. A secure routing protocol would result not effective to protect from these threats [2,1]. According to these assumptions, we can mainly focus on threats from internal intruders that generate control messages that are syntactically and semantically well-formed.

In summary, the main contributions of this paper are as follows:

- Application of our method to the detection of sinkhole and wormhole (hello flooding was considered in [4]);
- Extension to models that describe aggregate threats;
- Comparison of models that describe a single attack and models that describe more than one attack in terms of detection capability.

The remainder of this paper is organized as follows. In section 2 we present some background material on weak process models and show how it is applied to the problem of detecting sinkhole and wormhole. In section 3 we analyze false alarms and misdetection of single threat models compared to aggregated models. In section 4 we will present the design approach for the proposed WPM-based detection technique: mobile agents and enhancements to the execution environment in [31] have been proposed. Early implementations of the agent based secure platform are already available in our lab. Section 5 contains concluding discussion and future work.

2   Threat Detection and Alarm Generation

In our anomaly-based approach the anomaly rules are defined through inequality so that they define regions of the state space. This allows us to introduce a ranking among states that leads to a hierarchical structure. The number of false negative (mis-detection) is reduced since inequalities are satisfied by a larger number of values with respect to equalities. Also the number of false positive decreases given that we choose to associate an alert only to the state with the highest risk. States are classified according to two hazard levels, low potential attack (LPA) states and high potential attack (HPA) states. We also introduce a score mechanism to weight state sequences where LPA and HPA states contribute differently. Now we give formal definitions of WPMs, threat score, low potential attack and high potential attack.

A WPM, as any Markov model, can be formally represented using the canonical form:

$$\begin{cases} x^{k+1} = Ax^k \\ o^k = Bx^k \end{cases} \tag{1}$$

where:

- $X = (x_1, x_2, \ldots, x_3)$ *is the state set*;
- x^k is the *state* at step k. x^0 is the *initial state*;

- $O = (o_1, o_2, \ldots, o_q)$ is the *the set of observations*;
- o^k is the *observable o at step k* ;
- A is a $n \times n$ matrix representing *state transition distribution*. Matrix elements are defined as:

$$A_{i,j} = \begin{cases} 1 & \text{if } p(x^{k+1} = x_j | x^k = x_i) = 1 \\ 0 & \text{otherwise} \end{cases}$$

- B is a $q \times n$ matrix representing the *emission distribution*, that maps each observable with the states. Matrix elements are defined as

$$B_{i,j} = \begin{cases} 1 & \text{if } p(o^k = o_j | x^k = x_i) = 1 \\ 0 & \text{otherwise} \end{cases}$$

Definition 1. *Let s^k be the threat score after k observations. s^k is the result of a weighting mechanism applied to states and transitions belonging to the hypothetic state trace. Weights are represented by a square n x n matrix S, where is n the number of states in the model. The elements of the matrix are defined as follows:*

$$s_{ij} = \begin{cases} \text{weight assigned to the transition from } x_i \text{ to } x_j & \text{if } i \neq j \\ \text{weight assigned to the state } x_i & \text{if } i = j \end{cases}$$

Definition 2. *A Low Potential Attack (LPA) is an attack defined by a state x_j whose distance from the final state is at least 2 hops.*

Definition 3. *A High Potential Attack (HPA) is an attack defined by a state x_j whose distance from the final state is less than 2 hops.*

Let us assume now that, if a node represents a LPA state, then its score is L. If a node represents a HPA state, then its score is H and, if a node neither represents an attack state nor is the final state, then its score is 0. L and H are integers. We define the elements of the score matrix S as follows:

$$s_{ij} = \begin{cases} a_{i,j} \cdot (s_i - s_j) & \text{if } i \neq j \\ \{0, L, H\} & \text{if } i = j \end{cases}$$

where a_{ij} are the elements of matrix associated to the model describing the threat.

Let us define n_{hpa}^k and n_{lpa}^k the numbers of high potential and low potential states, respectively, reached in the observation interval. These numbers are not limited to a single trace, but include states belonging to all possible state sequences at time k. With the above assumptions the threat score at time k is

$$s^k = H \cdot n_{hpa}^k + L \cdot n_{lpa}^k \tag{2}$$

The choice of H and L depends on the length of the memory that we allocated to store the various states of the model. We call it WML, the weak process model

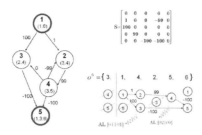

Fig. 1. Weak process model generating two alarms

length. If n is the number of states, then $n \cdot WML$ is the number of states to store. The worst case is when a single observable is associated to all $n \cdot WML$ states so that $\frac{H}{L} \geq n \cdot WML$.

In Figure 1 we show a model, the score matrix and the sequence of observations emitted at each step. The observable sequence is $o^6 = \{3, 1, 4, 2, 5, 6\}$. We assumed L=1 and H=100. At the bottom right is the correspondence between observables and associated states. The first observation must be discarded because the starting state can be reached only in the second observation. The two possible state traces are $Tr_1^6 = 1, 2, 4, 5$ and $Tr_2^6 = 1, 3, 5$. When the attack reaches state 3 or state 4 an alarm is issued (they are HPAs). Let us now compute the scores in state 3 and state 4. The state number 3 is reached with the third observation. The sequence of hidden states until the third observation has 1 high potential state (state 3) and 1 low potential state (state 1). Therefore, the score at state 3 is

$$s^3 = H \cdot n_{hpa}^3 + L \cdot n_{lpa}^3 = 100 \cdot 1 + 1 \cdot 1 = 101$$

The state number 4 is reached with the fifth observation. The sequence of hidden states until the fifth observation has 1 high potential state (state 4). We also have to consider the state (3). So we have two HPA states. This gives us the score at state 4

$$s^4 = H \cdot n_{hpa}^4 + L \cdot n_{lpa}^4 = 100 \cdot (1 + 1) + 1 \cdot (0) = 200$$

A cluster is a group of nodes that are interconnected. A dedicated node of the cluster is called cluster head. The cluster head is responsible for scheduling and dissemination of messages to the cluster members and for data aggregation when necessary [30]. In the rest of this paper we will concentrate on models with a minimal clustered topology composed by only three nodes: a cluster head CH, the generic cluster member M_i, and the attacking node n_e (figure 3).

An anomaly rule is a logic filter applied to incoming messages. If the filtering results in absence of anomalies, the message is processed further; otherwise, if an anomaly is detected, we are in the case of a threat. Any rule can be applied indifferently either to the cluster head and to the members as well. This scheme is scalable and avoids rule explosion.

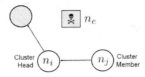

Fig. 2. Model with a minimal clustered topology

We follow a four step process when modeling a threat.

1. Analyze the behaviour of the threat;
2. Derive the Anomaly Rules;
3. Derive the WPM-based threat model;
4. Assign weights to WPM states and transitions.

Given the set of threat observables collected during two consecutive observation steps, the observable with the highest score back-propagates. In [4] we describe how to model the hello flooding attack and how WPMs are used to detect it. In this work we concentrate instead on the sinkhole and wormhole attack modeling and detection.

In the following threat scenarios, dotted arrows indicate the malicious traffic flow and the label refers to the anomaly rule used to detect it.

2.1 Sinkhole Modeling and Detection

In this threat nearly all traffic from a particular area is lured through a specific compromised node with unfaithful routing information [14]. Each neighbouring node of the adversary node is induced to forward packets directed to a base station through the adversary. The malicious node can then suppress, modify or redirect the packets. Geographic routing protocol are resistant to this threat since traffic is routed based on physical location. Protocols that construct a topology initiated by a base station are most susceptible to wormhole and sinkhole attacks. Those protocols that construct a topology on demand using only localized interactions and information are more resistant to these attacks. In [27] a light-weighted algorithm is proposed for detecting sinkhole attacks. It assumes a base station centric approach for network flow collection and intrusion detection. In [28] a distributed IDS is introduced using MintRoute as underlying not secured routing protocol (widely implemented in TinyOS [16]). The importance of monitoring the hop-count parameter in order to detect sinkhole attacks is presented in [29]. The authors also present a computationally efficient scheme for detecting abnormal route advertisements.

We assume that the attack is highly hazardous if at least 2 nodes in the network are attacked. The numeric labels that appears in Figure 3 refers to the corresponding observables listed in Table 1.

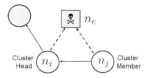

Fig. 3. Sinkhole attack. The attacker induces cluster members n_i and n_j to redirect messages to it.

Table 1. Anomaly rules description for sinkhole

ID	
AR1	If node n_i has authenticated node n_e but node n_e declares that $h_e < h_i$ with $h_i \neq 0$ (n_e declares it is the new cluster head of n_i but it is not) then $o^k = o_1$
AR2	If node n_i is the cluster head and (rule AR1 or rule AR2) in n_j is true then $o^k = o_2$

We introduce a counter R that is set to zero every time a new observation arrives. This is important to detect when observations are not arriving for more than a certain number of steps.

We indicate the malicious node with n_e, as evil. The attack is transparent if the compromised node n_e does not generate any anomalies and nodes n_i and n_j believe that they are supposed to connect with node e when instead their current cluster heads are alive. In [17] we stated the quantitative conditions among nodes hop distances h from the true sink to detect this anomaly: e.g. if node n_i is the cluster head of node n_j then $h_i = h_j - 1$ holds, where h_i and h_j are the respective distance hops from the sink.

The WPM-based sinkhole is represented in Figure 4. It has 4 states and 3 observables. The threat starts if observable 1 or 2 occurs and state SH_1 defines a LPA. If no more observables are identified in the following K steps (with K predefined threshold) then the threat is considered "reset", which means either that the attack is temporary suspended or there were no attack at all (SH_3). If either the observable 1 or 2 occurs again then the attack is dangerous. State SH_2 is high potential and an alarm is issued. If no more observables are identified in the following K steps then the attack is reset. The final state SH_4, labelled SUCCESSFULL ATTACK, is never reached so that the alarm remains on until an appropriate countermeasure has been taken or the threat returns reset.

The canonical form (1) and the score matrix can be specialized using matrices A_{SH} and B_{SH} and S_{SH} in (3).

$$A_{SH} = \begin{bmatrix} 0&0&0&0 \\ 1&0&0&0 \\ 1&1&0&0 \\ 0&1&0&0 \end{bmatrix} \qquad B_{SH} = \begin{bmatrix} 1&1&0&0 \\ 1&1&0&0 \\ 0&0&1&0 \end{bmatrix} \qquad S_{SH} = \begin{bmatrix} 1&0&0&0 \\ 99&-100&0&0 \\ -1&0&0&0 \\ 0&0&0&0 \end{bmatrix} \qquad (3)$$

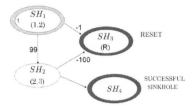

Fig. 4. WPM-based sinkhole model

2.2 Wormhole Modeling and Detection

In a wormhole attack a malicious node receives packets at one location in the network and tunnels them to another location (low latency link) in the network, where the packets are resent into the network generating denial of service, waste of resource, alteration on information semantics and other damages. In [25] wormhole attacks are detected by introducing the notion of a packet leash: a leash is any information that is added to a packet and is designed to restrict the packet's maximum allowed transmission distance. The authors distinguish between geographical leashes and temporal leashes: a geographical leash ensures that the recipient of the packet is within a certain distance from the sender; a temporal leash ensures that the packet has an upper bound on its lifetime, which restricts the maximum travel distance. Either type of leash can prevent the wormhole attack, because it allows the receiver of a packet to detect if the packet traveled further than the leash allows.

Figure 5 and Figure 6 depict two possible scenarios for wormhole attacks, where tunnel node end-points are located in the same cluster (intra-cluster attack scenario) or in different clusters (inter-cluster attack scenario) respectively. The

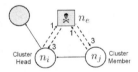

Fig. 5. Wormhole against nodes belonging to a cluster. The numeric labels refer to the corresponding observables listed in Table 2.

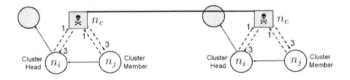

Fig. 6. Wormhole against nodes belonging to two different clusters

attacker emulates to be cluster head in order to receive traffic and to be cluster member to resend traffic or vice-versa. For example, in Figure 5 the sequence 1 - 3 (corresponding to the observable sequence $o_1, \ldots, o_3$) indicates a potential wormhole.

An informal description of the anomaly rules is provided in Table 2.

Observation o_R is emitted when no observables are detected for a certain number of steps. The last two anomaly rules, 3 and 4, describe a request to join a network. This can be an ordinary procedure as well as the precondition for a security attack. Therefore we suggest that the behavior related to AR3 and AR4 were consider normal and abnormal simultaneously. We retain as *ambiguous* threat observables with this characteristic. AR2 and AR4 enable the generation of the back propagation of the observables to the sink. This is important to detect complex threats attacking nodes that are distant to each other.

The WPM-based wormhole is represented in figure 7. The same considerations about RESET and SUCCESSFULLY ATTACK states made for sinkhole apply to this case. The number of states is 6 and the number of observables is 5. It is important to note that observables for sinkhole are a sub-set of those for wormhole. The canonical form (1) can be specialized using matrices A_{WH} and B_{WH} and the score matrix S_{WH} in eq. (4).

Table 2. Anomaly rules description for wormhole

ID	
AR1	If node n_i has authenticated node n_e but node n_e declares $h_e < h_i$ with $h_i \neq 0$ (n_e declares it is the new cluster head but it is not) then $o^k = o_1$
AR2	If node n_i is the cluster head and (rule AR1 or rule AR2) applied to n_j is true then $o^k = o_2$
AR3	If node n_i has authenticated node n_e but node n_E declare that $h_e \geq h_i$ with $h_i \neq 0$ (n_e declares it is the new cluster member but it is not) then $o^k = o_3$
AR4	If node n_i is the cluster head and (rule AR3 or rule AR4) applied to n_j is true then $o^k = o_4$

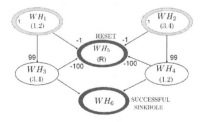

Fig. 7. WPM-based wormhole model

The threat starts with observables o_1 or o_2 or o_3 or o_4. If no more observables are identified in the next K steps the threat is considered suspended. If observables o_1 or o_2 or o_3 or o_4 occur again, then the attack moves to a high potential state.

$$A_{WH} = \begin{bmatrix} 0&0&0&0&0&0 \\ 0&0&0&0&0&0 \\ 1&0&0&0&0&0 \\ 0&1&0&0&0&0 \\ 1&1&1&1&0&0 \\ 0&0&1&1&0&0 \end{bmatrix} \quad B_{WH} = \begin{bmatrix} 1&0&0&1&0&0 \\ 1&0&0&1&0&0 \\ 1&1&1&0&0&0 \\ 0&1&1&0&0&0 \\ 0&0&0&0&0&0 \\ 0&0&0&0&0&0 \\ 0&0&0&0&0&0 \\ 0&0&0&0&0&0 \\ 0&0&0&0&1&0 \end{bmatrix} \quad S_{WH} = \begin{bmatrix} 1&0&0&0&0&0 \\ 0&1&0&0&0&0 \\ 99&0&0&0&0&0 \\ 0&99&0&0&0&0 \\ -1&-1&-100&-100&0&0 \\ 0&0&1&1&0&0 \end{bmatrix} \quad (4)$$

2.3 Aggregated Models

Single threat models can be aggregated in a multi threat model using boolean OR. The complete list of anomaly rules and the produced observables is the collection of the anomaly rules and observables related to single threats. We assume that cluster heads aggregate only the observable coming from the cluster members that has the highest score.

The aggregated threat model of hello flooding, sinkhole and a wormhole attack is shown in figure 8. When no more observables are identified in K consecutive observation steps the RESET state is reached. In that case the attack is suspended or there was no attack at all. Aggregated models allow to detect a larger class of attacks compared to single models.

In the next section we will show how the IDS proposed behaves in terms of false negative (mis-detection) or false positive (false alarms). The experiment investigates the accuracy of threat identification for single models and aggregated models.

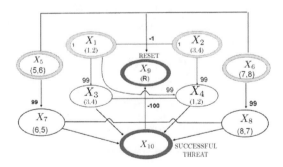

Fig. 8. Aggregated threat model for hello flooding, sinkhole and wormhole

3   Mis-Detection and False Alarm

It is important to check that if a threat occurs than an alarm is generated and that the number of false alarms is low. We investigate mis-detection and false alarm in the case of aggregated models in comparison to single threat models.

3.1   Mis-Detection Analysis

We apply the observable sequences produced by single hello flooding, sinkhole or wormhole. Each sequence will be applied to both single and aggregated model and their detection capabilities will be investigated. We assume 32 observables per sequence, $n \cdot WML \leq 100$ and $k = 3$. We consider the following observation sequences generated in the case of hello flooding, sinkhole and wormhole respectively.

$$\{5, 5, *, 8, 7, *, *, 6, 6, 8, 8, *, *, *, 8, *, *, 5, 7, *, *, 7, *, 6, 8, *, *, *, 5, 5, *, *\} \quad (5)$$

$$\{2, 1, *, *, *, 1, *, 1, 2, 2, *, *, *, 1, 2, *, *, 1, 2, *, *, *, 2, 2, *, *, 1, *, 1, *, *, *\} \quad (6)$$

$$\{2, 4, *, *, *, 3, *, 3, 1, 2, 2, *, *, 1, 3, *, *, 4, 4, *, *, *, 2, 2, *, *, 4, *, 3, *, *, *\} \quad (7)$$

It is important to note that there is no overlapping between observables from hello flooding and observables from sinkhole or wormhole. And the observables from sinkhole are observables from wormhole too.

Simulations provide the results graphically reported in figure 9, 10, and figure 11 respectively. Red bars refer to scores produced by individual threat models while yellow bars refer to aggregated threat models. To be noted that scores go to zero when the system is in a RESET state.

As expected the same outputs single model and aggregated model are obtained for threats not sharing any threat observables with each other. In fact figure 9 and figure 10 show that the aggregate and the single models have the same detection capability in cases of hello flooding and sinkhole respectively. Different

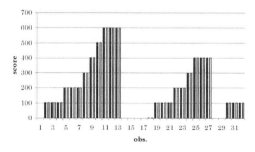

Fig. 9. Hello flooding detection scores when (5) is applied as input

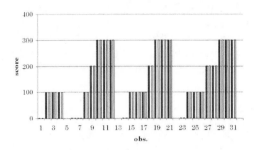

Fig. 10. Sinkhole detection scores when (6) is applied as input

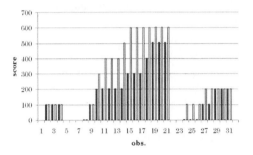

Fig. 11. Wormhole detection scores when (7) is applied as input

outputs are obtained for threats sharing at least one threat observables. For example sinkhole and wormhole in figure 10 and 11 share threat observables 1 and 2. In particular a sinkhole is an attack or is the initial step of a wormhole. Accordingly the score for wormhole in the case of the aggregated model is always greater than the score resulting from the single threat model (figure 11).

Attacks against distant nodes. Now we examine the capability of detecting the same threat attacking nodes that are not close to each other. In this test we assume a wormhole against nodes 4 and 5 in Figure 12. We consider the test successful if alarms were generated also in nodes 1, 2 and 3 (not directly attacked).

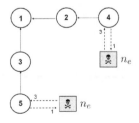

Fig. 12. Wormhole attack against nodes 4 and 5

Rule AR2, AR4 (from wormhole and the aggregate model) allow observable back propagation to nodes 4-2-1 and to nodes 5-3-1.

The criterion for the aggregation of observables is as follows. At the generic observation step k, the cluster head CH considers only observables with the highest score from neighbors. Accordingly, if the observable sequence 7 is produced in nodes 4 and 5, the following observables sequence 8 will be produced in nodes 1, 2 and 3:

$$\{2, 4, *, *, *, 4, *, 4, 4, 2, 4, *, *, 2, 4, *, *, 4, 4, *, *, *, 2, 2, *, *, 4, *, 4, *, *, *\} \quad (8)$$

Figure 13 shows the related threat scores. If no countermeasures are applied to nodes 4 and 5 observables propagates back from the compromised node to the sink until an alarm is triggered.

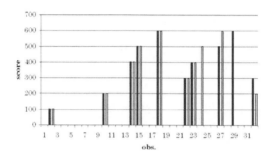

Fig. 13. Scores in nodes 1, 2, 3 from wormhole attack to nodes 4 and 5

3.2   False Alarm Detection

Test for positives will be performed through the analysis of the structure of the anomaly rules and the internal structure of the aggregated threat model in figure 8.

Among the anomaly rules in Table 2, AR3 and AR4 are associated to observables that can potentially produce false positives. This can lead to false alarms. But alarms be triggered only if the observations generate is a high potential attack. For example in figure 8, state X_3 is associated to observation o_3 or o_4 produced by AR3 and AR4 respectively. We propose two approaches reduce false positives.

1. *Introducing further states associated to certain threat observables in paths where at least one state is associated to ambiguous threat observables.* This approach lowers the probability for false positives ($p \mapsto 0$), as the longer the path to HPA the more reliable would be an alarm. A drawback is that long paths to HPA states, would reduce the reactivity in the monitoring service.
2. *Introducing a further class of states associated to ambiguous threat observables.* This approach cannot lower the probability for false positives, but

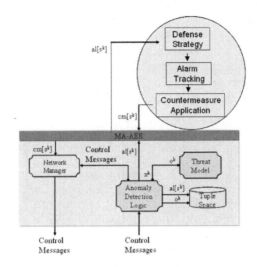

Fig. 14. WPM-based IDS component-based internal structure

"ad-hoc" lighter countermeasures can be applied to nodes where alarms from dubious observables are generated (e.g. node quarantine rather than link release).

4   Mobile Agent-Based Design

We adopt a mobile agent architecture to design and develop the proposed WPM-based intrusion detection. Resource constraints and topology dynamics in WSN imply restrictions for the software architectural choices where fundamental requirements are distribution, flexibility and scalability.

We will show that the agent based middleware proposed in [31] optimizes the design of distributed applications on clustered sensor networks. Cluster heads are not permanently assigned to specific nodes but dynamically re-assigned to any node according to eligibility criteria. This justify our choice of agents. A key concept from [31] is agent migration. During cloning, it copies its code and state to another node (strong cloning) and resumes executing on both the old and new nodes. Mobile agents support data-centric applications. Code migrates towards data independently from node addressing. Applications distribution through mobile agents results much less costly compared to traditional data broadcasting or code diffusion approaches. From [31] we will recall the concept of 'tuple space' as a local memory shared by local agents.

Figure 14 shows the basic functionalities of our intrusion detection system. Other functions related to intrusion reaction logic, including defence strategy, alarm tracking and countermeasures will be mapped into mobile agents as these functions will be performed at cluster level and data aggregation from neighbor nodes is mandatory. We denote this agent as 'Intrusion Reaction Agent' (IRA),

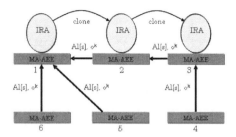

Fig. 15. IRA agent forward propagation vs. threat observables and alarms back propagation

represented by the oval in figure 14, which is hosted only by cluster heads. The mobile agent mechanism leads to forward propagation or diffusion from sink to leaves of IRA agents and to a back-propagation (from leaves to sink) of threat observables and alarms. In a clustered network, if IRA agent are hosted only on a cluster head, the agent diffusion mechanism across the network is described in figure 15 . IRA agent is initially hosted on node 1 and node 2 is a cluster member. The cluster head can read remotely threat observables stored on the tuple space of the neighboring node 2. When node 2 becomes cluster head, IRA (weakly) clones to it. The final agent distribution is depicted in figure 15. This mechanism allows each IRA to aggregate threat observables and alarms from cluster nodes, generate iteratively further observables and alarm. This aggregate and back-propagate mechanism for alarms and observables, leads to the detection of organized threats attacking nodes topologically distant. The ADL will store the produced observables and alarms into the 'local tuple' space. The middleware supporting the mobile agent execution environment is denoted as Mobile Agent Application Execution Environment (MA-AEE).

Our contribution is the definite verticality respect to WSN technology. Our approach to detection is fully distributed with a dynamic hierarchical architecture rather than centralized with a static hierarchical architecture. Security functions are executed autonomously by nodes in the network without any support from outside (like servers or database) as in [32,33], and complexity in IDS management is reduced due to the clustered tree topology which avoids overheads for loop checks and polling routines among neighboring nodes as in [34,35].

5   Conclusion and Future Work

In this paper we propose a new approach to anomaly detection and alarm generation logic using weak process models. Weak models are a simplified version of hidden markov models.

The proposed anomaly detection logic for threat modeling, threat identification, and alarm generation has been validated using MATLAB simulations.

Other threats are currently being modeled using the proposed formalism. The objective is the experimentation on a MicaZ cluster-based sensor network with a stepped implementation and deployment approach starting from few sensor nodes. Currently we are carrying on early experimentations on few MicaZ sensor nodes. Moreover we are packing ADL code for WSN development environment.

We are currently working on the capability of detecting a threat attacking nodes that are not close to each other. We showed in section 3 how the system performs when a wormhole was applied to distant nodes. We are currently extending this analysis to other attacks. Now the system uses only control messages to detect attacks. We plan to extend the proposed intrusion detection systems to include messages that contain monitoring data.

References

1. Roosta, T., Shieh, S., Sastry, S.: Taxonomy of security attacks in sensor networks. In: First IEEE International Conference on System Integration and Reliability Improvements, Hanoi, Vietnam, vol. 1, pp. 529–536 (2006)
2. Debar, H., Dacier, M., Wespi, A.: Towards a Taxonomy of Intrusion-Detection Systems. Computer Networks: The International Journal of Computer and Telecommunications Networking 31(9), 805–822 (1999)
3. Forney, G.: The Viterbi Algorithm. Proc. IEEE 61(3), 268–278 (1973)
4. Pugliese, M., Giani, A., Santucci, F.: A Weak Process Approach to Anomaly Detection in Wireless Sensor Networks. In: First International Workshop on Sensor Networks (SN 2008), Virgin Islands (2008)
5. Ephraim, Y., Merhav, N.: Hidden Markov Processes. IEEE Trans. Informmormation Theory 48(6) (2002)
6. Loo, C., Ng, M., Leckie, C., Palaniswami, M.: Intrusion Detection for Routing Attacks in Sensor Networks. International Journal of Distributed Sensor Networks (2005)
7. Doumit, S., Agrawal, D.: Self Organized Critically and Stochastic Learning Based Intrusion Detection System for Wireless Sensor Networks. In: Military Communications Conference, MILCOM (2003)
8. Jiang, G.: Robust process detection using nonparametric weak models. International Journal of Intelligent Control and Systems 10 (2005)
9. Yin, Q., Shen, L., Zhang, R., Li, X., Wang, H.: Intrusion Detection Based on Hidden Markov Model. In: International Conference on Machine Learning and Cybernetics, vol. 5, pp. 3115–3118 (2003)
10. Khanna, R., Liu, H.: System Approach to Intrusion Detection Using Hidden Markov Model. In: Proceedings of the international conference on Wireless communications and mobile computing, vol. 5, pp. 349–354 (2006)
11. Sheng, Y., Cybenko, G.: Distance Measures for Nonparametric Weak Process Models. In: IEEE International Conference on Systems, Man and Cybernetics, vol. 1, pp. 722–727 (2005)
12. Giani, A.: Detection of Attacks on Cognitive Channels. Ph.D. Thesis, Dartmouth College, Hanover, NH, USA (2006)

13. Silva, A., Martins, M., Rocha, B., Loureiro, A., Ruiz, L., Wong, H.: Decentralized Intrusion Detection in wireless sensor networks. In: Proceedings of the 1st ACM International Workshop on Quality of service and security in wireless and mobile Networks (2005)
14. Karlof, C., Wagner, D.: Secure routing in wireless sensor networks: Attacks and countermeasures. In: 1st IEEE International Workshop on Sensor Network Protocols and Applications, vol. 10 (2003)
15. Rabiner, L., Juang, B.: An Introduction to Hidden Markov Models. IEEE ASSP Magazine, 4–16 (1986)
16. http://www.tinyos.net/tinyos2.x/doc
17. Pugliese, M., Santucci, F.: Pair-wise Network Topology Authenticated Hybrid Cryptographic Keys for Wireless Sensor Networks using Vector Algebra. In: 4th IEEE International Workshop on Wireless Sensor Networks Security (WSNS 2008), Atlanta (2008)
18. Whitman, M., Mattord, H.: Principles of Information Security, 3rd edn. Thomson (2009)
19. Ross, A.: Security Engineering. Wiley, New York (2001)
20. Baker, Z., Prasanna, V.: Computationally-efficient engine for flexible intrusion detection (2005)
21. Dainotti, A., Pescape, A., Rossi, P., Palmieri, F., Ventre, G.: Internet Traffic modeling by means of Hidden Markov Models. Computer Networks 54, 2645–2662 (2008)
22. Al-Subaie, M., Zulkernine, M.: Efficacy of Hidden Markov Models Over Neural Networks in Anomaly Intrusion Detection. In: Proceedings of the 30th Annual International Computer Software and Applications Conference (COMPSAC), vol. 1, pp. 325–332 (2006)
23. Wang, W., Guan, X., Zhang, X.: Modeling program behaviors by hidden Markov models for intrusion detection. In: Proceedings of 2004 International Conference on Machine Learning and Cybernetics, vol. 5, pp. 2830–2835 (2004)
24. Luk, M., Mezzour, G., Perrig, A., Gligor, V.: MiniSec: A Secure Sensor Network Communication Architecture. In: Proceedings of the Sixth International Conference on Information Processing in Sensor Networks (IPSN) (April 2007)
25. Hu, Y., Perrig, A., Johnson, D.: Packet Leashes: A Defense against Wormhole Attacks in Wireless Ad Hoc Networks. In: Proceedings of the INFOCOM 2003 (2003)
26. Law, Y., Havinga, P., Johnson, D.: How to Secure a Wireless Sensor Network. In: Proc. of the International Conference on Intelligent Sensors, Sensor Networks and Information Processing Conference (2005)
27. Ngai, E., Liu, J., Lyu, M.: On the Intruder Detection for Sinkhole Attack in Wireless Sensor Networks. In: Proc. of the IEEE International Conference on Communications, ICC 2006 (2006)
28. Krontiris, I., Dimitriou, T., Giannetsos, T., Mpasoukos, M.: Intrusion Detection of Sinkhole Attacks in Wireless Sensor Networks. In: Proc. 3rd International Workshop on Algorithmic Aspects of Wireless Sensor Networks, AlgoSensors 2007 (2007)
29. Dallas, D., Leckie, C., Ramamohanarao, K.: Hop-Count Monitoring: Detecting Sinkhole Attacks in Wireless Sensor Networks. In: Proc. of the 15th IEEE International Conference on Networks, ICON 2007 (2007)
30. Brust, M.R., Andronache, A., Rothkugel, S., Benenson, Z.: Topology-based Clusterhead Candidate Selection in Wireless Ad-hoc and Sensor Networks. In: 2nd International Conference on Communication Systems Software and Middleware, COMSWARE 2007, pp. 1–8 (2007)

31. Fok, C.-L., Roman, G.C., Lu, C.: Agilla: A Mobile Agent Middleware for Sensor Networks. Tech. Report, Washington University in St. Louis, WUCSE-2006-16 (2006)
32. Balasubramainyan, J., Garcia-Fernandez, J.O., Isacoff, D., Spafford, E., Zamboni, D.: An architecture of Intrusion Detection using Autonomous Agents, Department of Computer Science, Purdue University TR 98-05 (1998)
33. Vahid Dastjerdi, A., Abu Bakar, K.: A Novel Hybrid Mobile Agent Based Distributed Intrusion Detection System. Proc. of World Academy of Science Engineering and Technology 35 (November 2008)
34. Ramachandran, G., Hart, D.: A P2P Intrusion Detection System based on Mobile Agents. ACM, New York (2004)
35. Zhou, C.V., Karunasekera, S., Leckie, C.: A Peer-to-Peer Collaborative Intrusion Detection System. In: Proc. of 13th IEEE International Conference on Communications, ICC 2005 (2005)

Key Establishment Using Group Information for Wireless Sensor Networks

William R. Claycomb[1], Rodrigo Lopes[1], Dongwan Shin[1], and Byunggi Kim[2]

[1] Secure Computing Laboratory, New Mexico Tech,
801 Leroy Place, Socorro, NM, USA, 87801
{billc,rodrigo,doshin}@nmt.edu
[2] College of Information Technology, Soongsil University,
511 Sangdo-dong, Dongjak-gu, Seoul 156-743, Korea
bgkim@comp.ssu.ac.kr

Abstract. Wireless sensor networks are commonly used for critical security tasks such as intrusion or tamper detection, and therefore must be protected. To date, security of these networks relies mostly on key establishment and routing protocols. We present a new approach to key establishment, which combines a group-based distribution model and identity-based cryptography. Using this solution enables sensor nodes to authenticate each other, and provides them with a structure to build secure communications between one another, and between various groups. Using our key establishment protocol, we show how to reduce or prevent significant attacks on wireless sensor networks.

Keywords: Group-based security, key establishment, wireless sensor networks.

1 Introduction

Wireless sensor networks (WSNs) have become commonplace in applications ranging from simple light, temperature, and sound measurements to sophisticated military and industrial applications. In some cases the security of the sensors, the data collection, and the communication of that data to a collection point is unimportant. However, for sensitive applications, the security of these tasks is paramount.

One of the core components to securing WSN data is the establishment of secret keys between sensor nodes in a network. In contrast to other mobile network applications, WSN have the property that key establishment information can be pre-loaded onto sensor nodes prior to deployment. However, the limitations of sensor nodes have traditionally limited key establishment and data encryption techniques to simple and symmetric cryptographic applications.

Recently, due to advances in sensor hardware, the field of asymmetric cryptography has become a realistic option for various operations in WSN.Using asymmetric cryptography for key establishment greatly simplifies many of the challenges currently faced by schemes relying on symmetric key establishment

S. Hailes, S. Sicari, and G. Roussos (Eds.): S-Cube 2009, LNICST 24, pp. 51–65, 2009.

protocols. For instance, node authentication is possible. Also, compromising even a large subset of nodes and communication keys does not compromise all communication keys for the network - a goal many of the solutions to date have strived to achieve. However, using asymmetric cryptography does not solve all the problems of WSN security. Specifically, three attacks that still present problems for WSN are *node replication*, *Sybil*, and *wormhole* attacks.

In this paper, we present a novel scheme for key establishment in WSN which combines the notion of *group-based* key predistribution with identity based cryptography (IBC). We show how this approach enables secure key establishment in WSN, and show how our solution improves upon the security of existing key establishment schemes. We discuss considerations in design for this type of WSN, including an analysis of group communication dynamics. We also demonstrate how our solution addresses various attacks on WSNs.

The remainder of this paper is structured as follows. Section 2 describes related work, including a description of identity based cryptography components. Section 3 describes our new key establishment protocol, followed by Section 4 which presents a detailed description of various attacks and how our solution addresses them. Section 5 presents a discussion of group distribution decisions and the impact to sensor nodes. In Section 6, we conclude the paper with a discussion of future work.

2   Background and Related Work

Key establishment in WSNs has been an active area of research for many years, and several approaches have been proposed. The simplest method of key establishment between nodes in a WSN is to preload each node with the same shared secret key, and use that key to secure transmission between every node pair. While this is simple in terms of protocol and storage requirements, it has the disadvantage that compromising a single node reveals all communication to an adversary. The simple solution to prevent this is to pre-load each node with a unique shared key for pairwise communication with every other node in the network. This is a more secure network than the previous one, as compromising a single node only reveals the data transmitted between it and its node partners. However, the storage overhead per node is unrealistic, particularly in the case of very large networks.

Several researchers have developed solutions for pairwise key establishment that fall between these two extremes. Recently, proposals have included the notion of *location-based*, or *group-based* schemes. These approaches observe that in large-scale sensor node distributions, nodes deployed in a group tend to end up near each other physically. By tailoring key predistribution to take advantage of this property, efficient schemes have been presented [1,2,3,4].

However, these solutions rely on symmetric key agreement protocols, and largely ignore the application of asymmetric key agreement methods. It has been commonly believed that the increased computational and time constraints required by asymmetric solutions are too costly for WSNs. Recently, though, researchers have studied implementations of asymmetric protocols such as elliptic curve cryptography (ECC) on sensor nodes [5,6,7,8,9]. Results have been promising, and various proposals for key establishment and key management using ECC-based approaches have been suggested [10].

2.1   Identity Based Cryptography

In [11], the authors propose using an *identity based cryptography* technique called *pairing* [12,13] to facilitate secure key establishment between nodes in WSNs. First proposed by [14], identity based cryptography (IBC), or *identity based encryption*, is similar to traditional public-key based cryptography systems, but instead of using a randomly generated public key, entities use unique strings or other short identifiers, such as email addresses, as their public key. For instance, to send an encrypted email to "bob@company.com," Alice would encrypt the message using the email address as the public key. Bob would obtain his corresponding private key from a *Private Key Generator* to decrypt the message. Therefore, IBC helps negate the use of public key certificate in PKC-based applications.

As one of the critical components to optimizing the performance of WSNs is minimizing data storage and transmission size, IBC is an excellent choice for exchanging key establishment information in this regard. The only thing necessary to begin key establishment is the identity of the source node, which only has to be large enough to ensure a unique ID among the entire network. A 16 bit ID would provide unique IDs for $2^{16} = 65536$ sensor nodes.

Definitions. The following definitions will be used in describing our solution:

p, q	large primes
$\mathbb{E}/\mathbb{F}_p$	An elliptic curve $y^2 = x^3 + ax + b$ over the finite field $\mathbb{F}_p$
$\mathbb{G}_1$	A q-order subgroup of the additive group of points of $\mathbb{E}/\mathbb{F}_p$
$\mathbb{G}_2$	A q-order subgroup of the multiplicative group of the finite field $\mathbb{F}_{p^2}^*$
$\hat{e}$	A mapping $\mathbb{G}_1 \times \mathbb{G}_1 \to \mathbb{G}_2$
H	A cryptographic hash function which maps to elements in $\mathbb{G}_1$
h	A standard cryptographic hash function
$A, B, ...$	Groups of sensor nodes
$x, y, ...$	Individual sensor nodes
ID_A	Unique ID of group A
ID_x	Unique ID of sensor node x
$K_{x:A}$	Secret key for node x among group A
K_{xy}	Shared pairwise key between nodes x and y
m_A	Master key for group A

The modified Weil pairing scheme in [12] is used for the basis of our key establishment protocol. This allows two sensor nodes to establish a shared secret key using only the knowledge of an individual secret key and the unique identity of the other node, as long as the secret key of the first node was generated using the same keying information as the identity information of the second node. The pairing is based on the *bilinear Diffie-Hellman Problem (DLP)*, which is proven to be computationally hard.

Pairing. A *pairing* is the mapping of two points P and Q, from separate subgroups of points on an elliptic curve, to a third point in a finite field, and is denoted $e(P, Q)$. Usually P and Q are linearly independent of each other, otherwise the pairing is considered degenerate, and $e(P, Q) = 1$. To use P and Q from the same group $\mathbb{G}_1$, a *distortion map* ψ is used to make the second element linearly independent of the first. This *distortion pairing* is denoted $\hat{e}(P, Q) = e(P, \psi(Q))$. The distorted pairing is *symmetric*, that is $\forall P, Q \in \mathbb{G}_1$, $\hat{e}(P, Q) = \hat{e}(Q, P)$. For a more thorough description of pairings over elliptic curves, please see [12,13].

Due to the distortion map, we can use a pairing which is a mapping $\mathbb{G}_1 \times \mathbb{G}_1 \rightarrow \mathbb{G}_2$. It has the following properties [12]:

– Bilinear: $\forall P, Q \in \mathbb{G}_1$ and $\forall a, b \in \mathbb{Z}$, $\hat{e}(aP, bQ) = \hat{e}(P, Q)^{ab}$.
– Non-degenerate: If P is a generator of $\mathbb{G}_1$ then $\hat{e}(P, P) \in \mathbb{F}_{p^2}^*$ is a generator of $\mathbb{G}_2$.
– Computable: Given $P, Q \in \mathbb{G}_1$, there is an efficient algorithm to compute $\hat{e}(P, Q) \in \mathbb{G}_2$

3   Group-Based Key Establishment

While some node deployment scenarios allow for manual or automated placement of nodes, or for key nodes to have known fixed positions [11], we believe that certain critical applications, such as battlefield deployments, do not provide such means. Therefore, it is desirable to have a solution which provides secure key establishment without requiring specific location knowledge for each node. Instead, we propose that in a group-based distribution, assuming nodes deployed together end up near each other [3,15], that each group of nodes deployed be pre-keyed using key information unique to that group. Doing so would allow nodes containing keying information for a specific group A to establish pairwise keys with nodes from group A. We will show that in order to establish this pairwise key, both nodes must have keying information for group A.

To detail our solution, we propose that a successful deployment of a WSN would consist of the following phases:

– Provisioning authority initialization
– Sensor key initialization (key pre-distribution)
– Sensor deployment
– Pair-wise key establishment

3.1   Provisioning Authority Initialization

A separate provisioning authority (PA) is created for each group of nodes to be deployed. A *master PA* is responsible for generating the pairing information for each PA. This information, as described in § 2.1, is $(p, q, \mathbb{E}/\mathbb{F}_p, \mathbb{G}_1, \mathbb{G}_2, \hat{e})$. The master PA also selects two hash functions, H and h, where H maps to nonzero elements in $\mathbb{G}_1$, and h is a secure cryptographic hash function. Then, for a group of sensors to be deployed, A, the master PA randomly selects m_A as the master secret for A. This sequence is loosely based on the work of [11], but has been modified to meet the specific needs of our solution.

3.2   Sensor Key Initialization

During this phase, we assume each group has a unique identity ID_A, and every node has a unique identity ID_x. The PA provides every sensor x, in group A, a unique identity-based key $K_{x:A}$. The unique key is calculated as $K_{x:A} = m_A H(ID_x)$. Along with the unique $K_{x:A}$, each node in A is pre-loaded with the public information for group A, $(p, q, \mathbb{E}/\mathbb{F}_p, \mathbb{G}_1, \mathbb{G}_2, \hat{e}, H, h, ID_A)$. Compromising a node will not reveal the group secret key m_A. This is due to the intractability of the discrete logarithm problem for elliptic curves (ECDLP). That is, consider an elliptic curve E defined over $\mathbb{F}_q$ and $P \in E(\mathbb{F}_q)$, which is a point of order n. Given $Q \in E(F_q)$, it is infeasible to find an integer $0 \leq d \leq n$ such that $Q = dP$. Therefore, it is also infeasible to find m_A, given $K_{x:A}$ and ID_x, since $K_{x:A} = m_A H(ID_x)$.

In addition to the unique key for group A, each node x is also pre-loaded with a unique key corresponding to each adjacent group B, which is calculated as $K_{x:AB} = m_A m_B H(ID_x)$. Nodes are also given the identifier for group B, ID_B. At this point, it is possible to pre-load x with additional unique keys and group identifiers for the groups beyond those immediately adjacent to A. The number of adjacent and surrounding group keys loaded on each node in A is determined by the needs of the network, noting that each additional layer of depth i adds 2^{i+2} public keys, if adjacent groups are arranged in a grid, as shown in Figure 1.

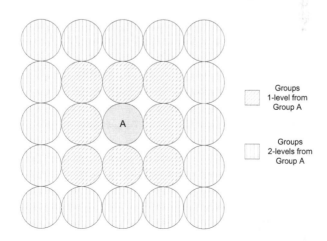

Fig. 1. Layers of sensor network groups

3.3   Sensor Deployment

Sensors are deployed in groups, in a predetermined pattern, over the intended area. No additional bootstrapping is necessary for nodes to begin generating pair-wise keys.

3.4   Pairwise Key Establishment

Pairwise keys between neighboring nodes can be established in one of two ways. The first, *intragroup* key establishment, involves pairwise keys generated between nodes in the same group. The second, *intergroup* key establishment involves nodes generating pairwise keys with nodes in different groups.

For the purposes of our solution, the elements of a pairing $\hat{e}(P, Q)$ are the private keying information of a source node, $K_{x:A}$, and the public keying information (identity) of the destination node, ID_y. Because of the symmetry of pairing, the private keying information of the destination node, $K_{y:A}$, and the public keying information (identity) of the source node, ID_x, will also produce the same value, as long as all elements originate in $\mathbb{G}_1$, due to the symmetry of the pairing.

Intragroup key establishment. To establish pairwise keys with neighboring nodes in the same group, node x broadcasts its identity ID_x, its group identity ID_A, and a random nonce n_x, and waits for responses from neighboring nodes within range. A node y receiving the broadcast from x first checks to see if it is in the same group A. If so, node y responds with its own identity ID_y, another random nonce n_y, and a verification of a shared key, $h_{K_{yx}}(n_x||n_y||1)$, where $K_{yx} = \hat{e}(K_{y:A}, H(ID_x))$. Because this is intragroup communication, the group ID ID_A does not need to be returned. The lack of group ID in the return message is a trigger to x that the return key information in intragroup. In this case, x is able to verify the identity of y, because $K_{yx} = K_{xy}$, due to the pairing symmetry. Node x responds with a verification message $h_{K_{xy}}(n_x||n_y||2)$, where $K_{xy} = \hat{e}(K_{x:A}, H(ID_y))$. This verifies to y that x has established the correct key.

Intergroup key establishment. To establish a pairwise key with a node in another group, B, node x follows a similar protocol. The initial broadcast step is the same: ID_x, the group identity ID_A, and a random nonce n_x. Upon receiving this message, node y, in group B, recognizes that x is in another group, A. y checks to see if it possesses a key corresponding to A, $K_{y:BA}$. If so, y responds with its own identity ID_y, its group identity, ID_B, another random nonce n_y, and a verification of a shared key, $h_{K_{yx}}(n_x||n_y||1)$, where $K_{yx} = \hat{e}(K_{y:BA}, H(ID_x))$. When x receives this message, it sees that a group identity was returned. x checks to see if it possesses a key corresponding to B, $K_{x:AB}$. If so, x responds with a verification message $h_{K_{xy}}(n_x||n_y||2)$, where $K_{xy} = \hat{e}(K_{x:AB}, H(ID_y))$. This verifies to y that x has established the correct key.

4   Attacks and Resistance

Various attacks on WSNs have been described in the literature. Some of the more difficult to defend against are the node replication, node addition, Sybil, and wormhole attacks. Our solution either prevents these attacks from occurring, or minimizes their impact to the point of inefficacy.

4.1   Node Replication Attack

A *node replication* attack [16] consists of an adversary compromising one or more existing nodes, duplicating (and perhaps modifying) the information retrieved, provisioning new nodes with the stolen information, and placing the replicated nodes into the network. Under simple authentication schemes, a network is unable to detect the duplicated nodes, particularly if they are placed far apart, and they are able to authenticate and interact with existing nodes. This provides the attacker with a means of intercepting communication, affecting network routing, or even skewing reputation-based trust management systems.

Our solution eliminates the node replication attack over multiple groups. To show this, consider a compromised node x, from group A. If placed in a group where nodes do not share keying information with A, the replicated node (denoted x') would be unable to establish any pairwise keys. To be successful, an attacker could only place x into a group where the nodes have shared key information with A. In a large network, the number of such groups is likely to be small. Additionally, placing x' into one of these groups would be likely to cause detection, as the real x is nearby, and nodes receiving another authentication request from a duplicate node proclaiming to be x would detect the attack.

4.2   Node Addition Attack

In a *node addition* attack [17], an adversary injects new nodes into a WSN. This differs from a node replication attack because the new nodes are not duplicates of an existing node, but rather are provisioned correctly as unique nodes in the network. To carry out this attack in a network with pairwise key establishment, an adversary must have access to keying information, such as a master key (m_A in our solution.) While some solutions allow the master key to exist for a short period of time on individual nodes during the distribution of a new network [11,17], ours does not allow m_A to exist on any node or base station in the network. Without m_A, an attacker can only gain information such as ID_x, $K_{x:A}$, ID_A, etc. Even with the pairing components (ID_x, $K_{x:A}$), m_A cannot be deduced, due to the properties of the pairing scheme.

4.3   Sybil Attack

The *Sybil attack* [18] describes a situation where an attacker generates multiple fake identities in one location, appearing to be many legitimate nodes, and uses those identities to influence the existing WSN. This influence can be against routing, trust management, reputation, or other elements of network management. In contrast to the node replication attack, the nodes in the Sybil attack are not real nodes, nor are they distributed throughout the network.

Our solution prevents this attack by preventing an attacker from spoofing legitimate nodes. Without the master key to generate pairing information, an attacker cannot generate correct pairing information. Without this information, a Sybil node cannot establish pairwise keys with any legitimate node in the network.

4.4   Wormhole Attack

One of the more interesting attacks in WSNs, the wormhole attack involves an attacker using a covert, high-speed side channel to tunnel information across the network. The effect is to allow two distant nodes to communicate with each other, fooling them into believing they are neighbors. This can disrupt network routing, potentially preventing critical messages from being received by the correct locations. It can also affect networks which use relative node location for decision-making. The wormhole attack is shown in Figure 2.

Detecting and preventing wormhole attacks are challenging issues. Most solutions to date involve the use of mechanisms based on the physical location of nodes, or the physical distance between them. These solutions use either location-fixing devices, such as GPS, or tight time synchronization between nodes to detect wormholes [11,19,20].

Our solution prevents wormhole attacks between nodes in distant groups because they do not share key information, and cannot form pairwise keys, as shown in Figure 3. However, a wormhole between two nearby groups is possible. Creating a wormhole for nodes within adjacent groups would have a limited effect, and would be physically more difficult, because creating a high-speed side-channel and processing information through it faster than the normal network routing becomes tricky as the distance between the wormhole ends grows smaller.

With this in mind, a network designer can carefully plan node group size to reduce the threat of wormhole attacks to an acceptable level. For instance, if an

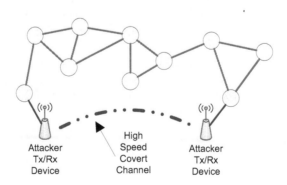

Fig. 2. A wormhole attack

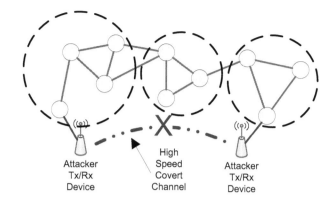

Fig. 3. A wormhole attack prevented in a group-based network

attack between nodes 50 m apart would not compromise the overall integrity of the system, then groups can be distributed with a diameter of 25 m, so the greatest distance between any two nodes allowed to communicate is 50 m.

Wormhole attacks can be prevented by a carefully designed security policy as well. If a policy is designed such that a group A only trusts connections to group B, then a wormhole attack is only possible from group A to group B. Because this is an asymmetric trust, a wormhole attack from B to A is not possible. This is an important step towards preventing a wormhole attack that seeks to "skip" a sensor or group of sensors in a sequence by generating a wormhole around it.

5   Discussion

The discussion of our solution will focus on two areas. The first part deals with the network design. Next, we discuss the impact to sensor nodes themselves.

5.1   Network Design

When looking at a group-based deployment, we must consider how the nodes will be distributed. Will they be distributed evenly over an area, or will they tend to be more densely populated near the center of an area? How does this affect the chances of multi-group communication? We attempt to answer these questions here.

Node distributions are not always uniform. Sometimes the reasons for this are simple physics (i.e. dropping a box of sensor nodes from an airplane at different heights, with different wind patterns, will result in greatly different distributions on the ground). Other times, the reasons for a certain distribution are more sophisticated, such as the desire to prevent a wormhole attack between nodes of a certain distance, n.

To help analyze communication between groups in our solution, we consider two variations of node distribution, one where nodes are distributed evenly over

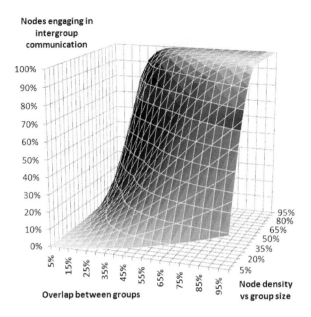

Fig. 4. Nodes able to communicate with other groups using an even distribution

the entire group, and one where nodes are distributed according to a normal (Gaussian) distribution.

Two key factors in determining how well two groups will communicate are the *node coverage* over the group, and the *overlap* between groups. Our simulation results show the percentage of nodes within a group able to communicate with adjacent groups, given the node coverage and overlap size of the network. Figure 4 shows the results for an even distribution of nodes over a group, and Figure 5 shows the results for a Gaussian distribution of nodes over a group.

Based on these results, it is clear that a more even distribution of nodes is desirable when implementing a group-based model. It is interesting to note the much higher percentage of nodes able to communicate in even distributions. The lower figure for the Gaussian distribution is due to the lower density of nodes distributed over the edge of the Gaussian group. Based on these results, we can make decisions regarding network architecture, taking into account the distribution method, and how nodes are likely to be distributed in their final state.

5.2 Sensor Impact

A critical analysis of any sensor network application must include the impact to the sensors in terms of space requirements, processing time, and power consumed. We believe the solution presented here has an acceptable footprint upon the sensor nodes. For analysis purposes, we will consider an implementation where p is a 512-bit prime and q is a 160-bit prime.

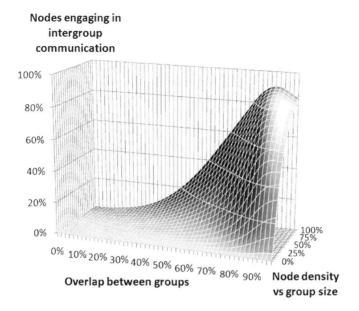

Fig. 5. Nodes able to communicate with other groups using a normal (Gaussian) distribution

Sensor memory requirements. The use of elliptic curve cryptography (ECC) based mechanisms means that less space is required to store key information. To achieve the same public key security as a 1024-bit RSA [21] implementation, only 160-bit keys are needed for ECC [6]. Standard ECC-based digital certificates, used in traditional key establishment, are ~530 bytes in size. This can be reduced to 86 bytes by removing all but the most important data [8]. Our proposal reduces this size even further, requiring only 40 bytes to store node identification and keying information. This improvement becomes even more important when we consider how much energy is consumed during data transmission - sending a singe bit of information can take the same power as 2090 clock cycles of execution [8].

However, in our solution, more than just one key is stored on each node. Adding keys for adjacent group key establishment depends on the topology of the network. Without loss of generality, we assume a topology similar to Figure 1. In this instance, the total number of keys to be stored on each node is $\sum_{i=1}^{n} 2^{i+2}$. To store 1 layer of key establishment information requires 160 bytes. For 2 layers, 480 bytes are needed. 3 layers require 1120 bytes. This must be considered in network design.

Group public information, $(p, q, \mathbb{E}/\mathbb{F}_p, \mathbb{G}_1, \mathbb{G}_2, \hat{e}, H, h, ID_A)$, must also be loaded onto each node. Due to space requirements, we will not detail each component, but will note that p is a 512 bit prime, $\mathbb{G}_1, \mathbb{G}_2$ are 160 bit primes, ID_A can be relatively small (16 bits), and the components relating to key generation code can be estimated at ~3.6KB [6] for 160-bit ECC operations.

We note that the Atmel ATmega128 [22], a common micro-controller used on many sensor devices, has 128KB of FLASH program memory. Another common sensor network node, the Crossbow Imote2 has 256KB of SRAM memory, 32MB of SDRAM memory, and 32MB of FLASH memory [23]. We believe sensor deployments where > 3 layers of shared key information are unlikely, so a total overhead of < 5KB seems reasonable for this application.

Processing time. Several works have analyzed processing time for ECC-based operation on various sensor devices. While some report times in excess of 30 seconds for generating shared secret keys [7], improvements in hardware, as well as algorithm design, have made significant improvements. In [6], an average time of 0.81s for 160-bit ECC operations is given.

Other papers have shown efficient implementations of pairing schemes. In [11], it is shown that a commonly used processor, the Intel PXA255, can generate a Tate pairing in approximately 62 ms. However, this is a 32-bit processor typically used on network gateway devices, such as the Crossbow Stargate, not on actual sensor nodes. Typical 8-bit sensor nodes take > 30 seconds on average to compute Tate pairings [24].

Recent advances in sensor nodes have included the addition of more powerful 32-bit processors at the node level. In [13], it is shown that it takes 290 ms to compute a Tate pairing on a 32-bit MIPS-32 based SmartMIPS architecture for smartcards, running at 36MHz. The Crossbow Imote2, uses a 32-bit Intel PXA271 scalable processor (13MHz - 416 MHz), and would require ∼23.2 ms for the same operation at its highest speed, 92 ms at 104MHz (normal operating speed), and 736 ms at 13MHz (low-power operating speed).

Processing power. We show the power consumption for various components of our solution, using an Imote2 sensor node running at the most conservative power level. The power consumption figures, including both computational operations and radio transmission, for establishing a pairwise key between two sensor nodes are shown in Table 1.

Transmission power. Because our solution uses such a small footprint for identity and group identification information, the transmission power necessary to establish a pairing is small. The total power required to establish a pairing,

Table 1. Power consumption of pairwise key establishment operations on an Imote2 Sensor node

Operation	Energy
All transmissions for pairing	203 μJ
Compute pairing (low power)	27.53 mJ
Compute pairing (normal power)	41.29 mJ

using a CC2420 IEEE 802.15.4 radio transciever [25], is approximately 203 μJ. This figure represents all transmission and reception power for a single node involved in the pairing operation, regardless of whether the node initiates the transaction or not.

6 Conclusion

We have demonstrated a method for key establishment in WSNs which leverages the properties of node authentication and group-based keys to strengthen the security of a network. Our solution is a novel approach to key establishment in WSNs that uses a group-based technique combined with identity based cryptography to provide node authentication and intergroup communication. We showed how our solution is resistant to some of the more difficult attacks to prevent in WSNs, including the node replication, Sybil, and wormhole attacks.

Future work will include multi-hop key establishment, which would further enhance the capabilities of a network of this type. Another interesting area of study would be to leverage the capabilities provided by this solution to establish a fine-grained security policy for WSN. Using knowledge such as authenticated node identity and group membership, this security policy could be fine-tuned to provide differing levels of access control to different sensors based on group membership.

Sensor networks will continue to be part of everyday life. As sensors become smaller and more capable, their potential uses will only increase. In many cases, the security of the networks they form is critical to maintain, and we believe this will continue to be an important area of research.

Acknowledgements

This work was partially supported at the Secure Computing Laboratory at New Mexico Tech by the grant from the National Science Foundation (NSF-CNS-0709437).

References

1. Du, W., Deng, J., Han, Y., Chen, S., Varshney, P.: A key management scheme for wireless sensor networks using deployment knowledge. In: INFOCOM 2004. Twenty-third AnnualJoint Conference of the IEEE Computer and Communications Societies, vol. 1, p. 597 (2004)
2. Huang, D., Mehta, M., Medhi, D., Harn, L.: Location-aware key management scheme for wireless sensor networks. In: Proceedings of the 2nd ACM workshop on Security of ad hoc and sensor networks, pp. 29–42. ACM, Washington (2004)
3. Liu, D., Ning, P.: Location-based pairwise key establishments for static sensor networks. In: Proceedings of the 1st ACM workshop on Security of ad hoc and sensor networks, pp. 72–82. ACM, Fairfax (2003)

4. Yu, Z., Guan, Y.: A key management scheme using deployment knowledge for wireless sensor networks. IEEE Transactions on Parallel and Distributed Systems 19(10), 1411–1425 (2008)

5. Gaubatz, G., Kaps, J., Sunar, B.: Public key cryptography in sensor Networks – Revisited. In: The Proceedings of the 1st European Workshop on Security in Ad-Hoc and Sensor Networks, ESAS (2005)

6. Gura, N., Patel, A., Wander, A., Eberle, H., Shantz, S.C.: Comparing elliptic curve cryptography and RSA on 8-bit CPUs. In: Joye, M., Quisquater, J.-J. (eds.) CHES 2004. LNCS, vol. 3156, pp. 119–132. Springer, Heidelberg (2004)

7. Malan, D., Welsh, M., Smith, M.: A public-key infrastructure for key distribution in TinyOS based on elliptic curve cryptography. In: 2004 First Annual IEEE Communications Society Conference on Sensor and Ad Hoc Communications and Networks, IEEE SECON 2004, pp. 71–80 (2004)

8. Wander, A.S., Gura, N., Eberle, H., Gupta, V., Shantz, S.C.: Energy analysis of Public-Key cryptography for wireless sensor networks. In: Proceedings of the Third IEEE International Conference on Pervasive Computing and Communications, pp. 324–328. IEEE Computer Society, Los Alamitos (2005)

9. Watro, R., Kong, D., fen Cuti, S., Gardiner, C., Lynn, C., Kruus, P.: TinyPK: securing sensor networks with public key technology. In: Proceedings of the 2nd ACM workshop on Security of ad hoc and sensor networks, pp. 59–64. ACM, Washington (2004)

10. Zhou, Y., Zhang, Y., Fang, Y.: Access control in wireless sensor networks. Ad Hoc Networks 5(1), 3–13 (2007)

11. Zhang, Y., Liu, W., Lou, W., Fang, Y.: Location-based compromise-tolerant security mechanisms for wireless sensor networks. IEEE Journal on Selected Areas in Communications 24(2), 247–260 (2006)

12. Boneh, D., Franklin, M.: Identity-Based Encryption from the Weil Pairing, pp. 213–229 (2001)

13. Scott, M., Costigan, N., Abdulwahab, W.: Implementing cryptographic pairings on smartcards. In: Goubin, L., Matsui, M. (eds.) CHES 2006. LNCS, vol. 4249, pp. 134–147. Springer, Heidelberg (2006)

14. Shamir, A.: Identity-based cryptosystems and signature schemes. In: Blakely, G.R., Chaum, D. (eds.) CRYPTO 1984. LNCS, vol. 196, pp. 47–53. Springer, Heidelberg (1985)

15. Liu, D., Ning, P., Du, W.: Group-based key predistribution for wireless sensor networks. ACM Trans. Sen. Netw. 4(2), 1–30 (2008)

16. Parno, B., Perrig, A., Gligor, V.: Distributed detection of node replication attacks in sensor networks. In: SP 2005: Proceedings of the 2005 IEEE Symposium on Security and Privacy, pp. 49–63. IEEE Computer Society, Washington (2005)

17. Zhu, S., Setia, S., Jajodia, S.: LEAP: efficient security mechanisms for large-scale distributed sensor networks. In: Proceedings of the 10th ACM conference on Computer and communications security, pp. 62–72. ACM, Washington (2003)

18. Douceur, J.R.: The sybil attack. In: Druschel, P., Kaashoek, M.F., Rowstron, A. (eds.) IPTPS 2002. LNCS, vol. 2429, pp. 251–260. Springer, Heidelberg (2002)

19. Hu, Y.-C., Perrig, A., Johnson, D.: Packet leashes: a defense against wormhole attacks in wireless networks. In: Twenty-Second Annual Joint Conference of the IEEE Computer and Communications Societies, INFOCOM 2003, vol. 3, pp. 1976–1986. IEEE, Los Alamitos (2003)

20. Lazos, L., Poovendran, R., Meadows, C., Syverson, P., Chang, L.: Preventing worm-hole attacks on wireless ad hoc networks: a graph theoretic approach. In: Wireless Communications and Networking Conference, vol. 2, pp. 1193–1199. IEEE, Los Alamitos (2005)
21. Rivest, R.L., Shamir, A., Adleman, L.: A method for obtaining digital signatures and public-key cryptosystems. Commun. ACM 21(2), 120–126 (1978)
22. Amtel Corporation, Amtel ATmega128 (2009),
    http://www.atmel.com/dyn/products/product_card.asp?part_id=2018
23. Crossbow Technology, iMote2 (2009),
    http://www.xbow.com/Products/Product_pdf_files/Wireless_pdf/
    Imote2_Datasheet.pdf
24. Oliveira, L., Aranha, D., Morais, E., Daguano, F., Lopez, J., Dahab, R.: Tinytate: Computing the tate pairing in resource-constrained sensor nodes. In: Sixth IEEE International Symposium on Network Computing and Applications, NCA 2007, pp. 318–323 (2007)
25. Texas Instruments, CC2420 (2008),
    http://focus.ti.com/lit/ds/symlink/cc2420.pdf

A Forward and Backward Secure Key Management in Wireless Sensor Networks for PCS/SCADA

Hani Alzaid[1], DongGook Park[2], Juan González Nieto[1], Colin Boyd[1], and Ernest Foo[1]

[1] Information Security Institute, Queensland University of Technology,
Brisbane QLD 4000, Australia
{h.alzaid,juanma,c.boyd,e.foo}@isi.qut.edu.au
[2] School of Information Technology, Sunchon University, Korea
dgpark6@sunchon.ac.kr

Abstract. Process Control Systems (PCSs) or Supervisory Control and Data Acquisition (SCADA) systems have recently been added to the already wide collection of wireless sensor networks applications. The PCS/SCADA environment is somewhat more amenable to the use of heavy cryptographic mechanisms such as public key cryptography than other sensor application environments. The sensor nodes in the environment, however, are still open to devastating attacks such as node capture, which makes designing a secure key management challenging. In this paper, a key management scheme is proposed to defeat node capture attack by offering both forward and backward secrecies. Our scheme overcomes the pitfalls which Nilsson et al.'s scheme suffers from, and is not more expensive than their scheme.

Keywords: Wireless sensor network, forward and backward secrecy, key management, process control systems, supervisory control and data acquisition.

1 Introduction

Process Control Systems (PCSs) or Supervisory Control and Data Acquisition (SCADA) systems are used to monitor and control a plant or equipment in industries such as energy, oil and gas refining and transportation. These systems encompass the transfer of data between the network manager and a number of Remote Terminal Units (RTUs), sensor nodes, etc. A SCADA system gathers critical information (such as where a leak in a pipeline has occurred) and then transfers this information back to the network manager. The network manager is responsible for alerting the home station about the leak and carrying out necessary analysis such as determining whether the leak is critical or not.

The owners and operators of SCADA systems aim to increase the monitoring sensitivity of their systems and reduce the day to day running cost wherever

S. Hailes, S. Sicari, and G. Roussos (Eds.): S-Cube 2009, LNICST 24, pp. 66–82, 2009.

it is possible. Due to the intelligent monitoring capabilities of Wireless Sensor Networks (WSNs), integration between SCADA and WSNs can be one way to achieve these aims. WSNs facilitate the monitoring process by performing specific tasks such as sensing physical phenomena at a remote field and then reporting them back to the network manager. They can form the "eyes and ears" of SCADA systems. Nodes, which are capable of performing functions such as gas detection and temperature sensing, provide information that can tell an experienced operator how well oil/gas pipelines are performing.

Roman et al. highlighted the role that WSNs can play in SCADA [14]. They argued that WSNs can aid SCADA's functionalities by providing monitoring, alerts, and information on demand. However, vulnerabilities related to WSNs can be introduced to SCADA. One of those potential vulnerabilities is the security compromise of sensor nodes given the lack of tamper resistance packaging [4]. An adversary can gain control of one or more sensor nodes and readily access sensitive information such as keys or passwords. The adversary therefore can easily get access to the plain text of the encrypted messages that are routed through the controlled nodes – this compromises the data confidentiality. The adversary may also inject their own commodity nodes into the network by fooling nodes so that they believe that these commodity nodes are legitimate members of the network. Another adversary activity is launching a selective forwarding attack where the node, that is under the control of the adversary, selectively drops legitimate packets in order to affect the overall performance of the system [5].

In this paper, we focus on strengthening the security level at the weakest component of the SCADA system which exists in remote fields [1]. The remote field has the weakest physical security requirements and consists of substations and intelligent electronic devices such as sensors (will be discussed in a later section). We propose a new key management protocol that updates the shared symmetric key between the network manager and a sensor node or between the network manager and a group of sensor nodes.

The rest of this paper is organized as follows. Section 2 provides an overview of SCADA systems. Section 3 explains the different types of the adversarial model. Section 4 discusses some of the related work. Section 5 explains the proposed key management protocol. Finally, the paper is concluded in Section 6.

2   SCADA

To best understand the added value of the proposed scheme, some understanding of SCADA is in order. Today's SCADA systems (the third generation) are a combination of legacy and modern technology [9]. It has become an open system architecture rather than a vendor controlled architecture as in the second generation of SCADA. It uses open standards and protocols which facilitate distribution of the functionalities of SCADA. We refer the readers interested in the differences between these generations to the paper by McClanahan [9]. Figure 1 shows a simplified SCADA system architecture which is composed of the following components:

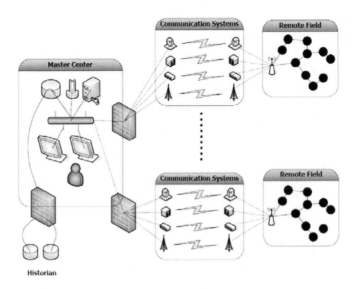

Fig. 1. The simplified version of PCS/SCADA

Master Center. The master center component contains the network manager, human machine interaction, database storage, processing server, etc. It has the highest physical security level compared to other components. Generally speaking, it receives monitoring information from remote fields (through the communication system component), processes it, and then makes decisions.

Historian. The historian is a backup for the SCADA system data which is often located in a separate subnet different to the one where the master center component exists. The master center component is able to access the historian in order to backup the data of the SCADA system.

Remote Fields. The remote fields are composed of substations (gateways) and intelligent electronic devices (IEDs) [1] which can be physically distant from the SCADA master center and in many cases are not physically secured due to the largeness or remoteness of the coverage area. The substation connects IEDs with the master center component through the communication component. It has a high degree of complexity and might have better physical security than IEDs. The IEDs can be sensor nodes, remote terminal units, or relays to name a few.

Communication System. The communication systems are responsible for transferring monitored data (control data) from remote field components (master center) to master center component (remote field components). This communication can be done via fiber optics, radio, satellite, etc.

3   Adversary Model and Security Concerns

When designing a key management protocol for WSNs, the most challenging and unique security threat would be *node capture*. With limited resources in sensor nodes, defeating this type of threat is very hard. Node capture will translate into compromise of all the credentials stored in the sensor node. Furthermore, the adversary can compromise all the *software codes* installed within the sensor node, especially random number generation functions. For example, he can modify the codes or replace them with his own codes to mislead functions related to SCADA/PCS use a fixed number for random numbers for input to security protocols, or launch a selective forwarding attack. However, the computation power of the adversary falls short of compromising the network manager and gateways which have reasonable physical security. Their physical security increases in proportion to the importance of the domain where a SCADA/PCS is deployed.

Our purpose in this paper is to design a key management scheme which is resilient to node capture: i.e., a scheme that enables sensor nodes to recover its secure status even after they have been captured and then released back. Consequently, we are interested in what the adversary can do both when a node is captured, and after it is released back. Key disclosure is technically simple [4]; what else should be done by the adversary to keep control of the node after he put it back to the field? He will hope that the node uses values of his choice for all cryptographic keys or keying materials. For this purpose, he may try to modify software components (especially the random number generation part), and monitor all or part of the subsequent key update messages. In this regard, we use the following criteria to classify the adversaries.

- The adversary can read and modify all the software codes and configurations, including secret keys, installed in the sensor node.
- The adversary can carry out seamless monitoring of all the subsequent key update protocol exchanges.

According to the above two criteria, we divide the adversaries into four distinct types as shown in Figure 2. Type I is the weakest adversary: neither seamless monitoring nor software compromise; Type IV is the strongest: seamless monitoring and software compromise. Type IV is so much powerful that it is unlikely to devise any practical cryptographic countermeasure for WSNs. The use of tamper-proof technology will be needed to cope with this type of adversary, but it is outside the scope of this paper. Our goal in the paper is to have a new key management scheme which is resilient to all the other three types of attackers only with cryptographic countermeasures.

One interesting point here is that the assumption of software modification is equivalent to that of software-based random number generation, in terms of their consequence in the context of cryptographic protocols. Software algorithm-based random number generation does not give true random numbers, which can only be obtained from a strong physical source of randomness. One consequence of this equivalence is that it makes no sense to use expensive tamper-proof technologies

Fig. 2. CLASSIFICATION OF ADVERSARIES. "Seamless monitoring" means the adversary keeps monitoring *every* subsequent key update message after compromising a sensor node; "software modification" includes alteration of any software installed in the node, especially the random number generator.

while true random number generation not used. Put a different way, we do not have to bother with true random number generation when software modification is assumed to be an easy work for the adversary.

Having identified different types of adversaries, we have the following concerns with regard to node capture and the consequent disclosure of all the internal data of the captured node:

– PAST KEY SECRECY: The past keys should not be compromised.
– FUTURE KEY SECRECY: The future keys should not be compromised.

The requirement of resilience to node capture rules out the use of any long-term keys; the keys must change or evolve continuously over time, with old prior keys deleted securely. In other words, we require a *key evolution* scheme in order to achieve past/future key secrecy against the threat of node capture.

TERMINOLOGY. To the best of our knowledge, the terms "past/future key secrecy" have never been used in previous literature. Similar terminology include "(perfect) forward secrecy" and "backward secrecy", which has always been quite confusing. The term "(perfect) forward secrecy" goes back to Günther [3]. The original term assumes a long-term key and session keys established by the key, and means that the current session key is not compromised by the "future" (thus, the expression "forward") exposure of the long-term key. This terminology, somehow, seems to have got a slightly different usage in the context of group key communication; it concerns about the contamination of a group key at a particular time by the compromise of an older/newer group key. The inherent ambiguity has brought a twin terminology: "backward secrecy". Some authors choose the term "backward secrecy" to mean "forward secrecy" called by other authors, and vice versa. To avoid all this confusion, we will use a new more concrete expression: "past/future key secrecy". The notation to be used in the rest of the paper can be found in Table 1.

4   Related Work

There are several papers dealing with key management designs for SCADA systems such as [2,12]. However, these designs either use heavy cryptographic

Table 1. Notations for the proposed scheme

Name	Description
M	Network manager.
N	Sensor node.
K_{MN}	Shared pairwise key between M and N.
s_0, t_0	Pre-installed global secret data in every N.
K_G^i	The i-th group key ($i \geq 0$).
r_X	Random nonce chosen by entity X.
(K_M^{-1}, K_M)	Asymmetric key pair of network manager.
$\{m\}_K$	Encryption of message m under the key K.
$h(\cdot)$	A cryptographic hash function.
$\mathrm{MAC}_K(m)$	A message authentication code function on m using the key K.

mechanisms, which do not suit resource constrained devices, or do not consider the integration of WSNs within SCADA.

To the best of our knowledge, the only existing key management in the wireless control environment, that considers the integration between SCADA/PCS and WSNs, has been proposed by Nilsson et al. [10]. They designed two key update protocols: the first one updates the pairwise symmetric key between the network manager M and a sensor node N (as described in Protocol 2) while the other scheme updates the global or group key among M and the whole group G of sensor nodes (as described in Protocol 1). They claimed that the protocols provide both forward and backward secrecy (or in our newly defined terminology, they provide both past and future key secrecy). It is unfortunately not the case.

Protocol 1. Group key update protocol from [10]

M: generates a new group key K_G' and a random number r_M

1. $M \rightarrow N : \{K_G', r_M\}_{K_{MN}}$
2. $M \leftarrow N$: $MAC_{K_G'}(N, r_M)$

To initiate the group key update protocol, M generates a new group key, K_G', randomly. It then encrypts it with another random number, r_M, and sends it over the network to the target group. No node in the group has any clue whether the received key is fresh or not. In other words, the freshness property, from the viewpoint of N does not hold since the two values (the new group key K_G' and the random number r_M) are random values chosen by M. It is both impractical and insecure for each sensor node to maintain a list of keys that have been used. Thus, an external adversary will be able to record a rekeying message and then re-inject it into the network, which leads to updating the group key with an old key. Consequently, the group enters a key mismatch phase where the key version that the group of sensors uses and what M has are different.

One good security practice is to minimize the damage caused by a compromised node. However, the authors did not consider common attacks in WSNs

---

Protocol 2. Pairwise key update protocol from [10]

N: generates a random number r_N

1. $M \leftarrow N$: $\{r_N\}_{K_M}$, $MAC_{K_{MN}}(\{r_N\}_{K_M})$

M, N: compute the new pairwise key $K'_{MN} = h(K_{MN}, r_N)$

---

that an adversary is capable of launching attacks such as selective forwarding [5] or node compromise [4]. If a single sensor node has the ability to affect the operation of a good number of sensor nodes, then the adversary will try to compromise that node. For example, if an adversary compromised a sensor node (say, node N_b) in a multi-hop path, then it would be able to enforce all other nodes downstream to enter the key mismatch phase. The adversary simply drops the rekeying message from M for the group key, and then use the new group key to calculate MACs on their identities and the received nonce, which results in a successful impersonation attack. We can easily fix the problem by replacing the MAC data with another one: e.g., $MAC_{K_{MN}}(K'_G, r_M)$.

Moreover, to initiate the pairwise key update protocol, N generates a random number, r_N, and encrypts it with K_M. It subsequently computes the MAC on the encryption result and sends this MAC and the encryption result over the network to M. The new pairwise key can be calculated, at the sender N and at the receiver M, by hashing r_N with the previous pairwise key. This means that the new pairwise key is always determined by N. The adversary consequently is able to know all the future keys once he compromised N. A closer look at the protocols, Protocol 1 and Protocol 2 reveals more serious defects of them.

- DEFECT I. The whole value of the new group key are directly carried by the protocol messages, encrypted under the pairwise key K_{MN}. The consequence is that compromise of the pairwise key for just one node leads to compromise of the group key for the whole group. This is a more serious problem than it might appear, because the pairwise key compromise does not necessarily require node capture.
- DEFECT II. The value of the new pairwise key K'_{MN} is only determined by the sensor node. When the adversary of Type II or IV (he can compromise the key generation codes stored in the node) captures the node, all the future pairwise keys for the node can be pre-determined by the adversaries. Namely, physical compromise of the node immediately leads to compromise of all the future pairwise keys if the adversary can modify the codes installed in the node. This, in turn, leads to compromise of all the future group keys as well because, as mentioned in Defect I, the group key is delivered encrypted under the pairwise key. Hence, contrary to their claim, the scheme does not provide "future key secrecy", against node compromise, for either the pairwise key or the group key.
- DEFECT III. Although not explicitly shown in the protocol descriptions above, the key input r_N for the new pairwise key K'_{MN} is not really random in their scheme; it is in fact a function of a pre-installed secret key and a counter value stored in the node. This means that, when the node is captured

and all the installed data including keys exposed to the adversary, all the past pairwise keys as well as the future keys can immediately be computed even without recording a single key update message! In fact, this disaster is not just because of Defect III, but also due to Defect II. Note that, due to Defect III combined with Defect II, the adversary does not have to modify the node's software at all in order to extract all the past and future pairwise keys. Hence no minimum level of past or future key secrecy against node compromise in their scheme. Moreover, the adversary can extract any group key in the past or future if he has got the records of the corresponding group key update message. Note also that, for this, "seamless" monitoring is not needed by the adversary. What does this mean? The scheme is, in terms of either kind of key, neither forward nor backward secure against node compromise for all the types of adversary I, II, III and IV (see Figure 2).

As for past key secrecy, we note two proposed schemes in the WSN context: Klonowski et al. [6] and Mauw et al. [8]. Both schemes use hash functions in order to achieve key evolution. Both schemes, however, are intended to be used not for group key update but for updating *pairwise* keys for node-to-node [6,13] or node-to-base station communication [8].

On the other hand, as for future key secrecy, Mauw et al.'s protocol does not provide this property. The protocol is based on a hash chain scheme originally proposed for RFID security [11]. In RFID environments, protecting secret tag information from tampering in the future is a big concern while it does not seem to be such a prime concern in WSNs. This is because it is more authentication and integrity than privacy that really matters in WSNs, especially SCADA/PCS. Hence, future key secrecy is more valued than past key secrecy. On the other hand, the protocol proposed by Klonowski provides future key secrecy in a "weak" sense; namely, it will be computationally hard for the adversary to compute a future key from the current compromised key if he fails to record, say ten, subsequent evolution steps [13].

5   The Proposed Scheme

Devising a key management for WSNs is not trivial and in particular may not be successfully accomplished by simple adaptation of security solutions designed for wired networks. This is because of the limited resources such as limited energy lifetime, slow computation, small memory, and limited communication capabilities which exist in WSNs [16,17]. In this section, we describe a key management scheme which secures communication between remote fields (where the WSN resides) and the master center (where the network manager resides) by considering vulnerabilities that are associated with WSNs.

5.1   Key Management Protocols

This paper focuses on updating two types of keys, which are the group key and the pairwise key, in the wireless process control environments. A pairwise key is shared between the network manager M and each sensor node N while the group key is shared among M and the whole group of sensor nodes.

Group Key Update Protocol. Our solution for group key rekeying also exploits the idea of key evolution using a hash chain in order to achieve past key secrecy. The protocol uses a hash chain, $h^i(s_0)$, where s_0 is a pre-installed key component at the pre-deployment phase and $i \geq 0$ denotes the index for key update phases.

As for future key secrecy, we use the *reverse hash chain* technique, which was first introduced by Lamport [7]. The network manager prepares in advance a hash chain of length n, starting from a random seed t_{n-1} and ending with the final value t_0:

$$t_{n-1},\ t_{n-2} := h(t_{n-1}),\ t_{n-3} := h(t_{n-2}),\ \ldots\ ,\ t_1 := h(t_2),\ t_0 := h(t_1)\,.$$

For reasons of convenience which will become clearer shortly, we write $h^{-i}(t_0)$ instead of t_i although h is not an invertible function and $h^{-1}(x)$ can only mean the set of all preimages of x in a strict sense. Roughly speaking, $h^{-i}(t_0)$ is the i-th preimage of t_0 in the reverse hash chain. The secret data, t_0, will be pre-installed into sensor nodes together with another key component s_0.

Protocol 3. The protocol for group key update

---
1. $M \rightarrow N$: i, $\{h^{-i}(t_0)\}_{K_{MN}}$
2. $M \leftarrow N$: $h_{K_{MN}}(K_G^i)$

M, N: update the value of the group key (i.e., $K_G^i = h^i(s_0) \oplus h^{-i}(t_0)$).

Now, with two secret key components s_0 and t_0 pre-installed within all sensor nodes, using Protocol 3, the group key K_G^i evolves as follows:

$$K_G^i = h^i(s_0) \oplus h^{-i}(t_0)\,,\ i \geq 0\,,$$

where we define $h^0(s_0) = s_0$ and $h^0(t_0) = t_0$. Figure 3 explains the key evolution in the protocol.

Any sensor node can easily compute the i-th hash image $h^i(s_0)$ from $h^{i-1}(s_0)$ while only the network manager knows the value of the i-th preimage $h^{-i}(t_0)$. Thus, it is only the network manager who can release the preimage into the sensor field. As a consequence, the first message in the protocol provides the sensor node with a weak form of signature from the network manager: the message could have been generated only by the network manager, not by any sensor nodes including the node itself. The check of the preimage (i.e., $h(h^{-i}(t_0)) = h^{-(i-1)}(t_0)$) also makes sure that the key update message is fresh.

After the i-th key update, the sensor node stores the index i and the secret data: $h^i(s_0)$, $h^{-i}(t_0)$ and K_G^i. Considering the highly lossy communication environment of sensor networks, the sensor node may sometimes fall behind the

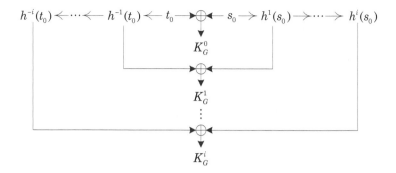

Fig. 3. Key evolution in the proposed protocol

group key update schedule. The sensor node, however, will soon be able to catch up at the next rekeying: it can compute the correct value of the new group key simply by checking the difference of two index values – the received and the stored – and applying the corresponding number of hash operations.

Now let's assume that the adversary has somehow extracted the current value of the group key, K_G^i. However, he cannot extract from this the previous key K_G^{i-1} because he cannot compute the value of $h^{i-1}(s_0)$. Note that this holds even when the adversary has recorded all the previous key update messages, and compromised all the previous manager-to-node pairwise keys. In fact, the node capturing and extracting all the stored secret data does not surrender the past group key to the adversary. This is because the previous values for $h^i(s_0)$ were never exchanged over the air, and were deleted after group key computation. Hence we can say that the protocol provides past key secrecy for any kind of compromise: group key compromise, pairwise key compromise, and the compromise of the node itself.

The protocol also provides future key secrecy in the sense that the adversary, just with knowledge of the current group key K_G^i, cannot predict the next group key K_G^{i+1}. The computation of K_G^{i+1} requires knowledge of $h^{-(i+1)}(t_0)$, which has not yet been exchanged. In the next step of the key update, the adversary, without knowledge of the pairwise key K_{MN}, will not be able to obtain the value of $h^{-(i+1)}(t_0)$ from the protocol message. In fact, the pairwise key compromise alone does not lead to the future group key compromise; it will only happen when the adversary captures a sensor node, thereby extracting the hidden component $h^i(s_0)$. Hence, the protocol satisfies future key secrecy in the face of group key and/or pairwise key compromise; simple delivery of the encrypted value of the new group key, as in [10], cannot provide this kind of resilience. The protocol will fail to provide future key secrecy only when the node is physically captured. Even in the case of capture, the adversary should listen to the key update message to extract the future group key. Furthermore, when the pairwise key is updated, any adversary of type I, II, or III will not be able to have any knowledge of the new pairwise key. This, in turn, leads to the adversary's failure to have any knowledge of the new group key established using the new pairwise key. Hence, we achieve the future group key secrecy even after node capture, as far as the adversary has no ability to modify the software codes stored in the node.

The protocol uses the pairwise key K_{MN} to encrypt the i-th preimage $h^{-i}(t_0)$ in the first message, and also to provide key confirmation by computing keyed hash of the new group key. This is in order to rule out any compromised or suspicious sensor nodes from group key update.

Our protocol, however, has one limitation: it is vulnerable to a kind of collusion attack. Assume that a sensor node was captured at a key update phase i, and another node was subsequently captured again at the phase $i + 10$. Then, the adversary can extract all the group keys for the phases i to $i + 10$. Of course, this compromise is limited to the past keys, not the future keys. We call this attack "*sandwich attack*" which will be considered in our future work.

Protocol 4. The protocol for pairwise key update

1. $M \rightarrow N$: i, $\{h^{-i}(t_0), g^{r_M}\}_{K_G^{i-1}}$ #*broadcast* message
2. $M \leftarrow N$: $\{g^{r_N}\}_{K_{MN}}$, $h_{K_{MN}}(g^{r_M}, g^{r_N})$

N: keeps the hashed value of the current pairwise key: $K_{MN}^1 = h(K_{MN})$.
M, N: increment the group key index from $i - 1$ to i, and update the values
of the pairwise key (i.e., $K_{MN} := g^{r_M r_N}$) and the group key (i.e., to K_G^i).

Pairwise Key Update Protocol.   Protocol 4 shows the rekeying protocol for the pairwise key shared between the network manager and the sensor. This protocol is based on Diffie-Hellman protocol which has recently become not only feasible on resource constrained nodes, but attractive for WSNs [15]. The network manager M first generates a secret random number r_M, and computes the Diffie-Hellman component g^{r_M}. It then *broadcasts* Message 1, which includes the index i of the next group key, and ciphertexts of the next group key component $h^{-i}(t_0)$ and a Diffie-Hellman component g^{r_M}, encrypted under the current group key, K_G^{i-1}.

The inclusion of the group key index i in the first message enables each sensor node to check if it keeps the current value of the group key; if not, the node can request the network manager to send the latest key component $h^{-i}(t_0)$. Thus, the group key rekeying protocol exchange as described in Protocol 3 can be inserted between Messages 1 and 2 of the protocol in the case of group key index mismatch.

After retrieving the plaintext of Message 1 using the group key, the node checks the preimage if $h(h^{-i}(t_0)) = h^{-(i-1)}(t_0)$. This check provides evidence for the node that M has really started the pairwise key update session. Considering that Message 1 is a broadcast message encrypted using the "group" key, it would be simply impossible to achieve this evidence without using the preimage as used here. Of course, using digital signature/verification is a different story.

Now the node constructs the second message of the protocol: it generates its own Diffie-Hellman component g^{r_N}, encrypts it, and generates the keyed hash of both Diffie-Hellman components under the current pairwise key K_{MN}. After sending the message to M, the node computes the new group key, $K_G^i = h^i(s_0) \oplus h^{-i}(t_0)$, increments the group key index from $i-1$ to i, and computes the Diffie-Hellman key $g^{r_M r_N}$ to be used as the new pairwise key, while keeping the hash $h(K_{MN})$ of the old pairwise key and safely deleting the old key.

On receiving Message 2, M decrypts g^{r_N}, and verifies the keyed hash from N. The inclusion of g^{r_M} and g^{r_N} in the hash provides M with confidence about the freshness and authenticity, respectively, of the message.

Use of Diffie-Hellman key agreement for the pairwise key update provides the past and future pairwise key secrecy; the key inputs are temporary randoms, and thus no relation to the previous or next key inputs. Even after node compromise, if the attacker is not able to modify the software codes in the node (i.e., the adversary of type I or III), or if he fails to record the key update messages (i.e., the adversary of type I or II), the node will escape from the control of the adversary to recover the secure status. Thus, our scheme satisfies past pairwise key secrecy for all the adversary types, and future pairwise key secrecy for any adversary type except type IV, even against node capture and its compromise.

IMPERSONATION ATTACK. If the adversary is in full control of a compromised node, in which he installed his own malicious attacking software, then the adversary's node can still impersonate M to some other victim node, succeeding in causing the victim to receive a fake Diffie-Hellman component, say g^x. But the attack is limited to that. The attacking node has only two options when receiving Message 2 of the victim node: (1) forward the message verbatim to M, or (2) cut out the message. In the former case, M will get not the expected hash $h_{K_{MN}}(g^{r_M}, g^{r_N})$ but a strange one $h_{K_{MN}}(g^x, g^{r_N})$. In the latter case, M will see no response from N. In both cases, M will issue Message 1 again through the unicast channel to N, which will finally lead to key agreement between M and N.

DELIVERY FAILURE MANAGEMENT. The delivery failure in the WSNs will lead to key mismatches of group keys and/or pairwise keys. With no long term key available in our key update protocols, key mismatch is a big concern and should be handled carefully. Simple retransmission of the protocol messages is not a solution; it may open the door to replay attacks. Moreover, it may require the sensor node to go back to the old key even after it has successfully updated the pairwise key. Consequentially, the node must keep two keys at the same time: the old key and the new updated key.

Our solution is to use key evolution here again. With no response from the node N, the manager M initiates Protocol 5 over the unicast channel to N. Here, $K_{MN}^j = h^j(K_{MN})$ is a hashed copy of the current key from M's viewpoint. For the time of the first protocol run, the index j is set to 1; it will be incremented by one whenever the protocol is retried. On receipt of Message 1 over the unicast channel, the sensor node N compares the received group key indice i, j with the stored indice i', j', and executes the required action as follows:

Protocol 5. The protocol to handle delivery failure

1. $M \rightarrow N$: $i, j, \{h^{-i}(t_0), g^{r_M}\}_{K^j_{MN}}$ # *unicast* message
2. $M \leftarrow N$: $\{g^{r_N}\}_{K^j_{MN}}, h_{K^j_{MN}}(g^{r_M}, g^{r_N})$

M, N: update the values of the pairwise key (i.e., $K_{MN} := g^{r_M r_N}$)
N: increments the indice i and j, and updates the values of the pairwise key
(i.e., $K_{MN} := g^{r_M r_N}$) and the group key (i.e., to K^i_G), and then keeps
the hashed value of old key: $K^{j+1}_{MN} := h(K^j_{MN})$

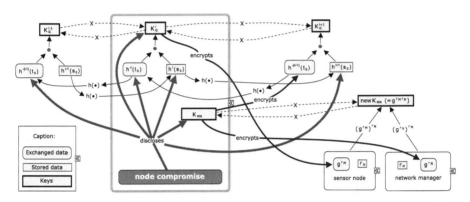

Fig. 4. Relations between keys and keying materials and the significance of node compromise

- CASE 1: $i = i'$ and $j \geq j'$. For simplicity, consider the case $j = j' = 1$.
The pairwise key update protocol (Protocol 4) has just been run, but the
reply message of the protocol failed to arrive at M. The node N has been
keeping the hashed copy $K^1_{MN} = h(K_{MN})$ of the old pairwise key, which is
applied to the ciphertext for Message 1 of Protocol 5. The retrieved value
of $h^{-i}(t_0)$ ensures the authenticity of the message; the entity other than N,
in possession of $h^{-i}(t_0)$ and K^1_{MN}, should be M. The node decrypts the
encrypted part of Message 1 using K^1_{MN}. Then, N follows exactly the same
step as in Protocol 4 except that it uses the hash of the old pairwise key
instead of the current pairwise key. At the end of the protocol run, N will
end up with a new pairwise key, and the hash of K^1_{MN}, i.e., K^2_{MN}; now $j = 2$.
The current pairwise key is simply deleted. One or more failure again will be
followed by reinitiation of the protocol by M with j incremented. It could
also happen that Message 1 itself fails to arrive at N, and subsequently M
retries the protocol. This will lead to the case $j > j'$.
- CASE 2: $i = i'$ and $j < j'$. This cannot happen; otherwise it is simply a
bogus message from another sensor node. N should ignore Message 1.
- CASE 3: $i > i'$. This happens when the node N has never been involved
in the pairwise key update protocol due to delivery failure of Message 1 of

Protocol 4 . In this case, N applies the hash to the current pairwise key j times, and uses the resulting value as the description key for Message 1.

- CASE 4: $i < i'$. This is another case of replay attack. N should ignore Message 1.

Now, the old key does not need to be kept just for handling key mismatch; Protocol 5 does not come with any breach of security.

5.2   Putting It All Together

In our scheme, the pairwise key is used for secure delivery of the group key update information in Protocol 3; the group key, in turn, encrypts the Diffie-Hellman components to establish a new pairwise key in Protocol 4. This combination helps the sensor networks to recover its security quickly after some sensor nodes are captured and their keys are compromised.

Figure 4 illustrates how all the keys and keying data are related to each other as they evolve over time. Note that no keys are delivered over the air; only their keying materials, such as $h^{-i}(t_0)$, are exchanged or even never exchanged over the air (e.g., $h^i(s_0)$). Thus, unlike the scheme of Nilsson et al. (see Defect I in Section 4), the pairwise key compromise alone does not lead to the group key compromise, and vice versa.

Using the inverse hash chain as well as the hash chain, we achieve both past/future group key secrecy at the same time; furthermore the group key update message provides an inherent message authenticity.

Both M and N contribute their Diffie-Hellman inputs to the computation of the new pairwise key, and thus the adversary can not determine the future values of the pairwise key even after node capture and the resulting compromise of the built-in software, which was not the case in the scheme of Nilsson et al. (see Defect II in Section 4).

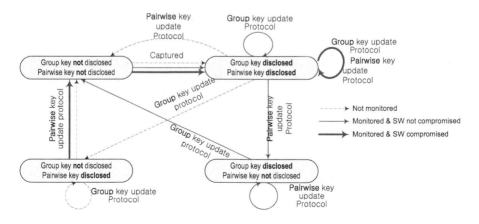

Fig. 5. State diagram of key disclosure

Carefully designed with node capture in mind, our scheme does not surrender all the key components required to retrieve the past/future group/pairwise keys. Only the adversary equipped with seamless monitoring and software compromise (i.e., the type IV adversary) can keep the control of the once-captured node.

Figure 5 shows how the node recovers its secure state with the help of the key update protocols, after it has been captured and all the keys in it are compromised. Without seamless monitoring (i.e., adversary types I and II), the adversary will soon lose all the control of the keys. Even with adversary type III (i.e., seamless monitoring but no software compromise), the node will eventually recover the secrecy of both keys. Only for adversary type IV (i.e., both seamless monitoring and software compromise), there is no path available back to the original secure state. We argue that a non cryptographic countermeasure such as tamper-proof technology is additionally required to fight against the strongest adversary of type IV.

6   Conclusion

Wireless sensor networks (WSNs) has brought a devastating security threat: node capture. The threat is so powerful that almost all existing key management protocols are just helpless because it overthrows the fundamental assumption for cryptographic system design: long term secret keys are securely stored. This is why so called forward secrecy and backward secrecy are required in cryptographic key management protocols for WSNs. Both terminologies are rather misleading and confusing, and so we propose more proper ones: future key secrecy and past key secrecy.

Nilsson et al. [10] have recently proposed a key management scheme for WSN applications in PCS/SCADA environments, which was incorrectly claimed to provide future and past key secrecies. Some proposals (only for pairwise key update) provide past key secrecy, but not future key secrecy [6,8].

We noticed that any cryptographic countermeasure alone cannot prevent the most powerful adversary in the WSN context; he can capture a node to extract all confidential data, modify any built-in codes, and seamlessly monitor to keep control of the node. This kind of attackers can only be fought by using tamper-proof technologies as well as cryptographic ones. The assumption regarding this type of adversaries, however, is by no means the most usual or reasonable assumption. Seamless monitoring requires the adversary not to lose every single session for group key or pairwise key update. The task of modification of random number generation codes will add another burden to that.

In order to measure the resilience of key management protocols, we derived four different types of adversaries varying in their capability with regard to seamless monitoring and software manipulation. As shown in Section 3, Nilsson et al.'s scheme, contrary to their claims, turned out to provide neither past key secrecy nor future key secrecy against node compromise by any type of adversaries.

We applied Lamport's reverse hash chain as well as usual hash chain to provide both past and future key secrecies. Our scheme avoids the delivery of the whole value of new group key for group key update; instead only the half of the value is transmitted from the network manager to the sensor nodes. This way, the compromise of a pairwise key alone does not lead to the compromise of the group key, which was not the case in the scheme by Nilsson et al. The new pairwise key in our scheme is determined by Diffie-Hellman based key agreement. As for the scheme of Nilsson's et al., it uses key transport, not key agreement, where the new pairwise key is determined by the sensor node and then delivered to the network manager by using public key encryption. This has brought a vital flaw to their scheme.

In short, our scheme provides a very strong resilience; both past and future key secrecies against node capture by all the adversary types except the strongest one, Type IV. A sensor node attacked by the adversary of Type IV, in theory, cannot be quarantined by a cryptographic method alone; a non-cryptographic countermeasure such as tamper-proof protection is needed together.

References

1. Beaver, C., Gallup, D., Neumann, W., Torgerson, M.: Key management for SCADA. Technical Report SAND2001-3252, Sandia National Laboratories - Cryptography and Information Systems Surety Department (March 2002)
2. Dawson, R., Boyd, C., Dawson, E., González Nieto, J.M.: SKMA: a key management architecture for SCADA systems. In: Buyya, R., Ma, T., Safavi-Naini, R., Steketee, C., Susilo, W. (eds.) ACSW Frontiers. CRPIT, vol. 54, pp. 183–192. Australian Computer Society (2006)
3. Günther, C.G.: An identity-based key-exchange protocol. In: Quisquater, J.-J., Vandewalle, J. (eds.) EUROCRYPT 1989. LNCS, vol. 434, pp. 29–37. Springer, Heidelberg (1990)
4. Hartung, C., Balasalle, J., Han, R.: Node compromise in sensor networks: The need for secure systems. Technical Report CU-CS-990-05, University of Colorado at Boulder - Department of Computer Science (January 2005)
5. Karlof, C., Wagner, D.: Secure routing in wireless sensor networks: attacks and countermeasures. Ad Hoc Networks 1(2-3), 293–315 (2003)
6. Klonowski, M., Kutylowski, M., Ren, M., Rybarczyk, K.: Forward-secure key evolution in wireless sensor networks. In: Bao, F., Ling, S., Okamoto, T., Wang, H., Xing, C. (eds.) CANS 2007. LNCS, vol. 4856, pp. 102–120. Springer, Heidelberg (2007)
7. Lamport, L.: Password authentification with insecure communication. Commun. ACM 24(11), 770–772 (1981)
8. Mauw, S., van Vessem, I., Bos, B.: Forward secure communication in wireless sensor networks. In: Clark, J.A., Paige, R.F., Polack, F.A.C., Brooke, P.J. (eds.) SPC 2006. LNCS, vol. 3934, pp. 32–42. Springer, Heidelberg (2006)
9. McClanahan, R.: SCADA and IP: is network convergence really here? IEEE Industry Applications Magazine 9(2), 29–36 (2003)
10. Nilsson, D.K., Roosta, T., Lindqvist, U., Valdes, A.: Key management and secure software updates in wireless process control environments. In: Gligor, V.D., Hubaux, J.-P., Poovendran, R. (eds.) WISEC, pp. 100–108. ACM, New York (2008)
11. Ohkubo, M., Suzuki, K., Kinoshita, S.: Cryptographic approach to privacy-friendly tags. In: RFID Privacy Workshop (2003)

12. Pietre-Cambacedes, L., Sitbon, P.: Cryptographic key management for SCADA systems-issues and perspectives. International Journal of Security and its Applications 2(3), 31–40 (2008)
13. Ren, M., Das, T.K., Zhou, J.: Diverging keys in wireless sensor networks. In: Katsikas, S.K., López, J., Backes, M., Gritzalis, S., Preneel, B. (eds.) ISC 2006. LNCS, vol. 4176, pp. 257–269. Springer, Heidelberg (2006)
14. Roman, R., Alcaraz, C., Lopez, J.: The role of wireless sensor networks in the area of critical information infrastructure protection. Information Security Technical Report 12(1), 24–31 (2007)
15. Szczechowiak, P., Oliveira, L.B., Scott, M., Collier, M., Dahab, R.: NanoECC: Testing the limits of elliptic curve cryptography in sensor networks. In: Verdone, R. (ed.) EWSN 2008. LNCS, vol. 4913, pp. 305–320. Springer, Heidelberg (2008)
16. Vieiral, M.A.M., Coelho Jr., C.N., Cecilio da Silva Junio, D., da Mata, J.M.: Survey on wireless sensor network devices, September 2003, vol. 1, pp. 537–544 (2003)
17. Walters, J.P., Liang, Z., Shi, W., Chaudhary, V.: Security in Distributed, Grid, and Pervasive Computing. In: Xiao, Y. (ed.) Wireless sensor network security: A survey, ch. 17. Auerbach Publications, CRC Press (2006)

Analysis of Channel Access Delay of Slotted CSMA/CA in a WSN

Alexandre Guitton and Nassima Hadid

LIMOS CNRS, Clermont University
Complexe scientifique des Cézeaux, 63173 Aubière Cedex, France
{guitton,hadid}@sancy.univ-bpclermont.fr

Abstract. Wireless sensor networks are often designed to operate on remote areas. Thus, sensor devices need to operate for years and have to save energy by switching their radio component off as often as possible. IEEE 802.15.4 is a standard that induces a low energy consumption. It divides time into an active period, where devices communicate, and an inactive period, where devices sleep. Many research has been done on how to optimize the medium access delay during the active period. Surprisingly, few studies take into account the inactive periods when analyzing the delay.

In this paper, we give a macroscopic analysis of the medium access delay of a low-power wireless sensor network that operates in the beacon-enabled mode of IEEE 802.15.4. We conduct multiple simulations in order to study the impact of the network parameters such as the number of devices in range and the traffic production. We also propose an estimation of the access delay in the case of a traffic uniformly distributed among devices, and in the case of a traffic non-uniformly distributed among devices.

Keywords: IEEE 802.15.4, slotted CSMA/CA, low-power WSN, medium access delay, estimation model.

1 Introduction

Recently, many industrial applications have been developed based on the technology of wireless sensor nodes. Sensor nodes are cheap energy-constrained devices that perform some monitoring tasks. They are often deployed in low populated or dangerous areas. The goal of such networks is to monitor the environment for several years without requiring to change the batteries of the devices. The IEEE 802.15.4 standard [IEE06] describes a medium access control (MAC) protocol that suits the requirements of such sensor nodes. The standard describes two modes of operation for the MAC sublayer, one of them being slotted CSMA/CA (which stands for Carrier Sense Multiple Access with Collision Avoidance), which is the focus of this paper.

Slotted CSMA/CA divides time into two periods: an active period and an inactive period. During the active period, all the devices can communicate together. They are often in competition for the medium access. During the inactive

S. Hailes, S. Sicari, and G. Roussos (Eds.): S-Cube 2009, LNICST 24, pp. 83–97, 2009.

period, they save energy by turning their radio component off. Low-power wireless sensor networks tend to have devices inactive most of the time. This has a clear impact on delay, as communications are only possible during the short active periods.

In this paper, we give a macroscopic analysis of the medium access delay of a low-power wireless sensor network that operates with the slotted CSMA/CA algorithm of IEEE 802.15.4. We conduct multiple simulations in order to study the impact of the network parameters such as the number of devices in range and the traffic production. We also propose an estimation of the access delay in the case of traffic uniformly and non-uniformly distributed among devices.

Section 2 describes the IEEE 802.15.4 standard and slotted CSMA/CA. It describes related analytical and experimental analyzes and shows that previous research mainly focuses on active periods, while we concentrate on inactive periods. In Sect. 3, we study the medium access delay in scenarios where the traffic is uniformly distributed among the data sources. In Sect. 4, we extend this study to scenarios where the traffic is non-uniformly distributed among the data sources. Then, we propose a linear estimation model for the delay in Sect. 5 and we present a discussion in Sect. 6. Section 7 concludes our work.

2   State of the Art

In this section, we first describe the IEEE 802.15.4 standard and slotted CSMA/CA. Then, we present the related work on slotted CSMA/CA that is devoted to the delay analysis, with analytical or experimental approaches.

2.1   Overview of the IEEE 802.15.4 MAC Layer

The IEEE 802.15.4 standard [IEE06] supports two operational modes: (i) the beacon-enabled mode in which periodic beacon frames are transmitted to synchronize nodes according to a superframe structure depicted in Fig. 1, and (ii) the non-beacon-enabled mode in which unslotted CSMA/CA is used. In this paper, we focus on the beacon-enabled mode as it is more energy-efficient than the non-beacon-enabled mode.

In the beacon-enabled mode, the active period (also called the superframe) is divided into two periods: the contention access period (CAP) during which slotted CSMA/CA is used to avoid collisions, and the contention free period (CFP) where nodes have guaranteed time slots ensuring a collision free transmission. Note that slotted CSMA/CA is only used during the CAP. The interval that separates two consecutive beacons (BI) and the superframe duration (SD) are determined by two parameters: the superframe order (SO) and the beacon order (BO). BI and SD are defined as follows:

$$\begin{cases} \text{BI} = \text{aBaseSuperframeDuration}.2^{\text{BO}}, \\ \text{SD} = \text{aBaseSuperframeDuration}.2^{\text{SO}}, \end{cases}$$

where $0 \leq \text{SO} \leq \text{BO} \leq 14$ and aBaseSuperframeDuration = 15.36 ms.

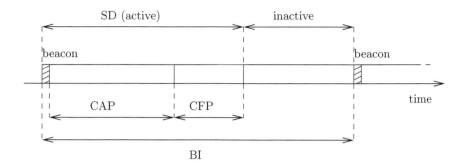

Fig. 1. Beacon interval in IEEE 802.15.4 beacon-enabled mode

Two topologies are proposed by the standard: star and peer-to-peer. The peer-to-peer topology suffers from beacon frame collisions when the beacon-enabled mode is used (see Task Group 4b [IEE] or [KCA07, CGM08]). Thus, in what follows we only consider the star topology.

2.2 Slotted CSMA/CA

In IEEE 802.15.4, the slotted CSMA/CA algorithm is applied before the transmission of any frame occurring during the CAP (except beacons and acknowledgements). This algorithm is based on a time unit called backoff period which lasts 320 μs. The boundaries of the backoff periods are aligned with the boundaries of the superframe slots, *i.e.*, the start of the first backoff period of all devices is aligned with the beacon transmission. Any activity of the MAC sublayer (such as the channel sensing and the transmissions) starts at the boundary of a backoff period.

The slotted CSMA/CA algorithm uses three variables: the first is NB (Number of Backoff periods), which is the number of times a backoff has been drawn for this transmission attempt. The second is CW (Contention Window length), which is the number of consecutive backoff periods during which a device senses the channel. The third is BE (Backoff Exponent), which defines the range of possible backoff periods a device waits for until it assesses the channel.

Figure 2 represents the stages of slotted CSMA/CA. In Step 1, the MAC sublayer initializes the three variables and locates the boundary of the next backoff period: NB is set to 0, CW is set to 2 and BE is set to 3. In Step 2, a random number of backoff periods is chosen from $[0; 2^{BE} - 1]$. In Step 3, the MAC sublayer assesses the channel by performing a clear channel assessment (CCA). The MAC sublayer asks the physical layer to perform two CCAs (since CW = 2) at the next backoff boundary. The next step depends on the result of each CCA. If the channel is assessed to be busy, the MAC sublayer goes to Step 4. Otherwise, it goes to Step 5. In Step 4, NB and BE are incremented by one, provided that BE does not exceed aMaxBE, and CW is set to 2. If NB exceeds macMaxCSMABackoffs (denoted by macMaxCB. on the figure), the algorithm

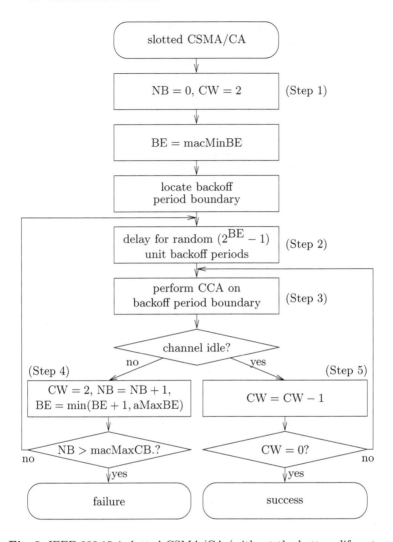

Fig. 2. IEEE 802.15.4 slotted CSMA/CA (without the battery life extension)

terminates with a channel access failure, otherwise it goes back to Step 2. In Step 5, CW is decremented. If CW becomes equal to zero, the transmission begins at the boundary of the next backoff period. Otherwise, the MAC sublayer returns to Step 3.

2.3   Analytical Analyzes of the Delay of Slotted CSMA/CA

Here, we focus on the papers that propose analytical models to evaluate the performance of slotted CSMA/CA. In all the following papers, authors focused on the evaluation of the delay during the active period. The key difference between their approach and ours is that we claim that the inactive period accounts for most of the delay.

In [PEE+06], the authors considered both saturated and periodic traffic scenarios in a star topology. They validated their analytical results on throughput and energy consumption by simulation. They simulated a long active period of 10^8 backoff periods, that is, of more than 8 hours.

In [PKC+05], the authors evaluated slotted CSMA/CA in terms of throughput and energy consumption, in saturation conditions in a star topology. They assumed that each time a frame is sent, a new frame arrives at the MAC sublayer. Their analysis is validated by simulations with the network simulator NS-2. Again, as the authors focused on the active period, they fixed a long beacon interval (BO = 10 which corresponds to 15.4 seconds).

In [TPGZ06], the authors proposed a Markov chain in order to analyze the throughput of slotted CSMA/CA. The authors developed a custom C simulator to validate their analysis. However, since no value for BO, SO, BI or SD is given, we assume that their simulation did not take into consideration the inactive period.

In [SS07], the authors studied the throughput and energy consumption of slotted CSMA/CA in both saturated and periodic traffic conditions. Their main contribution is the use of a single, simple, one-dimensional Markov chain while [PEE+06], [PKC+05] and [TPGZ06] use complex two-dimensional Markov chains. They validated their analysis through simulations. However, they simulated a single active period of 5.10^5 backoff periods, that is, of 160 seconds.

2.4 Experimental Analyzes of the Delay of Slotted CSMA/CA

Researchers have also performed simulation analyzes on slotted CSMA/CA. Among multiple parameters, they varied BO and SO and observed the impact on the performance of the protocol.

In [LKR04], the authors studied the delivery ratio, the throughput and the delay as a function of the duty cycle and the energy consumption of slotted CSMA/CA. Concerning the delay, they have shown that delay increases as the duty cycle decreases by plotting the average delay as a function of $2^{SO}/2^{BO}$, for a single source. In this paper, we propose a more detailed analysis of this phenomenon. Notably, we relate the medium access delay to the frame production time. We also study scenarios where multiple sources transmit data frames.

In [KAT06], the authors observed the effect of BO and SO on the behavior of slotted CSMA/CA and analyzed its impact on the average delay, the throughput and the number of collisions. However, in all their simulations, the values of BO and SO are the same. Thus, there is no inactive period.

In [CHGM09], the authors have shown that the deference mechanisms used towards the end of the CAP have a major impact on the delay of slotted CSMA/CA. Although deference mechanisms occur rarely, their penalty on delay is so large that deference becomes significant for short global cycles. In this paper, we encounter the same situation: the inactive period has a large impact on delay. We give here a macroscopic analysis of the medium access delay, as opposed to [CHGM09].

3   Analysis of Uniform Traffic

We start our analysis by a scenario where the traffic is uniformly distributed among the sources. After describing the simulation setup, we give results for a single source. Then, we extend the results to a scenario with multiple sources.

3.1   Simulation Setup

Our simulations are done with NS-2, version 2.31. We used a simple star topology with one coordinator and ten end-devices. We deployed the nodes so that they are in range of each other. We used the two-ray ground shadowing model with default parameters, and we used 1.33×10^{-6} W for the reception and carrier sense threshold. However, we deployed the nodes close enough to ensure that the propagation model has no impact on the reception of frames.

The PHY and MAC layers used in our simulation are those of the wpan module of NS-2, and correspond to IEEE 802.15.4 specifications. The coordinator generates periodic beacons, according to the value of BO. After all the end-devices are associated to the coordinator, some of them are chosen as traffic sources. Each traffic source periodically sends data frames to the coordinator. Data frames have a MAC payload of 30 bytes, plus 7 bytes added by the PHY layer. Each data frame is acknowledged. We set the size of the frame queues to 100 frames to reduce the effect of queue overflows (this is discussed in the following). Lastly, simulations are run 100 times and last for 100 seconds; frames in the queues when the simulation stops are discarded.

In the following, we consider two scenarios: one with a single traffic source, the other with multiple traffic sources. The varying parameters are described at the beginning of the corresponding subsection.

3.2   Single Source Scenario

In the single source scenario, only one end-device is configured as a traffic source. We set BO to 7, which results into a global cycle of $2^7 \times 15.36 = 1966.08$ ms (*i.e.*, about two seconds). In most simulations, we vary SO from 4 to 6, which results into activity durations from 245.76 ms to 983.04 ms (from 12.5% to 50% of the global cycle). This is a typical case for LP-WPANs. We also vary the traffic generation frequency from five frames per second to twenty frames per second.

Figure 3 shows a graphical representation of the medium usage on two sample simulations: one with a traffic frequency of five frames per second (referred to as low traffic), the other with a traffic frequency of twenty frames per second (referred to as high traffic), both with SO = 6. The medium usage is shown on a time axis for about 3 seconds, which is larger than one global cycle. Beacons,

Fig. 3. Medium occupation in the single source scenario, for low traffic (upper part) and high traffic (lower part). Medium occupation is high at the very beginning of the active period.

data frames and acknowledgments are represented by a vertical line at the time when they are transmitted. Active and inactive periods can be clearly seen on the figure. It can also be seen that the beginning of the active period is the period when the channel is the most busy. This is more obvious when the traffic frequency is high. The modeling of this phenomenon is the basis of this paper.

As we have seen, the medium is highly occupied at the beginning of the active period (which follows the beacon transmission), and is mostly idle the remaining of the time. This means that frames produced in the middle of the active period can be transmitted quickly, while frames produced at the beginning of the active period might experience larger delays. Our goal now is to quantify the delay of frames with respect to their production time.

Figure 4 shows the average medium access delay as a function of the traffic frequency. The delay is computed as the time that separates the frame production (at the application layer) to the frame transmission (at the physical layer). Note that in our simulation, the frame is only delayed at the MAC layer. The traffic frequency varies from five frames per seconds to twenty frames per second. Note that all times are normalized according to the beginning of the active period and are averaged over 100 simulations. Thus, each point of the figure represents the average of 5,000 global cycles (100 simulations for 100 seconds, with a global cycle of 2 seconds). Finally, times are rounded to 0.1 seconds.

Figure 5 displays the frame loss as a function of the traffic frequency. As the average medium access delay only takes into account the received frames, delay and frame loss have to be considered at the same time. As expected on this figure, frames are lost when the queues are full, that is towards the end of the inactive period, and at the beginning of the active period.

The active and inactive periods are shown very clearly on Fig. 4. As the active period directly follows the beacon frame transmission, it is normal that frames experience small delay on the left part of the graph. All the frames produced during the inactive periods experience large delays (reaching a peak at 1 second, which is the length of the inactive period).

There are two main results that can be extracted from Fig. 4 and from Fig. 5. First, it can be seen that the average delay decreases linearly during the inactive period, with a speed that depends on the traffic. When the number of frames accumulated during the inactive period is small, these frames are sent quickly by

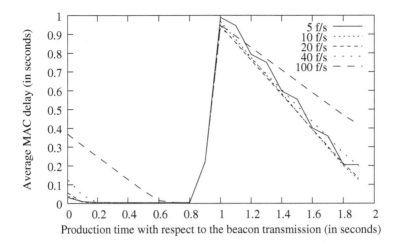

Fig. 4. The average medium access delay is very large for frames produced during the inactive period, but it can be large for frames produced at the beginning of the active period too

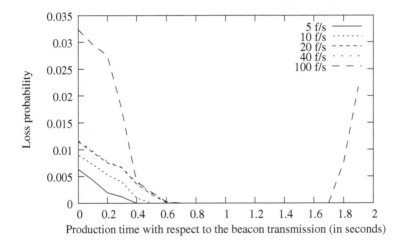

Fig. 5. Frames are dropped when queues are full, *i.e.*, at the end of the inactive period and at the beginning of the active period

slotted CSMA/CA. Thus, the average delay decreases from 1 s to nearly 0 s at the end of the inactive period. However, as more frames are accumulated, more time is required to send them, which delays all the remaining frames. Slotted CSMA/CA is not able to cope efficiently with more than 40 frames per second in our scenario.

Second, under high traffic conditions, frames produced at the beginning of the active period experience a large delay (and have a high probability of being lost). This is due to the fact that frames produced during the inactive period are already queued, and are trying to access the medium. When 100 frames are produced per second, more than 60% of the active period is devoted to transmitting the frames produced in the previous inactive period.

3.3   Multiple Sources Scenario

In the multiple source scenario, we varied the number of sources and kept the traffic constant. We used the following settings: 100 frames per second for one source, 20 frames per second for five sources, and 10 frames per second for ten sources. The overall traffic generated is 100 frames per second. Traffic production starts randomly within the first second for each source.

Results on delay are shown on Fig. 6. It can be seen that delay is reduced when the number of sources is increased. This general behavior is known for CSMA/CA algorithms. When a single node transmits data, it cannot use the medium very often. Indeed, it has to wait for the mandatory backoff (between 0 and 7 backoff slots) before transmitting any frame. Thus, it cannot use the medium to its full extent. When there are more sources in the network, the probability that one source transmits while the other performs the backoff is larger. This increases the medium usage, and reduces the average delay.

Results on frame loss are shown on Fig. 7. When there was only one source, queue overflow was the only cause of frame loss. As soon as multiple sources are competing for the channel, frame collisions appear. Many frames queued during the inactive period are dropped due to collisions. This number increases with the number of sources. The number of frames dropped due to queue overflows is negligible.

Slotted CSMA/CA is not very efficient in avoiding collisions. Let us consider a simple example when a collision occurs. Let us assume that the channel is idle, and two sources decide at the same time to perform the first CCA (this situation can happen even if the two sources have drawn different backoffs, provided that the difference of backoff cancels the difference of time when the decisions were taken). Both CCAs return idle, and both sources perform the second CCA. Again, both CCAs return idle. Then, the two sources start the transmission, and a collision occurs. Slotted CSMA/CA performs a few retries (four by default) before discarding the frame. Notice that in a real scenario, the capture effect might lessen this problem.

4   Analysis of Non-uniform Traffic

In this section, we used a non-uniform traffic in order to determine if the traffic distribution among sources had an impact on the average medium access delay. We used the same simulation setup as before, except for the traffic production. We decided to have five sources producing a total of 100 frames per second, that is an average of 20 frames per second and per source, but distributed among the sources in a non-uniform manner. Sources 1 and 2 produce 25 frames per second,

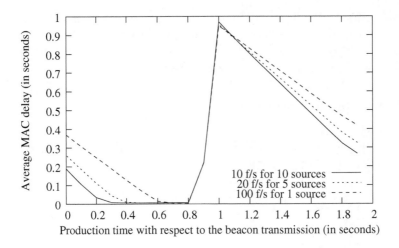

Fig. 6. The average medium access delay is reduced when several sources send traffic

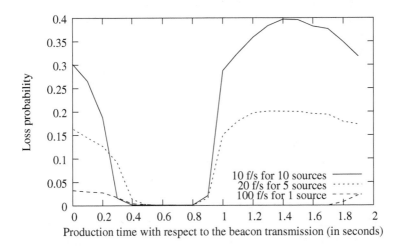

Fig. 7. The more sources, the more collisions

sources 3 produce 20 frames per second, and sources 4 and 5 produce 15 frames per second.

Fig. 8 present the medium usage for five sources on a sample simulation. It can be seen that sources 4 and 5, which produce less traffic than the other nodes, only suffer from the contention of the medium at the beginning of the CAP. The medium usage is high for sources 1 and 2 for more than a third of the active period. However, this medium usage snapshot is obtained only from one simulation.

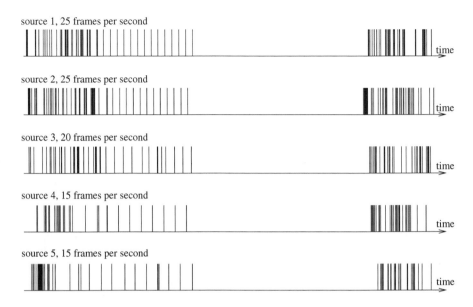

Fig. 8. Medium usage for five sources with non-uniform traffic load

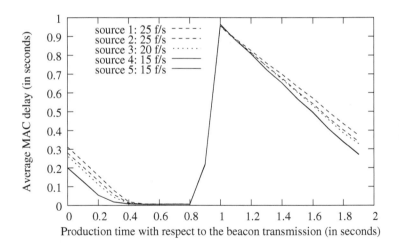

Fig. 9. The average medium access delay depends in a limited manner on the production of each source

Fig. 9 show the average medium access delay per source. Note that as the production of a source increases, its MAC delay also increases. As the traffic increases, the variation of delay also increases: sources 4 and 5 (having a small traffic production of 15 frames per second) experience a similar delay, whereas sources 1 and 2 (having a high production of 25 frames per second) experience a delay that slightly varies.

5   Linear Model of the Delay

As can be seen on Fig. 4, 6 and 9, the average MAC delay can be approximated as a linear function of the time. In this section, we propose such a model.

Figure 10 shows the important points of our model. Notice that O denotes the origin, that is, the beacon transmission time. b represents the beacon interval, and s represents the superframe duration (that is, the duration of the active period). Frames produced shortly before point A can be sent without a large delay. However, once the inactivity period starts, frames experience large delays. This is represented by point B. Frames accumulated during the inactivity period cannot be sent instantaneously at the beginning of the next active period. It takes up to a certain time, represented by point C, to have all the accumulated frames sent. We assume that the traffic load does not change a lot from one active period to the next active period. That is why our model uses in fact a point C', which corresponds to point C but in the current active period.

Our goal now is to determine the coordinates of each point. Trivially, $x_O = y_O = y_A = y_C = y_{C'} = 0$. We also have $x_B = x_A = b$ and $x_C = x_{C'} + b$. From the IEEE 802.15.4 standard, we know that $b = 15.36 \times 2^{BO} \times 10^{-3}$ seconds and $s = 15.36 \times 2^{SO} \times 10^{-3}$ seconds. As the nodes queues are traditionally of a first in first out (FIFO) type, the first frame that is queued at the beginning of the inactivity period is the first that is transmitted. This transmission occurs at the beginning of the active period (after waiting for a backoff and winning the competition for the medium). As the channel access time during the active period is negligible compared to the inactive period duration, the delay for the first frame (which is the highest delay) is equal to the inactive period duration. Thus, $y_B = b - s$.

The remaining value, $x_{C'}$, is computed using our experimental values, which are summarized in Table 1. Let n denote the number of sources and l the total

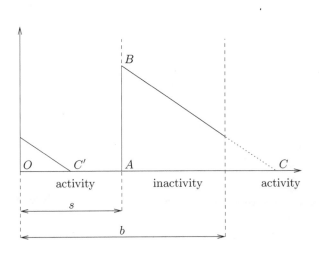

Fig. 10. A simple linear model of the average MAC delay

Table 1. Value of x_C as a function of the number of sources n and the traffic load l

Sources	Load	x_C	Sources	Load	x_C
1	5	0.1	5	100	0.35
1	10	0.1	10	100	0.25
1	20	0.1	5	40	0.15
1	40	0.15	10	40	0.15
1	100	0.6			

traffic load produced. From the values corresponding to $n = 1$, we have $x_{C'} \approx 6.5 \times 10^{-5} l^2 - 1.5 \times 10^{-3} l + 0.1$ (by using a polynomial regression of order 2). The number of sources only has a significant impact on the delay when l is high. That is why we started by expressing $x_{C'}$ as a function of l. From the previous expression of $x_{C'}$ as a function of l, we injected n in the following way. We noticed that:

- $x_{C'}$ for $n = 5$ and a given l is close to $x_{C'}$ for $n = 1$ and $6 \times l/8$,
- $x_{C'}$ for $n = 10$ and a given l is close to $x_{C'}$ for $n = 1$ and $5 \times l/8$.

Then, we found out a logarithmic fit for those values. We obtained the following formula for $x_{C'}$:

$$x_{C'} = 6.5 \times 10^{-5}(8.18 \times 0.94^n \times l/8)^2 - 1.5 \times 10^{-3}(8.18 \times 0.94^n \times l/8) + 0.1.$$

This model uses the total traffic load in the vicinity of the sensor, which can be obtained by overhearing, by computing the average number of clear channel assessments that failed, by computing the average number of frame failures or by other mechanisms.

Our model could be improved by determining the final equation as a function of n and l at the same time, rather than estimating it from l first, and adjusting it with n. Also, our model could be improved by taking into consideration the traffic load of each source independently, in addition to the total traffic load. However, from the results of Sect. 4, we expect only a small improvement in the approximation accuracy. A better improvement is certainly to model what happens at point C'. Indeed, the delay is not linear at this point, especially when the traffic load is high.

6 Discussion on Aperiodic Traffic

In this section, we discuss about non-periodic traffic. While all the simulations done for this paper concerned periodic traffic, we believe that the traffic distribution is not a parameter that has a significant impact on the results presented in this paper.

During the inactive period, the traffic is accumulated in the source queues. They serve as buffers, in the way of a leaky bucket: although they might be filled with aperiodic traffic, they are still emptied with linear speed (see the left part of Fig. 4 and 6).

During the active period, the traffic arrival distribution has an impact on delay. It is easier to deal with periodic frames in a fast manner than with burst of frames. However, this impact is limited. During the part of the active period when all the accumulated frames have been sent (or dropped), frames can be dealt with very efficiently. For example, we can see on Fig. 4 that it takes approximately 0.2 seconds for one node to transmit 40 frames (on the line with 40 frames per second, approximately 40 frames have been accumulated during the inactive period). Thus, even large bursts of 40 frames could be dealt with quickly. During the part of the active period when there are still some accumulated frames that have neither been sent nor dropped, the bursty frames accumulate with the previous frames, in the same manner as during the inactive period.

7 Conclusion

Low-power wireless sensor networks are designed to operate for years. The price to pay for the long energy autonomy of the devices is a larger medium access delay due to the long inactive periods. While many researchers have focused on optimizing the delay in the active period, we studied in this paper the impact of the inactive period on the delay.

We have shown that inactive periods cause a bottleneck at the beginning of the activity period. This bottleneck takes a significant amount of time to be dealt with, which increases the delay of all the waiting packets, and increases the frame loss probability. We have also shown that having more sources can reduce the delay, but at the cost of greatly increasing the frame loss probability. We have concluded our analyses by providing an estimation model of the average delay as a function of the number of sources and the traffic load.

References

[CGM08]   Chalhoub, G., Guitton, A., Misson, M.: MAC specifications for a WPAN allowing both energy saving and guaranted delay - Part A: MaCARI: a synchronized tree-based MAC protocol. In: IFIP WSAN (2008)

[CHGM09]   Chalhoub, G., Hadid, N., Guitton, A., Misson, M.: Deference mechanisms significantly increase the MAC delay of slotted CSMA/CA. In: IEEE ICC (2009)

[IEE]   IEEE 802.15 Task Group 4b. TG4b contributions, http://grouper.ieee.org/groups/802/15/pub/TG4b.html

[IEE06]   IEEE 802.15. Part 15.4: Wireless medium access control (MAC) and physical layer (PHY) specifications for low-rate wireless personal area networks (WPANs). Standard 802.15.4 R2006, ANSI/IEEE (2006)

[KAT06]   Koubaa, A., Alves, M., Tovar, E.: A comprehensive simulation study of slotted CSMA/CA for IEEE 802.15.4 wireless sensor networks. In: WFCS, July 2006, pp. 1–10 (2006)

[KCA07]   Koubaa, A., Cunha, A., Alves, M.: A time division beacon scheduling mechanism for IEEE 802.15.4/Zigbee cluster-tree wireless sensor networks. In: ECRTS (2007)

[LKR04]   Lu, G., Krishnamachari, B., Raghavendra, C.S.: Performance evaluation of the IEEE 802.15.4 MAC for low-rate low-power wireless networks. In: IPCCC, April 2004, pp. 701–706 (2004)

[PEE+06]   Pollin, S., Ergen, M., Ergen, S.C., Bougard, B., Van Der Perre, L., Catthoor, F., Moerman, I., Bahai, A., Varaiya, P.: Performance analysis of slotted carrier sense IEEE 802.15.4 medium access layer. In: IEEE Globecom, November 2006, pp. 1–6 (2006)

[PKC+05]   Park, T.R., Kim, T.H., Choi, J.Y., Choi, S., Kwon, W.H.: Throughput and energy consumption analysis of IEEE 802.15.4 slotted CSMA/CA. Electronics Letters 41(18), 1017–1019 (2005)

[SS07]   Shu, F., Sakurai, T.: Analysis of an energy conserving CSMA-CA. In: IEEE Globecom, November 2007, pp. 2536–2540 (2007)

[TPGZ06]   Tao, Z., Panwar, S., Gu, D., Zhang, J.: Performance analysis and a proposed improvement for the IEEE 802.15.4 contention access period. In: WCNC, April 2006, pp. 1–8 (2006)

Accurate Analysis of IEEE 802.15.4 Slotted CSMA/CA over a Real-Time Wireless Sensor Network

Wen-Tzeng Huang[1], Jing-Ting Lin[2], Chin-Hsing Chen[3], Yuan-Jen Chang[3], and You-Yin Chen[4]

[1] Department of Computer Science & Information Engineering
Minghsin University of Science & Technology
1, Hsin-Hsing Rd, Hsin-Fong, Hsin-Chu 30401, Taiwan, R.O.C.
[2] Department of Graduate Institute of Computer and Communication Engineering
National Taipei University of Technology
1, Sec. 3, Chung-hsiao E. Rd., Taipei, 10608, Taiwan, R.O.C.
[3] Department of Management Information Systems
Central Taiwan University of Science and Technology
No.666, Buzih Road, Beitun District, Taichung City 40601, Taiwan R.O.C.
[4] Department of Electrical and Control Engineering
National Chiao Tung University
1001 University Road, Hsinchu, 300, Taiwan, R.O.C
wthuang@must.edu.tw, kq13kq13@yahoo.com.tw,
{chchen,ronchang}@ctust.edu.tw, kenchen@cn.nctu.edu.tw

Abstract. Here, we present the collision probability of the IEEE 802.15.4 slotted Carrier Sense Multiple Access/Collision Avoidance (CSMA/CA) mechanism over a real-time wireless sensor network (RT-WSN), also called a synchronous network system. The "backoff," the random delay of CSMA/CA, can be used to create a probability model and to determine the average packet delay over RT-WSN. The proposed theoretical analysis model was nearly consistent with the simulation and with experimental results. This suggests that the slotted CSMA/CA mechanism cannot be applied effectively to RT-WSN because it cannot avoid a high collision rate with RT-WSN application requirements and, therefore, may waste a great deal of system bandwidth. We found that the packet collision rate increased up to 731% compared to an ideal model with more than 10 users within an RT-WSN. Without improvements in methodology, the high collision rate makes this slotted CSMA/CA mechanism unsuitable for RT-WSN applications.

Keywords: Real-time, wireless sensor network, collision, IEEE 802.15.4, CSMA/CA.

1 Introduction

The numerous advantages of wireless networking technology, including portability, no requirements for cables, flexibility, and low cost of constructing a network topology, have allowed it to be applied successfully in industry, medicine, transportation,

S. Hailes, S. Sicari, and G. Roussos (Eds.): S-Cube 2009, LNICST 24, pp. 98–110, 2009.

telemedicine, and home applications. Technological progress and the integration of wireless communication, batteries, and embedded processors have driven the development of Wireless Sensor Networks (WSN) [1]. In contrast with other types of wireless networks, the WSN data transmission method uses many sensing sources, called sensor nodes, routed to a single destination, called the sink node. The sensor nodes can detect various environmental parameters within their effective sensing distance, such as temperature, humidity, luminosity, wind speed, and pressure. The sensed information is gathered by the sink node, and then may be analyzed by network administrators and users. Recently, WSN has become increasingly widespread and its applications have expanded to sensor networks [2], industrial communication [3], home applications, and medical treatment [4]. This has produced ever-increasing demands for WSN. Real-time performance is sometimes required, especially in multimedia applications, and, to guarantee real-time execution, the access time of wireless media applications must occur within a maximum delay time. In many networks, packet faults can be revised by the acknowledge/retransmit mechanism of the protocol used. Such systems will become paralyzed by the uncertain delays experienced in real-time applications [5].

Medium access control (MAC) performance analysis of the IEEE 802.15.4 low-rate wireless personal area network (LR-WPAN) [6] is discussed in this study. The beacon mode with slotted Carrier Sense Multiple Access/Collision Avoidance (CSMA/CA) applied to real-time WSN (RT-WSN) was evaluated under real-time conditions in a star network topology. Singh et al. [7] analyses the performance under the IEEE 802.15.4 star topology. They found that the saturation throughput of n nodes can be calculated by an embedded Markov renewal process, and also the relation between the size of backoff and throughput. Therefore, they obtain an analytical model for the finite arrival rate case from the relation. This finite load model captures very well the qualitative behavior of the system. Finally, they used ns2 simulator to verify their model and simulation results. Kim et al. [8] studied the focus of the IEEE 802.15.4 unslotted CSMA/CA and proposed a simple mathematics model that utilized the wireless channel in the busy state to got the M/G/1 queueing system to make analysis. They can calculate the throughput, delay, and energy consumption in the bust state. Park et al. [9] proposed a new analysis model, which utilized the discrete time Markov chain to analyse the throughput and energy consumption of the slotted CSMA/CA. Timmons et al. [10] analysed the performance of the medical sensor body area networking context, which works in long-time operation. Hence, they focus on the power consumption issue.

The network performance parameters, time delay, throughput, and power consumption were also measured in these studies, and shown to affect the CSMA/CA RT-WSN. In this study, we evaluated the MAC performance required in real-time applications and then analyzed the effects of CSMA/CA RT-WSN when users need to use as much bandwidth as possible.

Sections 2 and 3 of this paper describe the IEEE 802.15.4 standard and the construction of the network model, respectively. Section 4 shows the mathematical analysis of our proposed network model. The performance results of the simulation and experiment are verified in Section 5. Section 6 presents our conclusions.

2 Overview of the IEEE 802.15.4 Standard

The new standard of 802.15.4 was used to develop two-layer protocol stacks, the physical layer (PHY) and MAC, for LP-WPAN applications [6]. This standard has a number of characteristics, as follows:

- The data transmission rate can be 250, 40, or 20 kbps through the air.
- Star or peer-to-peer operation.
- Allocated 16-bit short address, with a maximum of 65535 connections.
- CSMA-CA channel access.
- Acknowledged protocol for transfer reliability.
- Low power consumption.
- Energy detection.
- Link quality indication.
- 16 channels in the 2450 MHz band; 10 channels in the 915 MHz band; and 1 channel in the 868 MHz band.

Figure 1 shows the two-layer structure of a star topology sensor network consisting of one personal area network (PAN) coordinator and several sensor nodes. The data flow path is from leaf nodes, called sensor nodes, to the PAN coordinator.

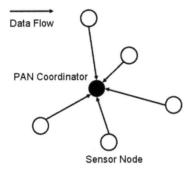

Fig. 1. The structure of a Star topology sensor network

There are two working modes, beacon and non-beacon, in the IEEE 802.15.4 standard. The beacon mode uses broadcast communication to synchronize the network. The coordinator periodically broadcasts the beacon frame to all of the sensor nodes. The superframe structure, which is largely designed to allocate the time distribution mechanism, is defined in the beacon mode, as shown in Figure 2 [6]. This causes all of the sensor nodes in the network to synchronize two functions, sleep and wake-up. As the network works only in the active state, the time in this state can be divided into 16 equal segments, called time slots. Any action involves the use of one time slot as the basic working unit. For example, the transmission operation costs three time slots, and the waiting operation costs five time slots.

The two-part active state consists of the contention access period (CAP) and the contention-free period (CFP). During the CAP, the system will allow the sensor nodes to compete freely to obtain channel access rights in the slotted CSMA/CA mechanism. Then, during the CFP, the system gives the sensor node exclusive access to the channel within its allocated time slot(s). Under these conditions, one node does not need to compete with other nodes to obtain access rights, guaranteeing the specificity of the sent data. The sensor node can also enter the power-saving mode to reduce power consumption during the inactive period. The lengths of the active and inactive periods can be adjusted by the superframe Order (SO) and Beacon Order (BO), respectively. According to the definition of the IEEE 802.15.4 standard, these can be set as follows: $0 \leq SO \leq BO \leq 14$, *aBaseSuperframeDuration* (which is a constant) = 960 as the default value, and one symbol (which is also a constant) = 16 μs in 2.4 GHz bandwidth operation. Therefore, the duration of the superframe is from 15.36 ms to 215.7 s. It does not use the superframe structure as SO = 15.

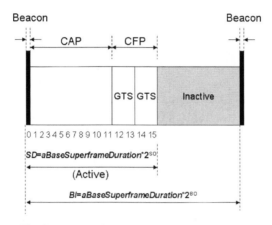

Fig. 2. The superframe structure of IEEE 802.15.4

During CAP, the sensor node competes with others to obtain channel access rights using the slotted CSMA/CA mechanism, as shown in Figure 3 [6]. The backoff period represents one unit of the time slots in CSMA/CA. In the slotted CSMA/CA, the backoff period boundaries of the sensor devices cannot be aligned with the time slot boundaries of the coordinator. Each sensor device maintains three variables, *NB*, *CW*, and *BE*. *NB*, which is used to determine when the channel is in the busy state, has an initial value of 0. *CW* indicates when the channel is empty and when it begins to transmit the data. PHY performing clear channel assessment (CCA) is used to detect whether the channel is idle or not. According to the range, $2^{BE} - 1$, CSMA/CA allows the sensor node to delay one random backoff period. As this allows sensor nodes to transmit without overlapping with each other, their collision probability can be effectively reduced. When the channel is in the busy state, it can reattempt access within the number of *macMaxCSMAbackoffs*, which is a constant. Then, *BE* will be incremented by 1 such that it can increase the random range. The competition fails when the retry number is greater than *macMaxCSMAbackoffs*. After ensuring that the channel is empty twice $(CW = 2)$, the node begins to access the channel for successful competition.

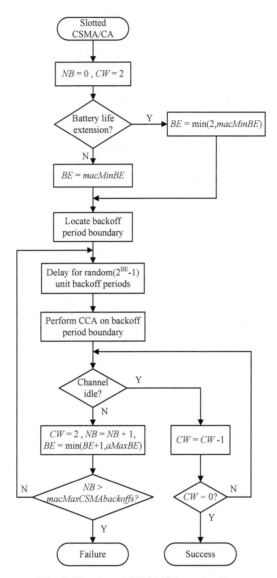

Fig. 3. The slotted CSMA/CA mechanism

Table 1. Default values of the CSMA/CA parameters

Parameters	Default Value
aMaxBE	.5
macMaxCSMABackoffs	4
macMinBE	3
macBattLifeExt	FALSE

CSMA/CA contains one other parameter, the binary constant *macBattLifeExt*. If the system needs to reduce the duty cycle of the network, *macBattLifeExt* can be set as "TRUE," which can reduce the delay of the backoff period and conserve battery energy. The default values of the CSMA/CA parameters are shown in Table 1.

3   Our Network Module

Our proposed network system is constructed as a star network consisting of one master node and many slave devices for monitoring. This protocol includes two classic tasks, a synchronous and an asynchronous task [11, 12]. The synchronous task involves periodic polling of each slave node for received data (*e.g.*, temperature, luminosity, humidity, pressure, rotation, and angle) from monitoring sensor devices. The asynchronous task does not involve periodic transmission and its transmission time is therefore fixed (event-driven). In comparison with previous systems, this type of system generally requires the ability to take the bounded time to be finished within the critical path.

In the synchronous task, data from the sensor nodes will be periodically and continuously sent to the coordinator. Generally, the system is capable of maintaining the sampling rate so that it can be implemented within the limitations of the memory buffer. For real-time requirements, the synchronous task of the sensor network is defined by RT-WSN.

The star topology sensor network of the IEEE 802.15.4 standard was employed in this study. Our system used the beacon-enabled configuration, which allows the coordinator to periodically broadcast beacons to all of the sensor nodes. After receiving the beacon, the sensor node performs the slotted CSMA/CA mechanism to obtain the access rights of the channel. Then, the successful node sends its packet to the coordinator. This is just one way to transmit the packet from the sensing node to the coordinator. Although the CSMA/CA mechanism can decrease the probability of collision, too many sensors and too heavy a traffic load within the network will cause a high collision rate. This results in the loss of the packet, increased delays and decreased the bandwidth, and the gradual degradation of network performance. To analyze, in detail, collision performance under the CSMA/CA mechanism, some terms of the network model are defined as follows:

- Maximize traffic load: The traffic load is equal to the maximum throughput of the system. Under the IEEE 802.15.4 standard at 2.4 GHz, the maximum bandwidth is 250 kbps. Throughput is possible in the saturate case, although the network simultaneously uses many sensor nodes.
- Fixed packet length: The length of all packets is set to a fixed value with a maximum of 128 bytes, according to the IEEE 802.15.4 standard.
- Without re-transmit/acknowledgment: Because of the requirements for real-time operation, the re-transmit mechanism settings do not provide redundant time for re-transmission by the network's sensor nodes [5]. When data are missing or the transmission is in error, the sensor node waits until the next beacon cycle to re-send the packet.
- Without inactive/sleep mode: When the system is operating at a high utilization rate or in a high duty cycle, it disables the sleep mode.

- Without packet loss rate: The packet cannot be lost in the normal case. Although some packets will be lost because of factors related to environment, distance, interference, and signal intensity, this study does not consider the effects of these factors.

When the sensor nodes are sent their packets passively according to the requirements of the coordinator, the maximum sampling rate of the system corresponds to the set

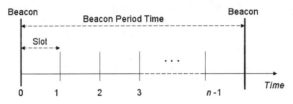

n : number of sensor nodes

Slot size : transmission time of packet

Fig. 4. Our network module

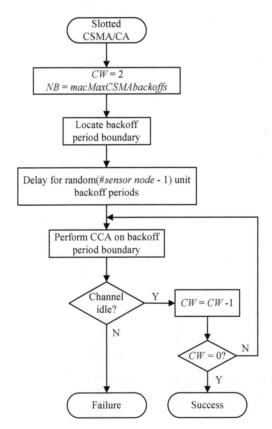

Fig. 5. The slotted CSMA/CA mechanism after adjusting

beacon period. To obtain real-time data in our model, we set the beacon period time equal to the sum of the packet transmission times of all of the sensor nodes. For example, when five sensor nodes are in the network, each with a packet transmission time of 4 ms, the beacon period is set to a minimum of $5 \times 4 = 20$ ms. In the beacon enabled mode, the superframe structure can be adjusted by our proposed method to reduce the redundant action. Hence, the length of one time slot equals the transmission time of one packet, and the number of time slots equals the number of sensor nodes, as shown in Figure 4.

In our module without collision, the packets of all of the sensor nodes can only be sent once during the beacon period. The system waits until the next beacon cycle to transmit, because collisions may cause the loss of the packet. In this case, this time slot cannot be used by any node, which wastes bandwidth. Although the backoff period is one random time slot length, it cannot run over the beacon period time. The maximum of the random variable is $(n - 1)$, where n is the number of sensor nodes. For example, the maximum length of the backoff period is four when the number of sensor nodes is five. With clear channel assessment (CCA), there is no time to compete again if the channel is in the busy state.

4 Mathematical Analysis

In this study, we propose a network analysis model to analyze the behavior of the slotted CSMA/CA over RT-WSN. Too many collisions cause time delays, which waste bandwidth and prevent the requirements of real-time operation. An analysis of the degree of network collisions therefore allows an evaluation system performance.

From the protocol of one packet, it will be allocated one random length of the backoff period during the competition case. Here, one unit of the backoff period is equal to the unit length of one time slot. There are n time slots during the beacon period, where n is the number of sensor nodes. The packet can randomly choose one of n time slots to access, as shown in Figure 6. Two sensor nodes will choose the random variables in the system. A collision will occur if more than two nodes choose the same random variable. In this case, both of the packets may be lost. This is one of the major causes of network performance degradation.

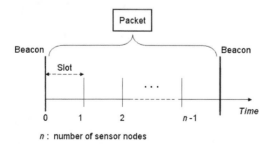

Fig. 6. Packets to be transmitted during any time slot

The following important parameters are defined for our model:

- n : Number of sensor nodes.
- $Network(i)$: There are i sensor nodes inour network model.
- $slot$: The time slot is equal to the packet transmission time.
- $\#slot$: Number of time slot.
- $D_{Avg}(n)$: Average of packet delay of the sensor node in n sensor nodes.
- $Collision(i)$: The number of sensor nodes that simultaneously choose the same random variable is "i," which will generate "i" collisions and lose "i" packets during the same "backoff" period.
- $P(e)$: Outcome probability of the event e.
- $S(e)$: One set contains the amount of all possible outcome samples during event e, also called "sample space" of the event e.

To analyze the collision probability within n sensor nodes over RT-WSN, or $P(Collision(n))$, the statistics of the sample space are be gathered first. We assume that one slot can be chosen as the candidate element among n sensor nodes. One candidate element among n time slots with n packets can be chosen, and all candidate elements can be counted by the statistics method as shown in (1).

$$S(Network(n)) = \# slot^n = n^n \tag{1}$$

Let $S(Network)$ be the total sample space over RT-WSN, containing a combination of collision and non-collision incidents. Let "$\#slot$" be the number of slots, and $Collision(0)$, ..., $Collision(n)$ be the collision probability of the nodes 0, 1, ..., n, respectively. Therefore, the sample $S(Network)$ of the network is the union of all incidents as shown in (2).

$$S(Network) = S(Collision(0)) \cup S(Collision(1)) \cup S(Collision(2)) \cdots \cup S(Collision(n)) \tag{2}$$

Let $Set(Collision(i))$ be the set number of $Collision(i)$. Hence, the collision probability within i sensor nodes, $P(Sollision(i))$, under $S(Network)$ is shown in Eq. (3).

$$P(Collision(i)) = \frac{S(Collision(i))}{S(Network(n))} \tag{3}$$

Therefore, $Collision(i)$ means that there are i time slots to be wasted. Then, it will take more cost of $i \times slot$ time delays. Hence, The average packet time delays under n sensor nodes, $D_{Avg}(n)$, is the summation of the wasted time delays of all possible collision probability as shown in Eq. (4).

$$\begin{aligned}
D_{Avg}(n) &= \big(P(Collision(0)) \cdot 0 + P(Collision(1)) \cdot 1 + \cdots + P(Collision(n)) \cdot n\big) \cdot slot \\
&= \left(\frac{S(Collision(0))}{S(Network(n))} \cdot 0 + \frac{S(Collision(1))}{S(Network(n))} \cdot 1 + \cdots + \frac{S(Collision(n))}{S(Network(n))} \cdot n\right) \cdot slot
\end{aligned} \tag{4}$$

First, to get $(n - i)$ elements without collision from n sensor node samples, let the amount of them be shown in Eq. (5).

$$C^n_{n-i} = \frac{n!}{(n-i)!(n-(n-i))!} \tag{5}$$

Second, let the permutation of $(n - i)$ elements within n time slots be shown in Eq. (6).

$$P^n_{n-i} = \frac{n!}{(n-(n-i))!} \tag{6}$$

Finally, let $D_{Avg}(n)$ be the average package delay with the collision case in n sensor nodes, and it can be derived from above equations and shown in Eq. (7), where $Set(G(i , i))$ will be shown in Eq. (8).

$$D_{Avg}(n) = \frac{slot}{n^n} \sum_{i=0}^{n} C^n_{n-i} \cdot P^n_{n-i} \cdot S(G(i,i)) \cdot i \tag{7}$$

Then, the recursion relation $S(G(i , k))$ can be defined as Eq. (8). There are 2 initial conditions are as follows. One, $S(G(0 , 0)) = 1$, is non-collision and the other, $S(G(1 , 1)) = 0$, is one sensor node with the collision case.

$$S(G(i,k)) = \begin{cases} 1 & \text{, if } i = 0, \\ 0 & \text{, if } i = 1, \\ k^i - \sum_{d=0}^{k-1} C^k_{k-d} \cdot P^k_{k-d} \cdot S(G(d,d)) & \text{, if } i > 1. \end{cases} \bigg|_{i=k} \tag{8}$$

5   Simulation and Experiment Results

To confirm our methodology, we verified our proposed theoretical analysis with simulation and experimental results. We found that the slotted CSMA/CA mechanism cannot be applied effectively to RT-WSN because it cannot avoid a high collision rate with real-time application requirements, and wastes a great deal of system bandwidth. We used the simulation tool Matlab to create the network model to be simulated. Figure 7(a) shows our implementation hardware [13] with the ZigBee RF module [14] and the MPS430 microcontroller [15]. The real experiments over RT-WSN within one office are shown in Figure 7(b). In our experiment, the transmission packet time was 8.706 ms and the number of sensor nodes ranged from 1 to 10.

A comparison among the numerical, simulation, and experimental results is shown in Figure 8(a); the number of sensor nodes is on the horizontal axis and the average transmission delay within one packet on the vertical axis. We found few differences among all three sets of results. The average delay per packet was 55 ms in the 10 sensor nodes. Therefore, the packet load was $(8.7 + 55) / 8.7 \times 100\% = 731\%$ that of the standard mode.

The real bandwidth effect of the measurement collision is shown in Figure 8. In this experimental platform, the access critical time of one packet was about 14.712 ms, and the length of one packet without the header was 115 bytes (IEEE 802.15.4 standard). Hence, the system bandwidth within one sensor node was 62 kbps.

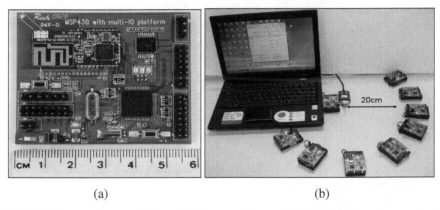

(a)   (b)

Fig. 7. (a) Our experiment platform. (b) The experiment of the RT-WSN environment with eight sensor nodes.

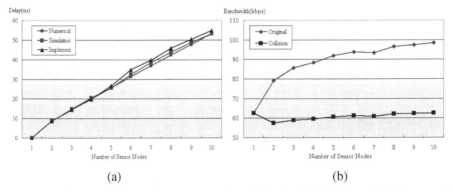

(a)   (b)

Fig. 8. (a) The average packet delay on 10 nodes. (b) The bandwidth effect of collision on 10 nodes.

6 Conclusions

In this study, we proposed an effective mathematical analysis methodology to be applied to real-time WSN under the IEEE 802.15.4 standard. Our theoretical analysis model was consistent with the simulation and experimental results indicating that this slotted CSMA/CA mechanism cannot be effectively applied to RT-WSN because it cannot avoid the high collision rate with real-time application requirements and wastes a great deal of system bandwidth. We found that the packet collision rate increased up to 731% compared to an ideal model with 10 users within RT-WSN.

Generally, most synchronous network systems possess real-time characteristics because they need to use as much network bandwidth as possible. We found that the slotted CSMA/CA mechanism is not a good choice for real-time applications, when the user wants to increase sensor nodes in the system to consider that there is the side effect of the high packet collision rate. The IEEE 802.15.4 standard is suitable for asynchronous system applications in distributed networks in the home, industry, and medical settings.

Acknowledgment

The authors would like to thank the National Science Council of the Republic of China for financially supporting this research under Contract No. NSC 97-2218-E-159 -002-, NSC 97-2622-E-027-009-CC3 and NSC 97-3114-E-002-003-.

References

1. Akyildiz, I.F., Su, W., Sankarasubramaniam, Y., et al.: Wireless sensor networks: s survey. Computer Networks 38, 393–422 (2002)
2. Callaway, E.H.: Wireless sensor networks: Architectures and protocols. CRC Press, Boca Raton (2004)
3. Willig, A., Matheus, K., Wolisz, A.: Wireless technology in industrial networks. Proc. IEEE 93, 1130–1151 (2005)
4. Golmie, N., Cypher, D., Rebala, O.: Performance evaluation of low rate WPANs for medical applications. In: Military Communications Conference 2004, pp. 927–933 (2004)
5. Van Den Bossche, A., Val, T., Campo, E.: Metrologie pour l'analyse comparative des performances temporelles des liens Bluetooth. Sciences of Electronic, Technologies of Information and Telecommunications 2005 (2005)
6. IEEE 802.15.4: Wireless LAN medium access control (MAC) and physical layer (PHY) specifications for low-rate wireless personal area network, LR-WPANs (2006)
7. Singh, C.K., Kumar, A., Ameer, P.M.: Performance evaluation of an IEEE 802.15.4 sensor network with a star topology. Wireless Networks 14, 543–568 (2008)
8. Kim, T.O., Park, J.S., Chong, H.J., Kim, K.J., Choi, B.D.: Performance analysis of IEEE 802.15. 4 non-beacon mode with the unslotted CSMA/CA. IEEE Communications Letters 12, 238–240 (2008)
9. Park, T.R., Kim, T.H., Choi, J.Y., Choi, S., Kwon, W.H.: Throughput and energy consumption analysis of IEEE 802.15. 4 slotted CSMA/CA. Electronics Letters 41, 1017–1019 (2005)
10. Timmons, N.F., Scanlon, W.G.: Analysis of the performance of IEEE 802.15.4 for medical sensor body area networking. IEEE SECON 4, 16–24 (2004)
11. Bertocco, M., Gamba, G., Sona, A.: Is CSMA/CA really efficient against interference in a wireless control system? An experimental answer. In: 13th. IEEE International Conference on Emerging Technologies and Factory Automation, pp. 885–892 (2008)
12. Bertocco, M., Gamba, G., Sona, A., Vitturi, S.: Performance measurements of CSMA/CA-based wireless sensor networks for industrial applications. In: IEEE Instrumentation And Measurement Technology Conference 2007, pp. 1–6 (2007)

13. Huang, W.T., Jeong, H.D.J.: A novel implementation of high-reliability wireless sensor network platform with serpentine-antenna design. In: The 3rd International Workshop on Intelligent, Mobile and Internet Services in Ubiquitous Computing (to be published, 2009)
14. Uniband Electronic Corp. (UBEC), U-Force Module User Manual, http://www.ubec.com.tw/product/U-Force.html
15. Texas Instruments Incorporated, MSP430x15x, MSP430x16x, MSP430x161x mixed signal microcontroller, http://www.ti.com/lit/gpn/msp430f1611/

Physical Characterization of Acoustic Communication Channel Properties in Underwater Mobile Sensor Networks

Andrea Caiti, Emanuele Crisostomi, and Andrea Munafò

ISME, Interuniversity Research Centre on Integrated Systems for the Marine Environment,
c/o DSEA, Dept. Electrical Systems and Automation, University of Pisa,
Largo Lucio Lazzarino (già via Diotisalvi 2), 56100 Pisa, Italy
{caiti,munafo}@dsea.unipi.it, emanuele.crisostomi@gmail.com

Abstract. A methodology to predict underwater acoustic channel communication properties (capacity, bandwidth, range) from the environmental conditions in the ocean is proposed. The methodology is based on the use of acoustic propagation models coupled to a set of equations proposed firstly by Stojanovic [1]. A parametric study of channel characteristics as a function of changing environmental conditions is presented, showing in particular how channel range and/or source transmission power are influenced by the relative position of source and receiver with respect to the ocean temperature thermocline. This kind of results is crucial to adaptively configure the relative position of mobile nodes (typically AUVs – Autonomous Underwater Vehicles) in underwater sensor networks, with the final goal of mitigating the effects of environmental changes on the network communication capabilities.

Keywords: AUV, underwater sensor networks, underwater communication, underwater acoustics, acoustic propagation.

1 Introduction

Since the seminal work of Curtin *et al.* [2], many progresses have been made toward the operational implementation of Autonomous Ocean Sampling Networks (AOSN). In particular, advances in miniaturization and embedded systems technology has now made possible the design and realization of low-cost Autonomous Underwater Vehicles (AUVs) [3], [4], that, equipped with appropriate oceanographic payloads, can act as a team in mapping specific areas of the ocean. Cooperation and coordination algorithms for mobile robotic vehicles have been successfully applied to teams of AUVs and/or oceanographic gliders [5]. Some large scale experimentation, in which networks of mobile and fixed sensors, autonomous or semi-autonomous, have been employed to monitor the evolution of ocean dynamics, have been successfully reported [6]. Nevertheless, the challenges posed by the ocean environments are such that there are still scientific and technological problems to be solved for the realization of the original AOSN vision.

S. Hailes, S. Sicari, and G. Roussos (Eds.): S-Cube 2009, LNICST 24, pp. 111–126, 2009.

One challenge not yet solved is related to the problem of communication among the underwater platforms, either fixed or mobile, composing the sensor network. Since electromagnetic waves are so strongly attenuated in salty waters to prevent any radio communication at distances exceeding few meters, acoustic waves are used for underwater communication. Hence, the physics of underwater acoustic propagation plays a key role in the determination of the communication channel characteristics. In turn, the physics of acoustic propagation is strongly influenced by the oceanographic conditions, since the sound speed in the water is a function of temperature, salinity and depth, and these quantities vary both in space and in time [7]. While several approaches have been proposed to model the underwater acoustic communication channel (see for instance [8] for a recent review), there still appears to be a gap in the scientific literature between the channel characterization which is required for communication system design, and the physical modeling of acoustic propagation.

In an attempt to bridge the above mentioned gap, Stojanovic [1] has proposed a set of expressions to determine maximum channel capacity and bandwidth as a function of the intensity loss of the acoustic signal. In [1], analytical computations are given for the case in which the medium (i.e., the ocean channel) is homogeneous and the intensity loss is due only to geometrical spreading and to the intrinsic attenuation of the medium. However, intensity loss is among the parameters computed by acoustic propagation codes: so, at least in principle, the approach of [1] can be extended in a straightforward manner by using appropriate numerical models of the acoustic channel.

The contributions of this paper are twofold:

- it is shown how indeed a specific computational code (the code "Bellhop", based on ray theory [7], [9]) can be used in order to derive communication channel characteristics following the approach of [1]; in doing this, we also discuss the set of modifications and/or caveat that have to be considered before transposing directly the results of the model into the channel equations.
- a parametric study based on the above mentioned channel modeling is performed to determine the variability of the communication channel performance as a function of the variability of the environmental conditions (and therefore of the acoustic propagation conditions).

The sensitivity study is directed toward the determination of optimal strategies for mobile nodes motion in an AOSN to maximize communication performance or to maintain team communication connectivity [10], [11]. While this latter problem is not treated in this paper, the results reported here are instrumental to the implementation of cooperative distributed motion algorithms in underwater sensor networks.

The paper is organized as follows: in the next section the main aspects of acoustic propagation relevant to the communication problem are briefly reviewed, the approach of [1] to the modeling of the acoustic communication channel reported, and the assumptions, validity limits and implementation choices adopted in coupling the physical model Bellhop to the communication channel equations illustrated. In Section 3 the simulative scenarios are described; in particular, we consider three cases, and in all of them sound speed changes only as a function of depth in the water column, but not of range between transmitter and receiver: in one case the sound speed is constant with depth (similar to the analytical case of [1]), in the other two cases a thermocline region is considered (i.e., a region in which temperature, and hence sound speed, has a constant gradient with depth), and transmitter and receivers are located within the thermocline, or on opposite sides of the thermocline. Simulations for the three cases are referred to two different scenarios, one taken from the original Stojanovic paper [1], and the other, considering higher frequencies and shorter ranges, corresponding to a more realistic operational configuration. Conclusions and future work are addressed in Section 4.

2 Acoustic Propagation and Communication Channel Characterization

In this section we first review the physics of acoustic propagation and the assumptions of the ray modeling approximation. Subsequently, the channel characterization proposed in [1] is reported and linked to the ray model.

2.1 The Physics of Acoustic Propagation

The pressure field generated by an acoustic (compressional) wave traveling in the ocean medium is governed, in the linear approximation, by the Helmholtz equation [7]:

$$[\nabla^2 + k^2(\mathbf{x})]\psi(\mathbf{x}, \omega) = f(\omega)\delta(\mathbf{x} - \mathbf{x_s}) \tag{1}$$

where ω is the angular frequency, $\mathbf{x}$ is the position in the space coordinate frame, ∇^2 is the Laplacian operator, $k(\mathbf{x}) = \omega / c(\mathbf{x})$ is the wavenumber, $c(\mathbf{x})$ is the sound speed in the medium as a function of geographical position, $f(\omega)$ is the forcing term due to a point source at location $\mathbf{x_s}$, δ is the Dirac's delta function, ψ is the wave potential. The pressure is related to the wave potential by the equation:

$$p(\mathbf{x}, \omega) = \rho\omega^2\psi(\mathbf{x}, \omega) \tag{2}$$

where ρ is the medium density, and it is considered constant in the following. To solve the Helmholtz equation it is necessary to specify the boundary conditions, in terms of sea surface and bottom depth, and the medium characteristics, in terms of the sound speed in the medium, which in practice depends on the ocean dynamics. The coordinate reference frame is usually taken with the origin at the sea surface and the z axis pointing downward toward the sea bottom. By assuming the existence of a solution to the homogenous Helmholtz equation of the form:

$$p(\mathbf{x}, \omega) = e^{j\omega\tau(\mathbf{x})} \sum_{h=0}^{+\infty} \frac{a_h}{\omega^h} . \tag{3}$$

and substituting (3) into equations (1) and (2), neglecting the terms where ω appears at the denominator, one gets the *ray-theory approximation* equations:

$$\left|\nabla^2 \tau(\mathbf{x})\right| = \frac{1}{c^2(\mathbf{x})} \qquad \text{(eikonal equation)} \qquad (4)$$

$$2\nabla \tau \cdot \nabla a_0 + (\nabla^2 \tau) a_0 = 0 \qquad \text{(transport equation)} \qquad (5)$$

where $\tau(\mathbf{x})$ is the time of arrival of an acoustic ray from the origin to the position $\mathbf{x}$. The above derivation has been outlined to emphasize that the ray theory approach, which is followed since now on, due to its intuitive appeal, it is an approximation which is valid only in the high frequency regime (usually above the KHz).

In qualitative terms, using the ray approximation, an acoustic wave traveling from a source in the ocean water column will manifest itself as a sequence of arrivals corresponding to the various rays (Fig.1, left). Different rays will arrive at the receiver following different paths (multi-path arrivals). The paths themselves will be determined by the sound speed in the medium through the Snell's refraction law (which is embedded in the eikonal equation). In (Fig. 1, centre) a typical sound speed profile as a function of depth is shown. The corresponding ray paths are shown in (Fig. 1, right) assuming cylindrical coordinates and sound speed constant with range.

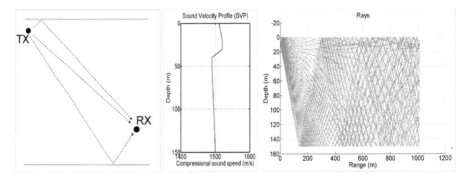

Fig. 1. The geometry of the transmitter and the receiver is shown on the left. Rays can arrive to the destination following different paths. A typical sound speed profile is shown in the middle, while the corresponding ray paths are shown on the right.

The acoustic intensity $I(\mathbf{x})$ is the power per unit surface of an acoustic wave, and it is proportional to the square of the pressure. The *transmission loss TL* of an acoustic wave is defined as:

$$TL(\mathbf{x}, \omega) = -10Log_{10}\left(I(\mathbf{x}, \omega)/I_0\right). \qquad (6)$$

where I_0 is the reference intensity. In underwater acoustics, the reference intensity is the intensity of a plane wave having rms pressure amplitude of $1\mu Pa$ at 1m distance from the source. By numerical solution of the transport equation, it is possible to numerically compute TL in the ray approximation. The computational code "Bellhop"

[9] is such a code; it is widespread in the scientific community, having passed the appropriate recognized benchmark tests. In the following of the paper, all the simulative results will be obtained through Bellhop. Moreover, in all our simulations we will refer to the so-called "range independent" environmental conditions: a cylindrical coordinate frame will be assumed, with axis r (range) and z (depth); the source is always placed on the $z = 0$ axis, and $c(r, z) = c(z)$.

It is important to remark that the Bellhop model includes the following physical mechanisms of intensity loss: the geometrical spreading, computed along the paths for each ray; the intrinsic attenuation, which is the attenuation due to mechanical and thermodynamic effects of pressure propagation in salty water, and which is frequency dependent; the wave interference patterns due to the superposition of different rays.

The transmission loss can be used to predict the intensity level S at the receiver due to a source of intensity SL through the so-called *passive sonar equation*:

$$S(\mathbf{x}) = SL - TL(\mathbf{x}) \tag{7}$$

By considering also an ambient noise term, the passive sonar equation can be formulated in terms of the Signal-to-Noise Ratio (SNR) at the receiver as follows:

$$SNR(\mathbf{x}, \omega) = SL - TL(\mathbf{x}, \omega) - N(\omega) \tag{8}$$

where all the above quantities are in dB ref $1\mu Pa$ @1m. The same SNR can be expressed in natural scale as: $snr(\mathbf{x}, \omega) = I(\omega)/n(\omega)$. The ambient noise term $N(\omega)$, or $n(\omega)$ in natural scale, may depend on a series of factors (ship traffic, wave motions,...) and the noise model defined in [1], [12], is considered in the remainder of this paper, with the same parameter choices of [1]. Space limitations prevent to report the model here.

For any given source position $\mathbf{x_s}$, and for any receiver position $\mathbf{x}$ and any frequency ω it is possible to define the channel transfer function $G(\mathbf{x_s}, \mathbf{x}, \omega)$ satisfying the following relation between transmitted and received pressure:

$$p(\mathbf{x}, \omega) = G(\mathbf{x_s}, \mathbf{x}, \omega) p_s(\omega). \tag{9}$$

where $p_s(\omega)$ is the source signal. The transmission loss can also be computed from the transfer function as:

$$TL = -20 Log_{10} |G(\mathbf{x_s}, \mathbf{x}, \omega)|. \tag{10}$$

while the SNR in terms of transfer function is given as:

$$SNR = -10 Log_{10}(snr) = -10 Log_{10}\left(\frac{p_s^2 |G|^2}{n}\right). \tag{11}$$

2.2 Acoustic Communication Channel Characterization

This section reports the definitions and equations proposed in [1] to characterize an acoustic communication channel on the basis of the transmission loss (equation (6)), of the SNR (equations (8) and (11)) and of the channel transfer function (equation 9). The original equations of [1] are slightly reformulated here to better link them to the physical description of the previous section, but preserving the same approach and considerations of [1]. We first note that, for any source-receiver geometric configuration $(\mathbf{x_s}, \mathbf{x})$ it is possible to define an optimal transmission frequency as:

$$\omega_0(\mathbf{x_s}, \mathbf{x}) = \arg\max_\omega \frac{|G(\mathbf{x_s}, \mathbf{x}, \omega)|^2}{n(\omega)}. \tag{12}$$

A *heuristic 3-dB bandwidth* $B_3(\omega_0)$ can then be defined as the range of frequencies in the neighborhood of ω_0 such that $SNR(\omega) > SNR(\omega_0) - 3$. For any given transmitted source signal $p_S(\omega)$, the source intensity in the bandwidth $B_3(\omega_0)$ is proportional to the square of the pressure spectrum integrated over the bandwidth:

$$I_S \propto \int_{B_3} p_s^2(\omega)d\omega. \tag{13}$$

The SNR, expressed in natural scale, within the 3dB bandwidth, is thus obtained by integrating the argument of the Log function in equation (11) over the bandwidth:

$$snr_{B_3}(\omega) = \frac{\int_{B_3} p_s^2(\omega)|G(\omega)|^2 \, d\omega}{\int_{B_3} n(\omega)d\omega}. \tag{14}$$

Equation (14) can then be used to dimension the source level (through $p_S(\omega)$) in order to achieve a prescribed SNR gain. In particular, assuming a constant source level p_3 over the 3dB bandwidth, in order to obtain a prescribed SNR γ (in natural scale) the following relation must hold:

$$p_3^2 \geq \gamma \frac{\int_{B_3} n(\omega)d\omega}{\int_{B_3} |G(\omega)|^2 \, d\omega}. \tag{15}$$

The corresponding channel capacity is given as:

$$C_3 = \int_{B_3} \log_2\left(1 + \frac{p_3^2 |G(\omega)|^2}{n(\omega)}\right)d\omega. \tag{16}$$

As observed in [1], the above heuristic definition does not guarantee the optimality in the energy distribution across the system bandwidth. Therefore, in [1] it is proposed also the following approach, termed *capacity-based bandwidth definition*, in which the bandwidth is indeed defined in order to maximize the channel capacity. In particular, under the assumption of time-invariance of the channel, by subdividing the bandwidth in sub-bands of width $\Delta\omega$ such that the channel transfer function G can be considered constant within the sub-band and the noise term n white within the sub-band, the channel capacity for a receiver located in $\mathbf{x}$ is given by:

$$C(\mathbf{x}) = \sum_h \Delta\omega \log_2 \left(1 + \frac{p_s^2(\omega_h)|G(\omega_h)|^2}{n(\omega_h)}\right). \tag{17}$$

The optimal energy distribution within the bandwidth is obtained by maximizing the capacity in equation (17) with the constraint of finite transmitted power $\int p_s^2$. The optimal signal power spectrum must satisfy the water-filling principle [13]:

$$p_s^2(\omega) + \frac{n(\omega)}{|G(\omega)|^2} = \kappa. \tag{18}$$

where the constant κ is determined from the resulting signal power. The SNR corresponding to the optimal energy distribution is obtained as:

$$snr(\omega) = \frac{\int_B p_s^2(\omega)|G(\omega)|^2 d\omega}{\int_B n(\omega)d\omega} = \kappa \frac{\int_B |G(\omega)|^2 d\omega}{\int_B n(\omega)d\omega} - 1. \tag{19}$$

and the transmitted power is:

$$P_S = \int_B p_s^2(\omega)d\omega = \kappa B - \int_B \frac{n(\omega)}{|G(\omega)|^2}d\omega. \tag{20}$$

Once a prescribed SNR γ (in natural scale) is given, the following iterative procedure can be employed to determine the optimal energy distribution:

1. For each receiver position $\mathbf{x}$, the optimal transmission frequency (equation 12) is determined; $\kappa(0)$ is initialized as $\kappa(0) = n(\omega_0)/2|G(\omega_0)|^2$ (note that κ will vary with receiver position)
2. given $\kappa(m)$, determine the bandwidth $B(m)$ as the region of frequencies around ω_0 such that $\kappa(m) > n(\omega_0)/|G(\omega_0)|^2$;
3. compute $snr(m)$ from equation (19) using $B(m)$ and $\kappa(m)$;
4. if $snr(m) < \gamma$, set $\kappa(m+1) = \kappa(m) + \varepsilon$, with ε (small) constant and go to step 2; otherwise, exit with $\kappa = \kappa(m)$ and $B = B(m)$

The optimal energy distribution is then given by equation (18) for $\omega \in B$, and it is zero outside the bandwidth B. The corresponding channel capacity, which will be referred as optimal channel capacity in the remainder of the paper, is given by:

$$C = \int_B \log_2 \kappa \frac{|G(\omega)|^2}{n(\omega)} d\omega. \tag{21}$$

2.3 Channel Performance from Acoustic Propagation Computation

The channel characteristics defined in the previous subsection can be determined by computation of the quantities defined in equations from (7) to (11) with a numerical code able to solve the Helmholtz equation (1). In particular, in the next section the code Bellhop, as already anticipated, will be extensively used. Bellhop solves equations (4) and (5), producing a high-frequency approximation of the solution of equation (1). One specific aspect has to be discussed when using the transmission loss computation from a numerical code as Bellhop to determine the communication channel performance: the evaluation of the multipath structure. In time domain the multipath structure reveals itself as a sequence of attenuated, delayed replicas of the first arrival, usually well separated in time (at least at high frequencies). Computational codes as Bellhop consider stationary sources and stationary waves; this implies, roughly speaking, that the signal intensity at the receiver position $\mathbf{x}_s$ is determined by adding up (with a coherent or incoherent procedure, depending if phase information is taken into account, and both options are available) the contributions carried on along each ray path to produce the total received intensity. As a result, in the case of coherent constructive interference, or in the incoherent case, multipath arrivals contribute to *decreasing* the transmission loss and *increasing* the SNR. While this makes sense in the usual application of acoustic propagation codes (determination of sonar ranges, etc.), it may not always be appropriate in the context of acoustic communication. An underwater acoustic communication signal will not transmit stationary waves, but it will use some kind of modulation. Multipath arrivals may not concur to enhance the SNR, but in fact, more often than not, will consist in a disturbance echo resulting in symbolic interference. Indeed, several receiving schemes proposed in the literature are based on the estimation of the multipath time-delay structure and on the suppression of the delayed arrivals [8].

It has to be noted, however, that there are propagation conditions in which only bottom reflected or surface reflected arrivals can reach the receiver; moreover, depending on the attenuation properties of the bottom (the "bottom loss"), a late surface reflected arrival may carry more power than a faster, bottom reflected arrival. In this case it is more useful to use the second arrival in decoding the transmitted signal.

Last but not least, it is worth to mention that other propagation codes, not based on the ray approximation, may cope with the same problem in a different way. For instance, when using normal mode-based computational codes, only the modes that effectively contribute to the useful part of the signal must be considered, while those contributing to symbolic interference must be discarded.

As a consequence of the above discussion, the decision whether to include the multipath arrivals in the computation of the transmission loss and of the SNR must ultimately depend on the modulation/demodulation algorithms and on anticipation of some peculiarities in the propagation behaviour. In the simulations reported in the next section, we have *not* considered multipath arrivals; all else being equal, inclusions of the multipath structure would have led to an increase in the estimated performance of the channel. This means that the results obtained are valid only for those demodulating schemes that suppress the delayed echoes due to the multipath structure and for situations in which a direct path is always present between transmitter and receiver.

3 Simulations and Sensitivity Analysis to Sound Speed Variation in the Water Column

In this section we consider two different scenarios and three cases for each scenario. The first case is indicated as "nominal scenario", and it is similar to that analyzed in [1]: frequencies vary from 10 Hz to 20 KHz, transmitter-receiver ranges vary from 1Km to 100Km. The nominal scenario has been included in order to allow an easy comparison between our computational results and the analytical results reported in [1]. The second case is indicated as "operative scenario", since it is closer to the expected frequencies and ranges that are or may be used in AOSN applications: frequencies vary between 20 and 50 KHz, and transmitter-receiver ranges vary from 100m to 6000m. In both scenarios, three cases are considered with different environmental conditions: constant sound speed profile (equivalent to the analytical case of [1]); presence of a thermocline with both transmitter and receiver in the thermocline region; presence of a thermocline with the transmitter above the thermocline and the receiver below. The transmitter depth is 300 m above the receiver depth in the nominal scenario, and 100 m above the receiver depth in the operational scenario. The results are always reported as a function of the *horizontal* range between transmitter and receiver. Water depth and bottom absorption do not play any role since we are considering only direct arrivals. The sound speed profile varies with depth (hence the presence of a thermocline) but not with range (*range independent* environmental conditions).

In both scenarios, the following results have been produced and presented as graphical output for the three cases considered: SNR as a function of frequency; optimal frequency as a function of range; heuristic bandwidth and capacity; optimal bandwidth and capacity; source power required to reach a 20 dB gain in SNR as a function of range.

3.1 Nominal Scenario

The three cases considered for the nominal scenario, in terms of relative position and sound speed profile in the water column, are reported in Fig. 2. The gradient in the sound speed profile corresponds to the thermocline region. In the simulations, frequencies from 10Hz to 20KHz have been considered, with 100Hz spacing starting from 100Hz. Horizontal range varies between 1 and 100Km; 200 range slices have been considered.

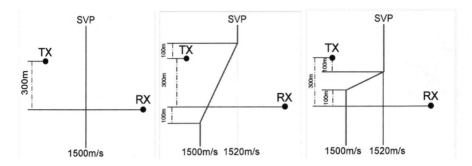

Fig. 2. The three cases considered, with different speed profiles as a function of depth, from the left to the right

In Fig. 3 the SNR as a function of range is reported for the three cases. The SNR decreases when propagation within the thermocline is considered. Note that in case 3, at 5 km distance, there is a direct path between the transmitter and the receiver that does not cross the thermocline.

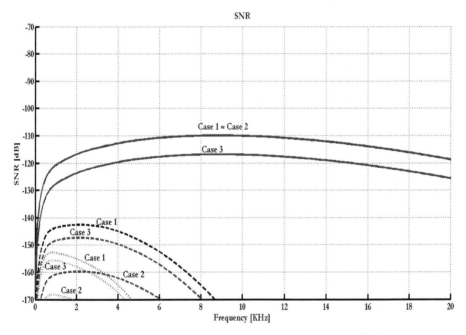

Fig. 3. SNR as a function of frequency. Solid lines refer to a range of 5 Km, dashed lines to range equal to 50 Km and dotted lines to 100 Km. For each of the three ranges, graphs corresponding to three cases are shown.

In Fig. 4 the optimal propagation frequency is indicated for the three cases; here it is worth to note that the optimal frequency is not influenced by the propagation condition.

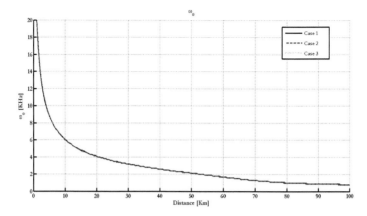

Fig. 4. Optimal frequency as a function of the range. There are not significant differences among the three studied cases.

Fig.s 5 to 8 show bandwith, capacity and power (in both heuristic and optimal definitions). Power is intended as the power required to achieve a 20 dB SNR gain. Similarly to the optimal frequency shown in Fig. 4, the bandwith is not influenced by the propagation conditions; this may appear surprising at first, since bandwidth does depend on the SNR. However, bandwidth depends on the relative differences of the SNR at adjacent frequencies; while the absolute SNR level is different from case to case, this is not so for the relative differences, hence the invariance of bandwidth with respect to environmental conditions. Differently from the bandwith, the reason why the capacity is apparently not affected by the propagation conditions in Figs. 7 and 8 is that here the source power compensates for SNR differences.

Finally, in Figs. 7 and 8, it can also be noted that at long ranges the environmental condition of case 2 (with both transmission ends within the thermocline region) is the one requiring the maximum power from the transmitter, while there are shorter ranges in which the most power consuming environmental conditions is the one of case 2 (transmitter and receiver on the opposite sides of the thermocline). In any case, the presence of the thermocline is detrimental to the system power consumption.

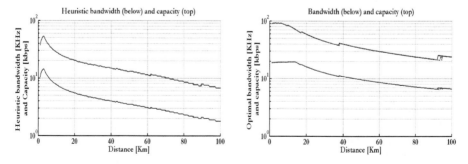

Fig. 5-6. The heuristic bandwith and capacity are shown on the left, while the optimal bandwith and capacity are on the right. There are not visible differences among the three studied cases.

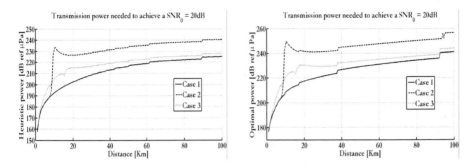

Fig. 7-8. On the left heuristic power and on the right optimal power required to achieve an SNR greater than 20 dB. Now differences among the three studied cases are evident.

3.2 Operational Scenario

The three cases considered for the operational scenario, in terms of relative position and sound speed profile in the water column, are reported in Fig. 9. In the simulations, frequencies from 20Hz to 50KHz have been considered, at 100Hz steps. Horizontal range varies between 100m and 6000m; 100 range slices have been considered.

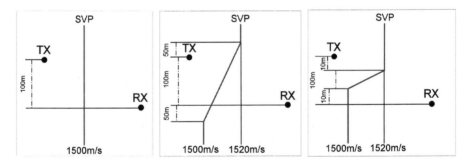

Fig. 9. The three cases considered, with different speed profiles as a function of depth, are shown from the left to the right

In Fig. 10 the SNR as a function of range is reported for the three cases; also in this scenario the SNR decreases when the direct path propagates through the thermocline.

In Fig. 11 the optimal propagation frequency is indicated for the three cases; while it is confirmed that also at higher frequencies the optimal frequency is not influenced by the propagation condition, here it is worth noting that the there is no optimal frequency above 38 KHz; the curve flattens at the 20 KHz value slightly above 1000m because 20 KHz is the inferior range considered in the scenario.

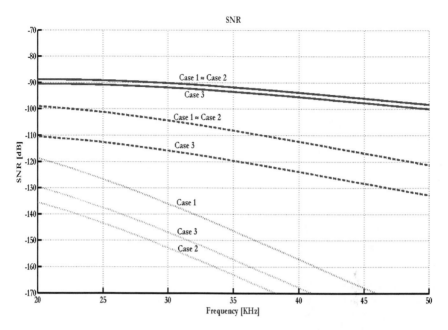

Fig. 10. SNR as a function of frequency. Solid lines refer to a range of 1 Km, dashed lines to range equal to 2 Km and dotted lines to 5 Km. For each of the three ranges, graphs corresponding to three cases are shown.

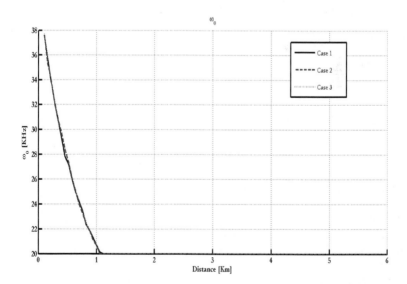

Fig. 11. Optimal frequency as a function of the range. There are not significant differences among the three studied cases.

Figs. 12 and 13, reports bandwidth and channel capacity (heuristic and optimal definition) while Figs. 14 and 15 report the required source power as a function of range to achieve a 20 dB SNR gain; here, in both cases, are more evident the nonlinear variations with range in the required power when propagation within the thermocline is considered.

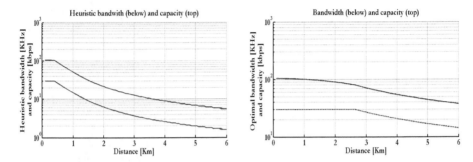

Fig. 12-13. On the left, heuristic bandwith and capacity as a function of the distance, while on the right the optimal bandwith and capacity are shown. There are not significant differences among the three studied cases.

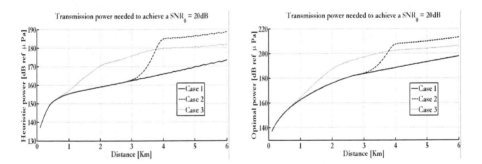

Fig. 14-15. On the left the heuristic power and on the right the optimal power required to achieve an SNR greater than 20 dB are shown. Now differences among the three studied cases are evident.

4   Discussion and Conclusions

In this work we have applied the theory developed in [1] to the computation of the underwater communication channel characteristics through the use of acoustic propagation simulators. In this way it is possible to consider the effective environmental conditions of the acoustic channel. This capability can be exploited in various ways: in the field, the on-line measurement of the sound speed profile in the water column (or equivalently the measurement of temperature and salinity) may be used to adapt on-line the characteristics of the communication system. At the design stage, sensitivity studies can be performed, similarly to what has been done in this contribution, analyzing particular environmental situations. In this paper such a sensitivity study has been carried out considering the very frequent situation in which a thermocline region is present in the water column. While the main result may not come as a surprise (the best situation, from the point of view of communication performance, is when both transmitter and receiver are either above or below the thermocline), the sensitivity analysis shows how the transmission power, and hence the source level, is influenced in order to achieve a prescribed SNR. The same results can be used to determine, with a given source level, what is the maximum range at which transmitter and receiver can be positioned to guarantee a prescribed SNR.

As discussed in the paper, the numerical results obtained are subject to a series of assumptions that may not apply to any underwater communication system or environmental situation. In addition to the multi-path arrival contribution to the SNR, discussed in section 2.3, another notable effect not included in this study and that must be part of a thorough analysis of communication strategies for an AOSN is the Doppler effect due to relative transmitter-receiver motion. Our future work will develop on two directions: on one side, we will enhance the communication-oriented modeling of the acoustic channel; on a parallel line, we intend to exploit the results of sensitivity studies similar to the one reported here in order to devise collective motion strategies in AOSN that guarantee some quality of service requirements in the communication and networking.

Acknowledgments. This work has been partially supported by European Union, project UAN – Underwater Acoustic Networks, 7th Framework Programme, grant agreement no. 225669.

References

1. Stojanovic, M.: On the Relationship Between Capacity and Distance in an Underwater Acoustic Communication Channel. ACM SIGMOBILE Mobile Computing and Communications Review (MC2R) 11(4), 34–43 (2007)
2. Curtin, T., Bellingham, J., Catopovic, J., Webb, D.: Autonomous Oceanographic Sampling Networks. Oceanography 6(3), 86–94 (1993)
3. Anderson, B., Crowell, J.: Workhorse AUV – A cost-sensible new Autonomous Underwater Vehicle for Surveys/ Soundings, Search & Rescue, and Research. In: Proc. IEEE Oceans 2005 Conference (2005)
4. Alvarez, A., Caffaz, A., Caiti, A., Casalino, G., Gualdesi, L., Turetta, A., Viviani, R.: Fòlaga: A low-cost autonomous underwater vehicle combining glider and AUV capabilities. Ocean Engineering 36(1), 24–38 (2009)
5. Paley, D.A., Zhang, F., Leonard, N.E.: Cooperative Control for Ocean Sampling: The Glider Coordinated Control System. IEEE Trans. Control Systems Technology 16(4), 735–744 (2008)
6. Curtin, T.B., Bellingham, J.: Progress toward autonomous ocean sampling networks, Deep Sea Research – Part II. Topical studies in Oceanography (2008) (in press), doi:10.1016/j.dsr2.2008.09.005
7. Jensen, F., Kuperman, W., Porter, M., Schmidt, H.: Computational Ocean Acoustics. American Institute of Physics (AIP), New York (1995)

8. Chitre, M., Shahabodeen, S., Stojanovic, M.: Underwater Acoustic Communications and Networking: Recent Advances and Future Challenges. Marine Technology Society Journal 42(1), 103–116 (2008)
9. Ocean Acoustic Library, http://oalib.hlsresearch.com/
10. Caiti, A., Casalino, G., Lorenzi, E., Turetta, A., Viviani, R.: Distributed adaptive environmental sampling with AUVs: Cooperation and team coordination through minimum-spanning-tree graph searching algorithms. In: Proc. IFAC Conf. Navigation, Guidance and Control of Underwater Vehicles, Killakoe, Ireland (2008)
11. Ghabcheloo, R., Aguiar, A.P., Pascoal, A., Silvestre, C.: Coordinated Path-Following Control of Multiple Auvs in the Presence of Communication Failures and Time Delays. In: Proc. IFAC Conf. Manoeuvering and Control of Marine Crafts, Lisbon (2006)
12. Coates, R.: Underwater Acoustic Systems. Wiley, New York (1989)
13. Telatar, I.E.: Capacity of multi-antenna Gaussian channels. Eur. Trans. Telecom. 10, 585–595 (1999)

A Code Generator for Distributing Sensor Data Models

Urs Hunkeler and Paolo Scotton

IBM Zurich Research Laboratory,
Säumerstrasse 4, 8803 Rüschlikon, Switzerland
{hun,psc}@zurich.ibm.com

Abstract. As wireless sensor networks mature, it becomes clear that the raw data collected by this technology can only be used in a meaningful way if it can be analyzed automatically. Describing the behavior of the data with a model, and then looking at the parameters of the model, or detecting differences between the model and the real data, is how experimental data is typically used in other fields. The work presented here aims at facilitating the use of sensor data models to describe the expected behavior of the sensor observations. The processing of such models can be pushed into the wireless sensor network to eliminate redundant information as early in the data collection chain as possible, thus minimizing both bandwidth requirements and energy consumption.

1 Introduction

Wireless sensor networks (WSNs) promise cheap sensor deployment to monitor an area of interest in great detail. WSNs are, for instance, being used to measure seismic activity at volcanoes [17] or the micro-climate of glaciers [3]. Such sensor network deployments generate data at a much greater spatial resolution than more traditional observation techniques such as wired networks or data loggers. In addition, the data generated by these networks is available for immediate use. However, the huge amount of data has to be processed. Nobody will look at every single sensor reading. Instead, the data is used to evaluate physical models of the observed phenomena, and to detect situations where such models do not represent the observed behavior accurately.

To illustrate this, let us consider a hypothetical sensor network deployment (partially based on a real case [2]). In this hypothetical deployment a mountain village experiences sporadic floods caused by a glacier. To predict floods and alert the population, climatologists install a sensor network to monitor the micro-climate of the glacier by observing the surface temperature of the ice, the duration and intensity of sunshine, the amount of precipitation, and other similar factors. Based on a model of the glacier's behavior the data from the WSN is used to predict floods. The model could describe how water accumulates, and under what conditions the ice barrier breaks and releases the water. The model will not accurately predict the behavior of the glacier if an unexpected event occurs. For instance, a nearby dirt avalanche could cause the glacier to be covered

S. Hailes, S. Sicari, and G. Roussos (Eds.): S-Cube 2009, LNICST 24, pp. 127–143, 2009.

with a small layer of dust. The dust could completely change the heat absorption rate of the glacier, and thus how much water is melted on a sunny day. This model rupture might be detected because the measured surface temperature of the glacier differs from the expected surface temperature.

To deal with the large amount of data generated by a WSN, it is necessary to use data models to simplify the analysis of this data. Currently, data models are processed on back-end systems. Many data models, especially if based on complex physical models, are computationally expensive and therefore cannot be processed efficiently on the low-power devices typically used for sensor networks. It is, however, possible to do a first part of the processing already within the WSN. In this way, only the data necessary for the model processing rather than every single sensor reading is transmitted. This helps both to reduce the power consumption and to resolve bandwidth bottlenecks. In addition, some data models are able to exploit redundancy in sensor readings to make the data assimilation of a sensor network more robust to transmission errors.

When using data models it is important to be clear about quality-of-information (QoI) needs. QoI has been defined [4] as a collection of attributes including timeliness, accuracy, reliability, throughput, and cost. A WSN has some obvious QoI characteristics, such as the amount of data to be transmitted and the measurement accuracy and frequency. Data models can increase the confidence in the data by combining information from multiple sensors. On the other hand, it is possible to increase the life-time of a WSN by allowing the QoI to be reduced.

We propose a framework that facilitates using data models to process sensor data, and that enables us to push part of the model processing into the WSN. The concepts behind this framework have been introduced in the positioning paper [11], which presented a model processing mechanism running entirely on the back-end system. In this paper we present a first implementation of a distributed model processing mechanism running partially inside the senor network, and in particular show how model descriptions can be compiled into a distributed program and how optimization techniques can be applied. The key contributions presented in this paper are: (1) the description of a framework to automatically process generic sensor data models, which also pushes part of the data processing into the WSN, (2) the presentation of the implementation of a concrete model called distributed linear regression, and (3) the lessons we learned by implementing this framework. Section 2 presents related work. Section 3 presents a data model based on linear regression that will be used throughout this paper to explain the concepts of the framework. Section 4 describes the network concept of WSNs and presents a concrete network topology that will be used in the examples. Section 5 introduces our model description language. Section 6 discusses distributed aggregation of linear functions. Section 7 explains how the distributed model-processing algorithm is generated. Section 8 describes the supporting services that are needed to run the model-processing algorithm. Section 9 presents the experience we gained by implementing the framework. Section 10 concludes the paper.

2   Related Work

TinyDB [14] is a framework based on TinyOS that lets users see the WSN as a database. Querying sensors results in data being acquired by the network. In some cases, queries using aggregation functions are calculated partially inside the network. TinyDB supports aggregation, energy-aware query constraints, and continuously running queries. However, TinyDB was never aimed at model-processing. The language is based on SQL and might not be intuitive for users of WSNs without a computer-science background. TinyDB is no longer maintained.

MauveDB [6] is an extension of Apache Derby, an open source relational database implemented in Java^{TM1}. MauveDB offers the user a novel kind of view that calculates its data based on a sensor data model. Currently, supported models are based on either linear regression or correlated Gaussian random variables. Model processing is done entirely on the back-end system.

In Distributed Regression [9], a model based on linear regression has been implemented to run entirely within the WSN. The observations are approximated with a base function that linearly combines model coefficients with functions of the query parameters. The network transmits the model coefficients describing the observations in the network to the sink. An application on the sink can then approximate values of the observations anywhere within the network. Using this linear regression model enables a significant reduction of the amount of data being transmitted in the network. The implementation is specific to and optimized for this type of models.

BBQ [5] implements a model based on multivariate Gaussian random variables that runs entirely on the back-end system. Sensor readings and correlations among the readings of different sensors are used to determine a query plan that uses the least amount of energy to gather just enough new information from the network to answer a query while respecting the error bounds given.

3   Linear Regression

The framework is designed to be applicable to a wide range of different sensor data models and processing algorithms. Throughout the remainder of this paper we will focus on linear regression [9] as our example to explain different concepts. In this section we introduce the model and show in detail how it can be applied to sensor data.

Linear regression is a method for finding a set of dependent variables such that the regression function best fits the data. Let $f()$ be the regression function, $x_1, \ldots, x_p$ the function arguments, $a_1 \ldots a_c$ the dependent variables, and $g_1() \ldots g_c()$ a set of functions that combine the arguments of the outer function. The linear regression function then has the basic form:

$$f(x_1, \ldots, x_p) = a_1 g_1(x_1, \ldots, x_n) + \cdots + a_c g_c(x_1, \ldots, x_n). \quad (1)$$

---

[1] Java and all Java-based trademarks and logos are trademarks of Sun Microsystems, Inc. in the United States, other countries, or both. Other company, product, or service names may be trademarks or service marks of others.

Let a data set D be composed of tuples, and let a tuple $d_i \in D$ be composed of the actual value v_i and a set of meta-data $x_{i,1}, \ldots, x_{i,p}$:

$$d_i = \{v_i, x_{i,1}, \ldots x_{i,p}\}. \tag{2}$$

Linear regression finds the dependent variables $a_1 \ldots a_c$ such that the sum of the squared difference between the values in v_i and the corresponding values from the regression function $f(x_{i,1}, \ldots x_{i,p})$ is minimized. If D consist of k tuples $d_1 \ldots d_k$, linear regression finds

$$\operatorname*{argmin}_{a_1, \ldots, a_c} \sum_{i=1}^{k} (v_i - f(x_{i,1}, \ldots x_{i,p}))^2 . \tag{3}$$

Let us use linear regression to model the temperature measured in a WSN as a function of the physical sensor locations and the measurement time. Let x and y be the Cartesian coordinates of the sensor's location (measured for instance in meters), and let t be the time of the measurement (for instance expressed in seconds since the start of the experiment). Throughout this paper, we will use the following function to model the temperature readings:

$$f(x, y, t) = a_1 + a_2 x + a_3 y + a_4 t + a_5 t^2 . \tag{4}$$

We call the linear regression function *model function*, as we use it to model the sensor data. Similarly, we call the dependent parameters $a_0 \ldots a_4$ *linear coefficients* or *model parameters*. The model function and the model parameters together fully define the model for a particular set of data. In our model, the functions $g_0(), \ldots, g_c()$ are

$$
\begin{aligned}
g_1(x, y, t) &= 1 & \text{(5a)} \\
g_2(x, y, t) &= x & \text{(5b)} \\
g_3(x, y, t) &= y & \text{(5c)} \\
g_4(x, y, t) &= t & \text{(5d)} \\
g_5(x, y, t) &= t^2 . & \text{(5e)}
\end{aligned}
$$

We define a query on the model to be equivalent to the evaluation of a model function with a set of arguments, and the set of arguments used in the query is called *query arguments*. In our example, the query arguments are x, y, and t. In most cases the model will not be perfect and will produce results that differ from the measured values. This modeling error is a measure of the ability of the model function to represent the data accurately.

Before the model can be used to answer queries, its parameters $a_1 \ldots a_5$ need to be determined. We call functions that determine the values of model parameters *learning functions*. To determine $a_1 \ldots a_5$ in our example, let S be a set of n sensors and for each sensor $s_i \in S$ let us consider a set of measurement values at times $t_1 \ldots t_r$ noted $\{v_{i,1} \ldots v_{i,r}\}$. In addition, for each sensor $s_i \in S$, let x_i

and y_i be its Cartesian coordinates. The model function and the measurements form the following equation system:

$$v_{1,1} = u_1 + u_2x_1 + u_3y_1 + u_4t_1 + u_5t_1^2$$
$$v_{1,2} = u_1 + u_2x_1 + u_3y_1 + u_4t_2 + u_5t_2^2$$
$$\vdots$$
$$v_{2,1} = u_1 + u_2x_2 + u_3y_2 + u_4t_1 + u_5t_1^2$$
$$\vdots$$
$$v_{n,r} = u_1 + u_2x_n + u_3y_n + u_4t_r + u_5t_r^2. \tag{6}$$

This linear equation system can be written in matrix form:

$$
\underbrace{\begin{bmatrix}
1 & x_1 & y_1 & t_1 & t_1^2 \\
1 & x_1 & y_1 & t_2 & t_2^2 \\
\vdots & \vdots & \vdots & \vdots & \vdots \\
1 & x_2 & y_2 & t_1 & t_1^2 \\
\vdots & \vdots & \vdots & \vdots & \vdots \\
1 & x_n & y_n & t_r & t_r^2
\end{bmatrix}}_{H}
\underbrace{\begin{bmatrix}
u_1 \\
\vdots \\
\\
\\
\vdots \\
u_c
\end{bmatrix}}_{\mathbf{u}}
=
\underbrace{\begin{bmatrix}
v_{1,1} \\
v_{1,2} \\
\vdots \\
v_{2,1} \\
\vdots \\
v_{n,r}
\end{bmatrix}}_{\mathbf{v}}. \tag{7}
$$

The factors of the linear equation system can be represented as a matrix H. The coefficients we would like to determine form the vector $\mathbf{u}$. The sensor readings are grouped into vector $\mathbf{v}$. The linear coefficients should be determined such as to minimize the overall error (see Equation 3). We can do this with the following equation:

$$(H^T H)\hat{\mathbf{u}} = H^T\mathbf{v}, \tag{8}$$

where $\hat{\mathbf{u}}$ represents the estimate of the linear coefficients minimizing the error. The matrix $\hat{H} = H^T H$ has the dimensions $c \times c$, where c is the number of unknowns in the equation system. This equation can easily be solved using Gaussian elimination.

The matrix $\hat{H} = H^T H$ and the vector $\hat{\mathbf{v}} = H^T\mathbf{v}$ have interesting properties that enable a distributed determination of their values. To simplify notations, let $\hat{g}_k(i, j) = g_k(x_i, y_i, t_j)$. Then the elements of $\hat{H}$ and $\hat{\mathbf{v}}$ are calculated with the following formulas:

$$\hat{H}_{l,m} = \sum_{i=1}^{n}\sum_{j=1}^{r} \hat{g}_l(i, j)\hat{g}_m(i, j) \qquad \forall l, m \in \{1, \ldots, c\}^2 \tag{9}$$

$$\hat{\mathbf{v}}_l = \sum_{i=1}^{n}\sum_{j=1}^{r} \hat{g}_l(i, j)v_{i,j} \qquad \forall l \in \{1, \ldots, c\}. \tag{10}$$

From Equation 9 it is clear that $\hat{H}$ is symmetric and thus only has $\sum_{i=1}^{c} i = \frac{c(c+1)}{2}$ unique elements. Consequently, the total number of unique elements from both $\hat{H}$ and $\hat{\mathbf{v}}$ that need to be known to solve the linear equation systems is

$$N_{tx} = \underbrace{\frac{c(c+1)}{2}}_{\text{for } \hat{H}} + \underbrace{c}_{\text{for } \hat{v}} = \frac{c(c+3)}{2} . \tag{11}$$

Both $\hat{H}$ and $\hat{v}$ are sums of elements only depending on information provided by a single sensor node. As we will see, sums are easy to aggregate, and breaking linear regression down in the way shown here is key to distributing the calculation of linear regression across nodes in the WSN.

4   Network Setup

To illustrate the concepts in this paper we will use a sample network setup, which is defined and described next.

A WSN consists of *sensor nodes*, which have as basic components a number of sensors, a processing unit, a wireless transceiver, and some form of power supply. Sensor nodes are sometimes called *motes*. In our work, we use the Tmote Sky nodes (also known as TelosB) equipped with sensors measuring temperature, humidity and light. As software environment we use TinyOS [10]. Programs are written in NesC, which is a C-like programming language with WSN-specific extensions to easily modularize programming. TinyOS itself is an operating system for embedded sensor devices. As it is available in source code, users can modify every aspect of the system.

A WSN is a set of sensor nodes organized as a meshed network. If a radio connection can be established between two sensor nodes of the network, these two nodes are said to be *directly connected*. In the remainder of this paper, we will assume that connections between nodes are always bidirectional. This assumption is based on link quality measurements in [16] and on our own observations. For a given sensor node, we will call *neighbors* the set of sensor nodes to which this node is directly connected. We will assume that the sensor network is not partitioned and that it provides a routing mechanism: if two arbitrary sensor nodes are not directly connected, then they can communicate through other nodes in the network.

A complete system consists of the WSN and a back-end system connected through gateways. The back-end system might consist of several computers and software components that can communicate over a network different from the WSN, for example over a company's local area network (LAN). As a gateway is present in both the WSN and the back-end system, it needs to be able to communicate with both networks. This is typically solved by connecting a *gateway sensor node* to a *gateway computer* over a serial or USB cable. In this paper we will assume that only one gateway exists and that all components of the back-end system run on the gateway computer.

Typically, most communications in a WSN send observation data from every sensor to a data *sink*. The collection tree protocol (CTP) [7] in TinyOS is an example of a routing protocol that lets any node in the WSN send data to a sink. For the purpose of this paper, we only consider the case of a single sink in the

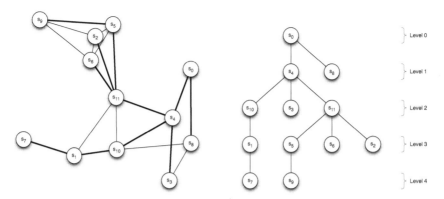

(a) A WSN topology. Thick lines are routes to the sink

(b) A hierarchical view of the WSN topology in Figure 1(a)

Fig. 1. A sample WSN configuration showing 1(a) the geographical distribution of motes and their connections, and 1(b) a hierarchical view of the routing tree

network. We further assume that the sink is also the gateway node connected to the back-end system. Routing algorithms based on the CTP principle operate as follows. The routing protocol establishes a spanning tree rooted at the sink and connecting all nodes in the network. When a sensor node wants to send data to the sink, it passes the data to its parent in the spanning tree. This operation is repeated by all parents of the node until the information reaches the sink. Therefore, to be able to communicate with the sink, a node only needs to know its parent in the spanning tree.

Figure 1(a) shows the geographic distribution of the sensor nodes in our sample WSN setup. The lines between the nodes indicate communication links; thick lines are links used for sending data towards the sink (s_0). Figure 1(b) shows the same network as a hierarchy of nodes. The top node is the sink. Nodes without children (s_2, s_3, s_6, s_7, s_8, and s_9) are leaf nodes. All other nodes relay messages from their children in addition to their own data.

5   Model Description Language

To describe sensor data models in an abstract way, we designed a model description language, whereby the aim was to design a language that is intuitive to use by people with little programming experience. For this reason we decided to develop a language similar to the mathematical languages used, for instance, in Matlab, SciLab or Octave. We presented this language in [11]. In this section, we explain the motivation behind these language design points that are specific to distributed model processing.

A model description essentially consists of the model function and the parameter-learning functions. In addition, it may contain configuration options that determine, for instance, the applicable QoI parameters. The basic concept of the language is the sensor node. As models usually operate on a set of sensors, the model description language has to be able to express sets of sensors. As a starting point for doing this, let S denote the set of all sensor nodes in the network. In addition, each sensor node object also has a **neighbors** set and a number of associated sensors. The language uses the **forall** qualifier to apply a given expression to all elements in a given set. The **forall** qualifier allows the specification of additional constraints with an optional **where** clause.

Sensor readings can be accessed through sensor objects associated to a given node. For instance, if a sensor node has a temperature sensor, the current temperature value can be read with an expression of the form **sn.temp**. It is possible to access the n-th value in the past with the syntax **sn.temp[n]**. An index of 0 is equivalent to reading the current value. If values of two different sensor nodes are accessed, then an appropriate synchronization mechanism ensures that the sensors are sampled at the same time.

Mathematical operations clearly are an essential part of any model description. In addition to the basic mathematical operators, the model description language supports a number of special operators often used in model descriptions. This set of operators will be expanded in the future as need arises. Currently we have predefined the functions **sum**, **avg** and **LMS**, which are used to calculate the sum and average over a set of values, and the best fit of a function to a set of data, respectively. The principle of the **LMS** operator was discussed in Section 3, and its implementation is the subject of Section 6.

Model parameters and model functions are declared with an assignment using the equals sign (=). Model parameters describe the state of the model based on the measured sensor values. They can be global (the same value is shared in the entire network) or local (the value is only valid for a particular sensor node). In addition, a model parameter can be defined for a pair of sensors, for instance, to express the covariance of their readings. Model functions, in contrast, have a list of function arguments. The arguments qualify what exactly should be modeled, e.g., which sensor value should be modeled. As querying the model involves evaluating a model function, we call the function arguments *query parameters*. The model function definition on the right-hand side of the assignment involves a computation based on the model parameters.

In our sensor data model language, the model (Equation 4) can be expressed as shown in Listing 1. The learning function for the model parameters (based on Equation 3) is shown in Listing 2.

The computation of the model function is obvious, but the learning function does not appear in an explicit form. LMS stands for least mean squares. This operator calculates the coefficients for a linear regression function over a data set. LMS operates on the sensed values and the factors of the regression coefficients as expressed in Equation 4. As for this minimization problem we consider all sensors simultaneously, LMS takes as arguments vectors whose elements correspond to individual sensors. The first element in the vector is the actual value to be approximated by the linear regression. In this example, the value of the

Listing 1. Model Function

```
1   b(float  x,  float  y,  int  t) = a[0] + si.x * a[1] +
2           si.y * a[2] + t * a[3] + t^2 * a[4];
```

Listing 2. Learning Function

```
1   a = LMS(forall  si  in  S,  t = 1 .. 5:  si.temp[t],
2           1,  si.x,  si.y,  t,  t^2);
```

first element in the vector, `si.temp[t]`, corresponds to $s(x, y, t)$. The remaining elements are the factors with which the coefficients are to be multiplied. In this example, the first factor is the numerical constant 1, which means that the coefficient a_0 stands by itself. The second and the third factor, `si.x` and `si.y`, are the x and y coordinates of sensor s_i. The forth factor is simply the time t, and the fifth factor is the squared time, t^2. In our example each vector contains six elements, or five factors, which means that the linear regression function has five coefficients. Thus, the `LMS` operator will return a five-element vector.

A data set given as argument to the `LMS` operator usually consists of more than one vector. In the example above, the data set contains a vector for every sensor $s_i \in S$ and for every time $t \in \{1, 2, 3, 4, 5\}$. The actual temperature readings and the x and y coordinates are associated with s_i.

The sensor data model language is designed such that it can represent any mathematical closed-form expression. As the compiler needs to be able to determine the cost of calculating a sub-expression on a mote, the language is designed to be deterministic and does not support jumps and non-deterministic loops. More complex functionality can be achieved, if needed, by including additional elementary functions. These additional functions should be implemented such that the cost of computing them, or at least an upper bound for the cost, is known.

6   Aggregation and Linear Regression

Often an aggregate value over a set of sensor readings is desired, such as average, minimum and maximum values, and standard deviation. Madden et al. [13] describe aggregation in three steps: determining a *partial state record* for individual sensor readings by applying an *initializer i*, then combining these partial state records using a *merging function f*, and finally calculating the value of the aggregation using an *evaluator e*. Aggregations in which the size of the partial state record is significantly smaller than the original data set potentially enable a reduction of the amount of data to be transmitted in the network. Instead of transmitting and relaying every sensor reading in the network, nodes only transmit partial state records based on the data from their own sensor readings and the partial state records of their children. This is particularly interesting for aggregations in which the size of the partial state record is constant, such as minimum and maximum values, averages, and sums.

The exact energy savings possible by using aggregation will have to be evaluated experimentally, as they strongly depend on the implementation details. In TinyOS, the energy consumption for message transmissions depends mainly on the number of messages sent rather than on the payload length of the messages. This is due to the default radio stack implementation, which senses the channel while waiting for a random back-off time prior to sending a message. As basis for comparing energy consumption, we take a very simple application that transmits a node's sensor readings using CTP [7]. CTP uses intermediate nodes to relay messages and does not alter these messages. For instance, in our network shown in Figure 1, the readings from sensor node s_7 would be relayed by the nodes s_1, s_{10}, and s_4 before they reach the sink s_0. Sending a message with readings from node s_7 results in a total of four message transmissions. Thus, if all nodes transmit their sensor readings, 28 messages are sent in the network.

With aggregation, each node only sends a single message that combines its readings with the readings of its child nodes. In our implementation we succeeded transmitting the partial state record of the LMS operator in a single message. Thus, each node waits for the partial state records of all its child nodes, combines the data, and then transmits a new combined partial state record to its parent. Sensor node s_{11}, for instance, sends a single message to its parent node s_4 instead of relaying the individual messages from nodes s_9, s_5, s_6, and s_2. Aggregating all the data within the network rather than transmitting every sensor reading results in only 11 message transmissions in our network. Aggregation thus can enable significant energy savings, especially in larger networks.

7   Compiling Models

To process a model, a program is generated that takes the sensor readings and calculates the model parameters. With this, queries from the user can be answered. In our example, a query is a call to the model function with specific values for the query parameters. The model function depends on the model parameters, which in this case are combined in a single vector a determined with the learning function. Once a is known, any query on the model can be answered. This section presents a method for generating the code to determine the model parameters in a partially distributed fashion.

A compiler takes a program as input, analyzes and transforms it, and produces the program in a different form as output. For our framework, the compiler reads a model description and produces code in the NesC and Java programming languages as output. To do this, the compiler reads the model description and forms an *internal representation* (IR) of the model by splitting the description into small pieces that each form a meaningful unit. Such units or *tokens* are, for instance, numerical constants, variable names, or mathematical operators. The compiler then analyzes and records the relationship between tokens. For instance, an operator operates on one or more input values and thus the token associated with it has a relationship with the tokens that describe the operator's input values. Certain tokens, such as parentheses, only serve to determine the relationships between other tokens and can be discarded once all relationships have been established. The resulting representation of the model can be seen as a tree (shown in Figure 2(a)) in which the root node represents the model as a whole. The child nodes of the model node represent the different learning and model functions that together form the model. The nodes representing these functions in turn have child nodes that represent, in the case of model functions, the arguments to the functions, and that describe the mathematical expressions used to calculate the function. The representation of a program, or in our case a model, in such a tree form is called *abstract syntax tree (AST)*. We use Java Compiler Compiler (JavaCC [12]) to help us generate the code for reading and analyzing the model description. Additional information about compiling in general can be found in [1].

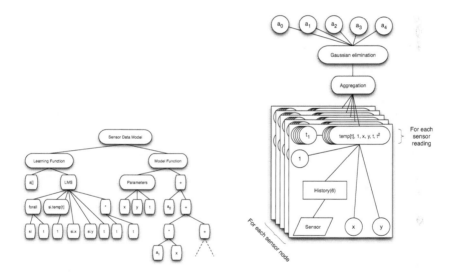

Fig. 2. (a) The linear regression model with (b) the learning function shown as abstract syntax trees. Note that because of space constraints not the entire model function is shown. In (b) the learning function has been arranged such that the multiplicity of the data sources and paths can be seen.

The basic AST plainly represents the model description. Before being able to generate distributed code to process this model, the AST must be augmented to include information related to specific nodes in the tree, such as the data type of each node. We distinguish between integer and floating point numbers, sensor nodes, sensors, vectors, and matrices. Vectors and matrices have associated dimensions and their elements in turn have associated data types. In the case of sensor nodes, the compiler needs to know which sensors are actually used and what information needs to be stored on the nodes. In addition, we need to determine how many sensor readings have to be retained. To do so, we start by determining the data types of the leaf nodes, and then work our way back up the tree. For constants and sensors, the data type is clear. Before we can determine the data type of a variable or model parameter, however, we need to determine the data type of the expression defining this variable or parameter. The data type of an expression is typically based on the data types of its arguments. Also, if all arguments of an operator are constants, the result of the computation represented by this operator can be calculated at compile time, and the operator can be replaced by a constant. Similarly, if a variable is assigned a constant, all of its occurrences can be replaced by this constant. Sometimes, information in one part of the tree affects a completely different part of the tree, for instance, when the data type of a variable is determined in one place but the variable is also used in a different place. It is thus possible that not everything can be determined in one pass. Therefore, we reiterate the passes for as long as there still exists information to be determined and new information is still obtained in every pass. If no new information is obtained, but not everything has been determined, the compilation process is aborted with an error.

A fundamental aspect of model processing is to get the source data (e.g., sensor readings). The compiler determines which sensors are accessed on a node and then includes the appropriate code to sample the sensors. For instance, the expression `si.temp[t]` in the learning function in Listing 2 tells the compiler that the temperature sensor is accessed. If an element of a sensor node is accessed, and that element is not a known sensor, the compiler assumes it to be a variable associated with the sensor node. For instance, the expressions `si.x` and `si.y` in the learning function do not refer to any known sensors. As no method has been defined to determine the values for x and y, the compiler adds the necessary code for the execution environment to configure these values (see Section 8).

For every sensor used by the model, the model processing code will reserve memory for storing a history of the sensor readings. By default, the history size is 1, which means that only the last (current) sensor reading is stored. The current sensor reading is accessed from the model either by simply accessing the sensor object (e.g., `si.temp`) or by specifying 0 as the time value (e.g., `si.temp[0]`). Older readings are accessed by specifying a time value greater than 0. To determine the amount of memory to be reserved for storing the sensor readings' history, the compiler analyzes how the sensor readings are accessed. In our learning function (Listing 2), the sensor readings are accessed with the expression `si.temp[t]`. The compiler then analyzes the potential values that t can take. The variable t is defined in the context of a **forall** statement, which declares t = 1 .. 5. Thus in the example above the compiler deducts that the values for t vary between 1 and 5, and therefore reserves memory space for 6 sensor readings[2].

With the information we extracted from the model definition so far, it is straightforward to generate code that takes sensor readings as input and com-

---

[2] The compiler also needs to store the current sensor reading.

putes the results for a given query. All that needs to be done is to calculate the expressions and update the model parameters. Our framework can produce code that reads sensor data from a variety of different sources and answers queries. We compared two different statistical sensor data models and published our findings in [11]. The next step is to generate code that can run in a distributed environment, such as a WSN. To do this, the compiler needs to determine for each node in the AST whether the node is to be processed in the network or on the back-end system.

Sensors obviously have to be sampled on the sensor nodes. Currently, our framework simply stores all sensor readings retained and all node variables on the sensor nodes themselves. Constants are located in the same place as the operator accessing them. This reduces the problem to determining where to locate the operators such that the overall energy consumption in the WSN is minimized. Once data has reached the back-end system, it makes little sense to send it back into the WSN to process it further. Thus, operators that are closely associated with sensor nodes are more likely to minimize overall energy consumption if they are also located in the WSN. If there is an aggregation operator somewhere in the data flow, then in most cases the optimal approach is to process all operators between the sensor readings and the aggregation inside the WSN, to perform a distributed aggregation, and then to compute the remaining operators on the back-end system. Therefore, the framework currently focuses on finding an aggregation operator, and then using it to separate the AST into a part to be processed in the WSN and a part to be processed on the back-end system. The operator placement for our model is shown in Figure 2(b). Every sensor node executes the code in the rectangle in the lower part of the AST (this multiplicity is indicated by overlapping rectangles). For a specific number of past sensor readings, a port of this code execution is repeated (again, the multiplicity is indicated in the graph). The aggregation is distributed among the nodes, and Gaussian elimination takes place on the back-end system.

Once the elements of the AST that should run in the WSN have been determined, the corresponding code has to be generated. The framework bases itself on TinyOS and thus generates code in the NesC programming language [8]. Besides generating the node processing code for the WSN, it also includes the appropriate modules from the execution framework (see Section 8). In particular, it includes code to allow the execution framework to configure node variables (such as the x and y coordinates for the linear regression model presented in Section 5), and the code to access the communication modules. The communication methods supported currently allow data to be sent to the sink as-is or perform distributed aggregation of the data.

The framework generates Java code for that part of the model processing that is performed on the back-end system. It includes the appropriate interface code to communicate with the WSN. The code generated offers a dynamic interface to the application to specify the query and change the configuration of the nodes. However, at this stage the code is not self-sufficient and needs an appropriate execution environment.

8   Execution Framework

While testing our framework with the linear regression model, we found that distributed model processing needs basic support services. Every sensor network needs to transmit data to a sink. If the network performs aggregation, then nodes need to know their parents and potentially also their children. For many applications, the physical position of each node needs to be known. To demonstrate the proper operation of the linear regression model, we thus implemented a configuration mechanism, a tree routing algorithm for aggregation, and a simple time synchronization method.

We implemented a configuration service that enables the setting of parameters for a particular node. With this service, we configure the x and y coordinates of the physical location of a node prior to starting the model processing. An alternative would be to estimate the physical location during run-time (see, for example, [15]). We decided to use a configuration service rather than a locationing service, as for most locationing algorithms some nodes need to know their position in advance and therefore still would have to be configured.

When compiling a model, the framework assumes that any variable for which no explicit means to determine its value exists, is a configuration parameter. It will then generate a configuration message type with fields for all parameters. An application can set a configuration parameter for a particular node through the framework. The framework checks the parameter name against the list of configuration parameters. If the parameter name specified is valid, the framework will set the corresponding field, include the identity of the targeted node in the configuration message, and broadcast the message in the network.

Data collected in a sensor network needs to be routed to a sink. To do this, WSNs form a collection tree. When processing a model instead of simply collection raw data, the data is often aggregated within the network. The routing structure for a network that aggregates the data is essentially the same as for a WSN collecting raw data, as the data still needs to reach the sink. The difference is that every node, instead of relaying the data of its children as-is, aggregates its own data with that from its children before sending the data to its parent (see Section 6). This means that for one data-collection epoch each node sends exactly one message to its parent. We call this setup an *aggregation tree*.

We use the collection tree protocol (CTP) [7] in TinyOS to establish the routing tree. Instead of letting the collection tree forward messages automatically, we intercept each message and signal that the message should not be forwarded. We aggregate the information in the message with the node's own information and the information received from the other children. The information is then sent to the node's parent.

Before sending data to the parent, a node has to receive data from all its children. To do this, a node could keep track of its children and which ones already sent data in the current epoch. Once all children have sent their data, the node in turn sends its data to its parent. The version of CTP provided in TinyOS does not maintain a list of a node's children. Also, with this method it would be difficult for a node to predict when a child node is ready to send data, which in turn makes it difficult for nodes to turn their radios off to save energy. Therefore, we adopted a time-synchronization strategy.

Synchronizing the clock of the nodes can be achieved by a variety of different protocols and algorithms. We found that one of the simplest approaches is also well suited to minimize energy consumption as determining required active periods for the radio is straight forward. In our implementation the network is synchronized by broadcasting the time from the sink node to the leaves of the tree. Based on the common view of the time, all nodes start the epoch at the same point in time. The nodes furthest down in the tree (level 4 in our sample network in Figure 1(b)) start by sending their data to their parents. After a fixed timeout, the nodes in the next higher level in the routing tree assume that all their children have sent their data, and send their aggregated data to their parent, until the data finally reaches the sink. This approach is simpler than explicitly waiting for data from all children, as nodes do not need to maintain a list of children. As the time period in which a node can expect transmissions from its children is well defined, nodes can turn off their radio when they do not expect transmissions, and thus achieve significant energy savings.

The basic services presented here are sufficient to implement the distributed linear regression model with the help of our framework. Other models might require additional services. A service can have multiple implementations, for instance, to optimize for speed, latency, reliability, or energy savings. We currently implemented very simple services as a proof of concept. Our framework facilitates uniting contributions from experts in different fields.

9   Results and Future Work

We implemented a framework for distributedly processing generic sensor data models. In this paper we focused on the model called distributed linear regression. The framework can be used for other models and we have, for instance, successfully implemented a model based on multivariate Gaussian random variables, which was inspired by [5].

The framework consists of the model description language, the compiler to generate the distributed code, and the execution framework that enables the code to run. During the implementation and testing process, we refined the model description language to make it easier to compile and also render it more intuitive to program. For instance, we removed a separate keyword for specifying model parameters. Instead, the compiler now recognizes model parameters by the form of their definition.

The implementation of the compiler also elucidated the key differences between normal programs and distributed WSN programs. Whereas for traditional ASTs it is sufficient to show the dependencies of nodes, for the distributed approach the dependencies themselves have properties that describe how the information flowing from the child to the parent is communicated and what the associated cost is. The main challenge in compiling distributed programs lies in optimizing this communication.

After having generated the distributed code, we realized that prior to running it we needed an execution framework for configuring the nodes, and for handling the communication between network and gateway. Especially communicating floating point values was challenging, as TinyOS does not directly support them. We solved this issue by copying a memory image of the variables holding floating point values. The `Float` class in Java has methods to convert between floating point numbers and byte arrays. Fortunately, the floating point representation of the TinyOS devices is compatible with Java's byte array representation.

Running linear regression as a distributed model in the current execution framework confirmed that the algorithm was running properly. However, sometimes CTP delayed messages, such that with the staged aggregation not all messages were received on time. We will have to analyze the exact reasons for this behavior. We will also implement our own version of a tree-routing algorithm that will enable us to turn off the radio when the mote is not expecting any messages. This will enable us to experimentally confirm the energy savings of our approach.

10   Conclusion

In this paper we presented an integrated approach for distributing the calculation of sensor data model processing. Our framework consists of a model description language, a compiler for this language that generates distributed code, and an execution framework needed for running the distributed programs. The framework is extensible and open for contributions from experts in very diverse fields. In contrast to previous work, which concentrated on studying a specific aspect of model processing and then optimizing it, our work is, to the best of our knowledge, the first holistic approach to generic model processing.

References

1. Appel, A.W., Palsberg, J.: Modern Compiler Implementation in Java. Cambridge University Press, New York (2003)
2. Barrenetxea, G., Ingelrest, F., Lu, Y.M., Vetterli, M.: Assessing the challenges of environmental signal processing through the SensorScope project. In: Proceedings of the 33rd IEEE International Conference on Acoustics, Speech, and Signal Processing (ICASSP 2008), pp. 5149–5152 (2008)
3. Barrenetxea, G., Ingelrest, F., Schaefer, G., Vetterli, M., Couach, O., Parlange, M.: SensorScope: Out-of-the-box environmental monitoring. In: Proceedings of the 7th ACM/IEEE International Conference on Information Processing in Sensor Networks (IPSN 2008), pp. 332–343 (2008)
4. Bisdikian, C.: On sensor sampling and quality of information: A starting point. In: Proceedings of the Fifth IEEE International Conference on Pervasive Computing and Communications Workshops (PERCOMW 2007), pp. 279–284 (2007)
5. Deshpande, A., Guestrin, C., Madden, S., Hellerstein, J.M., Hong, W.: Model-driven data acquisition in sensor networks. In: Proceedings of the Thirtieth International Conference on Very Large Data Bases (VLDB 2004), pp. 588–599 (2004)

6. Deshpande, A., Madden, S.: MauveDB: Supporting model-based user views in database systems. In: Proceedings of the 2006 ACM SIGMOD International Conference on Management of Data (SIGMOD 2006), pp. 73–84 (2006)
7. Fonseca, R., Gnawali, O., Jamieson, K., Kim, S., Levis, P., Woo, A.: The collection tree protocol (CTP), version 1.8 (February 2007),
   http://www.tinyos.net/tinyos-2.x/doc/html/tep123.html
8. Gay, D., Welsh, M., Levis, P., Brewer, E., Von Behren, R., Culler, D.: The nesC language: A holistic approach to networked embedded systems. In: Proceedings of the ACM SIGPLAN 2003 conference on Programming Language Design and Implementation (PLDI 2003), pp. 1–11 (2003)
9. Guestrin, C., Bodik, P., Thibaux, R., Paskin, M., Madden, S.: Distributed regression: An efficient framework for modeling sensor network data. In: Proceedings of the Third International Symposium on Information Processing in Sensor Networks (IPSN 2004), April 2004, pp. 1–10 (2004)
10. Hill, J., Szewczyk, R., Woo, A., Hollar, S., Culler, D.E., Pister, K.S.J.: System architecture directions for networked sensors. ACM SIGPLAN Notices 35(11), 93–104 (2000)
11. Hunkeler, U., Scotton, P.: A quality-of-information-aware framework for data models in wireless sensor networks. In: Proceedings of the First International Workshop on Quality of Information in Sensor Networks (QoISN 2008), September 2008, pp. 742–747 (2008)
12. JavaCC - a parser/scanner generator for Java (November 2008),
    https://javacc.dev.java.net/
13. Madden, S., Franklin, M.J., Hellerstein, J.M., Hong, W.: TAG: A tiny aggregation service for ad-hoc sensor networks. SIGOPS Oper. Syst. Rev. 36, 131–146 (2002)
14. Madden, S., Franklin, M.J., Hellerstein, J.M., Hong, W.: The design of an acquisitional query processor for sensor networks. In: Proceedings of the 2003 ACM SIGMOD International Conference on Management of Data (SIGMOD 2003), pp. 491–502 (2003)
15. Savarese, C., Rabaey, J.M., Beutel, J.: Locationing in distributed ad-hoc wireless sensor networks. In: Proceedings of the 2001 International Conference on Acoustics, Speech, and Signal Processing (ICASSP 2001), May 2001, pp. 2037–2040 (2001)
16. Srinivasan, K., Levis, P.: RSSI is under appreciated. In: Proceedings of the Third Workshop on Embedded Networked Sensors (EmNets 2006) (May 2006)
17. Werner-Allen, G., Lorincz, K., Johnson, J., Lees, J., Welsh, M.: Fidelity and yield in a volcano monitoring sensor network. In: Proceedings of the 7th Symposium on Operating Systems Design and Implementation (OSDI 2006), pp. 381–396 (2006)

Integer-Based Optimisations for Resource-Constrained Sensor Platforms

Michael Zoumboulakis and George Roussos

School of Computer Science and Information Systems
Birkbeck College, University of London
{mz,gr}@dcs.bbk.ac.uk

Abstract. In this paper we argue that the fundamental constrains of WSNs impose the need to re-discover programming optimisation techniques that were widely used a few decades ago but are less common today, at least in the conventional computing arena. Integer techniques, code tuning and profiling are absolutely essential in the world of the very small devices. We present three alternative methods of integer programming: scaling, fixed-point and rational arithmetic. These techniques are complemented by a brief review of bitwise and general optimisation techniques. As artifact of the usefulness of these techniques, we discuss the implementation details of a data mining algorithm that gained over a factor of 10 improvement in performance as a result of integer programming. We conclude by presenting a widely accepted time model adapted for a WSN platform.

Keywords: Wireless Sensor Networks, Optimisation, Integer Techniques, Fixed-Point Arithmetic, Rational Arithmetic, Data Mining.

1 Introduction

There was a time when programmers used to go to great lengths in order to ensure that their programs were efficient. Computers were slow and expensive pushing program performance optimisation very high on the list of software engineering priorities. As the years passed, advances in circuit design and memory density translated into faster machine speeds. Today we live in an era of powerful, transistor-dense, multi-core machines with abundant memory and storage. Inevitably, this fact had an impact in modern software engineering priorities: programmers chose to attach more gravity to other important goals such as stability, portability and maintainability whilst performance and efficiency gradually dropped towards the bottom of the priorities list.

However, the resource-constrained end of the Wireless Sensor Network (WSN) spectrum is comprised of devices whose datasheets are very similar to those of computers from a couple of decades ago. Furthermore, we know that the rate of growth of WSN nodes' capabilities is much slower than that of their consumer electronics counterparts. For instance, memory in low-cost, ultra-low power devices does not track Moore's law — a micro-controller RAM costs three

S. Hailes, S. Sicari, and G. Roussos (Eds.): S-Cube 2009, LNICST 24, pp. 144–157, 2009.

orders of magnitude more than PC SRAM and five orders more than PC DRAM [12]. Even more importantly, energy density does not seem to track Moore's law either — over a decade energy density of commercially available batteries has changed only modestly [4].

These fundamental constraints suggest that programming optimisation techniques widely used a few decades ago need to be re-discovered. Consequently, we address the importance of programming efficiency in WSNs and we discuss methods that contribute to the attainment of this goal.

In the remainder of the paper, we draw from our own experience of implementing an established data mining algorithm in a resource-constrained platform and we present the direct performance gains of applying a few straightforward coding techniques. Moreover, we focus on integer programming complemented by bitwise techniques and general code tuning — combined, they form a toolbox of techniques that can greatly improve program efficiency. Lastly, we adapt the conventional time model of [2] for a sensor platform with a view to identify costly operations and provide rough estimates of the time needed for typical tasks.

2   Case Study: TinySAX — Efficient Implementation of a Data Mining Algorithm

Symbolic Aggregate Approximation (SAX) [7] is a widely-accepted and mature algorithm used for data mining. Essentially SAX performs *Symbolic Conversion*: it maps an ordered sequence of sensor readings to a sequence of letters from a finite alphabet Σ according to a set of well-defined rules. Formally, the input is a sequence of readings $\bar{r} = \langle r_1, r_2, \ldots, r_n \rangle, r_i \in \mathbb{Z}$ and the output is a sequence of letters $\bar{s} = \langle s_1, s_2, \ldots, s_m \rangle, s_i \in \Sigma$ with $0 < m \leq n$. In this respect SAX is a discretisation technique.

Applying SAX to a time-series stream has many attractive properties such as dimensionality reduction due to the Piecewise Aggregate Approximation (PAA) that is central to the algorithm. A PAA representation has been found to rival more sophisticated dimensionality reduction techniques such as Fourier transforms and wavelets [6]. The core idea of obtaining a PAA from a sequence of readings is based on dividing the sequence into m equal-sized frames and taking the mean of the values that fall within each frame. The PAA representation comprises the vector of the mean values. The final step involves transforming the PAA into a sequence of equiprobable symbols. For this, SAX uses a sorted list of breakpoints (found in statistical tables) $\bar{\beta} = \langle \beta_1, \beta_2, \ldots, \beta_{\alpha-1} \rangle$, with $\alpha =$size of the alphabet, such that the area under a N(0,1) Gaussian curve from β_i to β_{i+1} is $1/a$ with β_0 and β_α set to $-\infty$ and ∞ respectively [14]. The final string is obtained according to the range of the PAA coefficients i.e. if a coefficient is less than β_1 it is mapped to 1, if it is lies between β_1 and β_2 is is mapped to 2 and so forth. The precise details of the PAA transformation and the further symbolic transformation are well-described in the SAX literature [7,6] (and references therein).

Table 1. Performance Times (in ms) for a Symbolic Conversion using naive implementation with floating-point operations

	Size					
Operation	*40*		*80*		*120*	
S2. STANDARDISE						
a. Mean	12ms	(10.62%)	24ms	(10.62%)	37ms	(11.01%)
b. Std Dev	42ms	(37.17%)	81ms	(35.84%)	120ms	(35.71%)
c. Subtract & Divide	25ms	(22.12%)	53ms	(23.45%)	78ms	(23.21%)
S3. GET PAA	24ms	(21.24%)	48ms	(21.24%)	73ms	(21.73%)
S4. GET SYMBOLS	10ms	(8.85%)	20ms	(8.85%)	28ms	(8.33%)
Total Time	113ms		226ms		336ms	
RAM Image Size (Bytes)	766		846		926	

One of the common uses of SAX is for *Anomaly Detection* in a time-series. We use SAX in the WSN setting for a similar purpose, namely *Complex Event Detection*. We use the following definition of Complex Events:

Complex Event. An interesting or unusual pattern in the data gathered and processed by WSN nodes that can be very difficult or even impossible to detect using threshold-based techniques.

This method allows us to detect many complex patterns simultaneously without significant overhead to the resources of the WSN nodes. We use SAX in an online fashion where sensor nodes continuously convert sliding windows of readings to symbols and then compare them against patterns of symbols submitted by users as event interests.

SAX relies on various operations involving floating-point numbers and a first implementation attempt was running prohibitively slow on the target platform (TMote Sky [16]). A single symbolic conversion was taking approximately 113ms for a sliding window of 40 readings. Profiling the code, by timing the entry and exit points of every function, provided the information shown on Table 1.

2.1   Refactoring SAX into TinySAX

This slow implementation had to be reviewed and re-written in a manner suitable for the constraints of the WSN. The outcome was TinySAX; an efficient integer-only implementation that reduced the active CPU time by more than a factor of 10. This was achieved by a combination of the following actions, listed in order of importance:

– **Integer Programming.** Firstly, all floating point variables were replaced by integers. Functions such as standardisation — that relies on the costly formula $\bar{z}_i = \frac{r_i - \mu}{\sigma}$ where μ is the mean and σ is the Standard Deviation of the sliding window $\bar{r}$ — were re-written with elimination of the division operation. Instead, the breakpoint vector $\bar{\beta}$ was scaled by σ. The size of

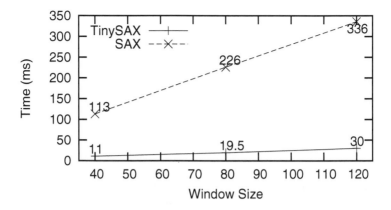

Fig. 1. Comparison of running times for two alternative implementations of the same data mining algorithm on a TMote Sky. SAX refers to an implementation that relies heavily on a number of floating point operations. TinySAX refers to an optimised implementation that has been re-written using integer programming.

the breakpoint vector is equal to the size of the alphabet. Since the latter is typically much smaller than the size of the sliding window, scaling the former involves significantly less operations than dividing each r_i by σ. Furthermore, as we will see in section 8, division is much costlier than multiplication especially for double words (i.e. 32-bit integers). Secondly, the breakpoints vector was *binary scaled* (i.e. multiplied by a power of 2) offline to map the floating point numbers to integers. To counteract this, the PAA coefficients were also scaled by the same scaling factor.

- **Bitwise Techniques.** Functions such as the square root were replaced by fast integer implementations coded in a manner that utilised bit-level operations. This gave an additional performance boost to the code.
- **General Optimisations.** Unrolling and consolidating loops and the choice of appropriate variables (i.e. unsigned *int*s for indices) trimmed off the final excess milliseconds from the implementation.

The results for TinySAX, in terms of time, are shown in Figure 1 — the difference in current consumption for a typical sliding window of length 40 is 73.7mA for the integer implementation compared to 251.74mA for the naive implementation (assuming a 1Hz sampling frequency).

In the sections to follow we are going to describe from a more general perspective some of the programming techniques used to transform SAX into TinySAX — an efficient data mining algorithm for constrained devices.

3   Optimisations: Strategies, Tools and Techniques

There are a few different alternatives when deciding to optimise for performance. One of the first things that should be decided is whether there is a need for optimisation: a fundamental questions is *"is the program good enough already"* [2].

The answer depends on the context in which the program must execute. If it has been stress-tested under different realistic workloads and it is found to perform well, then clearly there is little need to optimise. Aggressively optimising a program still in the early design stage can adversely impact the quality of the code and compromise its correctness. In the words of Donald Knuth [8]: *"we should forget about small inefficiencies, say about 97% of the time: premature optimisation is the root of all evil"*. A program should be subjected to an optimisation process once it has been profiled and its runtime behaviour is well-understood.

If optimisation passes the above suitability test, it should then be decided whether to opt for node-level optimisation, network-wide optimisation, or both. Node-level optimisation targets the specific program image that executes on a single node and attempts to re-design it so it is highly efficient. Network-wide optimisation, as the name suggests, targets the entire network: local decisions of individual nodes may be sub-optimal for the benefit of the whole network e.g. an example of this is distribution of processing load among nodes or avoiding bottlenecks such as the funnelling effect [1] that penalises nodes near a base station. Network-wide optimisation largely depends on application-specific factors and network characteristics such as density and therefore is beyond the scope of this paper. The techniques that follow are primarily aimed at node-level optimisation.

4   Integer Techniques

Integer techniques is a broad term for a family of methods relating to computer programs using integral data types. Although the term has been used to refer to techniques that sometimes use a mixture of floating-point and integer numbers, in this context we use it to refer to programs that use exclusively integers.

The motivation for re-introducing integer techniques into WSN programs stems from the following:

1. **Floating Point on Software.** The majority of low-end microcontrollers (MCUs) lack Floating Point Units (FPUs). Floating point numbers are represented in software and operations involving these data types are inherently slow and expensive.
2. **Lack of Standardisation.** Programs that use floats in WSNs are less portable since there exist variations in the floating point representation across different compilers and microcontrollers. Programs in heterogeneous networks that need to communicate floating point values over the radio, suffer from the added complexity that the lack of a common standard introduces.
3. **Application needs.** Many real-world applications have a requirement for operations involving real numbers — typical examples are object tracking and target estimation applications. In general, a large number of trigonometric and statistic functions are prime candidates for integer transformation.

In the following, we will discuss some of the specific techniques that are available to a programmer.

4.1   Scaling

We have briefly discussed scaling in section 2.1 where it was used in the implementation of TinySAX. Scaling is a well-understood technique that involves multiplying a floating point number by an integer, usually a power of two (binary scaling) to represent it as an integer. Arithmetic operations can then be performed using the scaled numbers and the result can be divided by the same scaling factor. As an example consider the floating point numbers -0.52 and 1.28. Scaling both by 2^{11} and rounding toward zero gives -1064 and 2621 respectively. Any arithmetic operation can be performed using the integers: i.e. multiplication would yield -2788744. If we divide the result by the same scaling factor we obtain -1361. To retrieve the floating point result we divide again and obtain 0.6645 (the exact floating point result is 0.6656).

Care must be taken to prevent arithmetic overflow. This is usually done by performing some analysis of the range of values that a program variable will take. The maximum of these values is taken and scaled. To accommodate the maximum value x_{max}, M bits will be needed with $\log_2 x_{max} \leq M$. Numerical precision requirements vary across applications, so N bits must be reserved to satisfy the accuracy requirements Δx with $2^{-N} \leq \Delta x$. The total number of bits that will be needed to represent the floating point number in an integer type within the accuracy requirements is therefore $M + N$. There is a tradeoff between the maximum range of a variable and the accuracy required [17], but this is very much application dependent.

Embedded operating systems such as TinyOS [13] employ scaling techniques in the design of certain components — an example of this is the implementation of Timers: a second equals 1,024 milliseconds. So if we need to represent the time value of 1.875 seconds we scale it by 2^{10} and use 1,920 to perform any arithmetic operations. This level of accuracy is good enough for many applications.

Generally speaking, there will always be a tradeoff between speed and accuracy: if an application requires very high numerical fidelity in its calculations then performance may need to be sacrificed, for instance by using arbitrary precision data types.

4.2   Fixed-Point Arithmetic

Fixed-point arithmetic is very closely related to the scaling technique but it involves slightly higher degree of programming effort. It is estimated that approximately 30 % of the software development for the first NASA Apollo space missions was spent on fixed-point arithmetic and scaling [3]. Nowadays, it is still widely used by DSP programmers, graphics developers, computer typesetting and other applications where there is a combined need for real-valued numbers and high performance.

In floating-point numbers the radix point is generally allowed to be determined dynamically or to "float" thus being capable of representing a wide range of values. Conversely, in fixed-point arithmetic the radix point is fixed. There is a fixed number of digits after the radix point reserved for the fractional part.

Let N represent the total number of bits needed to accommodate a fixed-point variable. We can then split a type of length N into Integer bits and Fractional bits. The integer bits are to the left of the hypothetical or implied binary radix point and the fractional bits are the remaining bits to the right. We use the notation (I, F)[1] to represent the Integer part and the Fractional part respectively. The number of bits needed for an unsigned type is $I + F$ and for a signed type $I + F + 1$. The range of unsigned fixed-point numbers is from 0 to $2^i - 2^{-f}$ while the range for singed fixed-point numbers is from -2^{i-1} to $2^{i-1} - 2^{-f}$, where i and f are the number of bits needed to represent the integer and fractional parts respectively. To obtain the value of unsigned and signed numbers in (I, F) (fixed-point) representation we use equations 1 and 2 respectively [19]:

$$x = 2^{-f} \sum_{n=0}^{N-1} 2^n x_n \tag{1}$$

$$x = 2^{-f} \left(-2^{N-1} x_{N-1} + \sum_{n=0}^{N-2} 2^n x_n \right) \tag{2}$$

Where x_n denotes bit n of x.

Consider the following example: an unsigned fixed-point data type of the form $(3, 5)$. This type can accommodate a range from 0 to 7.96875 and has the following representation:

← Integer Part →			←		Fractional Part		→
I	I	I	F	F	F	F	F

The number $(00101011)_2$ is then $2^{-5}(1 + 2 + 2^3 + 2^5) = 1.34375$. Similarly, if we were using a signed type $(3, 5)$ requiring $(I + F) + 1 = 9$ bits the range would become $-4 \leq x \leq 3.96875$, with the MSB reserved for sign in two's complement notation. The code (in C) needed for the transformation is shown below:

```
#define FB 5 /* (3,5) Representation */
float f=1.34375; uint8_t fp;
fp = (uint8_t)(f * (1<<FB) + (f>=0 ? 0.5 : -0.5));
f = (float) fp / (1<<FB); /* Fixed-point back to float */
```

All arithmetic operations are defined using the fixed-point representation but care needs to be taken to ensure that the types are in the same sign representation and that the result does not overflow. Operations can still be performed on numbers with different bit (I, F) representations but somewhat more effort is required for bit alignment.

Although measurable performance improvements can be gained by using fixed-point arithmetic, it suffers from certain disadvantages: it can hinder code portability. Moreover, it can make the programming task tedious resulting in error-prone code.

---

[1] Other common notations are (M, N) and Q.

Recently, there have been efforts to automate the floating-point to fixed-point conversion process. Notably, [11] and [15] suggest program translators that firstly monitor and collect statistics about the range of floating point variables and then automatically generate a fixed-point isomorphism.

4.3   Rational Arithmetic

An often overlooked alternative that lies between fixed point and floating point arithmetic in complexity, cost and capability is rational (or "no point") arithmetic [5]. In rational arithmetic two variables are used to store each number; A real number is therefore represented as a ratio (fraction) of two numbers. If arithmetic is done on fractions instead of approximations many computations can be performed entirely without any rounding errors or precision loss [9]. However, taking into account that it is advisable to avoid arbitrary precision arithmetic, some loss will occur if rational operations are bounded to a specific type length as it is the typical case.

Rational numbers are represented programmatically as pairs of integers $(u/u\prime)$ with u and $u\prime$ relatively prime and with zero represented as $(0/1)$. Arithmetic operations are defined on pairs of integers and they largely rely on the *greatest common divisor* algorithm. Euclid's algorithm which is by far the simplest for *gcd* calculation has $O(n^2)$ complexity, but a binary *gcd* implementation is somewhat faster.

An example of multiplication between $(u/u\prime)$ and $(v/v\prime)$ and result $(w/w\prime)$ involves the calculation of uv and $u\prime v\prime$. The resulting $(w/w\prime)$ may not be relatively prime but if we let $d = gcd(uv, u\prime v\prime)$ the answer is $w = uv/d$ and $w\prime = u\prime v\prime/d$ [9].

Rational arithmetic using bounded types offers the same range as fixed-point arithmetic and approximately the same accuracy. In terms of simplicity, the arithmetic operations of addition and subtraction are easier to implement [5] in fixed-point whilst division and multiplication have simpler implementations in rational arithmetic. An interface providing basic operations such as addition, multiplication, comparison, and so forth can be developed that offers the ability to use them in the same manner as calling library functions.

The advantage of rational arithmetic over fixed point is that it is more portable and less machine dependent. Of course this assumes that all helper functions (such as *gcd*) have machine-independent implementations.

5   Bitwise Techniques

Bitwise techniques involve the use of the bit-level operators: AND, OR, Exclusive OR (XOR) and left (<<) and right shifts (>>). The use of bit fiddling allows to operate at a much lower level and it can often assist in making programs more time and space efficient. Bit packing for example is a good technique for packing many values into one data type.

Consider an example from our implementation of TinySAX: the typical alphabet size used is 10 characters with a maximum size of 15 characters. The application has a requirement to send over the radio a string of characters. The smallest data type that a language provides is one byte, however 4 bits are sufficient to represent a character from an alphabet of size 15 (with range 0-15). The listing below shows a code example used to pack 4-bit nibbles into a 64-bit integer.

```
uint64_t y=0; /* 64-bit var to be packed with 16 nibbles */
for (i=0; i < length-1; i++)
  { y = (y+data[i]) << 0x4; }
y += data[length-1];
```

With this code we can encode twice the amount of information in a single variable. If there is a requirement to send such a variable once a second over the radio, in the course of a whole day we save 675 kilobytes (or little over 2 megabytes if we include the packet headers and footers) at the expense of a little computation. The packed value can be unpacked using the code below:

```
for (i=shift=0; i < length; i++, shift+=0x4)
  unpacked_data[(length-1)-i] = (y>>shift)%0x10;
```

Note that the modulo operation is inexpensive since it does not require division i.e. $x \bmod 2^n = x \& (2^n - 1)$ [10].

Bit fields such as the above are particularly useful in WSNs when there is a need to keep track of a neighbour table. For instance if neighbours with identification numbers 1,5,8 are awake, this can be encoded in a bit field in the following manner: $\{1,0,0,0,1,0,0,1\}$. This a very compact representation and individual bits from the field can be toggled, as neighbours appear or disappear, at a very small computational cost.

Furthermore, bitwise operations are useful for the reduction or elimination of *branching* — a part of the program where control flow is decided on evaluating some condition — in programs. For example the simple line x - ((x - y) & -(x < y)) can be used to determine the maximum of the two values (x, y) or (x ^ (x >> (16 - 1))) - (x >> (16 - 1)) to determine the absolute (abs) value of x (assuming 16-bit integers).

The usefulness of bit-level techniques in embedded devices is undisputed — in the words of the author of one of the leading works in bit fiddling [18] *"It is amazing what can done with binary addition and subtraction and maybe some bitwise operations"*. The main criticism for bit fiddling is that it can make programs less portable. The majority of bit-level operations depend on endianness (i.e. the byte ordering) and therefore can make programs platform-specific.

6   Profiling

Profiling or benchmarking is a useful form of empirical analysis that aims to identify which parts of a computer program consume the most time or other resources such as memory, registers or disk. With respect to time, a straightforward way of profiling a program is the use of timers at entry and exit points of

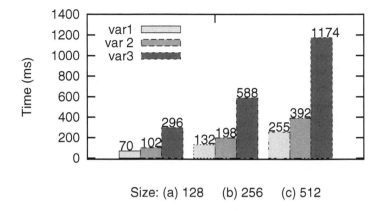

Fig. 2. Running time of 3 variance algorithms on a TMote Sky — Sets A, B, C represent vectors of 128, 256 and 512 random numbers respectively

functions. Timers are criticised of inaccuracy in conventional operating systems because a multi-tasking computer system is rarely idle and processes contend for CPU time. However this is not entirely true for the majority of low-end sensor nodes where a single-threaded application[2] is the *only* process in the system. Therefore, the use of timers is a fairly accurate profiling measure within the platform timer accuracy and precision envelope.

Theoretical complexity analysis of algorithms can be complemented by empirically obtaining execution times for real-world input. This process can aid in deciding which implementation to include in the final version of a program. As an example consider the results of the empirical analysis of three alternative variance implementations shown in figure 2.

The first algorithm (var1) is fast but slightly inaccurate: it has a relative error of .0011%, .037% and .092% on sets of random numbers A, B and C of sizes 128, 256 and 512 respectively. Algorithm 2 (var2) is precise and fairly fast while algorithm 3 (var3) [9] is a highly accurate and numerically stable algorithm.

The use of such analysis can annotate the accuracy-efficiency tradeoff with some numbers and can make the decision-making process easier.

7   Loop Unrolling

If a program performs an operation multiple times it is worth considering *unrolling* the loop — that is explicitly writing each iteration of the loop in sequence [2]. This can only be achieved when the terminating condition of the loop is known in advance.

An example of 2-way unrolling, provided SIZE is known in advance and it is an even number, is shown below:

---

[2] For the sake of simplicity, we ignore recent multi-threading abstractions such as TinyThreads and ContikiOS.

```
for (i=0; i < SIZE; i+=2)
 { c[i] = a[i]+b[i];
   c[i+1] = a[i+1]+b[i+1]; }
```

Table 2. Results from unrolling a basic loop that executes the one-line statement `c[i]=a[i]+b[i]` in its body

Degree of Unrolling	Time (ms)
Normal Loop	220ms
2-way Unrolling	173ms
Loop Elimination	112ms

The loop can be unrolled further as long as (SIZE *mod* increment) ==0 and it can even be eliminated altogether by writing out explicitly every instruction. The runtime results from unrolling the simple loop described above are shown on Table 2.

Another optimisation technique, involves removing any conditional expressions that are inside the body of a loop. This will reduce branching and the code can be re-factored by enclosing a copy of the loop inside the bodies of the if and else clauses respectively. Similarly, any expensive operations inside the loop body should be examined: for instance if a loop involves an expression that contains division, then this expression should be re-arranged to use multiplication e.g. $(u/u\prime) \leq (v/v\prime)$ is equivalent to $(uv\prime) \leq (vu\prime)$ — the latter is significantly cheaper, as we will see in the next section.

Generally speaking, loops are usually the first part of the program to target. Eliminating the loop completely will almost always yield a gain in performance. Critics of this technique assert that there is a side-effect of higher register usage to keep track of intermediate results. Empirical analysis suggests that this is highly compiler-dependent; run-time results can always assist in measuring the benefit for loop elimination.

8   A Time Model for WSNs

In this section, we apply the methodologies introduced by Bentley [2] for the construction of a time model that can be used to identify the relative cost of typical operations. The model is adapted so it tests various platform-specific components such as the time it takes to sample the on-board sensors. The results are shown in Table 3. Reported times are in milliseconds per 5,000 trials. As expected the arithmetic operations that are larger than the MCU word size (16-bit) are taking much longer. For example, 64-bit integer division is almost as slow as floating point division, while for other operations using a 64-bit type is cheaper than floating-point. 64-bit types can be useful for temporary storage i.e. holding results, when scaling is employed.

The lack of FPU slows down floating point operations — by a factor of 432 in the case of addition — making floating point operations unacceptably slow.

Table 3. Performance Times (in ms) for various operations executed by the TMote Sky (timed using TinyOS 2.x and msp430-gcc 3.2.3)

Operation	Arithmetic (Integer)		
	16-bit	*32-bit*	*64-bit*
Increment	6,734	12,824	67,271
Addition	7,955	15,319	88,301
Subtraction	7,969	15,310	87,985
Multiplication	145,020	159,060	316,755
Division	226,265	709,720	3,519,055
Remainder	225,375	706,875	3,540,080
	Bitwise		
AND	7,965	15,285	88,095
OR	7,985	15,325	88,360
XOR	7,955	15,315	88,310
SHIFT	56,735	62,880	573,665
	Floating Point Arithmetic		
Assignment & Cast	2,687,535		
Addition	3,438,530		
Subtraction	3,499,920		
Multiplication	4,841,490		
Division	4,041,785		
	Array Comparisons & Swaps		
Straight Comp	104,095		
Comp C Fcn	83,315		
Comp TOS Fcn	83,335		
Comp TOS task	159,055		
Swap C Macro	93,085		
Swap C Function	83,320		
	Max Function		
Straight Max	137,565		
Max C Macro	137,075		
Max C Function	79,110		
	Built-in Sensors		
ReadLight	327,510		
ReadTemperature	154,125		
ReadHumidity	154,175		
ReadIVoltage	321,635		
	External Flash Chip IO		
Reads (4-bytes)	158,750		
Writes (4-bytes)	191,280		

Surprisingly, bitwise operations are slightly slower than addition and subtraction but shifts are still considerably faster than division and multiplication.

Subscripted array operations are generally fast, and according to [2] this is due to favourable memory access predictability. A TinyOS function — which is platform-independent and hence portable — is infinitesimally slower (by 20ms) than a C function performing the same operation. However, a TinyOS task, which is placed on a separate FIFO queue, is somewhat slower — almost by a factor of 2 — than the C or TinyOS function. The debate of whether a function or a preprocessor macro is faster, appears to have settled on the fact that on a mote the C function is faster than its macro equivalent.

Sampling Light and Internal Voltage sensors is more expensive than sampling Temperature and Humidity — the internal temperature and humidity sensors are on the same chip, hence the similarity in terms of performance. Flash Input-Output is generally slow[3] and as expected writes and slower than reads. The reads are not cached, in contrast with traditional disks and flash chips.

Lastly, we expect this table to provide a suitable guide into the tradeoffs of operations and data types that partially determine the running time of programs.

9 Summary

There is a wide variety of real-world WSN applications that have a need for representation of real numbers in programs. However, many MCUs lack Floating Point Units (FPUs) and as a result computations are performed in software. This has the undesirable impact of slow performance and increased energy cost; both factors are burdensome in any embedded environment. Furthermore the lack of a common floating point representation across different node platforms and compilers can introduce runtime errors in heterogeneous networks that need to communicate such values over the air. In this paper, we focus on three main integer programming techniques: Scaling, Fixed-point and Rational-point Arithmetic. Each one of these varies in complexity, cost and implementation and a good understanding of their relative strengths and weaknesses is essential for designers who aim to shave off valuable time units from their implementations. Moreover, bitwise techniques and other optimisations such as loop unrolling can assist in compounding significant performance gains. We have highlighted the applicability of these methods, combined with integer techniques, by presenting a case study of an implementation of a data mining algorithm for a WSN platform. By re-writing the program with efficiency as the ultimate goal performance improved by a factor of more than 10. Finally, we assert that operational awareness of a program's performance together with application of an appropriate optimisation strategy are essential factors in software engineering for WSNs with direct implications to network and device lifetime.

References

1. Ahn, G.-S., Hong, S.G., Miluzzo, E., Campbell, A.T., Cuomo, F.: Funneling-MAC: a localized, sink-oriented MAC for boosting fidelity in sensor networks. In: SenSys, pp. 293–306. ACM, New York (2006)
2. Bentley, J.: Programming Pearls, 2nd edn. Addison-Wesley Pub. Co., Reading (1999)

---

[3] The results reported are using the `ConfigStorage` TinyOS component.

3. Kreide, H., Lambert, D.W.: Computation: Aerospace Computers in Aircraft, Missiles and Spacecraft. Space/Aeronaut 78 (1964)
4. Hellerstein, J.M., Hong, W., Madden, S.: The sensor spectrum: technology, trends, and requirements. SIGMOD Record 32(4), 22–27 (2003)
5. Horn, B.K.P.: Rational arithmetic for minicomputers. Softw. Pract. Exper. 8(2), 171–176 (1978)
6. Keogh, E., Lin, J., Fu, A.: HOT SAX: Efficiently Finding the Most Unusual Time Series Subsequence. In: IEEE International Conference on Data Mining, pp. 226–233 (2005)
7. Keogh, E., Lonardi, S., Ratanamahatana, C.A.: Towards parameter-free data mining. In: KDD 2004: Proceedings of the tenth ACM SIGKDD international conference on Knowledge discovery and data mining, New York, NY, USA, pp. 206–215 (2004)
8. Knuth, D.E.: Structured Programming with go to Statements. ACM Comput. Surv. 6(4), 261–301 (1974)
9. Knuth, D.E.: The Art of Computer Programming, 2nd edn. Seminumerical Algorithms, vol. II. Addison-Wesley, Reading (1981)
10. Knuth, D.E.: The Art of Computer Programming. F.1, Binary Tricks and Techniques, vol. 4. Addison-Wesley, Reading (2009)
11. Kum, K.-I., Kang, J., Wonyong, S.: AUTOSCALER for C: an optimizing floating-point to integer C program converter for fixed-point digital signal processors. IEEE Transactions on Circuits and Syst.—Part II 47, 840–848 (2000)
12. Levis, P., Brewer, E., Culler, D., Gay, D., Madden, S., Patel, N., Polastre, J., Shenker, S., Szewczyk, R., Woo, A.: The Emergence of a Networking Primitive in Wireless Sensor Networks. Communications of the ACM 51(7), 99–106 (2008)
13. Levis, P.A.: TinyOS: An Open Operating System for Wireless Sensor Networks (Invited Seminar). In: MDM 2006: Proceedings of the 7th International Conference on Mobile Data Management, Washington, DC, USA, p. 63 (2006)
14. Lonardi, S., Lin, J., Keogh, E.J., Chiu, B.: Efficient discovery of unusual patterns in time series. New Generation Comput. 25(1), 61–93 (2006)
15. Menard, D., Chillet, D., Sentieys, O.: Floating-to-fixed-point conversion for digital signal processors. EURASIP J. Appl. Signal Process. 2006, 77–77 (2006)
16. MoteIV (later renamed to Sentilla). TMote Sky Datasheets and Downloads, http://www.sentilla.com/pdf/eol/tmote-sky-datasheet.pdf
17. Tan, J., Kyriakopoulos, N.: Implementation of a Tracking Kalman Filter on a Digital Signal Processor. IEEE Transactions on Industrial Electronics 35, 126–135 (1988)
18. Warren, H.S.: Hacker's Delight. Addison-Wesley, Reading (2002)
19. Yates, R.: Fixed-point arithmetic: An introduction — digital signal labs, technical reference (2007), http://www.digitalsignallabs.com/fp.pdf

ProSe: A Programming Tool for Rapid Prototyping of Sensor Networks*

Mahesh Arumugam[1] and Sandeep S. Kulkarni[2]

[1] Cisco Systems, Inc., San Jose, CA 95134, USA
maarumug@cisco.com
[2] Michigan State University, East Lansing, MI 48823, USA
sandeep@cse.msu.edu

Abstract. We focus on application of abstract network protocols towards prototyping sensor networks. Such abstract programs exist for several applications, e.g., routing, tracking, dissemination, etc. These programs are often specified in terms of event-driven actions where the program responds to actions in the environment or previous actions taken by the program. Hence, they are easy to specify, verify and manipulate. However, they cannot be applied directly in sensor networks as the computation model in sensor networks (write all with collision) differs from that (read/write or shared memory) used in abstract programs. Towards this end, we propose ProSe, a programming tool that enables the designers to (1) specify protocols in simple, abstract models, (2) reuse existing fault-tolerant/self-stabilizing protocols from the literature, and (3) automatically generate and deploy code. ProSe hides the deficiencies of existing programming platforms that require the designers to explicitly deal with buffer management, stack management, and flow control. As a result, we expect that ProSe will enable rapid prototyping and quick deployment of protocols.

Keywords: Programming Tool, Network Protocols, Sensor Networks.

1 Introduction

Sensor networks have become popular due to their applications in border patrolling, critical infrastructure protection, habitat monitoring, structural health monitoring, and hazard detection. Furthermore, due to the development in MEMS technology, tiny low-power sensors can now be manufactured and deployed in large numbers. They have been successfully used in large scale deployments of several applications.

One of the important challenges in deploying sensor network applications is programming. Most of the existing platforms (e.g., nesC/TinyOS [2]) for developing sensor network programs use *event-driven programming model* [3]. As identified in [3–5], while an event-driven programming platform has the potential to simplify concurrency by reducing race conditions and deadlocks, the programmer is responsible for stack management and flow control. For example, in nesC/TinyOS platform, the state of an operation does not persist over the duration of entire operation. As a result, programmers need to manually maintain the stack for the operation. Moreover, the state of the

---

* A preliminary version of this paper appeared as a poster in [1].

S. Hailes, S. Sicari, and G. Roussos (Eds.): S-Cube 2009, LNICST 24, pp. 158–173, 2009.
© Institute for Computer Sciences, Social-Informatics and Telecommunications Engineering 2009

operation is shared across several functions. Hence, the designer has to manually control the execution flow. As the program size grows, such manual management becomes complex and is often the source of programming errors.

In addition, typical sensor network platforms require the programmers to manage buffers, contend for access to radio channel, and deal with faults. Hence, as mentioned in [6], programming in nesC/TinyOS platform is "somewhat tricky." In [6], the authors motivate the need for a simpler model that allows one to specify applications in terms of event-driven model (that hides several programming level issues).

To simplify programming sensor networks, several approaches are proposed (e.g., [6–24]). These approaches hide most of the low-level details of the network. (We refer the reader to Section 2 for more details on these approaches.) Existing work on macroprogramming primitives require implementation of such primitives in a target platform (e.g., nesC/TinyOS). Moreover, most of these primitives still require the designer to specify protocols in a target platform (though some intricate details are hidden).

Contributions of the paper. With this motivation, in this paper, we propose *ProSe*, a programming platform for sensor networks that allows designers to concisely specify sensor network protocols. ProSe is based on the theoretical foundation on computational model in sensor networks [25, 26]. In [25, 26], the authors model the computations in sensor networks as a *write all with collision* (WAC) model. In this model, in one atomic step, a sensor can write its own state as well as the state of all its neighbors. However, if two sensors try to update the state of a common neighbor (say, k) simultaneously then, due to collision, the state of k remains unchanged. Thus, this model captures the nature of communication in sensor networks. Moreover, in [25, 26], the authors proposed transformation algorithms that allow the designers to specify programs in abstract models (e.g., read/write model, shared-memory model) and transform them into WAC model (cf. Section 3.1 for a brief introduction to these models).

ProSe enables the designers to (1) specify sensor network protocols and macroprogramming primitives in simple, abstract models, (2) transform the programs into WAC model while preserving properties such as fault-tolerance and self-stabilization [27] of the original programs, and (3) automatically generate and deploy code. An advantage of ProSe is that it will facilitate the designer to use existing algorithms for automating the addition of fault-tolerance to existing programs. Moreover, since abstract models are used to specify protocols, ProSe allows the designer to gain assurance about the programs deployed in the network using tools such as model checkers [28].

Additionally, we observe that the work on distributed computing and traditional networking has focused on problems such as consensus, agreement in the presence of faulty/malicious sensors, reliable broadcast, routing, leader election, synchronization, and tracking. These problems (or variations thereof) also need to be solved in the context of sensor networks, either in the design of sensor network protocols or in the design of macroprogramming primitives. However, existing solutions to these problems are written in abstract models such as read/write model and shared-memory model. Since it is desirable to utilize the vast literature in this area, to speed up the development and deployment of sensor networks, ProSe enables the designers to reuse existing algorithms by automatically transforming them into WAC model.

Organization of the paper. In Section 2, we discuss the related work. In Section 3, we provide a detailed discussion on ProSe. Then, in Section 4, we discuss two case studies. Finally, in Section 5, we make the concluding remarks.

2   Background on Programming Platforms for Sensor Networks

Related work that deals with programming platforms include [6–24].

Macroprogramming. In [7], *collaboration groups* are proposed that hides the designer from issues such as communication protocols, event handling, etc. In [8–10], *macroprogramming* primitives that abstract communication, data sharing and gathering operations are proposed. These primitives are exposed in a high-level language. However, these primitives are application-specific (e.g., *abstract regions* for tracking and gathering [8] and *region streams* for aggregation [9]). And, in [11], *semantic services* programming model is proposed where each service provides semantic interpretation of the raw sensor data or data provided by other semantic services. In this model, users only specify the end goal on what semantic data to collect.

In [12], macroprogramming model, called *Kairos*, that hides the details of code-generation and instantiation, data management, and control is proposed. Kairos provides three abstractions; (1) node-level abstraction, (2) one-hop neighbor list abstraction for performing operations on the neighbor list, and (3) remote data access. In [13], programming language called *Pleiades* is proposed that extends C language with constructs for addressing nodes in a network and accessing local data from individual nodes. In [14], virtual node abstraction is proposed where the physical nodes in the network emulate the virtual node application (specified by the designer). The emulation is divided among three main components: (1) to elect a region leader in each region of the network, (2) to retrieve the current state of virtual node application, and (3) to keep the virtual node state synchronized with the physical nodes in the region.

While [7–14] are designed for simplifying programming application services such as tracking, aggregation, etc, ProSe is designed to simplify programming both network services (e.g., routing, clustering, leader election, distributed reset, etc) and application services. Furthermore, ProSe hides low-level details such as message collisions, corruption, sensor failures, etc. Moreover, unlike Kairos and Pleiades, ProSe does not require any runtime support. Additionally, ProSe enables reuse of existing algorithms while preserving properties such as self-stabilization of the input program.

Rule-based programming. In [15–18], rule based programming approaches are proposed. These approaches allow designers to specify programs similar to guarded commands format. However, unlike ProSe, approaches proposed in [15, 16] require designers to *explicitly* specify send/receive message actions of the sensors. As a result, the designers have to decide what messages to transmit (e.g., raw data vs. some interpretation of data), when message transmissions are scheduled (e.g., backoff based vs. timeslot based), and when to listen to the medium for new messages (e.g, always on radio vs. schedule based). In [18], a declarative sensor network programming paradigm called *DSN* is proposed. DSN uses *Snlog*, a high-level specification language based on facts and rules, for specifying programs. DSN provides an easy mechanism for inter-acting with the lower layers of the stack and components written in systems languages.

The approaches proposed in [15–18] do not facilitate the reuse of abstract proto-cols from the literature. Moreover, dynamic embedded sensing and actuation language (*DESAL*) proposed in [17] does not provide a mechanism for preserving properties of interest (e.g., fault-tolerance, self-stabilization) in the transformed programs. Addition-ally, unlike [18], ProSe does not require any runtime support.

Transaction-based programming. In [19], a transactional framework, called *TRANS-ACT*, is proposed for programming wireless sensor/actor networks. In this approach, an execution of a non-local method is of the form: *read[write-all]*. In other words, a non-local method consists of: (1) a read operation that reads the state of the neighbors and (2) a write-all operation that updates the state of all the neighbors. This model differs from WAC model as follows. Specifically, read action is modeled in [25] as a write-all action that updates the state of a sensor at all its neighbors. Therefore, expect for the write-all action, each method accesses only local variables. On the other hand, in TRASACT, designers have to specify what variables to read and what variables to update at the neigbhors in every method. As a result, TRASACT introduces unnecessary overheads in the implementation of read and write-all operations (e.g., read request, read reply, write-all, acknowledgment, conflict detection, cancellation, and c ancel acks).

Programming tools. Techniques like virtual machine (e.g., *Maté* [6]), middleware (e.g., *EnviroTrack* [20]), library (e.g., *SNACK* [21], *TASK* [22]), and database (e.g., *TinyDB* [23]) are proposed for simplifying programming sensor network applications. Another interesting approach for development of mobile sensor network applications is *CarTel* [24]. CarTel provides a simple querying infrastructure. However, these so-lutions are (i) application-specific, and/or (ii) restrict the designer to what is available in the virtual machine, middleware, library, or network. By contrast, ProSe provides a simple abstraction while allowing the designer to specify wide variety of protocols.

3   ProSe: Overview, Architecture, and Features

In this section, we present: (1) the theoretical background of ProSe, (2) the architecture of ProSe, (3) the internals of ProSe, and (4) the features of ProSe that simplify sensor network programming.

3.1   Preliminaries and Theoretical Background

Programs are specified in terms of guarded commands [29]; each guarded command (respectively, action) is of the form:

$$guard \quad \longrightarrow \quad statement,$$

where *guard* is a predicate over program variables, and *statement* updates program variables. An action $g \longrightarrow st$ is *enabled* when g evaluates to true and to execute that action, st is executed. A *computation* of this program consists of a sequence $s_0, s_1, \ldots,$ where s_{j+1} is obtained from s_j by executing actions in the program ($0 \leq j$).

A computation model limits the variables that an action can read and write. Program actions are split into a set of processes. Each action is associated with one of the processes. (Note that in this paper, the terms process and sensor are synonymous.)

Shared-memory model. In this model, in one atomic step, a sensor can read its state as well as the state of its neighbors and write its own variables.

Read/Write model. In this model, in one atomic step, a sensor can either (1) read the state of one of its neighbors and update its *private* variables, or (2) write its own state.

Write all with collision (WAC) model. In this model, each sensor consists of write-all actions. In one atomic step, a sensor can update its own state and the state of all its neighbors. However, if two or more sensors simultaneously try to update the state of a sensor, say k, then the state of k remains unchanged. Thus, this model captures the nature of communication in sensor networks (i.e., *local broadcast with collision*).

Transformations for WAC model. Recently, approaches have been proposed for transforming programs into WAC model. They can be classified as: (a) TDMA based deterministic transformation [25] and (b) CSMA based probabilistic transformation [26].

TDMA based deterministic transformation. In [25], Kulkarni and Arumugam proposed algorithms for transforming programs written in read/write model into programs in WAC model. In [25], the action by which a process (say, j) reads the state of process k in read/write model is modeled in WAC model by requiring process k to write the appropriate value at process j. However, if another neighbor of j is trying to write the state of j at the same time then, due to collision, none of the write actions succeed. In order to deal with this problem, in [25], time division multiple access (TDMA) is used to ensure that collisions do not occur during write actions. Specifically, in WAC model, each process executes the enabled actions and writes (broadcasts) its state to all its neighbors in its TDMA slots. Note that with TDMA based transformation, the model of computation does not change. Rather, TDMA avoids collisions during execution. However, if the slots are corrupted then collisions may occur during execution.

If the transformation uses a deterministic TDMA service (e.g., [30–32]) to implement the write-all action, the resulting program in WAC model is also deterministic. Additionally, in [25], the authors propose extensions for transforming programs written in shared-memory model into programs in WAC model.

TDMA based transformation algorithms proposed in [25] preserve self-stabilization property of the original programs. A program is self-stabilizing if starting from arbitrary initial states the program (eventually) recovers to states from where the computation proceeds in accordance with its specification. In [25], it has been shown that for every computation of the transformed program in WAC model there is an equivalent computation of the given program. Therefore, if the transformed program transitions into arbitrary states then there is a corresponding transition in the given program. Now, if the given program is self-stabilizing then it will recover to legitimate states. In the transformed program, if the TDMA slots are not corrupted then the transformed program will recover to legitimate states. Hence, if the TDMA algorithm is self-stabilizing (e.g., [30, 32]) then the transformation preserves self-stabilizing property.

CSMA based probabilistic transformation. In [26], Herman proposed *cached sensor transform* (CST) that allows one to correctly simulate a program written for shared-memory model in sensor networks. CST uses CSMA to broadcast the state of a sensor and, hence, the transformed program is randomized.

Dealing with lossy channels. The WAC model captures the nature of communication in sensor networks. However, in practice, messages may be lost due to various factors including corruption and varying signal-to-noise ratio. We argue that the transformations proposed for WAC model is valid in the presence of lossy channels.

Towards this end, first, we note that a message loss can be treated as a write action of a sensor did not update one or more its neighbors. This is equivalent to the computation of original program, say, in read/write model, where the sensor did not read the corresponding neighbor(s). Therefore, it follows that, for every computation of the transformed program in WAC model, there is an equivalent computation of the original program in read/write model.

In the presence of lossy channels, if a sensor executes the write-all action infinitely often then the state of the sensor is updated at all its neighbors infinitely often. In case of CSMA based transformation, thus, only probabilistic gurantees about the transformed programs can be provided in the presence of lossy channels. Likewise, in case of TDMA based transformation, although collisions are not a concern, the presence of lossy channels enable only probabilistic guarantees about the transformed programs. Additionally, since the transformation preserves the stabilization property of the original program, eventually, the transformed program in WAC model also self-stabilizes to states where each sensor correctly captures the state of all its neighbors.

3.2 Programming Architecture

The programming architecture of ProSe is shown in Figure 1. ProSe transforms the input guarded commands program into a program in WAC model. Subsequently, ProSe generates the corresponding nesC code (targeted for TinyOS). Furthermore, ProSe *wires* the generated code with a MAC layer to implement the write-all action in the WAC model. The MAC layer provides an interface for broadcasting (i.e., writing all neighbors) and receiving WAC messages. ProSe also wires the generated code with *NeighborStateM.nc* that maintains the state of the neighbors of each sensor. The designer can then use the nesC/TinyOS platform to build the binary of the nesC code that can subsequently be disseminated across the network using a network programming service.

Input guarded commands program. In the input program, the designer has to specify whether a variable is *public* or *private*. Also, the designer has to identify the sensor to which the variable belongs. For example, if sensor j accesses its local variable x, it is specified as $x.j$. Consider the *MAX* program (cf. Program 1). Each sensor maintains a public variable x. The goal of MAX is to eventually identify the maximum value of x across the network. Whenever $x.j$ is less than $x.k$, j copies $x.k$ to $x.j$. This allows j to update $x.j$ and, eventually, $x.j$ holds the maximum value of x.

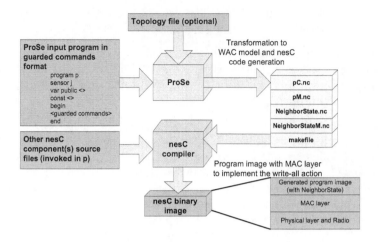

Fig. 1. Programming architecture of ProSe

Program 1. MAX program in shared-memory model

```
1 program max
2 sensor j;
3 var public int x.j;
4 begin
5     (x.k > x.j) -> x.j = x.k;
6 end
7 init state x.j = j;
```

Initial states. The designer also specifies zero or more initial states in the program. If initial states are not specified then the variables are initialized to arbitrary values. And, if the program contains more than one initial state then the variables are initialized to a randomly selected state. In the MAX program example, $x.j$ is initialized to j.

Topology information. ProSe *wires* a component (*NeighborStateM*) that maintains the state of the neighbors at each sensor, with the generated code. Each sensor should identify its neighborhood either dynamically using a neighborhood abstraction layer (e.g., [33]) or statically using a *topology file* which specifies the communication topology [34]. Then, ProSe configures the MAC layer and NeighborStateM.

3.3   Implementation

In the generated program, each sensor maintains a copy vector for each public variable of its neighbor (in NeighborStateM, the module that implements NeighborState interface to get/set copy vectors). Each copy vector captures the value of the corresponding variable at its neighbors. The size of this vector is determined using the neighborhood information of each sensor.

The actions of the input program are executed whenever a timer fires. Then, it marshals all the public variables as a message *wacMsg* and schedules it for transmission (broadcast). Depending on the transformation algorithm and the MAC layer selected by the user, ProSe configures when the timer fires and how *wacMsg* is transmitted. In case of a TDMA based transformation (e.g., [25]), ProSe configures the timer to fire in every TDMA slot assigned to the sensor and broadcasts *wacMsg* using a TDMA service (e.g., [30–32]). In case of a CSMA based transformation (e.g., [26]), it configures the timer to fire in a random interval whenever the sensor receives a message. And, it uses a CSMA service to broadcast *wacMsg*. Thus, as identified in Figure 1, ProSe generates the following nesC files: a *configuration* file, an *interface* file, and 2 *module* files.

Configuration file. Configurations wire components together, connecting interfaces used by components to interfaces provided by others [2]. ProSe generates *pC.nc*, given the input program *p*. *pC.nc* wires *pM.nc*, NeighborStateM.nc, network services (e.g., TDMA, CSMA, etc), and other interfaces required by the module.

Interface and module files. Modules provide the application code and implement one or more interfaces [2]. ProSe generates *pM.nc* (given the input program *p*) and (2) NeighborStateM.nc as outlined below. (For reasons of space, we refer the reader to [34] for the steps involved in the generation of these files.)

- *Initializing nesC modules.* ProSe generates NeighborState.nc that provides get/set functions for public variables of the program. For each public variable, ProSe generates a copy vector in NeighborStateM (with entries for all neighbors of a sensor). NeighborStateM.nc implements NeighborState.nc. In pM.nc, ProSe generates code to (1) initialize components (e.g., TDMA, CSMA, Timer, NeighborStateM) and (2) start network/middleware services (e.g., TDMA, CSMA, Timer).
- *Implementing the guarded commands.* ProSe generates the nesC code for the actions specified in the input program in *Timer.fired()* event. For each action $g \longrightarrow st$, it generates the corresponding nesC code of the form *if(g){st;}*. And, ProSe generates code for implementing the write-all action.
- *Updating the neighbor state.* ProSe generates code for updating NeighborStateM whenever it receives a message. The values of the public variables of the sender are updated in the corresponding copy vectors (in NeighborStateM).

Once code is generated, the designer can use the nesC/TinyOS platform to build the binary image. This image can then be deployed across the network.

3.4 Additional Features

Dealing with faults in protocol design. The normal operation of a network is affected by (1) failure of sensors, (2) state corruption, and (3) message loss. Regarding failure of sensors, ProSe provides an abstraction which allows a sensor (say, j) to determine whether its neighbor (say, k) is alive or failed. In the input program, sensor j can access the public variable $up.k$; if $up.k$ is *TRUE* (respectively, *FALSE*) then k is alive (respectively, failed). ProSe implements this variable using heartbeat protocol (e.g., [35]). For example, if j fails to receive update messages (i.e., WAC messages) for a pre-determined time interval from its neighbor k then j declares k as failed. Thus, designers can use this abstract variable to simplify the design of programs. Similarly, ProSe also models Byzantine sensors through abstract variables ($b.k$).

Regarding state corruption, ProSe permits arbitrary initial states. This allows the designer to model systems that are perturbed to an arbitrary state. When used in the context of a self-stabilization preserving transformation (e.g., [25, 26]), this feature enables the design of self-stabilizing protocols. Finally, regarding message loss, ProSe allows the designer to provide probability of transmission on any given link.

Priorities of actions. Consider a routing protocol. The actions in the protocol can be classified as either *heartbeat* or *protocol* actions. Heartbeat actions are responsible for checking the status of the neighbors and protocol actions are responsible for construction/maintenance of the routing structure. These two classes of actions may have different priorities, i.e., the frequency of execution of heartbeat actions may be different from protocol actions. Typically, in a network where failures are common, heartbeat actions have higher priority. To represent such actions, ProSe allows the designer to specify priorities for each action. Priority characterizes the frequency with which an action would be executed. And, priorities are specified along with the guarded commands.

Local component invocations. ProSe makes protocol design highly intuitive and concise. However, it is not always desirable to use guarded commands. For example, consider the design of a routing protocol, where the sensors maintain a spanning tree rooted at the base station. In this program, whenever the parent of a sensor fails, it chooses one of its active neighbors for which the link quality is greater than a certain threshold, as its parent. Towards this end, the sensor has to compute the link quality of each of its neighbors. Specifying this action in guarded commands is difficult. Moreover, nesC/TinyOS components may exist that provide the desired functionality.

To enable reuse of existing nesC/TinyOS components, ProSe allows component invocations in guarded commands. For example. in a routing protocol, the designer may invoke the interface *LinkQuality* (implemented by *LinkEstimatorM*) to compute the link quality. Thus, parent update action in the routing protocol can be specified in guarded commands as shown in Program 2. Note that LinkEstimatorM should be implemented in nesC/TinyOS. This component, however, uses only local data (e.g., using NeighborStateM). ProSe wires this component with the generated code.

Program 2. Illustration of local component invocation

```
1 ...
2 component LinkEstimatorM provides LinkQuality;
3 begin
4 ...
5 | (up.(p.j) == FALSE) && (up.k == TRUE) &&
6     (LinkQuality.quality(k) > THRESHOLD)
7  -> p.j = k; quality.j = LinkQuality.quality(k);
8 ...
9 end
```

4   ProSe: Case Studies

In this section, we present two case studies: (1) a routing tree maintenance program and (2) an intruder-interceptor program. (For reasons of space, we refer the reader to [34, 36] for a case study on prototyping a power management protocol.)

4.1   Routing Tree Maintenance Program (RTMP)

In this section, we specify routing tree program (RTMP) [37] in shared-memory model as shown in Program 3. In this program, sensors are arranged in a logical grid. The program constructs a spanning tree with the base station as the root. The base station is located at $\langle 0, 0 \rangle$. Each sensor classifies its neighbors as *high* or *low* neighbors depending on their (logical) distance to the base station. Also, each sensor maintains a variable, called *inversion count*. The inversion count of the base station is 0. If a sensor chooses one of its low neighbors as its parent, then it sets its inversion count to that of its parent. Otherwise, it sets its inversion count to inversion count of its parent + 1. Furthermore, to deal with the problem of cycles, if the inversion count exceeds a certain threshold (*CMAX*), the sensor removes itself from the tree.

Program 3. Routing tree maintenance program (RTMP)

```
 1 program RoutingTreeMaintenance
 2 sensor j;
 3 const int CMAX;
 4 var
 5   public int inv.j, dist.j;
 6   public boolean up.j;
 7   private int p.j;
 8 begin
 9 (dist.k < dist.j) && (up.k == TRUE) && (inv.k < CMAX) && (inv.k < inv.j)
10    -> p.j = k; inv.j = inv.k;
11 | (dist.k < dist.j) && (up.k == TRUE) && (inv.k+1 < CMAX) &&
12   (inv.k+1 < inv.j)
13    -> p.j = k; inv.j = inv.k+1;
14 | (p.j != NULL) && ((up.(p.j) == FALSE) ||   (inv.(p.j) >= CMAX) ||
15   ((dist.(p.j) < dist.j) && (inv.j != inv.(p.j))) ||
16   ((dist.(p.j) > dist.j) && (inv.j != inv.(p.j)+1)))
17    -> p.j = NULL; inv.j = CMAX;
18 | (p.j == NULL) && (inv.j < CMAX)
19    -> inv.j = CMAX;
20 end
```

In this program, each sensor (say, j) maintains three *public* variables: (i) $inv.j$, the inversion count of j, (ii) $dist.j$, the (logical) distance of j to the base station, and (iii) $up.j$, the status variable for j (indicates whether j has failed or not). ProSe provides implementation of $up.j$ using heartbeat protocol, as discussed in Section 3.4. Whenever

Table 1. Memory footprint of the generated RTMP program

	Program ROM (in bytes)	RAM (in bytes)
routingM + NeighborStateM	42	106
SS-TDMA	108	586
other components (Timer, FramerM, LedsC, etc)	15934	404

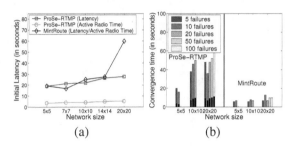

(a)   (b)

Fig. 2. Simulations results of the generated program. With 90% link reliability: (a) initial latency and (b) convergence time. Note that the black bars in the convergence time graph shows the active radio time during the convergence period. (The result was similar for simulations with 95% link reliability.

j finds a low/high neighbor that provides a better path (in terms of inversion count) to the base station, it updates its *private* variable, $p.j$, the parent of j, and inversion count $inv.j$. Whenever a sensor fails or inversion count is not consistent with its parent, the sensor sets its parent to *NULL* and its inversion count to *CMAX* (i.e., it removes itself from the routing tree). Subsequently, when it finds a neighbor with a better inversion count value, it rejoins the tree.

We used ProSe to transform the program and integrated SS-TDMA [32] with the generated program (cf. Table 1 for memory footprint of the generated program).

Simulation results. We simulated the generated program (ProSe-RTMP) and MintRoute [38] using TOSSIM [39]. (For experimental results, we refer the reader to [34].) In our simulations, the base station is located at $\langle 0,0 \rangle$ (i.e., sensor 0) and the inter-sensor separation is 10 ft. In the absence of any interference, we have observed that probability of successful communication is more than 98% among the neighbors. However, random channel errors can cause the reliability to go down. Hence, we choose conservative estimate of 90% link reliability (that correspond to the analysis in [40, 41]).

In our simulation, each sensor executes the write-all action of the program once in every 2 seconds. And, in MintRoute, the sensors exchange routing information every 2 seconds. Once the initial tree is constructed, we simultaneously fail some sensors and measure the convergence time. The simulation results are shown in Figure 2. The initial latency to construct the routing tree for ProSe-RTMP and MintRoute are similar. MintRoute maintains link estimates of the active links of a sensor and updates the estimate periodically. As a result, the radio is active all the time. By contrast, with ProSe-RTMP, the active radio time of the sensors during this period is significantly less (i.e., around 20% of the initial latency).

Figure 2(b) presents the convergence time of the protocols in the presence of failed sensors. MintRoute converges to a new routing tree quickly. By contrast, ProSe-RTMP converges within 30-50 seconds. We note that this behavior is *not* because of prototyping with ProSe. Rather, it is because of the nature of the original protocol specified with ProSe. More specifically, MintRoute is *pessimistic* in nature, i.e., it maintains a moving average of link estimates of all active links of a sensor all the time. Hence, when sensors fail, it converges to a new tree quickly. By contrast, RTMP is *optimistic* in nature. In other words, whenever a sensor chooses one of its neighbors as its parent, it does not change its parent unless the parent has failed or the tree is corrupted. As a result, when sensors fail, it takes sometime for the protocol to update the tree. On the other hand, the active radio time during recovery is small with ProSe-RTMP.

4.2 Pursuer-Evader Tracking Program

Sensor networks are often used in intruder-interception games, where the sensors guide the pursuer (e.g., a robot, a soldier, etc) to track and intercept the evader (e.g., intruder, hostile vehicle, etc). In this section, we specify the evader-centric program for intruder-interception from [42] in shared-memory model as shown in Program 4. In this program, sensors maintain a tracking structure rooted at the evader. The pursuer follows this tracking structure to intercept the evader. Whenever the pursuer arrives at a sensor (say, k), it consults k to determine its next move. Specifically, it moves to the parent of k. And, since the pursuer is faster than the evader, it eventually intercepts the evader.

Program 4. Pursuer-evader tracking program

```
1 program PursuerEvaderTracking sensor j; var
2   public int dist2Evader.j, detectTimeStamp.j, p.j;
3   private boolean isEvaderHere.j;
4 begin (isEvaderHere.j == TRUE)
5     -> p.j = j; dist2Evader.j = 0; detectTimeStamp.j = TIME;
6 | (detectTimeStamp.k > detectTimeStamp.j) ||
7     ((detectTimeStamp.k == detectTimeStamp.j) &&
8     (dist2Evader.k+1 < dist2Evader.j))
9     -> p.j = k; detectTimeStamp.j = detectTimeStamp.k;
10    dist2Evader.j = dist2Evader.k+1;
11 end
```

Each sensor (say, j) maintains three public variables: (i) *dist2Evader.j*, distance to the root of the tracking structure, (ii) *detectTimeStamp.j*, the timestamp that j knows when the evader was detected at the root, and (iii) *p.j*, the parent of j. Whenever j detects the evader, it sets *detectTimeStamp.j* to its current clock value (using the *TIME* keyword), *dist2Evader.j* to 0 and *p.j* to itself. If it finds one of its neighbors (say, k) has the latest detection timestamp, then it updates its public variables accordingly and sets its *p.j* to k. In Program 4, for simplicity, we do not show the actions of the pursuer. Since the pursuer can listen to the messages transmitted by the sensors, whenever the pursuer is near j, it reads the public variable *p.j* and moves to *p.j*.

Table 2. Memory footprint of the generated tracking program

	Program ROM (in bytes)	RAM (in bytes)
trackingM + NeighborStateM	N/A*	91
SS-TDMA	108	586
other components (Timer, FramerM, LedsC, etc)	14920	404

* The perl script `tinyos-1.x/contrib/SystemC/module_memory_usage` used to obtain

the breakdown of program ROM and RAM used by various components only provides the

RAM usage data for trackingM; it does not report the ROM usage for trackingM. We expect

this value to be small.

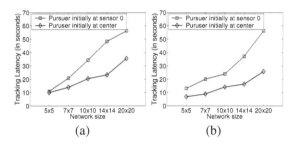

(a)   (b)

Fig. 3. Tracking latency of the generated program: (a) with 90% link reliability and (b) with 95% link reliability

We used ProSe to transform the program and integrated SS-TDMA [32] with the generated program (cf. Table 2 for memory footprint of the generated program). In this program, we need to *wire* components that detect whether the evader is present near a sensor. For example, if the goal is to intercept vehicles then we need to integrate components that can signal whether a vehicle is present or moving near a sensor (e.g., magnetometer components, accelerometer components). Based on this signal, the variable *isEvaderHere.j* at sensor j is either set or unset. Such components are independent of the design of a tracking service.

Simulation results. We simulated the generated program using TOSSIM [39]. The inter-sensor separation is 10 ft and the TDMA period in SS-TDMA is 0.78 seconds. Similar to Section 4.1, we choose the link reliability to be 90% and 95%. In our simulations, we use a *virtual* pursuer and a *virtual* evader. The evader moves randomly in the network. The variable *isEvaderHere.j* at j is set to $TRUE$ or $FALSE$ depending on the current location of the evader. The pursuer is twice as fast as the evader. We did two sets of simulations: (1) the initial location of pursuer is at $\langle 0,0 \rangle$ and (2) initial location of pursuer is at the center of the network. In both scenarios, the initial location of evader is at the corner (i.e., $\langle N-1, N-1 \rangle$ on NxN grid). From Figure 3, we observe that the tracking latency increases as the network size increases. The latency when the pursuer is initially near the center is significantly less than the case where the pursuer is initially at $\langle 0,0 \rangle$. And, the active radio time is at most 20% of the time required by the pursuer to intercept the evader. Thus, these results demonstrate the potential of ProSe to generate application-level services for sensor networks.

5   Conclusion

We expect that the programs generated by ProSe are competitive to related programs designed manually for sensor networks. Since ProSe hides low-level details from the designer, it allows rapid prototyping of sensor network protocols. Therefore, we expect that the development time of a typical application (composed of several protocols) is small. Furthermore, since ProSe automatically transforms the program in abstract model to generate the corresponding nesC/TinyOS code, it enables quick deployment of applications. We demonstrated this for (1) routing tree maintenance program (cf. Section 4.1), (2) pursuer-evader tracking service (cf. Section 4.2), and (3) power management protocol [36].

We note that program analysis of nesC/TinyOS programs is gaining attention recently as it assists in programmer understanding, error detection, and program validation (e.g., [43]). Specifically, in [43], program analysis is performed on state machines derived from nesC/TinyOS programs. Such analysis is straight-forward in ProSe as the programs are specified in a simple guarded commands format and several analysis tools and model checkers [28] are readily available.

There are several possible future directions to this work. First, we would like to to combine this work with [44] where the sensor network protocols are proposed in a model that is similar to the abstract models used in ProSe. Since [44] focuses on verification aspects of the abstract protocols, combining it with ProSe, will provide assurance guarantees about the deployed programs. Additionally, we are also focusing on integrating ProSe with tools that automatically synthesize fault-tolerant programs from their fault-intolerant versions (e.g., FTSyn [45]).

References

1. Arumugam, M., Kulkarni, S.S.: Prose - a programming tool for rapid prototyping of sensor networks. Poster at the Conference on Sensor, Mesh, and Ad Hoc Communications and Networks, SECON (2007)
2. Gay, D., Levis, P., von Behren, R., Welsh, M., Brewer, E., Culler, D.: The nesC language: A holistic approach to networked embedded systems. In: Programming Language Design and Implementation (PLDI) (June 2003)
3. Adya, A., Howell, J., Theimer, M., Bolosky, W.J., Douceur, J.R.: Cooperative task management without manual stack management or, event driven programming is not the opposite of threaded programming. In: USENIX Annual Technical Conference (June 2002)
4. Dunkels, A., Schmidt, O., Voigt, T., Ali, M.: Protothreads: Simplifying event-driven programming of memory-constrained embedded systems. In: Fourth ACM Conference on Embedded Networked Sensor Systems (SenSys) (November 2006)
5. Kasten, O., Römer, K.: Beyond event handlers: Programming sensor networks with attributed state machines. In: Fourth Internation Conference on Information Processing in Sensor Networks (IPSN) (April 2005)
6. Levis, P., Culler, D.: Maté: A tiny virtual machine for sensor networks. ACM SIGOPS Operating Systems Review 36(5), 85–95 (2002)
7. Liu, J., Chu, M., Liu, J., Reich, J., Zhao, F.: State-centric programming for sensor-actuator network systems. Pervasive Computing 2(4), 50–62 (2003)

8. Welsh, M., Mainland, G.: Programming sensor networks using abstract regions. In: Networked Systems Design and Implementation, NSDI (2004)
9. Newton, R., Welsh, M.: Region streams: Functional macroprogramming for sensor networks. In: Workshop on Data Management for Sensor Networks (2004)
10. Newton, R., Arvind, Welsh, M.: Building up to macroprogramming: An intermediate language for sensor networks. In: International Conference on Information Processing in Sensor Networks (IPSN) (April 2005)
11. Whitehouse, K., Zhao, F., Liu, J.: Semantic streams: A framework for composable semantic interpretation of sensor data. In: Römer, K., Karl, H., Mattern, F. (eds.) EWSN 2006. LNCS, vol. 3868, pp. 5–20. Springer, Heidelberg (2006)
12. Gummadi, R., Gnawali, O., Govindan, R.: Macro-programming wireless sensor networks using kairos. In: Prasanna, V.K., Iyengar, S.S., Spirakis, P.G., Welsh, M. (eds.) DCOSS 2005. LNCS, vol. 3560, pp. 126–140. Springer, Heidelberg (2005)
13. Kothari, N., Gummadi, R., Millstein, T., Govindan, R.: Reliable and efficient programming abstractions for wireless sensor networks. In: Programming Language Design and Implementation, PLDI (2007)
14. Brown, M., Gilbert, S., Lynch, N., Newport, C., Nolte, T., Spindel, M.: The virtual node layer: A programming abstraction for wireless sensor networks. In: International Workshop on Wireless Sensor Network Architecture (April 2007)
15. Sen, S., Cardell-Oliver, R.: A rule-based language for programming wireless sensor actuator networks using frequence and communication. In: Workshop on Embedded Networked Sensors (EmNets) (May 2006)
16. Terfloth, K., Wittenburg, G., Schiller, J.: Rule-oriented programming for wireless sensor networks. In: Conference on Distributed Computing in Sensor Networks (2006)
17. Arora, A., Gouda, M., Hallstrom, J., Herman, T., Leal, B., Sridhar, N.: A state-based language for sensor-actuator networks. In: International Workshop on Wireless Sensor Network Architecture (April 2007)
18. Tavakoli, A., Chu, D., Hellerstein, J., Levis, P., Shenker, S.: A declarative sensornet architecture. In: Workshop on Wireless Sensor Network Architecture (2007)
19. Demirbas, M., Soysal, O., Hussain, M.: TRANSACT: A transactional framework for programming wireless sensor/actor networks. In: International Conference on Information Processing in Sensor Networks (April 2008)
20. Abdelzaher, T., et al.: EnviroTrack: Towards an environmental computing paradigm for distributed sensor networks. In: International Conference on Distributed Computing Systems (ICDCS) (March 2004)
21. Greenstein, B., Kohler, E., Estrin, D.: A sensor network application construction kit (SNACK). In: Conference on Embedded Networked Sensing Systems (2004)
22. Buonadonna, P., Gay, D., Hellerstein, J., Hong, W., Madden, S.: TASK: Sensor network in a box. In: European Workshop on Wireless Sensor Networks (2005)
23. Madden, S., Franklin, M., Hellerstein, J., Hong, W.: TinyDB: An acquisitional query processing system for sensor networks. ACM Transactions on Database Systems, TODS (2005)
24. Hull, B., Bychkovsky, V., Chen, K., Goraczko, M., Miu, A., Shih, E., Zhang, Y., Balakrishnan, H., Madden, S.: CarTel: A distributed mobile sensor computing system. In: ACM Conference on Embedded Networked Sensor Systems, SenSys (2006)
25. Kulkarni, S.S., Arumugam, M.: Transformations for write-all-with-collision model. Computer Communications (Elsevier) 29(2), 183–199 (2006)
26. Herman, T.: Models of self-stabilization and sensor networks. In: Workshop on Distributed Computing (2003)
27. Dijkstra, E.W.: Self-stabilizing systems in spite of distributed control. Communications of the ACM 17(11) (1974)

28. Holzmann, G.J.: The model checker Spin. IEEE Transactions on Software Engineering 23(5), 279–295 (1997)
29. Dijkstra, E.W.: A Discipline of Programming. Prentice Hall PTR, Englewood Cliffs (1997)
30. Arumugam, M.: A distributed and deterministic TDMA algorithm for write-all-with-collision model. In: Kulkarni, S., Schiper, A. (eds.) SSS 2008. LNCS, vol. 5340, pp. 4–18. Springer, Heidelberg (2008)
31. Arumugam, M., Kulkarni, S.S.: Self-stabilizing deterministic time division multiple access for sensor networks. AIAA Journal of Aerospace Computing, Information, and Communication (JACIC) 3, 403–419 (2006)
32. Kulkarni, S.S., Arumugam, M.: SS-TDMA: A self-stabilizing mac for sensor networks. In: Sensor Network Operations. Wiley-IEEE Press (2006)
33. Whitehouse, K., Sharp, C., Brewer, E., Culler, D.: Hood: A neighborhood abstraction for sensor networks. In: ACM International Conference on Mobile Systems, Applications, and Services (MobiSys) (June 2004)
34. Arumugam, M.: Rapid prototyping and quick deployment of sensor networks. PhD thesis, Michigan State University (2006)
35. Gouda, M.G., McGuire, T.M.: Accelerated heartbeat protocols. In: International Confernece on Distributed Computing Systems, ICDCS (1998)
36. Arumugam, M., Wang, L., Kulkarni, S.S.: A case study on prototyping power management protocols for sensor networks. In: Datta, A.K., Gradinariu, M. (eds.) SSS 2006. LNCS, vol. 4280, pp. 50–64. Springer, Heidelberg (2006)
37. Choi, Y.-R., Gouda, M.G., Zhang, H., Arora, A.: Stabilization of grid routing in sensor networks. AIAA Journal of Aerospace Computing, Information, and Communication (JACIC) 3, 214–233 (2006)
38. Woo, A., Culler, D.: Taming the challenges of reliable multihop routing in sensor networks. In: Conference on Embedded Networked Sensing Systems (2003)
39. Levis, P., Lee, N., Welsh, M., Culler, D.: TOSSIM: Accurate and scalable simulation of entire tinyOS applications. In: First International Conference on Embedded Networed Sensor Systems (SenSys), November 2003, pp. 126–137 (2003)
40. Ganesan, D., Krishnamachari, B., Woo, A., Culler, D., Estrin, D., Wicker, S.: An empirical study of epidemic algorithms in large scale multihop wireless networks. Technical Report IRB-TR-02-003, Intel Research (March 2002)
41. Zuniga, M., Krishnamachari, B.: Analyzing the transitional region in low power wireless links. In: Conference on Sensor and Ad hoc Communications and Networks (2004)
42. Demirbas, M., Arora, A., Gouda, M.: Pursuer-evader tracking in sensor networks. In: Sensor Network Operations. Wiley-IEEE Press (May 2006)
43. Kothari, N., Millstein, T., Govindan, R.: Deriving state machines from TinyOS programs using symbolic execution. In: Seventh Conference on Information Processing in Sensor Networks, IPSN (2008)
44. Gouda, M.G., Choi, Y.-R.: A state-based model for sensor protocols. In: Anderson, J.H., Prencipe, G., Wattenhofer, R. (eds.) OPODIS 2005. LNCS, vol. 3974, pp. 246–260. Springer, Heidelberg (2006)
45. Ebnenasir, A., Kulkarni, S.S., Arora, A.: FTSyn: A framework for automatic synthesis of fault-tolerance. International Journal of Software Tools for Technology Transfer (STTT) 10(5), 455–471 (2008)

Energy-Aware Dynamic Route Management for THAWS

Chong Shen, Sean Harte, Emanuel Popovici, Brendan O'Flynn,
and John Barton

CLARITY Centre, Tyndall National Institute, Lee Maltings, Cork, Ireland
chong.shen@tyndall.ie
http://www.tyndall.ie/mai/

Abstract. In this research we focus on the Tyndall 25mm and 10mm nodes energy-aware topology management to extend sensor network lifespan and optimise node power consumption. The two tiered Tyndall Heterogeneous Automated Wireless Sensors (THAWS) tool is used to quickly create and configure application-specific sensor networks. To this end, we propose to implement a distributed route discovery algorithm and a practical energy-aware reaction model on the 25mm nodes. Triggered by the energy-warning events, the miniaturised Tyndall 10mm data collector nodes adaptively and periodically change their association to 25mm base station nodes, while 25mm nodes also change the inter-connections between themselves, which results in reconfiguration of the 25mm nodes tier topology. The distributed routing protocol uses combined weight functions to balance the sensor network traffic. A system level simulation is used to quantify the benefit of the route management framework when compared to other state of the art approaches in terms of the system power-saving.

Keywords: THAWS, Energy-aware, Routing, Energy model, Sensor network.

1   Introduction

The Tyndall Heterogeneous Automated Wireless Sensors (THAWS) tool has two types of nodes with different functions selected from a number of different node layers developed by Tyndall Nation Institute [1]. Two modular nodes have been designed with a size of 10 mm by 10 mm, and 25 mm by 25 mm [2]. These are referred to as the 10mm and 25mm nodes shown in Figure 1. Each node has a processing and transceiver layer. Sensor layers can then be connected with application specific sensors. In addition to sensors, a battery or energy harvesting device can be connected to provide a power supply and each node can also provide its own energy level reading.

The 25mm node has more powerful processing capabilities than the 10mm node. This is provided by a layer with an Atmel ATmega128 microcontroller with 128 kB of program memory. There is also an FPGA layer and a number of

S. Hailes, S. Sicari, and G. Roussos (Eds.): S-Cube 2009, LNICST 24, pp. 174–188, 2009.

Fig. 1. 10mm (left) and 25mm (right) modular Tyndall nodes

different layers for RF communications. In the 2.45 GHz frequency band there is a layer using a Nordic nRF2401 transceiver and another layer using an Ember EM2420 ZigBee 802.15.4 compatible transceiver. There is also a 433/868/915 MHz layer using a Nordic nRF905 transceiver, which allows a longer range, of up to 3.8 km in line-of-sight conditions, compared to the 2.45 GHz options, which have a maximum range of about 200 m [1]. The drawback is that bandwidth is limited to 50 kbps, compared to 1000 kbps for the Nordic nRF2401. The tradeoff between data rate and bandwidth is that a small bandwith requires the radio transmit for a longer time, which consumes more energy. The 10mm node is currently a single transceiver layer, which uses a Nordic nRF9E5 chip. The chip has a radio that is compatible with the Nordic nRF905 so this allows heterogeneous networks to be built. This chip also has an integrated 8051-compatible microcontroller with a limited 4kB program memory. However, the 4KB memory is more than enough to be programmed to read and transmit sensor data, and handle 25mm association and deassociation in the THAWS. Meanwhile, the small size of the 10mm nodes allows a greater range of application with cheaper cost due to reduced PCB size, the lower component count, and cheaper assembly costs. The range of the 10mm node is less as the antenna does not perform will with such a small ground reference, and also less than optimal design of the balun circuitry in order to fit it into such a small area [2].

The core of the THAWS is an application generating tool, which has two main parts. The first of these is a software library containing modules of code that act as primitives in building up a WSN application. The second part is a description of the desired application. The second step of developing the THAWS tool is to propose energy-aware adaptive communication protocol considering self-organised medium access and energy-oriented dynamic routing path discovery as the key enablers. In this paper we propose a distributed route management

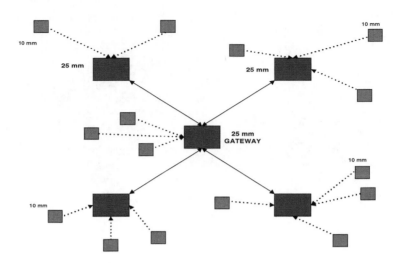

Fig. 2. Two-tiered heterogeneous network. The 25mm Tyndall nodes compose the first tier and some of them serve as gateway. The 10mm Tyndall nodes compose the second tier.

protocol and an efficient energy model specifically for the THAWS tool, where the 25mm nodes are exclusively used as the base station nodes creating the first network tier, and the 10mm nodes are used as the normal data collectors creating the second tier. Figure 2 presents an example THAWS tool topology with two tiers. Each 10mm node is associated with a 25mm node. It only has part of the 25mm communication functionalities. The 10mm only transmits collected data to its serving(associated) 25mm node base station. Complicated tasks such as data dissemination, topology control, fault recovery, internet gateway connection, etc. can be solely carried out at the 25mm nodes tier with more computation power when compared to the 10mm nodes tier. In the rest of the paper, we first review the state of art energy-aware routing protocols for the heterogeneous wireless sensor networks in Section 2. An energy model and a distributed network layer routing protocol will be detailed in Section 3. Section 4 provides the simulation models and protocols performance result with discussion. And finally in Section 5, a conclusion will be made with future research outlook.

2   Related Work

Current research is making an effort to improve the heterogeneous wireless sensor network overall lifetime at the network layer. The sensor networks can be classified as one type of ad hoc networks but the ad hoc routing protocols e.g. Ad hoc On-Demand Vector (AODV) and Direct Source Routing (DSR) [6] can not be imported directly due to problems such as power constraints, limited microcontroller computation capability, different radio access methods, Radio Frequency (RF) modules, etc. In order to find a path from the source node to the destination node, usually, flooding is a classical way to propagate and disseminate data but it always results in the broadcast storm problem, high message exchange overhead and fast node power consumption, which are unacceptable in wireless sensor networks.

Different proposals provided solutions for those problems mentioned above. Gossiping [3] is a probabilistic based flooding scheme, which tries to overcome the broadcast storm problem locally but at the cost of reliability. The use of gossiping method for unstable sensor networks routing may increase the overall or partial system failure rate. Sensor Protocol for information via negotiation (SPIN) [4] is a flat data centric routing technique based on exchange of meta-data before actual transmission. The meta-data exchange via data advertisements has proven to be very useful in overcoming the broadcast storm problem including redundancy, overlapping, and resource blindness. However, SPIN does not guarantee information delivery if intermediate nodes between the source node and destination node are not interested in the data advertisements. This disaccord the objective of Tyndall 25mm nodes tier guaranteed Quality of Service (QoS) data delivery. Directed Diffusion [5] is an important paradigm for the event monitoring of sensor networks. It uses attribute value pair for naming the data and queries the nodes or sensors in an on demand fashion by using the naming scheme and has achieved many fold energy efficiency as compared to classical flooding techniques but its emphasis on life time of an overall system is less. The THAWS tool prefers system-wide power saving rather than reduced individual node power consumption. On the other hand, The gradient set up phase is also expensive in terms of latency and energy consumption. Moreover, being a query driven data model, directed diffusion is not very efficient in applications where data is sent to the sink on continuous basis while the THAWS tool requires the 10mm tier continuously sends data to the 25mm tier.

For the AODV and DSR as mentioned previously, nodes periodically transmit routing table updates and generate networking traffic. As network size grows, the size of the routing tables and the bandwidth required to update them grows. The AODV is a reactive routing protocol, which uses sequence numbers of the destination that results in loop free topologies. Routes are acquired on demand, which results in extra delay known as route acquisition delay. Moreover, a large volume of message overhead is incurred if the routing information is changed when nodes are moved, but the power-aware THAWS tool constantly copes with the situations e. g. 25mm node failure or medium access slot failure. The DSR is very similar to the AODV, which is based on source routing where the source specifies the complete path to be taken by a packet. The Energy Aware Routing (EAR) [7] argues that using the minimum energy path all the time depletes the node energy on this path and result in a disconnected network topology. It instead uses a probabilistic approach in selecting the path to the destination by keeping more than one path toward the destination. The problem associated with the probability can be magnified when the THAWS scales to a large number of nodes. First of all, the multiple routing path storage requires sensor memory, which is not adaptive and consumes a lot sensor power. Secondly, we can not treat the 25mm and 10mm equally and nevertheless, it is impractical to have a big routing table at each 10mm Tyndall node. There are few other complex routing protocols available such as gradient based routing, rumor routing, which are also not adaptive for a sensor system with ultra low power design objective.

3   Energy-Aware Route Management for THAWS

With the aim to provide energy-aware and energy-efficient sensor network applications through the THAWS tool, we at the Tyndall National Institute (TNI) first identify and investigate a fixed heterogeneous sensor network infrastructure where all the positions of 25mm nodes and 10mm nodes are fixed thus the node mobility issues are not considered. The infrastructure, as a IEEE 802.15.4 compatible sub-network along with other different sub-networks at the Dublin City University (DCU), will be eventually connected to the University College Dublin (UCD) Internet database via IEFT IPv6 over Low power wireless Personal Area Networks (6LowPan) technology within the Science Foundation Ireland funded CLARITY [9] project. Figure 3 presents the cooperation plan between different institutes at different locations.

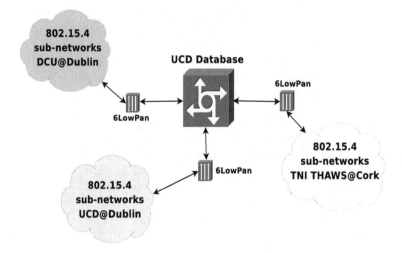

Fig. 3. The CLARITY project 6LowPan and IEEE 802.15.4 based system

As specified in previous description for the 25mm nodes and 10 nodes at Section 1, due to the hardware limitation for the miniaturised 10mm node, it doesn't support 802.15.4 using Nordic radio mircocontroller. Therefore, the 6LowPan gateway connections and distributed route management functions for the THAWS tool have to be handled at the 25mm nodes.

3.1   Node Energy Model

The goal of the use of an energy model control is to periodically monitor 25mm base station nodes energy consumption status in order to maintain some property

of the communication graph, while dynamically change the number of 10mm
nodes association as the energy consumed by the communications between the
serving 25mm node and its associated 10mm nodes is one of the primary sources
of energy consumption. The Tyndall 25mm node can also adaptively change
the transmission range to achieve a good energy efficiency using different RF
modules. The route management protocol considers the THAWS power efficiency
as the primary optimisation objective, and packet transmission delay and packet
successful delivery ratio as the secondary optimisation objectives. Therefore, a
practical three states energy model is first proposed for the 25mm nodes.

The THAWS topology has been analysed as shown in Figure 4. Based on
the energy mapping technology for both 25mm nodes and 10mm nodes, given
energy levels of the nodes, the THAWS tool can roughly predict future state of
the network. The spatial and temporal energy gradient of the network nodes may
also be modelled. Coupled with network topology, this can be used to identify
"weak areas" of the network. Most importantly, each 25mm node decides how
many 10mm nodes it serves at first instance and exchanges information with
other 25mm nodes to handover or accommodate 10mm nodes.

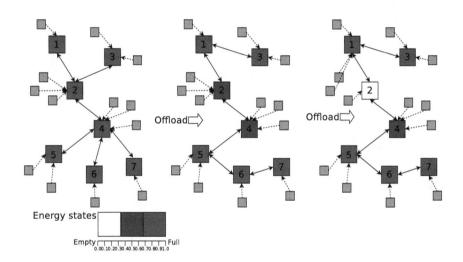

Fig. 4. The Tyndall 25mm nodes practical energy model based traffic offloading
illustration

The 25mm distributed energy-aware offloading mechanism includes two sub-
algorithms in respect to the node energy states as presented in Figure 4. The
energy-model at each 25mm node uses a linear energy function to describe the
energy level:

$$E = 1 - T_a C_a - T_s C_s \qquad (1)$$

Where 1 stands for full energy level. T_a and T_s are the Tyndall 25mm node usage
time accumulated in the active mode and sleep mode, respectively. C_a and C_s

are the 25mm typical energy used at the active mode and sleep mode. The 10mm node uses a similar energy-model and it shuts down when the energy is empty. Two hard boundaries, which are 0.33 and 0.67, have been introduced to trigger the two sub-protocol named Level 1 Offloading (L1O) and Level 2 Offloading (L2O). The three energy states are Full $E = (0.67, 1]$, Normal $E = (0.33, 0.67]$ and Restricted $E = (0, 0.33]$. The reason to only have two sub-protocols with two hard boundaries is the energy saving consideration because the frequent network topology and unnecessary information exchange must be avoided.

As shown in Figure 4, the example network (cluster) consists of 7 first tier 25mm nodes and a number of second tier 10mm nodes connected to the 25mm nodes. When 25mm node 2 and node 4 change the energy state to Normal (red coloured) state, the L1O protocol is triggered:

L1O. A 25mm node searches other first tier 25mm nodes using Routing Request (RREQ) message to reduce the number of intra-tier connections, which result in the node energy saving since the time spent on active transmission mode will be reduced. In order to retain the connectivity of the entire network, a spanning tree [10] algorithm is used. To avoid flooding information through the entire 25mm node tier, it is divided into several clusters and each cluster includes a number of 25mm nodes e.g. 7 nodes. Therefore in a sensor node mapped graph (a cluster) there is a subgraph which is a tree and connects all the vertices together. A single graph can have many different spanning trees. We assign a energy model based weight function to each edge, which is a number representing how unfavorable it is, and use this to assign a weight to a spanning tree by computing the sum of the weights of the edges in that spanning tree. We also assign a higher energy weight upon the links associated with state change. A minimum weight spanning tree is then a spanning tree with a weight less than or equal to the weight of every other spanning tree.

Using the L1O protocol, the connection within the seven 25mm nodes cluster has been changed after node energy based weight calculation at each link. Node 1 connects to node 3 and node 3 disconnects from node 2. Node 2 disconnects from node 3. Node 4 disconnects from both node 6 and node 7. Node 5 connects to node 6. Node 6 connects to node 5 and disconnects from node 4. Node 7 connects to node 6 which has a higher energy left and disconnects from node 4.

When 25mm node 2 changes the energy state from Normal state to Restricted (write coloured) state, the L2O protocol is triggered:

L2O. A 25mm node searches other first tier 25mm nodes using Routing Request (RREQ) message to reduce the number of inter-tier connections and shift a number of its associated 10mm nodes to its neighbouring 25mm nodes, after acknowledged answer from the neighbouring 25mm nodes through Routing Reply (RREP). The neighbouring nodes will not reply RREP to the requesting 25mm node unless two conditions are satisfied, which are the transmission range of a candidate 10mm node & available medium access slots.

Using the L2O protocol, as indicated in 4, 25mm node 2 with restricted energy state disconnects two of its associated 10mm nodes. The two 10mm node are then connects to 25mm node 1. The other 10mm node can not be connected to node 1 due to the transmission range problem.

3.2   Energy-Aware Power Saving Protocol

The Energy-aware power saving protocol for the THAWS operates distributedly. It comprehensively considers three parameters: Energy Consumption (E), Packet Delivery Delay (D) and Packet Successful Delivery Ratio (S) to the distributed protocol. The shortest path between the source node to the sink node (or say hop distance) is usually a critical parameter for a dynamic environment, but for the nodes position fixed THAWS it is not necessary. A function is assigned to each 25mm node and the routing path between the source 25mm node and the destination 25mm node is based on the calculation of a function:

$$F_n = \alpha E_n + \beta D_n + \gamma S_n \tag{2}$$

Where n is the node number or an identifier assigned to a 25mm node. Each parameter has been given a weight factor, which are α for energy consumption), β for packet Delivery Delay and γ for packet successful delivery ratio depending on different wireless sensor network application requirement, and the add sum of $\alpha + \beta + \gamma = 1$. A localised flooding technique is used to find next hop neighbouring 25mm node distributedly and system-wide probing message flooding is prohibited to reduce data exchange overhead. For example, if an application requires a guaranteed packet delivery with a time restriction, we can assign a higher weight factor value to β and γ while reducing the value of α. Instead of reacting to the environmental change (power level) in a reactive manner as in the proposed energy model based L1O & L2O, the protocol operates proactively to balance traffic within the THAWS. For example, as shown in Table 1 with 7 nodes scenario, we first assign 0.5, 0.25 and 0.25 to α, β and γ to prioritse an energy-efficient sensor network application. We also assume node 1 is the source node and node 7 is the destination node (sink) which connects to the 6LowPan based IP network.

The label routing concept and routing table style originated in ATM networks [11] and has been introduced to the protocol since the position of the 25mm node

Table 1. An example weighted function calculation for 7 nodes

	αE	βD	γS	F
Node1	0.50	0.25	0.25	1.00
Node2	0.48	0.25	0.25	0.98
Node3	0.37	0.24	0.24	0.85
Node4	0.46	0.25	0.25	0.96
Node5	0.42	0.24	0.24	0.90
Node6	0.39	0.25	0.25	0.89
Node7	0.50	0.25	0.25	1.00

Table 2. An example label based added value calculation for 7 nodes

	Node1	Node2	Node3	Node4	Node5	Node6	Node7
Node1	N/A	1.98	1.85	N/A	N/A	N/A	N/A
Node2	1.98	N/A	1.83	1.94	N/A	N/A	N/A
Node3	1.85	1.83	N/A	N/A	N/A	N/A	N/A
Node4	N/A	1.94	N/A	N/A	1.86	1.85	1.96
Node5	N/A	N/A	N/A	1.86	N/A	1.79	N/A
Node6	N/A	N/A	N/A	N/A	1.79	N/A	1.89
Node7	N/A	N/A	N/A	1.96	N/A	1.89	N/A

is fixed and the label based switching provides faster packet forwarding than IP based indexing or other mature reactive routing protocol such as AODV and DSR. Instead of finding the next relay node hop by hop, the path from the source node to the sink node is identified by multiple labels where the label is represented by the added value of two neighbouring nodes $L_{a.b} = F_a + F_b$. Then the next actual node the source node is hopping to is decided by a comparison of the added value between next hopping neighbours as shown in Table 2. We can also understand that the path is separated by several labelled segments. The routing table at each 25mm node has seven message types: Label in, Label out, Source node, Destination node, Destination Sequence, Hop count and Time to live (TTL). The relay nodes only need to find the available entry indexed by label in the packet, swap it with respective label out of this entry, and then send it out to the next relay node.

Figure 5 illustrates the label exchange over seven 25mm nodes scenario. After compare the added weight value function $L_{a.b}$, source node 1 checks the sequence

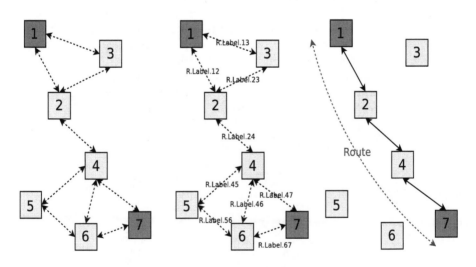

Fig. 5. The energy-aware power saving routing protocol illustration with fast label exchange

number (SEQ) of the destination node 7 in the current path in order to avoid old path information. It should be at least as great as the value entry in the current request otherwise the existing path in the table will be discarded. Another function of the SEQ is to compare with its older value to increase the hop count, e.g. if the source node can not find the destination node, it will increment the hop count by one and then broadcast it to its neighbours. The hop distance is not necessarily considered due to the fixed infrastructure and eventually balanced traffic distribution. However, it is defined that the path keeps the hop count as small as possible to avoid abused path violation. Meanwhile, the label request will repeat once for each connection request. The second plot in Figure 5 presents the propagation mechanism and the label based routing path segmentation. The third plot presents that the routing path has been established between the source Node 1, Node 2, Node 4, and the destination Node 7 after label message exchange and weight functions comparison.

4   Simulations

Before deploying C based code to both 10mm and 25mm Tyndall nodes, a discrete event simulation tool known as OMNeT++ [8] is used for the evaluations. The simulation provides facilities to model the communications between the nodes. It serves as a validation and optimisation tool for THAWS fast sensor network applications development and deployment.

In the experiment, 98 25mm nodes are modelled and placed in a 3000 m x 3000 m area and 196 10mm nodes are also randomly distributed. Each 10mm node is first associated with a 25mm node. For 25mm base station nodes, 7 of them are grouped as a cluster therefore 14 clusters are formed. The gateway (or say clusterhead for 6LowPan deployment) is randomly positioned at the cluster boundaries. At the beginning of the simulation, all 25mm nodes starts with full energy unit (1 Unit). With every reception, transmission and message exchange a 25mm node constantly decreases the energy at the active mode otherwise it is in the sleep mode. The 10mm node also starts with full energy unit. Node only periodically transmits data and then puts itself in sleep mode. Free space propagation model and Additive White Gaussian Noise (AWGN) environment are used. Each 25mm transmission range is set to 3 km while 10mm is set to 100 m. The network stack consists of physical layer, Address Resolution Protocol (ARP) module, modified 802.11 based slotted medium access module, link layer and interface priority queue. The bandwidth is fixed at 2 Mbps for a higher bound optimisation. The data is transmitted at Constant Bit Rate (CBR) at payload of 512 bytes with different deadlines. Data packets are generated at the source at a rate of 0.5, 1.0, 1.5, 2.0, 2.5 and 3.0 packets/s.

We have compared the performance of our THAWS energy-aware label based routing management (THAWS-R) with EAR and a modified classic AODV (without mobility header packets) protocol. The energy-model with L1O and L2O mechanisms proposed is also used at each 25mm node.

4.1 System Lifetime

Figure 6 compares the system lifetime for different route management approaches as it is a critical objective for the THAWS-R to achieve. The system life time parameter is scaled from 0-100 according to the system power left at all Tyndall 25mm and 10mm nodes. We first define system failure as the time after which 33% of sensor nodes run out of batteries that resulting in a routing hole. In the result, the simplified AODV presents the worst performance as expected because the system wide flooding produces a large number of signalling exchange over-head. The sensor system consumes a large amount of power at 25mm base station nodes when active. It has been proved that the protocol is neither adaptive nor energy-efficient also due to the route change latency. On the other hand, as a lin-ear energy model is used in each 25mm node, the rate of partial or system wide 25mm nodes power drainage is increased, which resulting in a shorter system lifetime. EAR gives a higher priority to energy-efficiency therefore it presents a better performance than AODV. However, it implements multicast instead of unicast, and does not consider a restricted neighbouring path finding mechanism with weight functions as compared to THAW-R, both the 25mm and 10mm will have to spend more time at active mode. As evident by the graph, the THAWS-R management is the most energy-efficient protocol when compared to the other two. It is able to balance node energy utilisation system wide and also accounts for the delay critical to real-time applications by using label routing mechanism.

Figure 7 presents the average active mode rate of all 25mm and 10mm nodes after a simulated 70 hours run. All packets are transmitted at 2 packets/s. From the results we notice that the node active mode rates using simplified AODV increase rapidly after 30 hours run. The trend is approaching the maximum when the simulation is finishing. The 25 sensor node consumes a large amount of battery power to find a route to the sink node. After a long run, many sensor nodes even go down if the detected events are not arriving at the sink node

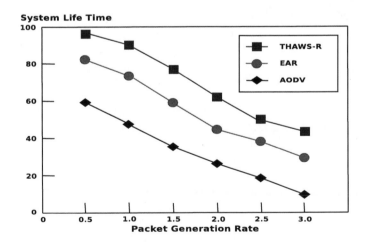

Fig. 6. System lifetime for different route management schemes and protocols

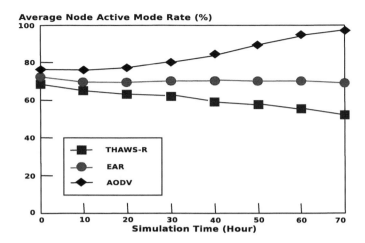

Fig. 7. Average nodes at active mode rate for different route management schemes and protocols

or due to power drainage. The rest of the sensor nodes have to make effort on path finding repeatedly and data forwarding, which results in more sensor nodes works at active mode. EAR protocol without an adaptive localised routing functions, presents a slight better results than the simplified AODV. During the 70 hours run, the average rate that nodes at active mode is smooth. Less nodes go down due to issues such as power drainage and the traffic is reasonably distributed across the system. However, this probability based approach mainly considers power criteria but not the packet delivery rate, delivery delay and link establishment speed. The proposed THAWS-R route management protocol, again, gives the best results against the other two. The active sensor node rate using distributed weight functions and label based route establishment even decreases with increasing simulation time. This is because the restricted flooding (local neighbour finding) and label routing help to construct adaptive routes to sink nodes across the system. The label indexing other than direct next hop indexing, greatly reduces the time that nodes spend on active mode.

4.2 Packet Delievery

For the packet level data delivery, it is important that traffic should reach the destination within the deadline, otherwise the data must be resent or recollected, which consumes nodes power. Our route management strategy is aware of packet delivery using the weighted Equation 2 thus low-rated routes (packet delivery error-prone paths) are avoided largely to make sure packets reaching the destination before the deadline proactively. AODV sends packet by different routes that increases the reliability. This is evident in Figure 8, where we have compared the packet delivery percentage with the deadlines. When the deadline is long enough, all three schemes achieve a satisfactory packet delivery percentage. When the

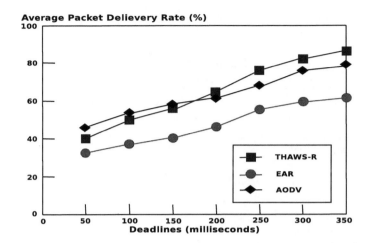

Fig. 8. Packet delivery ratio for different route management schemes and protocols

deadlines are configured more and more aggressive, the results show the delivery percentage reduces drastically for EAR protocol. The proposed THAWS routing scheme has a slightly higher successful delivery ratio than AODV with aggressive deadlines (starting from 200 milliseconds) due to its adaptivity. However, as stated previously, the THAWS weight function based routing can enhance one performance metric while worsening another. Therefore choosing the routing approach is greatly influenced by the performance qualification metrics, which are highly dependent on the nature of sensor network applications. If data delivery loss rate is of great interest, and latency and energy conservation are of concern, one might pick a higher weight factor to further enhance the system packet delivery rate.

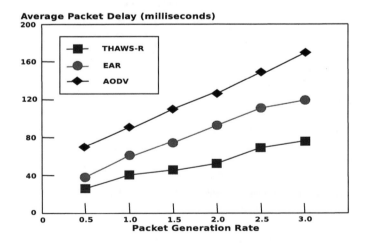

Fig. 9. Average packet delay for different route management schemes and protocols

For the average packet delay evaluation, the THAWS route management, again, gives the best performance when compared to the other two schemes as indicated in Figure 9. This is expected as the delay function has been included in the protocol to find the next hop node, the traffic has been evenly distributed with reduced congestion and the fast label routing speeds up the route establishment process. Meanwhile, AODV gives the worst result as it tries to exhaustively flood the system with large number of hops. This makes packets visit multiple nodes incurring more transmission and queuing delay. EAR presents a slightly better result than AODV but it also tries to minimise the transmission power by taking shorter distance, is not aware of system wide power utilisation, and chooses the next hop node solely based on geographic information with energy mapping.

5   Conclusions

This paper has presented a practical route management framework specifically for the Tyndall heterogeneous automated wireless sensor tool. The analysis and simulation results confirm that the proposed protocol and the 25mm tier energy model based dynamic load balancing significantly improve the platform performance in terms of node energy consumption, packet delivery delay and packet successful delivery ratio. Moreover, the lifetime of the overall THAWS tool is considerably increased. Future work will look at the deployment issues for the 10mm nodes and 25mm nodes and Tyndall nodes based embedded system software development and hardware updates.

References

1. Harte, S., Popovici, E., O'Flynn, B., O'Mathuna, C.: THAWS: Automated Design and Deployment of Heterogeneous Wireless Sensor Networks. WSEAS Trans. Circuits and Systems 7(9), 829–838 (2008)
2. Harte, S., O'Flynn, B., Martinez-Catal, R., Popovici, E.: Design and Implementation of a Miniaturised, Low Power Wireless Sensor Node. In: Proc. 18th Euro. Conf. Circuit Theory and Design, Seville, pp. 894–897 (2007)
3. Akyildiz, I., Su, W., Sankarasubramaniam, W., Cayirci, E.: Wireless Sensor Networks: a Survey. Computer Networks Elsevier Journal 38(4) (March 2002)
4. Heinzelman, W., Kulik, J., Balakrishnan, H.: Adaptive Protocols for Information Dissemination in wireless sensor networks. In: Proc. of IEEE MobiCom., Seattle, WA (August 1999)
5. Wattenhofer, R., Li, P., Wang, Y.: Distributed Topology Control for Power Efficient Operation in Multihop Wireless Ad Hoc Networks. In: Proc. of IEEE InfoCom (April 2001)
6. Ganesan, D., Govindan, R., Shenker, S., Estrin, D.: Highly-Resilient, Energy-Efficient Multipath Routing in Wireless Sensor Networks. Mobile Computing and Communications Review, 1–2 (1997)
7. Shah, R., Rabaey, J.: Energy Aware Routing for Low Energy Ad Hoc Sensor Networks. In: Proc. of IEEE WCNC, Orlando, FL (March 2002)

8. Varga, A.: Using the OMNeT++ Discrete Event Simulation System in Education. IEEE Trans. on Education 42(4) (1999)
9. CLARITY: The Centre for Sensor Web Technologies Bringing Information to Life, http://www.clarity-centre.com
10. Chazelle, B., Rubinfeld, Trevisan, L.: Approximating the Minimum Spanning Tree Weight in Sublinear Time. Computation Journal, 1370–1379, 34 (2005)
11. Leon-Garia, A., Widjaja, I.: Communications Networks. McGraw-Hill, New York (1999)

All Roads Lead to Rome: Data Highways for Dense Wireless Sensor Networks[*]

David Lowe[1,2] and Daniele Miorandi[2]

[1] Centre for Real-Time Information Networks, UTS, Ultimo, NSW 2007, Australia
`david.lowe@uts.edu.au`
[2] CREATE-NET, v. alla Cascata 56/D, 38123 – Povo, Trento, IT
{`daniele.miorandi,david.lowe`}`@create-net.org`

Abstract. The design of efficient routing algorithms is an important issue in dense ad hoc wireless networks. Previous work has shown that benefits can be achieved through the creation of a set of data "highways" that carry packets across the network, from source(s) to sink(s). Current approaches to the design of these highways however require a–priori knowledge of the global network topology, with consequent communications burden and scalability issues, particularly with regard to reconfiguration after node failures. In this paper we describe an approach to generating these data highways through a distributed reaction-diffusion model that uses localised convolution with activation-inhibition filters. The result is the distributed emergence of data highways that can be tuned to provide appropriate highway separation and connection to data sinks. We present the underlying models and the algorithms for generating the highways, as well as preliminary simulation results.

Keywords: Wireless sensor networks, routing, data highways, activation–inhibition mechanisms, reaction–diffusion patterns.

1   Introduction

A key issue in dense ad hoc wireless networks is the design of efficient routing algorithms. This can affect the performance of the resultant system in terms of power efficiency, communication latency and robustness. For example, an efficient routing algorithm can lead to reductions in both the number of network nodes that need to remain awake to route traffic and the total transmission power required for the multi–hop communication along the routing path from data source to data sink.

Previous work [10] has shown that the creation of a set of wireless "backbones" or data highways that carry packets across the network, from source to sink, can provide a network capacity that follows the same pattern for randomly located nodes as can be achieved for arbitrarily placed nodes. In effect, the highways are

[*] This work has been partially supported by the European Commission within the framework of the BIONETS project EU-IST-FET-SAC-FP6-027748, `www.bionets.eu`

S. Hailes, S. Sicari, and G. Roussos (Eds.): S-Cube 2009, LNICST 24, pp. 189–205, 2009.

constructed such that every source node is within range of at least one highway (implying it can access it in a single hop). The highways then drain packets to the sinks along a series of shorter length hops, with correspondingly lower power requirements and hence a lower interference footprint.

In previous work, these highways have been constructed based on approaches such as percolation theory [10]. This has the disadvantage that it requires an a–priori analysis of the entire network structure, with the consequence that the approaches cannot readily accommodate randomly placed nodes unless there is a mechanism for determining and communicating node location — a constraint that adds a layer of complexity and a performance burden. It also typically makes the network less robust, as any change (such as a failure or location change of a highway node) requires a global recalculation of the routing pathways.

In this paper we discuss an approach to addressing this problem through distributed determination of the data highways based on an activation-inhibition diffusion that generates optimal highway separation. We argue that this approach represents a significant contribution, insofar as it will improve robustness and allow localised self–healing of the data highways — an important characteristic of dense networks with randomly placed nodes.

In section 2 we discuss previous work in this area and in particular on the application of distributed diffusion model for engineering the emergence of patterns in large–scale networks. Following this, in section 3, we consider the models that underpin the highway generation and the mechanisms that we have used for their distributed construction. Section 4 discusses the way in which data is then routed within this data highway system, and section 5 presents preliminary results and analysis showing the performance of the approach. Finally, we present our conclusions in section 6.

2   Related Work

Wireless sensor networks (WSNs) [1] have become an important tool in many real–world settings. For example, they are being increasingly used for the monitoring of environmental parameters, where nodes are deployed over space, each node sensing a given environmental parameter (temperature, light, level of pollutants etc.). In most real–world settings multiple sinks are present, each sink being connected, usually through some form of long–range wireless communications, with a remote data center where information is processed. When fine–grained information is needed, the net result can be – from a communications perspective – the formation of dense WSNs.

Current state–of–the–art routing schemes for WSNs, for communicating sensory data to the sinks, are most often based on the construction of trees, a structure that lends itself naturally to perform en route aggregation of data [7]. For dense WSNs, various authors have proposed optimal routing strategies based on the use of a continuum model of node placement over space. In particular, routing strategies based on analogies with physical phenomena have been proposed (optics [12,6] and electromagnetism [17]), as well as routing strategies built using models inspired by road traffic engineering [2].

In their seminal work, Gupta and Kumar [11] proved that the communication capacity of (dense) ad hoc networks, with n nodes within a given area, can scale, in terms of per source–destination throughput, as $\frac{1}{\sqrt{n}}$ bit/s in the case of arbitrary node placement and as $\frac{1}{\sqrt{n \log n}}$ in the case of randomly (uniformly) located nodes. The existence of such a gap gave rise to various investigations, aimed at finding suitable strategies for closing it. This is particularly important given that many (indeed possibly most) sensor networks are likely to have nodes that are randomly placed.

In a series of papers, Franceschetti et al. [10] demonstrated, using tools and results from percolation theory, that such a gap could be closed by introducing non–uniform transmission power schemes. The concept of data highways was introduced in [10], where it was shown that it was always possible to build high–throughput paths crossing a given section of the network. Such paths result in high–throughput as they can be operated at very low transmission power, hence limiting self–interference. The optimal routing strategy would then be: (i) from a source reach the closest highway with a single (possibly high–power) hop; (ii) route packets along the highway using low–power hops; (iii) drain packets from the highway to the appropriate sink when in proximity. Such a scheme was shown to be able to attain a throughput per source–destination pair of the order of $\frac{1}{\sqrt{n}}$, thereby effectively closing the gap in the Gupta–Kumar result. A sample representation of a set of data highways is reported in Fig. 1 (taken from [10]).

The intuition behind such a result is that by using highways it is possible to limit mutual interference among nodes in the network. To the best of the authors' knowledge, however, such a result has not yet found any application to routing problems in realistic environments. The main difficulty is the construction of highways. In order to have a feasible solution (in terms of scalability and complexity), the formation of highways should be achieved by means of a distributed process based on local information only. Rather than a global design of the highways, the nodes should self–organize to achieve the desired spatial

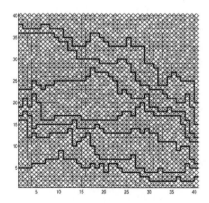

Fig. 1. Typical data highways through a 40x40 grid, obtained using a bond percolation model (from [10])

structures that can in turn be used to generate the data highways. This raises the question of what form of self–organising process may be relevant in this particular scenario?

The use of self–organizing processes has seen wide consideration. For example, their use for building "spatial" computers was at the heart of the MIT's Amorphous Computing initiative[1]. One of the application scenarios envisioned for the (programming) techniques developed within the framework of such an initiative was to engineer the emergence of structures in sensor–actuator networks [4].

The use of related self–organizing spatial processes for building overlays found applications in various networking fields. In WSNs, Bicocchi et al. proposed to use a field–based mechanism for aggregating WSNs into logical neighborhoods [5]. In peer–to–peer systems, probabilistic distributed mechanisms were proposed by Jelasity et al. for dynamically rewiring links in overlays [14,13]. In particular, it was shown that, by relying on local interactions only, it was possible to build system–level structures with desired topological properties.

In [16] Saffre and Shackleton propose the use of an embryogenies–inspired mechanism for efficiently allocating 'roles' in an autonomic manner in a peer–to–peer service infrastructure. In such a work, nodes communicate via gossiping techniques, and differentiation decisions are taken at each node based on the nodes' current status and the status of neighbours. The mechanism is reported to be able to build efficient structures (in terms of topology and role assignments).

Possibly the most relevant form of self-organising process to our particular problem are reaction-diffusion processes. These processes are at the basis of various natural mechanisms that result in the emergence of patterns, in particular of cell differentiation and morphogenesis [3]. The use of reaction–diffusion processes (and in particular of activation–inhibition mechanisms) has been proposed in the context of ad hoc networks to deal with activation problems. In particular, it has been proposed by Durvy and Thiran for dealing with activation at the MAC level [9] and by Neglia et al. for addressing clustering problems in WSNs [15]. In both cases, the pattern to be created presents isolated activation peaks (corresponding to 'active nodes') divided by large valleys. Such patterns are different from those needed to engineer data highways, which require the creation of zebra–like stripes, which should furthermore converge to one of the sinks present in the network. We will consider these processes in more detail, and how we might adapt them, in the following section.

3   Models and Mechanisms for Data Highways Formation

3.1   Reaction Diffusion Modeling

As outlined above, we wish to develop self-organising processes that lead to the natural emergence of data highways through a wireless network. These highways need to be optimally spaced such that all nodes are within a single hop of a highway, but the highways themselves utilise short-range hops to transport data

---

[1] http://groups.csail.mit.edu/mac/projects/amorphous/

to any data sink. This concept was shown in Figure 1. Further, the highways should be able to be derived only through local interactions between nodes.

In developing an approach to this problem, we have taken inspiration from mechanisms that utilise activation-inhibition reaction-diffusion [3,9,15]. These mechanisms describe how a field strength variable or substance concentration within each cell or node can vary in space and time under a pair of competing influences – a short range positive activation region within which the field of neigbouring cells is strengthened, and a longer range negative inhibition region within which the field of neighbour cells is retarded – with the resultant emergence of specific patterns when the effects are diffused through the network. The resultant models have been used widely to describe behaviours in biological and physical processes (see [8] for a discussion). The simplest formulation of this approach, using a single field variable, is modelled in the discrete time domain as follows:

$$u(\mathbf{k}, t+1) = g\left(\varphi_s u(\mathbf{k}, t) + \sum_{\mathbf{j} \in R_i} \varphi_i(\mathbf{j}) u(\mathbf{k}+\mathbf{j}, t) + \sum_{\mathbf{j} \in R_a} \varphi_a(\mathbf{j}) u(\mathbf{k}+\mathbf{j}, t)\right) \quad (1)$$

where $u(\mathbf{k}, t)$ is the field strength in cell $\mathbf{k}$ at time t, R_i is the region over which the inhibition function φ_i is applied, R_a is the region over which the activation function φ_a is applied, and $g()$ is a limiting function. The activation functions are time invariant, and applied uniformly across the sensor field. Note that this is equivalent to the convolution of $u(t)$ with the sum of φ_i, φ_a and the self-activation value φ_s. Note also that, in general, it is assumed that φ_i takes negative values, while φ_a and φ_s take positive values.

As discussed in the previous section, recent work has adapted reaction diffusion models to the design and/or configuration of wireless networks. As an example, Neglia and Reina [15] have used activator-inhibitor diffusion to select active nodes within a dense wireless sensor network. The nodes have deeply overlapping sensing fields, and hence only a small number of nodes are required to be active in order to adequately provide full data on the region to be sensed. The operation of this approach can be seen in Figure 2. A random dense wireless sensor network (Figure 2a) is repeatedly convolved with a symmetric 2-dimensional diffusion filter (Figure 2b). The resultant field strength after 20 iterations of a filter[2] (Figure 2d) is then analysed to determine local maxima (Figure 2e) – which represent the nodes to be activated. All other nodes can be switched to a low-power non-sensing state. The result is a distributed process for identifying a subset of nodes to be activated, such the nodes are suitably distributed.

The repeated filter convolution causes the emergence of the peaks in the activation field by activating localised regions whilst inhibiting the areas between these regions. The width of the inhibition zone controls the separation of the resultant peaks and the width of the activation zone controls the kurtosis of

---

[2] The filter used in this case was a simplified version, with a central self-activation strength $\varphi_s = 2$, a flat activation ring of strength $\varphi_a = 1$ and radius 1, and a flat inhibition ring of strength $\varphi_i = -0.1$ and radius 6.

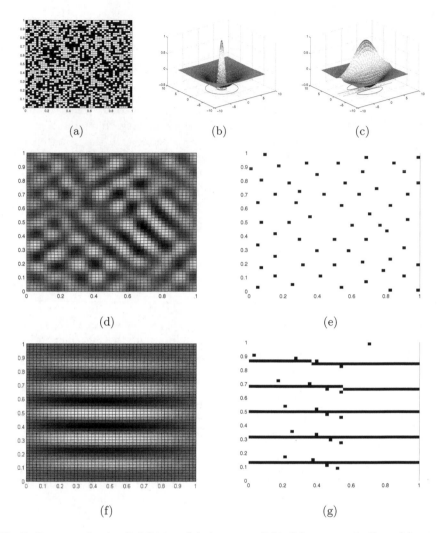

Fig. 2. Sensor activation/inhibition: (a) the sensor field; (b) symmetric filter; (c) rotationally asymmetric filter; (d) activation field resulting from symmetric diffusion filter; (e) detected peaks in field; (f) activation field resulting from asymmetric diffusion filter; (g) detected ridges in field

the peaks. It is therefore possible to select filter parameters that ensure that an optimal density of active nodes is obtained. The filter used in the activation-inhibition diffusion can be readily implemented in a distributed fashion, provided each node has knowledge of the diffusion filter parameters to be used. Each node communicates with its neighbours, and acts to either strengthen or weaken their resultant activation field. The nodes also can then through comparison with neighbour nodes' current activation strengths, determine whether they are at a local maxima and hence should be active. This means that this approach can be fully distributed within a wireless network, leading to active node selection with no network-wide oversight.

3.2   Highway Generation

What we are seeking in the design of the data highways is analogous to this – the localised selection of the nodes which form the highways without any global design or control. The natural question to ask is therefore whether or not an activation-inhibition diffusion model can be adapted such that the result is connected nodes that together make data highways, rather than single active nodes.

The solution is based on changing the nature of the diffusion filter. Previous work on wireless networks has used symmetric filters, leading to the emergence of patterns that have isolated peaks in the sensor activation field. Work in other areas (e.g. [8]) has shown that changing the nature of the diffusion filter can lead to changes in the patterns that emerge in the activation field. As an example, consider the bottom row of Figure 2. In this case the random dense wireless sensor network is repeatedly convolved with a rotationally asymmetric filter that has a dominant horizontal activation axis, whilst inhibiting along the vertical axis (Figure 2c). The resultant field strength patter after 20 iterations of a filter that has this structure is shown in (Figure 2f). This has developed a striped pattern of ridges and troughs, with the orientation controlled by the orientation of the activation axis in the filter and the separation determined by the range of the filter inhibition. The ridges in this pattern can then be used to determine local ridge maxima (Figure 2g) – giving the potential data highways that we are seeking. Nodes at ridge maxima become highway nodes, and all other nodes communicate with the highways in order to deliver data to desired data sinks. By tuning the filter parameters appropriately, we can control the separation between the highways, and thereby ensure that all non-highway nodes are within a single hop of a highway.

3.3   Controlling Highway Orientation and Destination

Having demonstrated that it is possible to generate 'striped' patterns that can be used to generate highways, we next consider the question of how we orient these stripes so that the highways converge on data sinks. One possibility is to construct artificial "bridges" between the highways and relevant sinks (taking into account the overall topology as well as load balancing between the sinks). These bridges can be either multi-hop paths, or could be a single high-power connection. In either case, this solution requires the artificial construction of additional routes[3].

An alternative is to investigate whether it is possible to control the directions of the highways such that as the ridges are generated during the diffusion process,

---

[3] This is actually the solution originally discussed in [10].

they naturally converge to the data sinks. Given that the orientation of the ridges are controlled by the orientation of the activation axis in the filter, we should therefore be able to create ridges that converge on a sink by making the direction of the filter activation axis spatially dependent.

Consider the case of a network field with a single sink. Each node in the network determines the direction to that sink, and rotates its local instance of the diffusion filter so that the activation axis is aligned with the direction to the sink. The diffusion filter contains a square inhibition zone R_i of dimension $2R \times 2R$ (with an inhibition level of φ_i), and a wedge-shaped activation zone R_a with an angular size ρ (with an activation level of φ_a). We rotate the filter by rotating just the activation band within the overall square filter.

Applying this filter so that the activation band is always oriented towards the single sink gives an activation field as shown in Figure 3a, with all ridges having a dominant orientation towards the sink. Performing a ridge detection on this then gives the ridges shown in Figure 3b[4]. A simple growth of any ridge point that is at the end of a ridge can be used as a final step in connecting any isolated data highways, to form a connected data highway network.

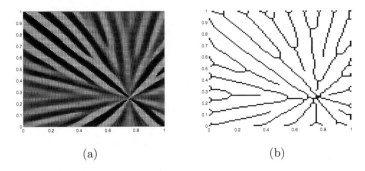

(a)   (b)

Fig. 3. Sensor activation/inhibition with local filters rotated towards a single sink: (a) activation field resulting from rotated filters; (b) detected ridges in field

If we add additional data sinks then the filter orientation, and hence the activation field orientation, can be derived based on a gravitational attraction model. For each node, the activation field direction should be a weighted sum of the directions to each sink, with the weight inversely proportional to the square of the distance to the sink. In other words, the direction of the diffusion filter at node N_i can be given by the vector D_i:

$$D_i = \frac{\sum_{j \in \mathcal{S}} (N_i - S_j)|N_i - S_j|^{-2}}{\sum_{j \in \mathcal{S}} |N_i - S_j|^{-2}} \tag{2}$$

where $\mathcal{S}$ is the set of sink nodes S_i.

---

[4] It is worth remarking that, whereas for the detection of single points a 2-dimensional local maxima was used, in this case the ridge detection is done by looking for local maxima in only one dimension perpendicular to the filter orientation.

As with the previous example, this approach is still able to be implemented in a distributed fashion. The only aspect that unavoidably requires global knowledge is the relative location of the data sinks – or rather, whilst each node does need to know its own location, it does need to know the direction and (network) distance to each sink. Without this knowledge it would be impossible to locally orient the filter, and hence activation bands and the resultant highways. Knowledge of the sinks can however be readily achieved through a broadcast beacon signal from each sink node when it activates. The beacon propagates through the network, with each node recording the number of hops to each sink from each of its neighbour nodes, and hence the distance and dominant direction. In the next section, we will present a distributed procedure for gathering such information at each node in the network.

4   Routing on Data Highways

Let us now consider the algorithms for implementing the models discussed above, as well as how the resultant highways are then used to route data. We assume the following:

- Nodes are assigned a unique identifier;
- Nodes can tune dynamically their transmission power level P_{tx} in the range $[P_{min}, P_{max}]$;
- The network is connected when all nodes use $P_{tx} = P_{min}$;
- Nodes transmit at P_{min} unless otherwise specified.

Each node maintains the following data structures:

- A database of all data sink(s), called $sinkDB$, having entries of the type $< sinkID, distance >$, where $distance$ denotes the (minimum) distance in terms of number of hops from a given sink;
- a database for the state of neighbouring nodes, where the size of the neighbourhood is determined by the filter to be applied, as detailed in Sec. 3. We denote by $nodeDB$ such a database, whose entries have the form $< nodeID, distance, state, sinkDB >$, where $nodeID$ is the identifier of a node in the neighbourhood, $distance$ is its minimum distance (in hops) from the given node, $state$ is its current state (activation level) and $sinkDB$ is a data structure containing information on distance from the sinks present in the network.

We first detail the algorithms necessary for initializing the network and setting up the highways. The algorithms work in two steps. First, sinks need to announce their presence, and nodes to compute their distance from them. To accomplish such a task, sinks broadcast a beacon message ($sinkBeacon$) containing both their $sinkID$ and a $distance$ field in the header. The field $distance$ is initialised to one. Nodes receiving the beacon check if an entry with the same $sinkID$ is present in their $sinkDB$. If there is no entry, or the $distance$ field in the received beacon is less than the $distance$ in the stored entry, then the $sinkDB$ is updated, the *distance* field is incremented by one and the beacon is forwarded on. In such a way, the field *distance* in the sinkBeacon corresponds to the minimum distance (in hops) from the corresponding sink. At the end of the process each node has the complete list of sinks in the network and the corresponding distance from any of them. Such an information is needed for setting up the filter, as outlined in Sec. 3. A detailed description of the algorithm is reported in the App. A (Alg. 1).

The next step is to let nodes construct their neighbourhood map, according to the filter parameters (in particular the dimension of the activation/inhibition neighbourhood, denoted by the filter radius R parameter[5]). In order to do so, they need to collect information about the state of their k–hop neighbours ($k \leq R$) and their distance from the sinks present in the system, as outlined in the previous section. Such a procedure is then repeated periodically to maintain an updated view of the system state. This process is carried out using a gossip–based mechanism for spreading information about nodes' state in a distributed fashion. Each node periodically broadcasts a *nodeQuery* message, where it includes its own ID, current activation state and the information contained in the sinkDB (i.e., distance from any sink). Upon reception of a *nodeQuery* message, one–hop neighbours first update the state field of the corresponding nodeDB entry. Then, they query their own nodeDB for information about the state of nodes that are at distance (in hops) less than or equal to $(R-1)$. This retrieves all information that is at most R hops from the node issuing the original query. The information collected is then included in an acknowledgment message that is sent back to the node originating the query. A detailed description of the algorithm is reported in the App. A (Alg. 2)[6]. Once each node has the relevant filter information they are able to recalculate their activation level, and subsequently compare this to neighbouring values to determine if they are a "ridge" node, and hence on a highway.

Given the mechanisms for building data highways, we now need to introduce mechanisms for routing messages containing sensed data from any node to one of the sinks present in the system. The routing protocol envisioned can be broadly divided in two phases. In the first phase, nodes not belonging to an highway have to find a way to reach one. This is done by simply broadcasting a beacon message with increasing transmission power (and hence communication range) until a node on an highway is reached and sends back an acknowledgment message. Such a node will constitute the entry point to the highway. From that moment on, all messages generated will be forwarded to the entry point. A detailed description of the algorithm is reported in the App. A (Alg. 3). Note that if at

---

[5] The parameter R, which roughly correspond to the distance among highways, should be chosen in such a way to ensure that, by transmitting at P_{max}, a node will be able to join an highway.

[6] With such a procedure, information on the state of nodes is received incrementally, each round bringing information to nodes located one hop further. When bootstrapping the system, it takes R rounds to acquire the knowledge necessary for building the filter.

any point there is a failure in a highway node, the source node can repeat the above process to locate a new highway entry point.

The second phase is concerned with the routing of messages along an highway, in order to reach an appropriate sink. In general, following the procedure highlighted in the previous section, we will achieve highways connected to one single sink. However, the activation–inhibition mechanism presented in Sec. 3 cannot prevent highways to be connected to two or more sinks. In order to optimize the usage of resources, messages should be directed towards the closest sink.[7] Once the highway setup phase is completed, nodes on the highway(s) will reset their sinkDB data base. Sinks will then broadcast a beacon message (*beaconSinkH*), which will be propagated only by nodes belonging to an highway. Such messages will include a *distance* field that will be initially set to 1. Upon reception of such a message, nodes on the highway(s) will check their internal sinkDB data base; if an entry corresponding to the sink ID is already present, it is updated if the distance contained in the beacon is smaller than that maintained in the corresponding entry of the data base. The beacon message is then relayed, after having increased by one the value of the *distance* field. A detailed description of the algorithm is reported in the App. A (Alg. 4).

As with reconnecting of source nodes to highways, the highways themselves are also able to self-heal. When the failure of a highway node is detected by a neighbouring highway node being unable to route traffic to the failed node, the neighbour can trigger a new localised diffusion process, that leads to the emergence of new highway in the local region of the failed node. Given the local nature of this process, this resultant highway will be operational, but may not be optimal. Whilst the highway is being used, further diffusion can progressively refine the highway route. The result is an inherent self-healing of the network.

5   Numerical Example

In order to illustrate the approach we have developed, we provide a simple example. Figure 4a shows a sample 200×200 wireless node grid. We have then allocated three sink nodes at $(25, 140)$, $(120, 180)$, and $(175, 25)$. We have assumed a maximum communication desired range of 5 units (from a non-highway node to a highway node). Consequently a distributed diffusion filter is implemented by each node, with a radius $R = 5$ hops. Other parameters used were a self-activation factor $\varphi_s = 1.5$, a constant mutual activation factor $\varphi_a = 0.7$, a constant inhibition factor $\varphi_i = -0.3$, and an activation band with angular width $\rho = \pm 20 \deg$. This was then simulated in Matlab. Note that the simulation assumed a simple communication model that focused on routing behaviours, and assumed communication links that varied within a fixed range. Further work will need to investigate the validity of these assumptions. and the consequences when they fail.

---

[7] It is worth remarking that the 'distance' in this case has to be understood as distance along the highway, and not as distance on the connectivity graph of the network as computed at system initialisation phase.

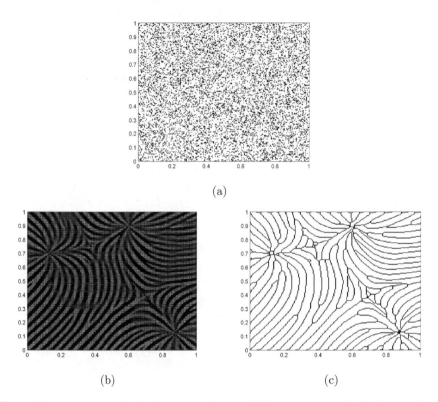

(a)

(b)   (c)

Fig. 4. Determination of wireless network data highways in a multiple sink environment: (a) Example node field (200 x 200 grid); (b) resultant activation field; (c) derived data highways from ridges in activation field

The resultant activation field after 20 iterations of the simulated convolution is shown in Figure 4b. From this it is possible to see clearly the pattern of ridges that form, and in particular, the way in which the mechanism for calculating the directionality of the diffusion filter has led to ridges that converge on the data sinks. In numerous cases, as the ridges converge on the sinks, two or more ridges merge into a single ridge, thereby keeping the spatial separation of the ridges constant.

It is also worth noting that the resultant pattern exhibits some unusual artefacts. For example, there are several unusual bands that run orthogonally to the main ridges. We are still investigating these, though our current hypothesis is that they arise from the interactions that are occurring when different localised ridge patterns spread, and meet, during the diffusion process. These localised ridge patterns emerge early due to high local node densities. These artifacts do not appear to be problematic, though we are currently investigating this further.

From the ridge patterns we are then able to extract local ridge maxima, and then post-process these ridge maxima to ensure full connectivity is achieved. The result of this is shown in Figure 4c. As can be seen from this figure, we have a connected network of localised highways that can carry data to one or more data sinks. No non-highway node is further than 5 units from the nearest highway node, as desired.

Note that we have not yet evaluated the performance load that this approach places on the network. We are current implementing an OMNeT++ simulation to investigate this issue.

6   Conclusions and Discussion

As outlined in Section 1, the design of efficient routing algorithms is a key issue in wireless ad hoc networks. In this paper we have described an approach to the distributed design of data highways for use in routing data within dense wireless sensor networks. The algorithms developed allow these data highways to emerge naturally from localised processing in the network, without requiring network-wide knowledge or oversight, while still ensuring that design criteria are met. In particular, the highways will converge to the data sinks and ensure a maximum highway separation that allows all non–highway nodes to be within a desired maximum distance of a data highway.

As discussed in Section 4 it is expected that this approach will lead naturally to self-healing of the network – in terms of regeneration of the highways in the event of a sink failure, localised recalculation of highway routes in the event of the failure of a highway node, and reconnection of source nodes to the highways when necessary. Ongoing work will explore these self-healing characteristics.

Other questions that remain open, and represent ongoing research, relate to refining the mechanisms for determining the local diffusion mechanisms and on considering the impacts of the sink locations.

In terms of the local filter orientation, our current implementation assumes that each node is aware of its location and that of each sink, and can hence directly calculate the orientation of the activation band in the diffusion filter. As discussed in Section 3.3 it is possible for local nodes to obtain sufficient information about sink distance and direction through a sink beacon process. We are currently exploring the implementation of a simulation based on this principle.

A further refinement that is yet to be analysed in depth involves a modification to the convolution process that removes the need for local knowledge of the sink directions and only requires distance information. Rather than applying the diffusion as a direct convolution of a fixed (albeit locally rotated) filter, it may be possible to directly diffuse the activation-inhibition data, and the receiving node determines itself whether to treat the diffusion from a neighbour as an activation or an inhibition based on distance parameters. If the distance from the receiving node to the nearest sink is similar enough to the distance from the diffusing node to the sink, then the diffusion is treated as an inhibition (since both need not be on a highway). Conversely, if the distances are sufficiently different, then it is treated as an activation, since they can be on the same highway. Further investigation will explore whether this approach is feasible.

Finally, another key avenue for further exploration is to consider the impact of sink location on the structure of the data highways. In particular, it may be possible to selectively position the sinks in order to allow the highways to be tuned, and the data loads across the highways to be optimally balanced.

References

1. Akyildiz, I.F., Su, W., Sankarasubramaniam, Y., Cayirci, E.: Wireless sensor networks: a survey. Computer Networks 38(4), 393–422 (2002)
2. Altman, E., Bernhard, P., Silva, A.: The mathematics of routing in massively dense ad-hoc networks. In: Coudert, D., Simplot-Ryl, D., Stojmenovic, I. (eds.) ADHOC-NOW 2008. LNCS, vol. 5198, pp. 122–134. Springer, Heidelberg (2008)
3. Bar-Yam, Y.: Dynamics Of Complex Systems. Westview Press (2003)
4. Beal, J., Bachrach, J.: Infrastructure for engineered emergence on sensor/actuator networks. IEEE Intelligent Systems 21(2), 10–19 (2006)
5. Bicocchi, N., Mamei, M., Zambonelli, F.: Towards self-organizing virtual macro sensors. In: Proc. of IEEE SASO, pp. 355–358 (2007)
6. Catanuto, R., Toumpis, S., Morabito, G.: Opti{c, m}al: Optical/optimal routing in massively dense wireless networks. In: Proc. of IEEE INFOCOM, pp. 1010–1018 (2007)
7. Ciciriello, P., Mottola, L., Picco, G.P.: Efficient routing from multiple sources to multiple sinks in wireless sensor networks. In: Langendoen, K.G., Voigt, T. (eds.) EWSN 2007. LNCS, vol. 4373, pp. 34–50. Springer, Heidelberg (2007)
8. Deutsch, A., Dormann, S.: Cellular automaton modeling of biological pattern formation: characterization, applications, and analysis. Birkhäuser, Basel (2005)
9. Durvy, M., Thiran, P.: Reaction-diffusion based transmission patterns for ad hoc networks. In: Proc. of IEEE INFOCOM, pp. 2195–2205 (2005)
10. Franceschetti, M., Dousse, O., Tse, D.N.C., Thiran, P.: Closing the gap in the capacity of wireless networks via percolation theory. IEEE Transactions on Information Theory 53(3), 1009–1018 (2007)
11. Gupta, P., Kumar, P.R.: The capacity of wireless networks. IEEE Transactions on Information Theory 46(2), 388–404 (2000)
12. Jacquet, P.: Geometry of information propagation in massively dense ad hoc networks. In: Proc. of ACM MobiHoc, pp. 157–162 (2004)
13. Jelasity, M.: Engineering emergence through gossip. In: Proceedings of the Joint Symposium on Socially Inspired Computing, AISB Convention, Hatfield, UK, pp. 123–126 (2005)
14. Jelasity, M., Babaoglu, O.: T-man: Gossip-based overlay topology management. In: Brueckner, S.A., Di Marzo Serugendo, G., Hales, D., Zambonelli, F. (eds.) ESOA 2005. LNCS (LNAI), vol. 3910, pp. 1–15. Springer, Heidelberg (2006)
15. Neglia, G., Reina, G.: Evaluating activator-inhibitor mechanisms for sensors coordination. In: Proc. of Bionetics, Budapest, Hungary, ICST (2007)
16. Saffre, F., Shackleton, M.: "Embryo": an autonomic co-operative service management framework. In: Bullock, S., Noble, J., Watson, R., Bedau, M.A. (eds.) Artificial Life XI: Proceedings of the Eleventh International Conference on the Simulation and Synthesis of Living Systems, pp. 513–520. MIT Press, Cambridge (2008)
17. Toumpis, S., Tassiulas, L.: Packetostatics: deployment of massively dense sensor networks as an electrostatics problem. In: Proc. of IEEE INFOCOM, pp. 2290–2301 (2005)

A   Detailed Algorithms Description

Procedure at the sink(s)
$distance \leftarrow 1$ {Set distance field to 1}
broadcast($sinkBeacon, sinkID, distance$) {Sink broadcasts beacon}

Procedure at other nodes
receive($sinkBeacon, sinkID, distance$) {Node receives a beacon}
if $sinkID$ already present as $sinkDB(k)$ **then**
  if $sinkDB(k).distance < distance$ **then**
    return {Terminate, as already have a shorter path}
  else
    $sinkDB(k).distance \leftarrow distance$ {Store new shorter path}
  end if
else
  $sinkDB.create(sinkID, distance)$ {Add new sinkDB entry}
end if
broadcast ($sinkBeacon, sinkID, distance + 1$) {Node forwards beacon}

Algorithm 1. Sink(s) announcement procedure

Announcement procedure at each node
$nodeDist \leftarrow 1$
broadcast($nodeQuery, R, nodeID, state, sinkDB$)

Response to a query message
receive($nodeQuery, R, nodeID, state, sinkDB$)
if $nodeID$ already present as $nodeDB(k)$ **then**
    $nodeDB(k).state \leftarrow state$ {Update state}
else
    $nodeDB.create(nodeID, 1, state, sinkDB)$ {Add new nodeDB entry, distance field
    set to 1}
end if
create empty list tmp
for all entry k in nodeDB **do**
    if $nodeDB(k).nodeID \neq nodeID$ & $nodeDB(k).nodeDist + 1 \leq R$ **then**
        $tmp.add(< nodeDB(k).nodeID, nodeDB(k).distance + 1, nodeDB(k).state$
        $, nodeDB(k).sinkDB >)$ {Add entry k of nodeDB to the list}
    end if
end for
send($nodeQueryACK, list$) {Send response}

Update of nodeDB at each node
receive($nodeQueryACK, < nodeID_1, nodeDist_1, state_1, sinkDB_1 >, \ldots,$
$< nodeID_h, nodeDist_h, state_h, sinkDB_h >)$ {Node receives an ACK message with
information on state of neighbours}
for all $i = 1$ to h **do**
    if $nodeID_i$ already present as $nodeDB(k)$ **then**
        $nodeDB(k).state \leftarrow state_i$ {Update state}
        if $nodeDB(k).distance > nodeDist_i$) **then**
            $nodeDB(k).distance \leftarrow nodeDist_i$ {Update distance}
        end if
    else
        $nodeDB.create(nodeID_i, nodeDist_i, state_i, sinkDB_i)$ {Add new nodeDB en-
        try}
    end if
end for

Algorithm 2. Initialisation and update of filter at each node

---

At nodes not on highways
$nextHop \leftarrow 0$
while $nextHop = 0$ **do**
  send($beaconNotHighway, nodeID$)
  if no reply within τ **then**
    increase P_{tx} until P_{max} is reached
  else
    receive($beaconNotHighwayACK, nodeHighwayID$)
    $nextHop \leftarrow nodeHighwayID$
  end if
end while

At nodes on highways
receive($beaconNotHighway, nodeID$)
send($beaconNotHighwayACK, ID$)

Algorithm 3. Routing along highways

Initialisation: at the sink node(s).
$distance \leftarrow 1$
broadcast($sinkBeaconH, ID, distance$)

Initialisation: at the highway nodes.
reset sinkDB
receive($sinkBeaconH, sinkID, distance$)
if $sinkID$ already present as $sinkDB(k)$ **then**
  if $sinkDB(k).distance < distance$ **then**
    return {Terminate, as already have a shorter path}
  else
    $sinkDB(k).distance \leftarrow distance$ {Update distance}
  end if
else
  $sinkDB.create(sinkID, distance)$ {add new sinkDB entry}
end if
broadcast($sinkBeaconH, sinkID, distance + 1$) {Node forwards beacon to other nodes on the highway.}

Highway nodes announcing distance
$myDistance \leftarrow \arg \min_{sinkDB} distance$ {Computes minimum distance from a sink.}
broadcast($beaconHighway, nodeID, myDistance$)

Highway nodes updating next hop
receive($beaconHighway, nodeID, distance$)
if $distance = myDistance - 1$ **then**
  $nextHop \leftarrow nodeID$
end if

Algorithm 4. Building routes: procedures for nodes on highways

Sensor Data Fusion for Activity Monitoring in Ambient Assisted Living Environments

M. Amoretti[1,5], F. Wientapper[2], F. Furfari[3], S. Lenzi[3], and S. Chessa[3,4]

[1] R&S INFO, Parma, Italy
michele.amoretti@unipr.it
[2] Fraunhofer IGD, Darmstadt, Germany
folker.wientapper@igd.fraunhofer.de
[3] CNR-ISTI, Pisa, Italy
{furfari,lenzi,chessa}@isti.cnr.it
[4] Computer Science Dep., Univ. of Pisa, Italy
[5] Dep. of Information Engineering, Univ. of Parma, Italy

Abstract. We illustrate the PERSONA context-awareness framework applied to a major problem in Ambient Intelligence, namely user activity monitoring, that requires to infer new knowledge from collected and fused sensor data, dealing with highly dynamic environments where devices continuously change their availability and (or) physical location. We describe the Sensor Abstraction and Integration Layer (SAIL), we introduce the Human Posture Classification component, which is one particular context information provider, and finally we describe the Activity Monitor, which is a reasoner that delivers aggregated/derived context events in terms of the context ontology.

Keywords: Ambient intelligence, context-awareness, data fusion, artificial vision, activity monitoring.

1 Introduction

The concept of Ambient Intelligence (AmI), which refers to a digital environment that proactively supports people in their daily lives, was introduced by the Information Society Technologies Advisory Group (ISTAG) of the European Commission [13]. AmI overlaps with other concepts, such as ubiquitous computing, pervasive computing, context awareness, embedded systems and artificial intelligence [7].

In the AmI context, the European Commission recently started the Ambient Assisted Living (AAL) technology and innovation funding programme, aiming at improving the quality of life of older people in their homes, by increasing their autonomy and assisting them in their daily activities, and by letting them feeling included, secure, protected and supported. AAL spaces are physical places featured with AmI enabling technologies, including the intelligence which supports

S. Hailes, S. Sicari, and G. Roussos (Eds.): S-Cube 2009, LNICST 24, pp. 206–221, 2009.

the services. Examples of AAL spaces are the home where the user lives, the neighborhood, the town, but also the body of the user itself. The technical challenge is to develop an integrated technological platform that allows the practical implementation of the AAL concept for the seamless and natural access to those services indicated above, to empower the citizen to adopt ambient intelligence as a natural environment in which to live.

For the creation of AmI environments, it is essential to have a framework supporting context-awareness. The scope of the contextual information spans the situational user context (his or her identity, capabilities, preferences, tasks, and state) over temporal, spatial, and environmental parameters (*e.g.* time, location, temperature, etc.), the available and accessible resources, and their capabilities and states. In general, context sources are manifold (several sensors, different profiles, and still others not enumerated explicitly), and the data coming from these sources must comply with a shared data model (the context ontology) in order for them to be used further by the consumers. In particular, some multidimensional (*i.e.* non-binary) sensors such as cameras, microphones, inertial sensors, must have a conversion of their data (pixel values, bit-encoded acoustic signals, etc.) into basic but at least meaningful, ontological states. Moreover, there must be an aggregation and reasoning mechanism aimed at deriving more significant context information, and there must be a subscription and notification mechanism aimed at triggering actions within an AmI system.

In this paper we illustrate a modular solution for sensor data fusion, allowing run-time connection and disconnection of components (sensors, data filters, reasoners, actuators). This is made possible by the PERSONA context awareness framework (introduced in section 2), which defines the concept of *context bus*, shared by specialized software components that produce and consume context events characterized by different granularity. Some components are directly connected to hardware sensors, and publish raw data in the context bus. Such basic context events are consumed by specialized data filters and reasoners, that infer high-level knowledge. The PERSONA middleware enables data fusion and aggregation at three levels: network, virtual network and application.

Such a modular approach allows to cope with a wide range of context awareness problems. In this paper we focus on user activity monitoring, that needs to infer new knowledge from collected and fused sensor data, dealing with highly dynamic environments where devices continuously change their availability and (or) physical location (*e.g.* those which are carried or worn by the user). In Section 3 we describe the Sensor Abstraction and Integration Layer (SAIL), with a specific discussion on the integration of ZigBee devices. Then, in Section 4, we introduce one particular context information provider, the Human Posture Classification component, which processes images coming from a camera in order to retrieve static estimates about meaningful, ontological posture states of a person being in the field of view. Finally, in Section 5, we describe the Activity Monitor, which is a reasoner that delivers aggregated/derived context events in terms of the context ontology (in particular, the action ontology). In the final section we summarize the work presented in this paper and discuss future work.

2   The PERSONA Framework for Context Awareness

PERSONA (Perceptive Spaces prOmoting iNdepentent Aging) [2] is a EU-funded research project (FP6) started in 2007, aiming at developing a scalable open standard technological platform to build a broad range of Ambient Assisted Living (AAL) Services. In this context the main technical challenge is the design of a self-organizing middleware infrastructure allowing the extensibility of component/device ensembles in an ad hoc fashion. In order to achieve this goal the communication patterns of the infrastructure must be able to execute distributed coordination strategies in order to provide the necessary service discovery, service orchestration and service adaptation functionalities.

The components of a PERSONA system are interfaced with the PERSONA middleware that enables the allocation of a different number of communication buses, each of them adopting specific and open communication strategies. Components linked with the PERSONA middleware may register with some of these communication buses, find each others and collaborate trough the local instances of the buses. Figure 1 shows the conceptual architecture of PERSONA. Input and output buses support multi-modal user interactions with the system. The context bus is an event-based channel to which context sources are attached, in particular the Wireless Sensor Networks (WSN) [5] are attached to this bus. Published events may be re-elaborated and transformed in high level events (situations) by components that have subscribed to the bus (*e.g.* context reasoners).

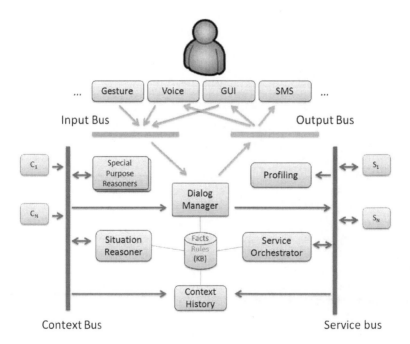

Fig. 1. The PERSONA Abstract Architecture

The service bus is used to group all the services available in the AAL-space, being them atomic or composite (whose availability is managed by a Service Orchestrator component). Services belonging to the service bus may be requested by the Situation Manager in consequence of situation detections and rules stored in the Knowledge Base of the system. Generally, devices are attached to both the context and service bus. The former is used to send notifications of status changes, the latter to answer to status query or execute actions (*e.g.* switch on the light device). Many other basic components are foreseen in PERSONA system, but their discussion is out of the scope of this paper (see [11] for details).

As in other international research projects (Gator Tech [17], Amigo [4], Socam [14]), we developed a middleware implementation based on the OSGi Platform [1]. The OSGi specification provides a standardized way to manage the software life cycle of Java applications. OSGi implementations are containers running on top of a JVM which enable installation, removal, start, and stop of components at run time. An OSGi component is a JAR file called *bundle* which contains Java classes, resources and metadata describing the dependencies with other bundles. A feature of the OSGi platform that is useful to recall here is the OSGi service model. A component can register with the OSGi Registry instances of services implementing specific interfaces and described by key-value properties. Every other component interested to monitor the presence of a particular service can register listeners with filter properties that will be notified by the OSGi framework when there is a match.

3   Sensor Abstraction and Integration Layer

The artifacts composing AAL-spaces can be classified in *stationary, portable* and *wearable components*. The first ones run on desktop PCs, Set Top Boxes, Residential Gateways or they belong to the environmental infrastructures like Home Automation sub-systems; *portable components* are, for instance, medical devices or mobile/smart phones, while *wearable components* are based on garments equipped with sensors. The PERSONA middleware targets small but reasonably powerful devices, therefore not all the components can be integrated by using an instance of the PERSONA middleware. Typically, wearable components, as well as nodes of WSNs or Home Automation Systems (HAS) require a different approach because of their limited computation resources; in such cases PERSONA adopts a solution based on a gateway, which allows the PERSONA application layer to share information by communicating with other application layers resident on different network infrastructures (*e.g.* ZigBee [5] or Bluetooth applications). Due to the features of the OSGi Platform[1], it is sufficient to write a bridging component that interacts from one side with the PERSONA middleware and from the other side with the software drivers that access the networked devices. In the following, we briefly introduce the Sensors Abstraction and Integration Layer (SAIL) developed in PERSONA, by highlighting different aspects

---

[1] Initially OSGi was designed as a framework to develop Open Service Gateways.

and requirements of sensor network applications. A specific section related to the integration of ZigBee devices concludes the chapter.

3.1 Wireless Sensor Networks

Wireless Sensor Networks are an important technological support for smart environments and ambient assisted applications. Up to now, most applications are based on ad-hoc solutions for WSNs, and solutions providing uniform and reusable applications are still in their youth. Note that AAL spaces can be populated by many sensor networks (*e.g* ZigBee or IEEE 802.15.4 standard, and Bluetooth). The main requirements, in the integration of WSN into PERSONA, are:

- R1: *Integration of the different sensor network technologies.*
- R2: *Sharing of communication medium by concurrent sensor applications.*
- R3: *Management of different applications on the same WSN.*
- R5: *Dynamic discovery of sensor applications.*
- R6: *Management of logical sensors.*
- R7: *Configuration and calibration of sensor applications.*

The requirement R1 is usually satisfied by enabling the dynamic deployment of ad-hoc network drivers in the system, while we can assume that requirements from R2 to R5 largely depend on the operating systems and middleware used for the sensor nodes programming (*e.g.* ZigBee, TinyOS, TinyDB, TeenyLIME and others [22]). The requirement R6 concerns the possible virtualization of the sensors deployed either in the environment or worn by the users. For example, let's consider an application that detects the user's posture by means of a number of accelerometers placed on the body: in this case, the posture can be represented by a single logical sensor, which aggregates information produced by all the accelerometers for producing the state of the user (sitting, walking, etc.). In this example, the accelerometers may not even be visible to the application layer. Such a virtualization can be implemented directly on the sensor network or implemented at application level within the gateway.

   In order to face these requirements, we developed SAIL [12] an architecture organized in three layers, namely the *Access*, *Abstraction*, and *Integration layer*, constructed over the OSGi platoform. The Access layer is a collection of drivers that provides basic access to WSNs. The Abstraction layer, if needed, can be used to elaborate the data received by the sensors before of exporting them at application level, and the last layer exposes the sensors to one or more access technologies, that in the context of PERSONA project is the middleware.

3.2 ZigBee Networks Integration

A diagram of the current SAIL architecture with ZigBee networks is depicted in figure 2. The ZigBee Base Driver is a network driver in charge of executing the scan of the network, getting the description of the ZigBee devices, and registering a proxy service for accessing the discovered remote services. This proxy

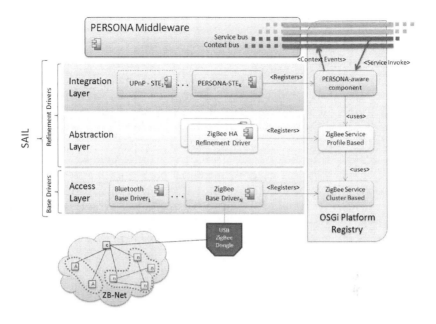

Fig. 2. The SAIL layered architecture

is a generic ZigBee service, registered with the OSGi Platform, which exposes
the properties retrieved during the network inquiry. It enables the access to the
remote service by means of simple primitives (*e.g.* invoke(byte[] payload))
that have to be filled by the proper cluster message. The components on the upper layers may act as Refinement Drivers (in OSGi terms). By using the OSGi
Framework facilities, as soon as a service implementing a known cluster is registered, these drivers refine the service by registering another service proxy with
a more detailed interface (*e.g.* action/command based). Thus the second layer is
specialized to represent the service according to a specific profile, for instance the
Home Automation profile. The upper layer integrates the ZigBee services within
PERSONA. It is composed of Sensor Technology Exporters (STE), which discover the services by implementing standard or extended profiles and registers
proxies that are PERSONA-aware components[2]. The mapping between services
compliant to the ZigBee model and PERSONA model is realized at this level;
these proxies send events or register service callees according to the PERSONA
ontologies.

In conclusion, the abstract layer is populated by custom drivers which may
combine and process the sensed data to instantiate logical sensor services and
refine the cluster-based services. All the code for ZigBee network access will be
released with OS license as soon as the integration with a commisioning tool will
be completed.

---

[2] The same approach can be used to expose the services according other access technologies (*e.g.* UPnP).

4 Vision-Based Human Posture Classification

Concerning the *acquisition* of context information, some sensors require a transformation of their output into meaningful, ontological states such that reasoning mechanisms may work upon it. In this section we will we introduce one particular context information provider that has been developed in the course of the PERSONA project. The Human Posture Classification (HPC) component is a camera based solution designed to retrieve static estimates about discrete (*i.e.* ontological) posture states of a person being in the field of view of the camera. "Static" means that the postures are derived from single images and are related to one concrete time instant. Furthermore, in contrast to the main research stream on human pose estimation (see [21] and [25] for in-depth reviews) no continuous pose is estimated. So instead of estimating the configuration of the skeletal configuration of the articulated body in a parameterized fashion *e.g.* by means of expressing it by joint angles of limbs and the general body orientation, the postures are directly classified according to a finite set of discrete posture states such as "Sitting", "Standing", "Bending", etc. Such a representation is needed to support higher level reasoning within a semantic / ontological AAL-architecture like the PERSONA framework.

Compared to related work in the field of discrete posture classification for domestic services ([10],[9],[23]), our approach is characterized by its simplicity and effectiveness. Firstly, we do not require multiple cameras in order to resolve ambiguities arising from self-occlusion of the body parts or to handle difficulties caused by poor segmentation when using conventional color based cameras. Instead, we advocate the use of Time-Of-Flight cameras which produce a three-dimensional, geometric representation of the scene. This reveals much better segmentation results and provides additional information for ambiguity handling. Secondly, we do not use a particular model of the human body in order to estimate a complete, parameterized body configuration prior classification. In fact, only few image processing steps are needed to obtain a low resolution feature image which in turn is used to train a recently proposed machine learning approach. It is clear that due to the high amount of computational effort needed for image processing applications, the HPC-component should run on a dedicated machine. It is the output of this preprocessing step - the extracted context information (posture states) - which is fused within the communication framework for Activity Monitoring.

In the following two subsections a brief overview over the particular advantages of using TOF-cameras instead of conventional types is given. Next, we explain the image processing steps for obtaining feature vectors that are used for training and online classification. Technical details and an evaluation of the solution are presented in [30].

4.1 Advantages of Time-of-Flight Cameras

Common to most of the human pose estimation approaches is the assumption that the camera is placed at a fixed spot in the room. This allows for applying a background-foreground segmentation (or background-subtraction) technique to obtain a silhouette image of the person. The basic idea is that the appearance of the scene is learned once beforehand, without any person in the field of view of the camera. While processing the live image the foreground can in turn be segmented by identifying changes with respect to the background model.

In fact, most pose estimation approaches rely heavily on a good segmentation result. However, despite many years of research (see [24] for a review on background segmentation), in practical, realistic environments conventional cameras still pose certain difficulties to obtaining a clear silhouette. These difficulties include the following:

- noise in the image,
- similar colors of the background and the clothes worn by persons,
- shadows that result in additional, unwanted variations between the background model and the live images,
- changing lighting conditions (*e.g.* when someone switches a light on or off) and,
- completely dark environments, as in the case of monitoring the behaviour of people at night, where conventional cameras are not applicable, at all.

Due to these difficulties we propose to use images coming from Time-Of-Flight (TOF) cameras ([20]), instead. TOF cameras produce a three dimensional, geometrical representation of the scene by emitting infra-red light and measuring the time the light takes to returning back to the camera.[3] With TOF-cameras most of the abovementioned difficulties are overcome, as the representation of the scene is based on its geometry and not on its visual appearance, thus making it more robust and more applicable in realistic scenarios.

4.2 Time-of-Flight Image Feature Extraction, Learning and Classification

The implemented algorithmic solution to camera based posture classification comprises four main steps which are briefly summarized, subsequently:

1. *Background subtraction and connected component merging*: Although TOF-cameras directly produce a cloud of 3D-coordinates of the perceived scene as output, each depth value is also associated to a pixel-coordinate. Thus many of the conventional image processing techniques may be applied to TOF-images in a similar fashion, including background-subtraction. However, compared to grey-level images from conventional cameras, the pixel values (depth-value) have much higher and very heterogeneous noise. To account to these peculiarities we adopted a recently proposed algorithm [26] that estimates the mean and covariance for each pixel in the background model (see figure 3, top-right). Next, the perceived differences between the

---

[3] More precisely, a TOF camera emits sinusodial light impulses and measures the phase shift of the returning light for each pixel.

background and the live image are grouped into connected pixel regions ("blobs"). This step is used to remove any false positives arising *e.g.* due to image noise. A simple threshold is applied to the size of the connected components, *i.e.* blobs below a certain size are simply discarded. Furthermore the largest blob among the remaining is assumed to be the one corresponding to a person.

2. *Subimage cropping, resampling and vectorization*: Based on the previous region-of-interest detection, a sub-image is cropped in such a way that it contains as much foreground as possible. The sub-image is centred and resampled to a low resolution while keeping the aspect ratio constant (see figure 3, bottom-left). The cropped and resampled sub-image is interpreted as a high dimensional feature vector with each pixel value being one element of the vector (*e.g.* a 20-by-24 image results in a 480 dimensional vector).

3. *Learning a transformation from image space to posture space (offline)*: In order to infer the posture from the high dimensional feature vectors, a recently proposed machine learning approach is used ("Locality Preserving Projections") [15][4]. A set of reference images needs to be captured and annotated manually according to their corresponding discrete states ("sitting", "standing", etc.). The machine learning approach is closely related to Principal Component Analysis (PCA), but, by contrast, takes into account neighbouring relations between the feature vectors, and thus, can also be used in a supervised manner (refer to [27] for details). It works by finding an optimal transformation from high dimensional feature space to a low dimensional representation. Image vectors belonging to the same or similar state are mapped to nearby points in the low dimensional space, such that points belonging to same states form clusters (see figure 3, bottom-right). For each cluster the mean and covariance is computed, which are used later for classifying the transformed image vectors into the corresponding states.

4. *Feature projection and classification (online):* The optimal projection derived from the training data is applied to the online image vectors. This projected online feature is then classified according to the closest mean vector of the projected training data. Furthermore we apply a threshold on the Mahalanobis distance between the online feature vector and the covariance of the projected training data of each class (see figure 3, bottom-right). *I.e.* if the normalized distance to the closest mean exceeds a certain threshold, the state is considered to be "Unknown". As we can show on real data, the machine learning approach has good generalization capabilities, *i.e.* previously unseen images not contained in the training set are correctly projected and classified.

---

[4] Wang and Suter ([28], [29]) already adopted LPP in the context of human monitoring. However their approach differs from ours in that they use it to obtain a parameterization of the image manifold and, in turn, use the evolution of the projected feature vectors to classify dynamic activities.

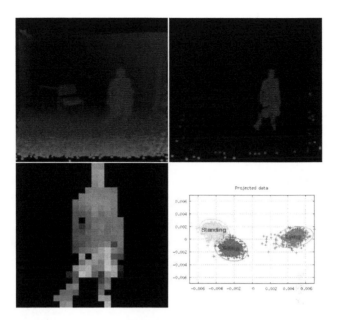

Fig. 3. Illustration of the image processing and classification steps for the human posture recognition (best viewed in color): Color encoded visualization of the 3D raw data coming from a TOF-camera (tl), result after background-subtraction (tr), cropped feature-image with grey-valued encoded relative depths (bl), projected training data for three states, "Standing", "Sitting and "Lying" (cyan, purple and blue), and the projection of the current feature image on the left (red point above the "Sitting" caption)(br)

5   Data Fusion for User Activity Monitoring

Understanding of human behaviors may be thought as the classification of time varying feature data, *i.e.* matching an unlabeled set of context events and other useful information with a group of labeled reference sets representing typical behaviors. A distinction between *static* and *dynamic* activities is necessary. Static activities like "standing" or "sitting" can be inferred directly from low-level data at a particular time instant (such as the pose of the person at a certain time using some kind of thresholding mechanism on the pose estimate). By contrast dynamic activities, such as "moving around", are usually composite activities requiring a monitoring of a full sequence of low-level data (*e.g.* context events describing ongoing sub-activities). Low-level data needs to be stored for several time frames (in a context buffer), as the whole sequence is needed to infer that activity from an evolution of the low level data. For example: "cooking" may be composed of several low-level data at different time instances: "opening the fridge", "closing the fridge", "standing in front of the oven", etc.

The existing body of literature in automatic reasoning can be decomposed according to two basic approaches. A pure "rule-based" approach that is a composition of several "If...Then..." conditions. *E.g.* for "cooking", it might be used "fridge has been opened for several times" && "hotplate was on for > xx minutes" && "activity of person in the kitchen" && "...". A "supervised learning" based approach [18], where the system is trained with a history of low-level data and corresponding output states (the low-level data is labeled with corresponding output states). Usually such supervised learning methods work by finding a decision surface in the high-dimensional (labeled) input data. Supervised learning (a.k.a. inductive machine learning) applied to human behavior detection has two advantages. First, the system can be configured (trained) by performing the activities themselves instead of programming the rule-based conditions. Second, the system can updated/trained online, for example by asking the person if the inferred activity was correct. Then with the confirmation/disagreement of the user, the training space (*e.g.* decision surface) is updated.

Our approach is based on probabilistic rules, with absolute probabilities of high-level actions can be automatically updated by means of long-term behavior detection (which is not discussed in this paper). The Activity Monitor (AM) is a reasoner that delivers aggregated/derived context events in terms of the context ontology (in particular, the action ontology). Thus the AM registers to the context bus (c-bus) both as subscriber and publisher in order to use context events from lower levels, and produces context events on a higher level. In details, the AM is a special-purpose reasoner that aggregates context events related to basic user activities (AtomicActions), recognized by the HPC component, and to user localization, as well as information about the status of user-controlled devices, such as the TV, to produce context events describing complex user activities such as "eating", "watching tv", etc (CompositeActions).

Figure 4 summarizes the internal architecture of the AM, which is registered on the c-bus as context subscriber for many user-related context events (*e.g.* those published by the HPE). When a context event of type AtomicAction is received, the Classifier decides whether to consume it immediately (to infer a CompositeAction and publish it as context event) or to store it in the Action Archiver, for later use.

The Classifier is based on a Bayesian network (BN) approach [16,19]. A Bayesian network is a graphical model enabling the description of probability relationships among a set of variables (features). The graph allows the user to understand which variables affect which other ones, and also serves as the backbone for efficiently computing marginal and conditional probabilities that may be required for inference and learning. Because a Bayesian network is a complete model for the variables and their relationships, it can be used to answer probabilistic queries about them. For example, the network can be used to find out updated knowledge of the state of a subset of variables when other variables (the evidence variables) are observed. The process of computing the posterior distribution of variables given evidence is called probabilistic inference.

We illustrate how BNs have been used to implement the Activity Monitor with a simple example. Then we briefly illustrate the classification algorithm implemented in the AM.

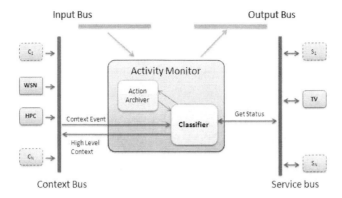

Fig. 4. The internal architecture of the Activity Monitor

5.1   Case Study

Different context events may allow to infer that the user is involved in a telecommunication: he is talking, he is facing TV, the TV is switched on in "communication mode". Being in the living room, with TV switched on may also mean that the user is watching TV programmes. From the point of view of the Activity Monitor, user actions (A_i) and localizations (L_j), as well as and device states obtained from the s-bus (S_k) are boolean random variables. The idea of inferring situational knowledge from a set of answers to "Y/N" questions comes directly from Shannon's information theory. In this context, asking more questions means merging more c-bus and s-bus data, that allows to infer more detailed knowledge.

The BN in figure 5 illustrates the dependencies among the variables considered for the case study. Those representing composite actions are placed as roots in the acyclic graph, while sub-actions and device states are always leaf nodes (since they are considered to be implied by composite actions).

The BN designer has to fill the conditional probability tables (CPTs) for each variable. For example, when a "Telecommunicating" action is ongoing, the probability that the user is in the living room is 0.5, otherwise it is 0.2. These values

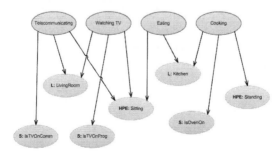

Fig. 5. Bayesian network for the case study

can be set taking into account the average time spent by the user, each day, to perform the composite actions of interest (cooking, watching TV, etc.), observed by relatives, caregivers and friends. Their values can be updated automatically, by using long-term behavior detection.

The Activity Monitor is thus able to compute, for example:

P("Telecommunicating" | "L:LivingRoom"=T, "S:IsTVOnComm"=T)

i.e. "what is the likelihood that the user is telecommunicating, given that he is in the living room, and the TV is in communication mode?".

5.2   Implementation of the Activity Monitor

To implement the classifier based on BNs, we adopted the Weka library (version 3.5.8) [3,6], which is a collection of machine learning algorithms for data mining tasks. The algorithms can either be applied directly to a dataset or called from Java code. For Bayesian network design and management, Weka provides a Java API and a graphical editor.

The Weka BN GUI allows to create Bayesian networks and to store them on files in XML BIF format [8]. To create a BN, nodes can be placed and linked together in a free space, and CPTs can be defined. A BN stored in a XML BIF file can be read, modified and stored in a new file by means of the Weka API.

Context events describing simple actions (such as "Sitting") are used by the AM to infer the CompositeAction context events. If a simple action does not contribute immediately to the inference of a composite action, it is stored in the Action Archiver, which is a continuously updated list.

When a context event describing a basic Action is intercepted, the BN is explored and the composite action with higher marginal probability is returned, using the following algorithm:

1. get node i from the BN, such that (descr(i) == descr(theAtomicAction))
2. get the set N_i of parents of node i
3. for each node in N_i compute the marginal probability P_m, considering other evidences
4. select node j in N_i with the highest marginal probability $P_m(j)$
5. return descr(j) and $P_m(j)$

Step 4 is the most important. It requires to take into account, for each node in N_i, the current values (evidences), whether they are available, of all its child nodes (that do not always represent context events, but information to be requested on the s-bus). For example (still referring to the case study), suppose the "Sitting" event has been detected. Its parent set N_i includes "Watching TV", which has two more child nodes, one describing the presence of the user in the living room, the other describing the programming state of the TV. By invoking an appropriate service, the AM can retrieve the current value of the variable represented by the "S:IsTVOnProg" node (T or F). Moreover, the AM can check its internal location archive, searching for recent evidence of use presence in the living room. These facts are then used to compute the marginal probability of the considered parent node, *e.g.*

P("Watching TV" | "Sitting"=T, "L:LivingRoom"=T, "S:IsTVOnProg"=F)

If a parent node has, among its child nodes, other context events representing actions, the AM inspects the Action Archiver, looking for recent evidence of such actions. If no recent evidence of actions related to a composite action is found in the archive, the evidence of those actions is set to F.

6   Conclusions

The PERSONA framework that we presented in this paper addresses three major issues for user related context awareness in an AmI environment.

We presented a general *communication framework* that allows to exchange context information, thus supporting context reasoning and data fusion in a distributed manner. A key concept is the context bus, to different components may subscribe for publishing and consuming context events. Within this paper a special focus has been given to the design of the wireless sensor network integration. The framework supports data fusion and aggregation at three levels of abstraction: network, virtual network (SAIL) and application level.

We addressed the problem of *context data acquisition, i.e.* the preprocessing of sensor output in order to obtain meaningful, ontological information such that high-level reasoners may work upon it. Here we focused on a particular problem in computer vision: the acquisition of posture information of the user when captured by a camera. We suggested to use Time-Of-Flight cameras to circumvent several difficulties (*e.g.* changing lighting conditions) that usually decrease the robustness of any solution in realistic and practical situations. Furthermore, we adopted a machine learning approach that can be trained to detect a variety of different posture states of interest. Of course, postures of persons are of special interest for activity monitoring as they provide important clues about the activities being performed.

Finally, a powerful and flexible *context data fusion* approach was introduced, *i.e.* the Activity Monitor. It is a reactive component that produces information about ongoing user activities, merging context events such as human postures and localization, with information about the status of user-controlled devices. The Activity Monitor is composed by a classifier and a short-term context archiver. The classifier is based on a Bayesian network (BN) approach, which allows to infer high-level knowledge with associated marginal probability. To improve the component, we are studying mechanisms for allowing to dynamically update the absolute probabilities of composite actions, taking into account the results produced by another PERSONA reasoner which is the Long-term Behavioral Analyzer (whose development is in progress).

Acknowledgements

This work has been partially funded by the EU IST Project PERSONA (FP6 contract N.045459).

References

1. OSGi web site, http://www.osgi.org
2. PERSONA project web site, http://www.aal-persona.org
3. Weka 3: Data mining software in java, http://www.cs.waikato.ac.nz/ml/weka/
4. AMIGO project. Ambient intelligence for the networked home environment (September 2004), http://www.amigo-project.org
5. Baronti, P., Pillai, P., Chook, V.W.C., Chessa, S., Gotta, A., Hu, Y.F.: Wireless sensor networks: A survey on the state of the art and the 802.15.4 and zigbee standards. Computer Communications 30(7), 1655–1695 (2007)
6. Bouckaert, R.: Bayesian network classifiers in weka for version 3-5-8 (July 2008)
7. Ramos, D.S.C., Augusto, J.C.: Ambient intelligence - the next step for artificial intelligence. IEEE Intelligent Systems 23(2) (March/April 2008)
8. Cozman, F.G.: The interchange format for bayesian networks, http://www.cs.cmu.edu/~fgcozman/research/interchangeformat/
9. Cucchiara, R., Grana, C., Prati, A., Vezzani, R.: Probabilistic posture classification for human-behavior analysis. IEEE Transactions on Systems, Man and Cybernetics, Part A 35(1), 42–54 (2005)
10. Cucchiara, R., Prati, A., Vezzani, R.: Posture classification in a multi-camera indoor environment. In: ICIP (1), pp. 725–728 (2005)
11. Fides-Valero, Á., Freddi, M., Furfari, F., Tazari, M.-R.: The PERSONA framework for supporting context-awareness in open distributed systems. In: Aarts, E., Crowley, J.L., de Ruyter, B., Gerhäuser, H., Pflaum, A., Schmidt, J., Wichert, R. (eds.) AmI 2008. LNCS, vol. 5355, pp. 91–108. Springer, Heidelberg (2008)
12. Girolami, M., Lenzi, S., Furfari, F., Chessa, S.: SAIL: a Sensor Abstraction and Integration Layer for Context Aware Architectures. In: Proceedings of the 34th EUROMICRO Conference on Software Engineering and Advanced Applications (SEAA 2008), Parma, Italy, pp. 374–381. IEEE, Los Alamitos (2008)
13. I. A. Group. Scenarios for ambient intelligence in 2010, european commission (2001)
14. Gu, T., Pung, H.K., Zhang, D.Q.: A middleware for building context-aware mobile services. In: IEEE Vehicular Technology Conference, pp. 2656–2660 (2004)
15. He, X., Niyogi, P.: Locality preserving projections. In: Advances in Neural Information Processing Systems, vol. 16. MIT Press, Cambridge (2003)
16. Heckerman, D.: A tutorial on learning with bayesian networks. In: m. i. (ed.) Learning in graphical models. Kluwer, Dordrecht (1998)
17. Helal, S., Mann, W., El-Zabadani, H., King, J., Kaddoura, Y., Jansen, E.: The gator tech smart house: A programmable pervasive space. IEEE Computer 1(3), 64–74 (2005)
18. Kotsiantis, S.: Supervised machine learning: A review of classification techniques. Informatica Journal 31, 249–268 (2007)
19. Madden, M.: The performance of bayesian network classifiers constructed using different techniques. In: Proc. of european conference on machine learning, workshop on probabilistic graphical models for classification (September 2003)
20. MESA Imaging (February 2009), http://www.mesa-imaging.ch/
21. Moeslund, T.B., Hilton, A., Krueger, V.: A survey of advances in vision-based human motion capture and analysis. Computer Vision and Image Understanding 104(2), 90–126 (2006)
22. Molla, S., Ahamed, M.M.: A survey of middleware for sensor network and challenges. In: Proceedings of nternational Conference on Parallel Processing Workshop (ICPP 2006) (August 2006)

23. Pellegrini, S., Iocchi, L.: Human posture tracking and classification through stereo vision and 3d model matching. J. Image Video Process. 8(2), 1–12 (2008)
24. Piccardi, M.: Background subtraction techniques: a review. In: 2004 IEEE International Conference on Systems, Man and Cybernetics, vol. 4, pp. 3099–3104 (2004)
25. Poppe, R.: Vision-based human motion analysis: An overview. Comput. Vis. Image Underst. 108(1-2), 4–18 (2007)
26. Porikli, F., Tuzel, O.: Bayesian background modeling for foreground detection. In: VSSN 2005: Proceedings of the third ACM international workshop on Video surveillance & sensor networks, pp. 55–58. ACM, New York (2005)
27. Wang, H., Chen, S., Hu, Z., Zheng, W.: Locality-preserved maximum information projection. IEEE Transactions on Neural Networks 19(4), 571–585 (2008)
28. Wang, L., Suter, D.: Analyzing human movements from silhouettes using manifold learning. In: IEEE Conference on Advanced Video and Signal Based Surveillance, vol. 7 (2006)
29. Wang, L., Suter, D.: Learning and matching of dynamic shape manifolds for human action recognition. IEEE Transactions on Image Processing 16(6), 1646–1661 (2007)
30. Wientapper, F., Ahrens, K., Wuest, H., Bockholt, U.: Linear-projection-based classification of human postures in time-of-flight data. IEEE Transactions on Systems, Man and Cybernetics (October 2009)

Trade-off Analysis of a MAC Protocol for Wireless e-Emergency Systems

Óscar Gama[1], Paulo Carvalho[1], J.A. Afonso[2], and P.M. Mendes[2]

[1] Department of Informatics,
University of Minho, Braga, Portugal
{osg,pmc}@di.uminho.pt
[2] Department of Industrial Electronics,
University of Minho, Guimarães, Portugal
{jose.afonso,paulo.mendes}@dei.uminho.pt

Abstract. Wireless sensor networks are envisioned to be deployed in health-care. Since emergency and intensive care applications need to assure reliable and timely data delivery, they have increased demands for quality of service, including at the MAC layer. Amongst MAC protocols available for WSNs, the Low Power Real Time (LPRT) presents suitable characteristics to be deployed in emergency platforms due to its rational bandwidth allocation, low energy consumption, and bounded latency. Yet, this protocol may present a significant packet loss ratio in a wireless channel with bit error ratio. In order to define a MAC protocol more robust to bit error conditions and able to fulfill the required quality of service, solutions based on short size beacons and multiple retransmissions are proposed and tested. The results showed that such strategies led to meaningful improvements regarding packet loss ratio, without compromising significantly the energy consumption.

Keywords: e-Emergency, Quality of Service, Wireless Sensor Networks.

1 Introduction

An e-health monitoring system commonly grounds on a group of sensors attached non-invasively to a patient in order to monitor some physiological parameters. In case of emergency clinical scenarios, a healthcare network should provide quality of service (QoS) facilities since these clearly demand for high reliability, guaranteed bandwidth and short delays [1]. Therefore, communication protocol layers need to assure a reliable and timely data delivery.

Many Medium Access Control (MAC) protocols have been developed for wireless networks using contention or multiplexing-based algorithms. Traditional contention-based protocols assume traffic is distributed stochastically. As traffic in a wireless sensor network (WSN) tends to be highly correlated and dominantly regular, conventional Carrier Sense Multiple Access (CSMA) protocols are not advised for WSNs [2]. S-MAC [3] and WiseMAC [4] are typical examples of CSMA-based protocols designed for low duty-cycle WSNs, developed to help saving energy in applications whose nodes remain idle for long time until an event is detected (e.g. surveillance).

S. Hailes, S. Sicari, and G. Roussos (Eds.): S-Cube 2009, LNICST 24, pp. 222–235, 2009.
© Institute for Computer Sciences, Social-Informatics and Telecommunications Engineering 2009

These protocols are convenient for WSNs having usually low traffic loads. Consequently, these MAC protocols are inadequate for networks requiring high throughput and low latency.

Amongst multiplexing-based protocols, Time Division Multiple Access (TDMA) is a commonly used technique. Time is divided into slots, which are used by motes (wireless sensor nodes) to transmit data without the need to contend for the medium. If a base-station (BS) is available to keep the WSN scheduling and synchronization, then TDMA-based MAC protocols are usually a preferable choice to satisfy the QoS requirements of e-emergency systems, as QoS is easier assured in a collision-free environment than in a contention-prone medium. Within TDMA-based MAC protocols, LPRT [5] is a convenient choice to provide efficient bandwidth allocation, low energy consumption, and bounded latency, as required by e-emergency wireless networks. However, it may present a significant packet loss ratio in a wireless channel affected by errors. In order to improve its robustness to bit errors, new solutions based on short size beacons and multiple retransmissions are proposed and verified in a WSN simulator.

The remaining of this paper is organized as follows; the related work is discussed in Section 2; proposals to improve LPRT protocol are presented in Section 3; the simulation testbed setup is described in Section 4; the results are discussed in Section 5; and, finally, the conclusions are presented in Section 6.

2 Related Work

TDMA-based protocols available for WSNs include IEEE 802.15.4/GTS [7], LMAC [8], TRAMA [9], and LPRT.

The IEEE 802.15.4 standard specifies the physical layer and the MAC sublayer, allowing the optional use of a TDMA-based superframe structure. However, the low granularity of the time slots leads to poor bandwidth efficiency, making it unsuitable to e-emergency scenarios [1].

LMAC allows a WSN to self-organize in terms of slot assignment and synchronization, without requiring a central manager, through a distributed algorithm running in every mote. Nodes wake up at the start of each slot to stay synchronized and to listen to a message. If the message is not addressed to the node, it will sleep until the next slot. Since each node has only one slot assigned and one transmission per superframe (32 slots) allowed, LMAC is inadequate to e-emergency systems.

TRAMA uses a distributed election scheme based on information about the traffic at each node to decide which node can transmit at a particular slot. It avoids the assignment of slots to nodes without traffic to send, and also allows nodes to decide when they can sleep. It is well suited for applications that require high-delivery guarantee and energy efficiency, without being delay sensitive. The latter characteristic impairs the support of real-time applications.

LPRT is a simple, beacon-based protocol that uses dynamic and efficiently the available bandwidth. Its highly-grained superframe (Figure 1) starts with the transmission of a beacon frame (B) by the BS, followed by the Contention Access Period (CAP), also called Contention Period (CP). The CAP may be used for the (dis)association or configuration of a body sensor network (BSN). The Contention

Free Period (CFP) follows the CAP. The CFP is composed by the Normal Transmission Period (NTP) and the Retransmission Period (RP). The NTP is used for motes to transmit new data. Lost data are retransmitted in the RP. Data packets are sent in contiguous slots of the CFP. The slots attribution in the CFP is announced through a list of allocation fields carried in the payload of every beacon. Each allocation field contains the association identification and the initial transmission slot (ITS) for every mote in the WSN. Data frames transmitted to the BS during the NTP are acknowledged by the ACK bitmap present in the beacon of the next superframe.

The beacon size may become relatively large, since it is directly dependent on the number of motes associated with the BS. A mote transmits data in the superframe only if the corresponding beacon carrying the list of allocation fields is received, and a single retransmission procedure is used in case of transmission failure. These characteristics may lead to a significant packet loss ratio if communications occur in a wireless channel with an appreciable bit error ratio (BER). In order to improve its robustness against bit errors, a solution based on short size beacons is proposed.

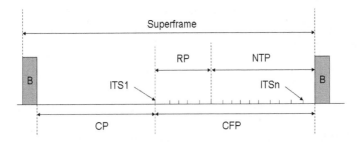

Fig. 1. Superframe structure in the LPRT protocol [5]

3   Proposals to Improve LPRT

In order to define a more robust MAC protocol to channel errors, solutions based on short size beacons and multiple retransmissions were added to LPRT. For this purpose, the RP is placed between the CAP and the NTP. RP is defined after the CAP so that a packet is retransmitted away from an eventual burst error condition responsible for the transmission failure occurred during the last NTP. RP is not placed after the NTP to avoid a mote transmitting in the NTP with a variable packet size.

Short size beacons. To assure a good performance of the e-emergency WSN, the percentage of lost beacons should be very low. A strategy to accomplish this goal is to send beacons with a convenient transmission power, since the BER of the channel decreases as SNR increases. In addition, the beacon frame length should be as small as possible. So, whenever possible the beacon payload contains only the ACK bitmap to acknowledge the frames correctly received during the NTP of the last superframe, and the CAP size of the current superframe (assuming the start slot of the CAP is known). In this case, motes must run an algorithm to compute which slots should be used to (re)transmit data without interfering each other, in accordance with a predefined order schema. Using this strategy, the energy consumption in each BSN improves too, since smaller size beacons are received by the motes.

According to the received ACK bitmap, each mote must calculate the corresponding superframe slots to transmit its data. If a mote does not receive a beacon or a short sequence of beacons, it may continue to send its new data in the NTP, since a mote clock drift in the order of microseconds should permit the WSN to continue synchronized during a few consecutive beacon intervals. However, the mote cannot retransmit any data in the RP because the ACK bitmap is not available and so it does not know how the RP slots are being allocated to the motes.

In order to save energy, it might be tempting to retransmit the lost data aggregated to the new data sent in the NTP, instead of retransmitting it in the RP. However such strategy should be avoided because the number of slots allocated in the NTP to each mote becomes variable. Consequently, if a mote does not receive the beacon, it has no way to know *a priori* which slots to use for transmission. Indeed, if a mote does not receive the ACK bitmap, it does not know which motes are going to transmit aggregated data in the current superframe, making impossible to compute the new slot allocation schema. This situation does not occur if the NTP is used only to transmit new data packets. Hence, aggregated retransmissions in the NTP are not recommended, except in cases where aggregation does not imply taking more slots, such as packets carrying temperature data.

Besides the ACK bitmap and the CAP size, a beacon may need to send reconfiguration instructions if a new clinical situation is detected in some BSN. For instance, higher monitoring activity and lower delay transmission of the vital signals might be required when a patient´s clinical situation changes from non-critical to critical. In this case, the BS should inform all motes about the new situation and eventually reconfigure the WSN. To perform this action all motes must follow a reconfiguration scheme, such as the algorithm proposed in [6].

Retransmission in the RP. The retransmission order in the RP depends on the ACK bitmap received from the BS. Using an increasing slot sequence, firstly data of all motes having the highest-priority and the bit false in the ACK bitmap are retransmitted successively. Then, data of all motes having the second higher-priority and the bit false in the ACK bitmap are retransmitted successively, and so on. If slots are not enough to permit all required retransmissions, then schedule truncation is done in order to guarantee that no retransmission occurs in the NTP. It should be noted that retransmissions may not be the appropriate error recovery mechanism if losses are due to fading.

Retransmission in the CAP. If a mote does not receive the beacon then it fails to receive the ACK bitmap, and therefore it does not know if the BS correctly received the packet sent in the NTP of the last superframe. Retransmitting properly that packet in the RP is impossible because such mote cannot compute the slot allocation schema of RP. A solution to overcome this problem is to retransmit it during the CAP using the slotted CSMA/CA [7]. This procedure should improve the packet loss ratio at expense of some energy consumption and CAP slots waste, since the mote may be transmitting a duplicated packet. Indeed, a packet already received by the BS may be retransmitted again in the CAP of the next superframe if the mote does not receive the beacon.

4 Simulation Testbed

To test the solutions proposed in the previous section and to compare them with LPRT, the Castalia simulator [10] was used. For that purpose, a case-study and distinct MAC protocol operation modes were programmed in Castalia.

4.1 Castalia Simulator

Castalia is a discrete event-driven simulator designed specifically for wireless sensor networks. It uses the communication model proposed by Zuniga *et. al.* [11]. In a wireless channel the BER is variable because errors may occur in long bursts due to fading or shadowing. Castalia does not support currently these time-varying effects.

Castalia provides a tuneable CSMA-based MAC protocol in order to model several link protocols. However this protocol was built for broadcast communications, not unicast, and so it does not currently support acknowledgements. For this reason, acknowledgements are performed at the application level.

In order to compute the total energy consumed by a mote, Castalia takes into account not only the consumed power while the radio is in listening, sleeping, transmitting or receiving state, but also the power consumed by state switching. It also accounts the energy consumed per sample by the sensing devices present at each node. CPU energy consumption and memory access cost are not accounted in the current version of Castalia.

4.2 Case-Study

The testbed is based on a hospital room containing six beds with one patient per bed. Each patient is monitored by a body sensor network, and a BS collects and analyses the vital signals of all patients. The signals being monitored are temperature (T), oximetry (OXI), arterial pressure (ART), respiration rate (RR) and electrocardiography (ECG). Each signal is collected and transmitted by a dedicated mote. The MAC protocol deployed in the network must guarantee a maximum latency below 500 ms, low packet loss ratio, 10.5 kbps of bandwidth to each BSN and low energy consumption [1].

4.3 Operation Modes

In order to compare different MAC strategies, five operation modes were defined in the simulation testbed: 0, 1, 2, 3, and 4. In all modes, frames transmitted at the NTP are acknowledged through the ACK bitmap sent in the payload of the next beacon. Also, a mote may transmit data in the NTP even if a short size beacon is not received.

In operation mode 0, there are no retransmissions of lost frames. This mode is used as the worst-case, as no error control mechanism is present in the system.

In operation mode 1, lost packets are retransmitted once at the RP and these retransmitted packets are not acknowledged. This mode differs of LPRT, because in this protocol a mote only transmits data in the NTP if a relatively large size beacon is received. Hence, if the channel BER is not null, the packet loss ratio in a WSN operating at mode 1 is lower than using LPRT.

In operation mode 2, packets with a payload size above a fixed threshold may be retransmitted during RP at most twice. The threshold was set to 40 bytes, so ECG and ART motes have two chances to retransmit the lost data. The second retransmission occurs only if the frame is not correctly received by the BS during the first retransmission. Hence, the first retransmission must be acknowledged, although the second one does not need to be. Packets with a payload size below the threshold may be retransmitted once in the RP and they are not acknowledged.

In operation mode 3, packets with a payload size above a fixed threshold may be retransmitted at most three times in the RP.

Operation mode 4 is similar to operation mode 2, but if a mote does not receive a beacon, it tries to send in the CAP the packet transmitted in the NTP of the last superframe. A minimum CAP size is available in all superframes.

4.4 Testbed Setup

The relevant setup and parameterization steps followed in the simulation testbed are presented next.

Wireless Channel. Since the room considered in our case-study is relatively small (10mx10m), the BER given by the simulator was always null, meaning that all motes worked in a good connected region. In order to test the robustness of the diverse protocols to different BERs, an additional random error generator was introduced in the wireless channel module of Castalia to force the degradation of the bit error probability.

Radio Model and Operating States. In the present protocol implementation, a mote radio is normally in the sleeping state. It switches automatically to the transmission state whenever it has a packet to send and enters in listening mode five slots before the ending of the superframe to receive the next beacon. The BS never enters in the sleeping state because conserving energy is not a concern for this device.

The CC2420 radio model, used by the popular TelosB motes, and a transmission power level of -10 dBm were chosen.

Beacon Interval and Superframe Time-Slots. The number of slots in the superframe should be as high as possible to tune accurately the time division allocated to each mote and so minimizing the bandwidth waste, but not too high so that the slot duration is beyond the mote timer resolution. Since this is typically in order of microseconds, it was chosen 512 slots per superframe, which means that the duration of each slot is around 0.43ms, considering a beacon interval of 0.220s. This period was chosen for ECG packets to be sent with the payload almost fully-loaded to save energy, and it must not be above 0.250s to respect the maximum delay of 0.500s imposed to all signals, including the retransmitted frames [1].

Physical, MAC, and ACK Frames. Since many commercial motes use ZigBee, a physical layer frame having a total maximum size of 133 bytes (B) was assumed, the same length as specified in IEEE 802.15.4. Its physical header of 6B was also adopted: preamble sequence (4B), start frame delimiter (1B), and frame length (1B).

A MAC header of 6B was tailored to this case-study, containing the fields: frame control (1B), sequence number (1B), destination address (1B), source address (1B), WSN identification (1B), and frame check sequence (2B).

The ACK frame has a MAC header of 6B and payload size null.

Data Packet Payload. ECG motes sample the physical signal at 250 Hz, ART motes at 120 Hz, OXI motes at 60 Hz, RR motes at 20 Hz, and T motes at 2 Hz [1]. The samples of every mote have a resolution of 16 bits. Consequently, packets transmitted from ECG, ART, OXI, RR, and T motes present a payload of 110B, 54B, 28B, 10B, and 2B, respectively.

Transmission in the NTP. The number of slots N_s each mote occupies in the NTP of the superframe to transmit data is:

$$N_s = \text{ceil}(t_{tx}*S/ t_{SD}) \tag{1}$$

where t_{tx} is the transmission duration (in seconds), S is the total number of slots in the superframe, and t_{SD} is the superframe duration (in seconds). The ceiling function ceil(x) returns the integer part of the argument rounded up. For a packet with a physical header P_h, a MAC header M_h, a MAC payload length M_p bytes, and a transmission rate R bps:

$$t_{tx} = (P_h+M_h+M_p)*8/R \tag{2}$$

Considering a null overhead for the layers above the MAC layer,

$$M_p= t_{SD}*F*r/8 \tag{3}$$

where F is the sample rate (samples/s) of a specific mote type, and r is the sampling resolution in bits. As S=512 and R=250 kbps, each ECG, ART, OXI, RR, T frame takes respectively 10, 5, 3, 2, and 1 slots in the superframe.

When allocating each set of slots in NTP to the motes, two additional slots are included for safeguarding purposes. The slots in the superframe are occupied in the following order:

Beacon I CAP I RP I T(5-0), RR(5-0), OXI(5-0), ART(5-0), ECG(5-0) I

--------------- NTP ---------------

where ECG(5-0)=ECG(5,4,3,2,1,0) represents the following transmission sequence in NTP: after ECG mote of BSN 5 (ECG5) transmitting its packet, then ECG4, ECG3, ECG2, ECG1, and ECG0 transmit successively their data. The same criterion is applied to the remaining types of motes.

Retransmission in the RP. The retransmission order in the RP depends on the ACK bitmap received from the BS. Using an increasing slot sequence, firstly the data of ECG motes having the bit false in the ACK bitmap are retransmitted successively. Then, if the respective ACK bits are false, ART motes retransmit their data, followed by the OXI motes, the RR motes, and finally the T motes. The number of slots allocated in RP to the motes includes two slots for safeguarding purposes, plus two slots if ACK receiving is required.

In case of no more slots available to be allocated for retransmission, the less important vital signals should not be retransmitted. Since body temperature changes slowly along time, this signal is the first to be discarded in such situation.

One, two or three consecutive set of slots may be used for a single retransmission, according to the operation mode used. In mode 2, the second set of slots is used for retransmission if the packet is not correctly received by the BS during the first retransmission. Accordingly, the first retransmission must be acknowledged. If a packet is sent with success during the first retransmission, then the slots reserved for the second retransmission are unused, resulting in bandwidth waste. The second retransmission is not acknowledged. The same reasoning is applied for mode 3.

Retransmission in the CAP. In operation mode 4, a minimum CAP size of fifty slots is defined for every superframe so that motes have a chance to retransmit data in case of not receiving a beacon. To free some slots, T motes are not allowed to retransmit data in the CAP. The remaining operation modes have no minimum CAP size.

5 Simulation Results

In order to study the improvement obtained in LPRT when short size beacons and multiple retransmissions are deployed in this protocol, several simulation tests were carried out for different operation modes. Packet loss ratio, energy consumption, CAP availability, and scalability were the parameters under test. The performance of a WSN using beacons with different sizes was tested as well.

For each test run, a simulation time of one hour was defined. Extending the simulation time would not affect significantly the results. During that time period, the BS sends around 16363 beacons, carrying in the payload only the ACK bitmap (4B). It is assumed that BER is equal in both communication directions.

In some graphics the probability P of a fully-loaded packet to be received at destination is used instead of the BER. Both parameters are related by:

$$BER = 1 - P^{1/(8*MPS)} \qquad (4)$$

where MPS is the maximum physical frame size. Considering MPS=133B, the BER changes between 0 and around $6.5*10^{-4}$ as P decreases from 1 to 0.5 along the simulation runs. Typical values for BER in a good real wireless channel are of the order 10^{-5} and in a bad channel may be less than 10^{-3}.

5.1 Performance of a WSN with Short Size Beacons

The beacon size should be as small as possible to improve the performance of the WSN. In order to evaluate the impact of the beacon size in a WSN, the loss ratio of ECG packets for the beacon payloads of 4B (the minimum size to contain a bitmap for 30 motes, as required by the case-study), 36B, 68B, and 100B, were tested in the testbed using operation mode 2. The results are presented in Figure 2. It is observed that as the beacon payload becomes larger, the beacon loss probability increases, and so the packet loss ratio.

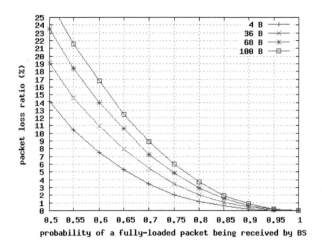

Fig. 2. ECG packet loss ratio for several beacon payload sizes (in steps of 32B)

Moreover, considering that samples performed by sensing devices consume no energy, simulations show that, for operation mode 0 and P=1, ECG motes save around 14% of energy when the BS sends short size (4B) beacons instead of sending in the beacon payload all information (68B) specifying concretely which slots the sensors should take in the CFP.

These results confirm that the performance of a WSN improves significantly in terms of energy saving and packet loss ratio if short size beacons are used.

5.2 Packet Loss Ratio

LPRT may present significant packet loss ratio in wireless channels with bit errors. In order to study how the proposals presented in Section 3 may help to improve this drawback, the Packet Loss Ratio (PLR=100-Packet Delivery Ratio) for the traffic generated by all types of motes were obtained for every operation modes.

Figure 3 presents the packet loss ratio curves for the traffic produced by both the ECG motes and the T motes. The information presented for ECG traffic is calculated by taking into account all packets generated by all ECG motes in the WSN. This criterion holds true also for the other mote types, such as ART motes whose loss ratio curves are presented in Figure 4, and also for OXI and RR motes (Figure 5). By doing so, one may evaluate how the traffic produced by the diverse mote types is affected by operating in a given mode. Yet in a real situation, attention should be paid to the traffic coming from each individual BSN since the traffic treatment may be different for each BSN, according to the degree of the patients' emergency state. However, for easiness of dealing with the whole information produced by the simulator, a global analysis for each type of traffic generated in the WSN is done. This procedure will not affect the main conclusions obtained from the simulation results.

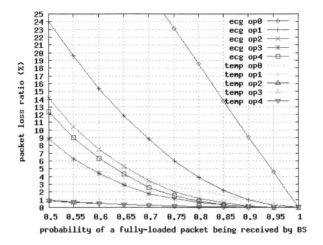

Fig. 3. Packet loss ratio for ECG and T traffic

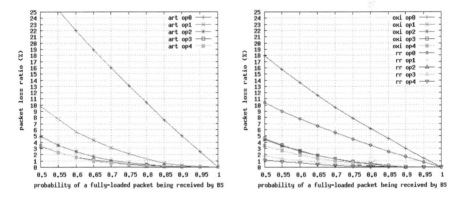

Fig. 4. Packet loss ratio for ART traffic   **Fig. 5.** Packet loss ratio for OXI and RR traffic

Comparatively to mode 1, Figures 3 and 4 illustrate clearly the improvement achieved when the WSN operates in modes 2, 3, or 4. These operation modes present an ECG packet loss below 1% when probability P > 0.8. Such improvement is due to the multiple retransmission process occurred in the superframe. The ECG traffic presents a lower loss ratio in a WSN operating in mode 3 than in mode 4. However for ART traffic it is almost irrelevant to work in mode 3 or 4. This occurs because the probability of losing an ART packet is lower than the probability of losing an ECG packet, as the packet size is smaller in the former.

Since OXI, RR, and T motes may only retransmit once in RCFP, no significant difference is detected in such traffic by operating in modes 1, 2, or 3. However an improvement is noticed at OXI and RR traffic by operating at mode 4. T traffic does not have such improvement because it cannot make use of the CAP.

5.3 Energy Consumption

Since WSNs are operated by low-capacity batteries, energy preservation is important to guarantee that the e-emergency WSN operates for a long time. In order to evaluate the impact of the diverse operation modes on the energy consumption, the lifetime of the motes was studied.

To better evince the impact of each operation mode on the energy cost of the WSN, the consumption due to samplings performed by the sensing devices is ignored initially. For every operation mode, Figure 6 presents the average lifetime per initial energy of the battery for each mote type relative to the simulations run with a probability P=0.75. To know how many minutes a type of mote would live in such conditions, the values in the y-axis must be multiplied by the available energy in the battery (in Joules) when the mote started working. The available energy E in a battery with n cells, having each cell V Volts and a capacity of C mAh, is: $E=n*V*C*3.6$ J. For instance, one 3V, 1000 mAh lithium coin battery (CR2477) contains 10800 J of initial energy. So, according to Figure 6, an ECG mote operating in mode 4 and powered by that battery would live for 3.68*10800 min = 662.4 hours.

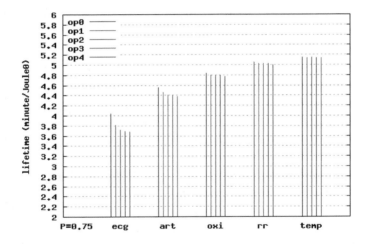

Fig. 6. Lifetime ignoring the sensing consume

For every mote type, the energy consumption does not change significantly with probability P > 0.75 and operation mode 1, 2, 3, or 4.

Figure 7 presents the results when each sampling performed by a sensing device consumes 0.01 mJ of energy. As shown, the effect of the sampling rates on the lifetime of the motes is notorious. As ECG motes have both the highest sampling rate and the largest transmitted packet size, the energy drainage is faster than in the other mote types. However, the lifetime differences observed in each mote type for the diverse operating modes are almost negligible.

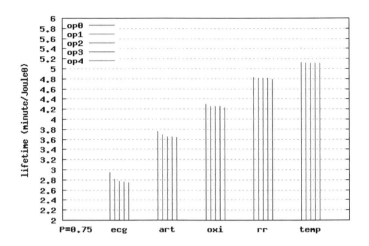

Fig. 7. Lifetime for a sensing consume of 0.01mJ

5.4 CAP Availability

The association or disassociation of a BSN in the WSN is done during the CAP. To see how long is the CAP available for these operations, Figure 8 shows the percentage of superframes containing a CAP with a given size using P=0.75 and operation mode 3, the most limited mode regarding CAP size. In the y-axis, S_1 is the number of superframes with n free slots. For example, a CAP with 255 slots is available in 6.45% of all superframes. It is also shown that information considering groups of slot intervals (bar graph). The values are calculated performing the discrete integral along the specified slot interval. In this case, the values in y-axis must be multiplied by ten, and S_{intv}

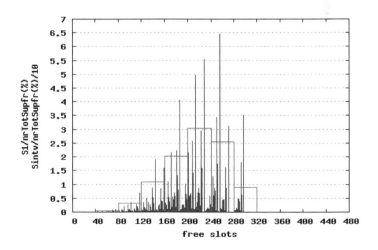

Fig. 8. Free slots for operation mode 3, P=0.75

is the number of superframes with free slots in each interval. For instance, 30.5% of all superframes have a CAP size comprised between 200 and 239 slots.

It is observed that 99.3% of all superframes contain a CAP size above 80 slots, which are enough to perform (dis)association operations. Since CAP size is variable, the beacon should carry the superframe CAP size to inform the motes wishing to associate to the WSN about the available contention slots. It is assumed that the start slot of the CAP is fixed and known previously.

5.5 Scalability

The WSN must be scalable in order to admit additional BSNs. In a LPRT-based system, scalability may be evaluated from the CAP available beyond the minimum CAP size. Indeed, if all superframes have a CAP size bigger than the minimum CAP size, it means that RP and NTP do not take all slots, which eventually may be used by an additional BSN. Figure 9 presents the percentage of superframes with a CAP size equal to the minimum value for several operation modes. This minimum value is fifty slots for operation mode 4, and null for the remaining modes. It is observed that a WSN operating in modes 1, 2, 3, and 4 may admit respectively 5, 3, 1, and 2 additional BSNs without losing significant performance.

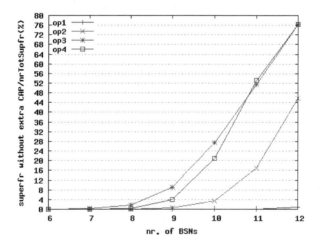

Fig. 9. Evaluation of scalability for P=0.75

5.6 Latency and Goodput

Since all packets are delivered to the BS with a delay below 500ms, the graphs reporting this parameter are not presented. In this slotted framework, goodput is correlated with the packet loss ratio, therefore goodput graphics are not shown too.

6 Conclusions

The deployment of LPRT in e-health systems leads to low power consumption, controlled latency, and throughput efficiency. However, as simulations have shown, LPRT is unreliable if the wireless channel is affected by appreciable bit errors. In order to define a MAC protocol more robust than LPRT, different approaches based on short size beacons and multiple retransmissions have been proposed and tested. The results have shown that such approaches lead to meaningful improvements regarding packet loss ratio, without compromising significantly the energy consumption.

Despite of presenting the best performance regarding packet loss ratio, a network operating in mode 3 faces scalability problems, since significant waste of time slots occurs in the RP. The results have revealed that operation mode 4 offers a better scalability and a good compromise in terms of packet loss. Therefore, we believe that LPRT operating in this mode will enhance QoS in e-health networks. Currently, we are implementing this operation mode in a real testbed for experimental analysis.

Acknowledgments. Óscar Gama is supported by FCT (SFRH/BD/34621/2007), Portugal.

References

1. Gama, O., Carvalho, P., Afonso, J.A., Mendes, P.M.: Quality of service in wireless e-emergency: main issues and a case-study. In: Proc. of 3rd UCAmI, Salamanca, Spain (October 2008)
2. Akyildiz, J.F., Su, W., Sankarasubramaniam, Y., Cayirci, E.: A survey on sensor networks. IEEE Communications Magazine, 102–114 (August 2002)
3. Ye, I., Heidemann, J., Estrin, D.: MAC with coordinated adaptive sleeping for wireless sensor networks. IEEE/ACM Trans. Networks 12(3) (June 2004)
4. El-Hoiydi, A., Decotignie, J.D.: WiseMAC, An ultra low power MAC protocol for the Wise-NET wireless sensor network. In: Proc. of 1st ACM SenSys Conf., USA (November 2003)
5. Afonso, J.A., Rocha, L.A., Silva, H.R., Correia, J.H.: MAC protocol for low-power real-time wireless sensing and actuation. In: 13th IEEE International Conference on Electronics, Circuits and Systems, Nice (December 2006)
6. Gama, O., Carvalho, P., Afonso, J.A., Mendes, P.M.: An Improved MAC Protocol with a Reconfiguration Scheme for Wireless e-Health Systems Requiring Quality of Service. In: 1st Wireless Vitae 2009, Aalborg, Denmark (May 2009)
7. IEEE Std 802.15.4-2003, Wireless Medium Access Control (MAC) and Physical Layer (PHY) Specifications for Low-Rate Wireless Personal Area Networks (October 2003)
8. van Hoesel, L.F.W., Havinga, P.J.M.: A lightweight medium access protocol (LMAC) for Wireless Sensor Networks. In: Proc. 3rd Information Processing in Sensor Networks, Berkeley (April 2004)
9. Rajendran, V., Obraczka, K., Garcia-Luna-Aceves, J.J.: Energy-Efficient, Collision-Free MAC for Wireless Sensor Networks. In: Proc. ACM SenSys 2003, LosAngeles, USA (November 2003)
10. Castalia Simulator, http://castalia.npc.nicta.com.au
11. Zuniga, M., Krishnamachari, B.: Analyzing the transitional region in low power wireless links. In: 1st IEEE Annual Conference on Sensor and Ad Hoc Communications and Networks (October 2004)

An Underwater Robotic Network for Monitoring Nuclear Waste Storage Pools

Sarfraz Nawaz[1], Muzammil Hussain[1], Simon Watson[2], Niki Trigoni[1],
and Peter N. Green[2]

[1] Oxford University Computing Laboratory
Wolfson Building, Parks Road,
Oxford OX1 3QD
{Sarfraz.Nawaz,Muzammil.Hussain,Niki.Trigoni}@comlab.ox.ac.uk
[2] School of Electrical and Electronic Engineering
University of Manchester
Sackville Street Building
Manchester M60 1QD
simon.watson@postgrad.manchester.ac.uk,
peter.n.green@manchester.ac.uk

Abstract. Nuclear power provides a significant portion of our current energy demand and is likely to become more wide spread with growing world population. However, the radioactive waste generated in these power plants must be stored for around 60 years in underwater storage pools before permanent disposal. These underwater storage environments must be carefully monitored and controlled to avoid an environmental catastrophe. In this paper, we present an underwater mobile sensor network that is being developed to monitor these waste storage pools. This sensing system will also be used in very old storage pools to build maps of their internal structure which can then be used for waste removal and pool decommissioning. In this paper, we outline the unique challenges of our application scenario which include robot localization in cluttered underwater environments and the effect of location errors on environment mapping. We also list other industrial applications that can benefit from our underwater sensor network.

1 Introduction

According to the World Nuclear Association [1], there are a total of 437 operational nuclear reactors around the world supplying approximately 15% of the total electricity consumption. In the UK alone, there are 19 nuclear power plants generating electricity for civilian use and 25 old power plants that are in various stages of shutdown and decommissioning. As the world population grows, increased energy demand is likely to make nuclear energy generation more wide spread. However, the biggest issue associated with nuclear power is the generation of radioactive waste which must be managed and stored over a long period of time. This radioactive waste can be classified as low level waste (LLW), intermediate level waste (ILW) and high level waste (HLW). Low level waste contains paper, tools, clothing and other material that produce very small amount

S. Hailes, S. Sicari, and G. Roussos (Eds.): S-Cube 2009, LNICST 24, pp. 236–255, 2009.

of radioactivity. It is generally incinerated or processed as ordinary waste. Intermediate level waste comprises of chemicals, resins and metal fuel cladding. It contains higher amounts of radioactivity and thus requires shielding. It is sometimes stored in short term storage facilities for a few weeks or months before being solidified and buried in near surface trenches. Spent nuclear fuel and products of the fission reaction form high level waste. It generates the highest amount of radioactivity and thus requires shielding and careful handling. It is held in interim storage for 20 to 60 years before it can be transferred to permanent disposal sites. Some of these high level wastes can have a half-life ranging from hundreds of thousands to millions of years and thus require special treatment. The most popular proposal is deep geological disposal in which the waste would be solidified in glass or ceramic through a process called vitrification and then buried in very deep rock formations ranging from 300m to 800m below the earth surface [2]. There are also some proposals to bury these wastes under the seabed [3].

Although, deep geological disposal is in its advanced stages of research, there are no fully functional waste disposal repositories available at present. Even if such repositories were available, it is still necessary to store this waste in cooling ponds for 20 to 60 years to remove the heat that is continuously generated by this waste. After this extended underwater storage, the amount of heat generated is reduced to a level that is suitable for deep rock burial. During this extended underwater storage, the cooling ponds must be carefully monitored for temperature hot-spots and leakage in storage canisters. We are developing an underwater mobile sensor network for these nuclear waste storage pools in collaboration with our partners at University of Manchester and the National Nuclear Laboratory. This network will consist of a swarm of small scale robots. Each robot will be approximately 10cm in diameter and will collaborate with other robots to monitor the conditions inside the storage pool. The cluttered underwater environment of these pools presents significant difficulties for accurate robot localization. Inaccurate robot positions in turn influence the higher layer tasks of environment mapping and high density spatial sampling. In this paper, we discuss these challenges in detail and highlight these issues with our preliminary results. We also list underwater processes in other industrial applications outside the nuclear domain that can benefit from our mobile sensing system.

The rest of this paper is organized as follows. Section (2) introduces the overall architecture and design of our mobile sensing system. Section (3) outlines the issues faced by robot localization algorithms and some preliminary experiences. Section (4) discusses the challenges in performing mapping and exploration tasks. Section (5) outlines the open issues and a research vision that we intend to pursue. Section (6) presents the simulation environment that has been set up to test and analyze the performance of various algorithms. Section (7) lists other industrial applications of our mobile sensor network. Section (8) reviews related work and Section (9) concludes this paper.

2   System Architecture

In this section, we describe our application environment in detail and outline a high level architecture of our mobile sensing system. There are two different types of storage pools that we are targeting. In the following, we describe the differences between these two types and then present our system design.

The first type of storage ponds are modern, well maintained and clean pools. These are generally indoor concrete structures that are designed to be resistant to movements generated by events like earthquakes. Their sizes vary with the largest ones approaching the dimensions of an Olympic sized swimming pool i.e. 50m×25m. These pools can be as deep as 20m and are equipped with pumps and heat exchangers. The waste is sealed in steel flasks and then put in large skips. These skips are stacked on top of each other with the help of an overhead crane assembly. This creates an underwater landscape of rows of towers of skips. The distance between the surface of water and the top of skip towers is generally one to two meters. This thick layer of water prevents any radiation from escaping the pool. Pools are also equipped with cleaning systems to control water quality that is necessary to prevent any corrosion of storage skips. Fig. (1) shows a photograph of one such storage pool at a reprocessing facility in the UK. In these ponds, our mobile sensor network will be used to perform dense spatial sampling of temperature, pH and radioactivity. It will also be used to monitor for any leakages. Our specific research objective is to accurately sample temperature and radioactivity fields in these storage ponds using a swarm of resource constrained robots.

The second type of storage ponds are very old ponds that were built during the early 1950s and used until late 1980s. Over the years, a lot of intermediate and high level waste has been dumped in these ponds. The metal structures

Fig. 1. Modern Storage Pool

and spent fuel rods in these ponds have decomposed and formed a thick sludge that has settled on the bottom over time. This sludge may contain pockets of hydrogen and other solid objects. Visibility inside these ponds is very poor because of the suspended particulates. Skip towers have also toppled over and the internal structure is not known. There are no detailed records regarding the exact contents of these ponds. Some of these ponds are extremely hazardous and only very little human activity is allowed in the vicinity of these ponds. It is necessary to gain more information about the internal structure of these ponds so that the waste can be removed and stored in modern well maintained ponds until deep geological disposal is available. In these ponds, our specific research objective is to build accurate maps of the internal structure of the ponds using a swarm of resource constrained robots. Both tasks of spatial sampling (in new ponds) and mapping (in old ponds) require robots to be able to localize themselves within the pond. The main questions discussed in this paper are, how the presence of clutter - stored nuclear waste - impacts localization errors, and how these errors influence the spatial sampling and mapping processes.

Fig. (2) shows an overall architecture of our underwater mobile sensing system. The storage pond is instrumented with a number of fixed anchor nodes. These anchor nodes periodically transmit acoustic beacons that are used by mobile nodes to determine their position inside the pool. These nodes also act as collection sinks and are used to receive data transmitted by robots on the acoustic channel. Robots can also communicate with each other and perform distance measurements among themselves using acoustic signals. This allows the robots to collaborate with each other during the localization, sensing and mapping tasks. Both the payload and propulsion system of the underwater robots are currently under investigation. At this point, it is envisaged that the the payload will initially consist of a pressure sensor to measure depth, a temperature sensor and a number of obstacle detection sensors that will be based on the

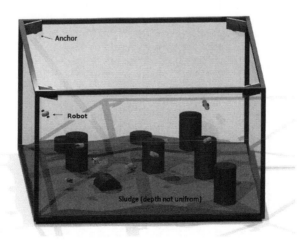

Fig. 2. Underwater Sensor Network Architecture

(a) Robot Internals   (b) Robot size   (c) Prototype Robot

Fig. 3. Size comparison of prototype robot

communication and positioning acoustic transducers. There will also be a hardness sensor based on the same technology and an optical based turbidity sensor. The propulsion system is split into the z plane and x-y plane and will provide at least 4 degrees of freedom (surge, sway, heave and yaw) [4]. Movement in the z-plane will come from propellers while the x-y plane movement will be achieved by a combination of propellers and/or miniaturized vortex ring thrusters [5]. The propulsion systems will be controlled by an embedded system in the form of a 32-bit microprocessor with DSP. Each robot is expected to be approximately 10cm in diameter. Fig. (3) shows an initial prototype version of our robot.

Fig. (4) shows how different components of the software system interact with each other and the hardware components. The lowest layer consists of various hardware components that include acoustic communication and ranging, various sensors and propulsion system. These hardware components are in various stages of development. Middle level layers are responsible for localizing the robot and for performing reactive obstacle avoidance. These middle layer components have been implemented in a simulation environment. The higher layer consists of our two distinct applications i.e. spatial sampling in new ponds and exploration and mapping in old ponds.

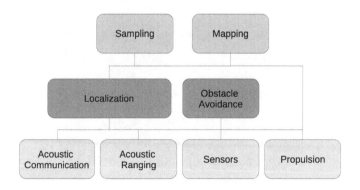

Fig. 4. Software Architecture

3   Robot Localization

3.1   Background

Location awareness is a basic requirement for a robot swarm to explore and map an enclosed underwater environment such as a nuclear waste storage pond. It is necessary for the robots to have accurate position information not just for actual mapping but also for navigating through the pond. Anchor nodes, nodes connected to external reference systems that supply positional information, enable the use of *trilateration* for localizing robots. The technique exploits geometrical constraints, given the locations of a number of anchors and distances to them, to calculate the position. Even though for three-dimensional positioning we require at least four anchors, the underwater robots we are designing have pressure sensors which can be used to determine the depth (z-coordinate) of the robot. This obviates the need for a fourth anchor.

Distance measurements to the anchors, in noisy environments, have small Gaussian errors [6], thus introducing an error in the calculated position. In large networks, where the number of anchors is small compared to the remaining non-localized nodes, it could be the case due to the limited transmission range of the acoustic communication and the attenuating effects of cluttered environments, that *all* anchors would not be heard by *all* the nodes in the network. It is possible that a particular unpositioned node cannot *hear* the required number of anchors in order to calculate its position thus requiring neighbouring nodes which have already been localized (owing to their proximity to the required number of anchors) to assist them. These neighbouring nodes are used as **virtual anchors** and the process is called *iterative localization*. However these virtual anchors, having previously localized themselves, contain inherent errors in their own positions. These errors, compounded by the noisy distance measurements, could propagate via successive iterative localization steps. It is vital to control the propagation of error due to noisy distance measurements and inaccurate virtual anchors positions.

Iterative localization has been a well researched topic for the past few years. *Collaborative* multi-lateration is introduced in [7] where location information from across multiple hops is used to localize a node. In [8], the authors propose a method to quantify the errors introduced by virtual anchors and noisy range measurements. Each node can thus prevent the accumulation of localization errors by maintaining a registry of its neighbouring anchor nodes and using those anchors in trilateration that have the smallest errors. Another approach [9] to quantifying error in iterative localization takes into account the geometric relationships between the anchors during selection. Localization in underwater environments has also been an active area of research [10]. However, almost all of this work deals with localizing sensor nodes in open sea environments [11,12]. Our research, on the other hand, deals with localizing sensing robots in cluttered underwater environments. This is discussed in detail in the following subsection.

3.2   Localization in Cluttered Underwater Environments

One of the primary areas of interest in this project is the challenges faced by a network of robots in exploring cluttered environments. Clutter is generally irregularly shaped obstacles that obstruct acoustic propagation paths between robots or worse introduce multipath acoustic communication.

The underlying concept behind range-based localization is that the distance between the robot and the anchors can be obtained by sending a communication signal between them and the distance is derived from the characteristics of the received signal. In case of acoustic/ultrasound signals, the propagation time translates into the distance travelled, assuming that we know the velocity of sound in that particular medium accurately. This, however, hinges on the assumption that the signal travels straight from the anchor to the non-localized robot along the shortest path, without bouncing off any obstacles in between. Such signals are called **Line Of Sight (LOS)** signals. The measurements from such signals would yield the least distance errors. However in reality, in cluttered environments with obstacles between the transmitter and receiver, it is possible that a large number of signals are **Non Line Of Sight (NLOS)**. Such signals have large distance measurement errors.

There has been extensive research in the mitigation of non line-of-sight measurements, particularly in cellular network research. It was motivated by the requirement put forth by Federal Communications Commission (FCC) to cellular operators to be able to locate a mobile handset within an accuracy of 300 meters for 95% of calls [13]. In current literature [14,15,16,17,18,19,20,21] there are three general methods to deal with NLOS readings. The first method attempts to identify and use only LOS measurements. Distinguishing NLOS from LOS distance measurements could either be done using a time-varying hypothesis test [14], a probabilistic model [18] or residual information [15,21]. The second method incorporates both LOS and NLOS distance measurements with appropriate weighting to minimize the contribution of NLOS observations. Here the primary assumption made is that the number of LOS readings is much greater than the number of NLOS readings [16,17], which may not be the case in our underwater cluttered environment. The third method advocates the use of scattering models. This method takes into account the propagation characteristics of the channel and then directly determines the actual line-of-sight distance using the NLOS readings using a scattering model [19,20]. However this requires perfect knowledge of the underwater environment, including the topology and type of clutter, which may not be possible in most cases.

We have simulated robot localization in the presence of LOS signals and NLOS signals in Fig. (5). In Fig. (5a), we see that the smallest localization error is obtained when only LOS distance measurements are used. In Fig. (5b) we see that localization error increases with a smaller number of LOS distance measurements, even though we have filtered out NLOS measurements. Fig. (5c) shows that using NLOS measurements in addition to LOS measurements gives a large localization error. Hence we can conclude that not only should we filter out NLOS measurements but also have enough LOS measurements to get an accurate position estimate.

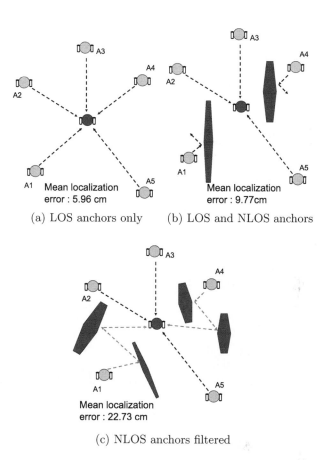

(a) LOS anchors only   (b) LOS and NLOS anchors

(c) NLOS anchors filtered

Fig. 5. Robot localization errors when LOS distance estimates have a small Gaussian error ($\sigma = 6.5$cm) [6] and NLOS distance estimates have a large constant error (30 cm)

From the preliminary experiments we have conducted, we envisage two scenarios as illustrated in Fig. (6). In the first scenario, the clutter is impermeable to acoustic signals. Here only reflected non line-of-sight (NLOS) signals, which have large errors in distance estimates, are present. These have to be detected and filtered from the remaining range measurements before calculating the position. In the second case, the clutter is actually permeable to acoustic signals whereby the signal can 'resonate' through the obstacle without losing all the energy. In this case, the distance estimate of the NLOS signal would be comparable to that of a LOS signal.

When the majority of the NLOS measurements are of the first type i.e., reflected NLOS, it may be the case that filtering out NLOS measurements (anchors) could lead to a non-localized robot not having access to the required number of anchors. For example, in Fig. (5c), if three of the five measurements had been NLOS, the non-localized robot would not have been able to calculate

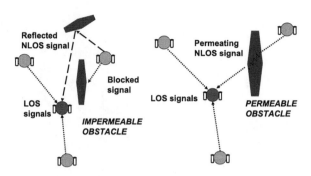

(a) Non-Permeable Obstacles   (b) Permeable Obstacles

Fig. 6. Possible types of obstacles in a nuclear storage tank. Permeable obstacles giving rise to 'near-LOS' NLOS range measurements.

its position. Also the reduced number of LOS anchors increases the error in the position estimate. In this scenario it may become necessary to develop a strategy to deploy previously localized robots to help their non-localized neighbours to localize, so as to maximize the chances that a node, at any given position in the underwater pond, can localize itself accurately. At first we would want to work with the static case where the robots are stationary. Here emphasis is put on the initial position of the robots so as to enable all/most of the robots to be localized.

Now that we have introduced the challenges of robot localization in cluttered underwater environments, in the next section, we discuss how these localization errors effect the mapping task.

4   Exploration and Mapping

Creating maps of the bottom of old waste storage ponds where sludge and other particulate material has settled down over long periods of time is an important aspect of our mobile sensing system. In order to create these maps, the robots must be aware of their surroundings as well so that they can safely move around in the pond without colliding with the waste storage canisters. Thus, to accomplish this task, the robots must explore and map the entire pond. These robots must also collaborate with each other to map the environment efficiently. In this section, we discuss some related work on robotic mapping and exploration, and outline the challenges of performing the mapping task in the pesence of robot localization errors. We also present some preliminary simulation results that highlight these issues.

When a robot is placed in an unknown environment and it does not have access to any location information, it has to determine its location and build the map of the environment at the same time. This problem is known as Simultaneous Localization and Mapping (SLAM) or Concurrent Mapping and Localization

(CML) and has received considerable attention from the robotics research community. Smith and Cheeseman [22] used an Extended Kalman Filter (EKF) to solve the SLAM problem for the first time and since then it has been a highly active field of research. Thrun [23] provides an extensive survey of SLAM techniques.

When the location information is available to a robot, the problem of mapping the environment becomes easier as compared to SLAM. However, noisy sensor measurements and complex environments can still pose significant challenges to mapping and exploration algorithms. The most widely used family of algorithms used to map environments with known robot locations is called *Occupancy Grid Mapping*. Occupancy grid based mapping was introduced by Elfes [24] and later a Bayesian statistical basis of this approach was developed by Moravec [25]. Moravec [26] also extended this approach to build three-dimensional maps using stereo cameras. Occupancy grids have also received a wider acceptance in robotics because they are commonly used as input to algorithms for path planning, collision avoidance, sensor fusion etc. In our system, a group of anchor nodes provide an infrastructure that is used by robots to determine their positions. Therefore, we use occupancy grids for building the maps of underwater environments of the storage pools.

The basic idea of occupancy grid mapping is that the space that has to be mapped is divided in small uniform sized cells, for example, 10cm $\times$ 10cm. For each cell, the robot maintains a probabilistic belief about the occupancy of the cell. In the beginning, no information is available and the status of each cell is unknown. As the robot moves around, it gathers measurements from its perception sensors (e.g. sonar, laser range finder, stereo cameras or some other sensor) and the corresponding cells are updated with these measurements according to a Bayesian reasoning approach. In order to determine which cells to update, the robot must know its position in the environment and the characteristics of its sensors. For example, if a robot is using a sonar sensor to perceive its environment, then all the cells m_i of the occupancy grid that lie within the beamwidth of sonar sensor are updated according to the Bayes rule using the log odds representation as,

$$l_{t,i} = l_{t-1,i} + \log \frac{p(m_i|x_t, z_t)}{1 - p(m_i|x_t, z_t)} \tag{1}$$

where x_t is the location of the robot at time t, z_t is the sonar measurement and p is the occupancy probability derived from a sensor model given the range measurement z_t returned from the sonar and $l_{t,i}$ is

$$l_{t,i} = \log \frac{p(m_i|x_{1:t}, z_{1:t})}{1 - p(m_i|x_{1:t}, z_{1:t})} \tag{2}$$

Generally, the log odds of prior probability l_0 is set to zero for all cells m_i. The log odds representation provides an easy update rule in the form of Eq. (1). When it is required to determine whether a cell m_i is occupied or free, the probability $p(m_i|x_{1:t}, z_{1:t})$ can be recovered as

$$p\left(m_i | x_{1:t}, z_{1:t}\right) = 1 - \frac{1}{1 + \exp\left(l_{t,i}\right)} \tag{3}$$

and compared against thresholds `thres-occ` and `thres-free` to decide on its occupancy,

$$p\left(m_i | x_{1:t}, z_{1:t}\right) \begin{cases} \geq \texttt{thres-occ} & m_i \text{ is occupied} \\ \leq \texttt{thres-free} & m_i \text{ is free} \\ \text{otherwise} & m_i \text{ is unknown} \end{cases} \tag{4}$$

The probabilistic belief for each cell in the grid is derived using sensor measurements and robot location. Therefore, any measurement or location error affects the occupancy grid. We have shown in Section (3) that the cluttered environment of the storage pools can introduce significant errors in estimated robot positions. These location errors in turn introduce anomalies in the storage pool maps built by robots in the form of occupancy grids. Fig. (7a) shows a 6m × 6m simulated pool where two towers of storage skips have been placed. Anchor

(a) Simulated Cluttered Pond

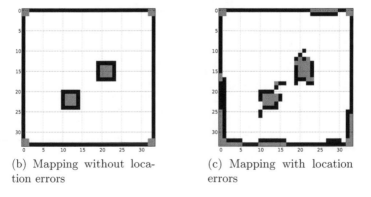

(b) Mapping without location errors

(c) Mapping with location errors

Fig. 7. Mapping in cluttered ponds

nodes have been placed at four out of the eight corners of pool and a single robot moves through this lightly cluttered pool localizing itself through single-hop trilateration. For direct line of sight distance estimates, a small error from a normal distribution $N(0, \sigma)$ with $\sigma = 5$cm is introduced. For non line of sight distances between the anchors and robots, a uniform distribution $U(0, b)$ with $b = 30$cm is used to introduce errors. The robot uses sonar measurements and its estimated location to build a 2D map of the simulated pool using frontier based exploration and mapping [27]. A number of such 2D maps can be built at various depths to create a three dimensional map of the environment. Further details of our simulation environment are described in Section (6). Fig. (7b) shows a 2D map that is built using the perfect location information without any errors. Fig. (7c), on the other hand, shows a map when the estimated robot location contains significant errors due to non line of sight (NLOS) distance estimates between the robot and the anchor nodes. These location errors not only distort the map but since the partial map is also used by the robot for exploration and path planning, they also affect the efficiency of the mapping process. Our aim is to quantify the effect of these errors on the mapping process and then develop efficient exploration strategies that can mitigate the effect of these errors on the mapping process.

5   Open Research Issues

Now that we have described the specific challenges of robot localization and its effects on mapping and exploration tasks in the previous two sections, we now present a vision that we intend to pursue in our future research. We envisage three different types of environment mapping systems using our swarm of robots. In the following, we outline these three systems and the individual questions that we intend to answer for each of these systems.

Our first system consists of robots that have been classified in two different categories depending on their role. We term the robots belonging to the first category as *localizers* and those belonging to the second category as *explorers*. The role of the localizer robots is to position themselves in such a manner that the explorer robots can localize themselves and thus explore the cluttered environment. The main challenge of this approach is to optimally place localizers so that the explorers can build an accurate map of the environment.

In our first system, there is no feedback mechanism between the localization and the exploration tasks. Explorers only explore those regions where the localizers are available to provide positioning infrastructure. In the second system that we envisage an explicit feedback mechanism is available between the explorers and localizers. Thus the explorers can request the localizers to move to a certain region to provide positioning infrastructure so that that region can be explored and mapped. The main challenge of this approach is to design efficient resource allocation strategies that can be used to assign localizers to explorers.

In our third system, there is no distinction of roles and each robot performs both of the tasks simultaneously i.e. each robot not only explores and maps the environment but it also helps its neighboring robots to localize themselves. Thus in this final system, these tasks are very tightly coupled. The main challenge of this approach is to design an efficient coordination strategy among the robots that maximizes the accuracy of the built map.

The specific question that we would like to answer is which one of these three systems can perform environment mapping more accurately given a fixed number of robots, limited energy and the harsh cluttered environment.

6   Simulation Environment

The target scenario of our research project is cluttered underwater environments. This is a unique application scenario that has not been extensively addressed in research literature. Although, there is a large body of work on underwater robots, most of the readily available robot simulators do not provide any means of simulating underwater environments. Stage is probably the most widely used simulator in robotic research community. It provides a 2D environment in which virtual robots can be spawned and controlled by clients. It is generally used with Player [28] which provides a set of standard interfaces. Stage uses very simple and computationally efficient models for the virtual robots and sensors. The advantage of this approach is that the simulation can be scaled to a very large number of robots. However, these simple models do not provide enough details to emulate actual environments and robot behaviours. The 2D nature of the simulator is also very limiting if the robots have higher mobility, for example, three dimensional movement. This limitation makes it unsuitable for our research where the robots are being specifically designed to move in a three dimensional space. Gazebo [29] is an open source 3D simulator that can be used with Player. It uses an open source physics engine called Open Dynamics Engine [30] to provide detailed simulation of Newtonian physics of rigid body systems. The three dimensional virtual environment is described in XML format in a world file. Gazebo seems to address the issues with Stage by providing 3D environments and detailed dynamics simulations. However, the most limiting factor of Gazebo is the use of a text based world file for describing the virtual environments. This approach makes it extremely difficult to design and test complex scenarios.

USARSim is based on a commercially available industrial strength game engine called Unreal by Epic Games [31]. The game can be bought at a small cost of £20 to £30 and the simulator is an open source free software. Unreal gaming environment has an integrated physics engine called Karma [32] that provides high fidelity Newtonian physics simulations for rigid bodies and joint systems. An additional benefit of using the gaming engine is the availability of good quality graphics rendering and visual feedback. By off loading these two important tasks to the gaming engine, USARSim makes it easy for a user to focus on algorithm development for the application. However, the user is still forced to make realistic assumptions due to the high fidelity simulation of the behaviour of robot and its interaction with the surrounding environment. USARSim relies on Gamebots [33] to provide a TCP/IP interface to the outside world. This allows

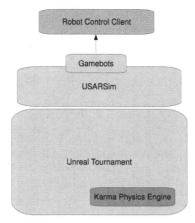

Fig. 8. Structure of USARSim

the controller programs to connect to the simulation environment and spawn and control different robots. Fig. (8) shows the overall structure of USARSim simulator and how different components fit together.

Unreal gaming engine also ships with a 3D editor UnrealEd that can be used to easily create 3D virtual environments. It includes all the necessary facilities to easily create the target environments for our research. The most important of these facilities is the ability to create a *Water Volume*. A water volume is a region of space where the physics engine modifies its behaviour to simulate a fluid. Thus, in a water volume, a robot experiences fluid friction and buoyancy in addition to gravity. It is also possible to change the default values of these parameters to match those of an actual pond. Using UnrealEd, we have created virtual 3D storage pools. We can also create towers of skips and other clutter of different sizes in these simulated pools. Therefore, this simulation set up can faithfully reproduce the actual storage pools in the virtual simulated environment.

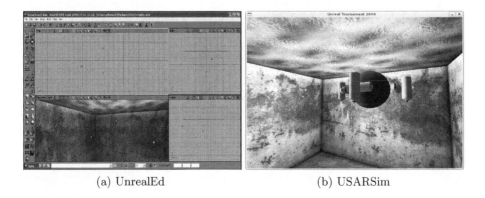

(a) UnrealEd   (b) USARSim

Fig. 9. Screenshot of the simulated pond and the robot

Due to the above mentioned benefits, we decided to use USARSim for investigating the mapping, exploration and localization algorithms for our underwater mobile sensing system. Fig. (9) shows a screen shot of one of the pools in UnrealEd and a robot moving around in this pool in the USARSim simulator.

7   Other Industries

The technologies and the algorithms developed during the course of this research can be used in a wide range of applications in addition to nuclear waste monitoring. In this section, we outline some of the potential industries that operate aqueous environments similar to waste storage ponds and thus can significantly benefit from a networked mobile sensing system for these underwater environments.

Industrial scale process monitoring in chemical industry is an area that can benefit from our contributions. A large portion of these processes involve large scale vessels where different chemicals are mixed together. For these processes, the chemical engineers are generally interested in temperature, pressure, concentration of chemicals, turbidity and other parameters inside the vessel. At the moment, the only technique available to measure some of these parameters is tomography where sensors are placed outside the vessel. However, only some of the above parameters can be estimated using tomography. Another disadvantage of tomography is that it offers very limited spatial and temporal resolution. A swarm of our submersible robots can be placed inside such vessels to perform high density spatial measurements of all of these parameters. These measurements would allow the chemical engineers to develop a better understanding of these chemical processes. This data can then also be used to redesign and improve the chemical processes in terms of energy savings and material usage. The robots can also be used to monitor the wear and tear of reaction vessels from the inside.

Almost all of the chemical plants have large scale settling ponds that are used to clean water after it has been used in a chemical process. These ponds are generally outdoors and could be as big as 100m in diameter. These settling ponds are filled with water and the particulates in water are allowed to settle down. The water is then drained off and recycled. Any leakage in these ponds can have a detrimental effect on the surrounding environment. Therefore, it is necessary to monitor these ponds for any such leakages. Current methods used for these inspections are manual and thus expensive and time consuming. Our system of networked robots can be used to continuously monitor the pond for any anomalies at significantly reduced costs.

Another industry where our mobile sensor system can be used is sewage wastewater treatment. The wastewater generated by our cities and communities is on average 99.94% water by weight and only 0.06% solid waste [34]. Wastewater treatment plants collect this sewage and process it in an extensive network of chambers and ponds to separate these solid wastes from the water. The first stage of this network is similar to settling ponds mentioned above where the water is held for few hours and the solid waste is allowed to settle down. The second stage consists of a large number of aeration ponds where microorganisms are used to breakdown the dissolved waste materials. This process is similar to essentially what happens in nature. However, in a wastewater treatment plant the speed of this process has to increased to process the large quantities of water. Therefore, it is necessary to create optimum conditions for microorganisms in these ponds. This includes mixing the right quantities of oxygen and nutrients in these ponds. Our mobile sensor network can be used in these ponds to monitor the concentration of these substances. Using these observations, the plant engineers can control the amount of oxygen and nutrients injected into the ponds as the wastewater concentration changes every few hours during the course of the entire day.

8   Related Work

In this section, we outline some of the related work to put our research in proper perspective. We discuss some underwater autonomous robots and robotic swarm systems and highlight the challenges that differentiate our research from these efforts.

It is generally more difficult to work with underwater environments as compared to the terrestrial one and therefore the development of underwater robots and especially autonomous underwater vehicles (AUVs) has been relatively slow. However, the military, scientific and commercial applications of these autonomous underwater vehicles has contributed to a very rapid progress in recent years. A database of currently available AUVs hosted by Autonomous Undersea Systems Institute lists a total of 103 AUVs available from 51 different manufacturers [35]. More sophisticated systems that consist of swarms of cooperating AUVs, nodes anchored to the seabed and floating buoys have also been developed. Autonomous Ocean Sampling Network [36] and Autonomous Systems Network [37] are a couple of examples of such underwater networked sensing systems. The deployment and coverage analysis of such underwater sensing systems has also been studied [38]. However, almost all of these platforms and networked systems are targeted towards and deployed in open ocean environments. Open sea is an extremely vast environment that presents its own unique challenges. The AUVs used in this environment are relatively large in size and have significant movement, sensing and computational resources available on board. Networks of such vehicles are also of relatively large size with individual communication links usually stretching to tens of kilometers. Our application, on the other hand, requires the development of very small scale robots that can move in cluttered aqueous environments with dimensions ranging from tens to a few hundred meters. In addition to being small, these robots must have enough resources to safely navigate, sense and map these constrained cluttered ponds.

Serafina is a small scale AUV developed at Australian National University [39]. It is 50cm long and weighs around 5kg. It has five fixed thrusters with two in horizontal and three in vertical configuration. These thrusters provide five degrees of freedom of movement to the AUV. An inertial sensor and a compass are used to perform attitude control and communication among different nodes is achieved through a long wave radio with a carrier frequency of 122.88kHz. The relative distance and heading of nearby nodes in a swarm of Serafina vehicles is determined by using a pair of hydrophones to receive acoustic signals. However, the performance of these techniques has only been measured in a small tank with clear line of sight and without any clutter [40]. Kalantar and Zimmer [41] have also proposed swarming algorithms to track and map environmental fields like chemical concentration spread and ocean bottom mapping.

Researchers have always looked towards nature to draw inspiration for their own creations and this has resulted in various bio-mimetic robots. The robotic fish [42] developed at University of Essex is one such underwater autonomous robot. It uses the oscillatory movement of its body just like an actual fish to propel itself through water instead of using the traditional propeller based propulsion systems. It can move autonomously in an unknown environment in a complete 3D manner. Researchers at University of Essex are proposing to use these autonomous robots for pollution monitoring in sea ports. The current generation of this robot is 52cm long. Three servo motors and mechanical joints are used to generate the oscillatory movement of the body. Four IR sensors and one sonar sensor is used for obstacle detection. However, at the moment there is no communication functionality available to exchange information between different robotic fishes. Therefore, these robots cannot collaborate with each other to form swarms of mobile sensors.

Hydron was developed as part of the Hydra project [43]. It is a very small underwater robot that has a roughly spherical shape with approximately 11cm diameter. Movement in the horizontal direction is achieved by expelling water that is drawn in through an impeller from one of the four nozzles selected through a rotating collar. A syringe is used to draw in or expel the water through the bottom. This alters the buoyancy of the robot and thus allows movement in vertical direction. Each hydron robot can communicate with other units with short range optical transceivers. Hydron robots were developed as basic units that could act as building blocks to automatically form more complex structures by rearranging themselves around each other. However, these units are not equipped with localization facilities that could allow them to determine their position in the aqueous environment.

The cluttered nature of industrial ponds creates a very harsh environment for communication and positioning systems and the focus of our research is to address this challenge at each individual layer of our mobile sensing system ranging from low level distance estimation to application level mapping and exploration algorithms. This is a unique application scenario and to the best of our knowledge has never been addressed before. The robotic platforms and sensing systems that we discussed in this section are either too large for our purposes or have never been tested in our unique application scenario.

9   Conclusion

In this paper, we discussed a novel application of nuclear waste storage pool monitoring and outlined a detailed architecture of our proposed underwater mobile sensor network for monitoring these pools. We described the difficulties faced by robot localization and environment mapping algorithms due to the cluttered and enclosed nature of these underwater environments with preliminary results. We outlined the future research challenges of our unique application and also highlighted various other industrial applications that can potentially benefit from our underwater mobile sensor network.

Acknowledgements. This work is supported by the EPSRC grants EP/ F064209/1 and EP/F064578/1 on Actuated Acoustic Sensor Networks for Industrial Processes (AASN4IP). We would also like to thank the National Nuclear Laboratory (NNL) for their contribution to this paper.

References

1. World Nuclear Association, http://www.world-nuclear.org
2. Roberts, L.E.J.: Radioactive waste management. Annual Review of Nuclear and Particle Science 40(1), 79–112 (1990)
3. Hollister, C.D., Nadis, S.: Burial of radioactive waste under the seabed. Scientific American (January 1998)
4. Fossen, T.I.: Guidance and Control of Ocean Vehicles. John Wiley & Sons, Chichester (1994)
5. Krieg, M., Mohseni, K.: Thrust characterization of a bioinspired vortex ring thruster for locomotion of underwater robots. IEEE Journal of Oceanic Engineering 33(2), 123–132 (2008)
6. Whitehouse, K., Karlof, C., Woo, A., Jiang, F., Culler, D.: The effects of ranging noise on multihop localization: an empirical study. In: Fourth International Symposium on Information Processing in Sensor Networks, IPSN 2005, pp. 73–80 (2005)
7. Savvides, A., Han, C.C., Strivastava, M.B.: Dynamic fine-grained localization in ad-hoc networks of sensors. In: Proceedings of the 7th annual international conference on Mobile computing and networking, pp. 166–179. ACM, New York (2001)
8. Liu, J., Zhang, Y., Zhao, F.: Robust distributed node localization with error management. In: Proceedings of the 7th ACM international symposium on Mobile ad hoc networking and computing, pp. 250–261. ACM, New York (2006)
9. Yang, Z., Liu, Y.: Quality of Trilateration: Confidence Based Iterative Localization. In: The 28th International Conference on Distributed Computing Systems, ICDCS 2008, pp. 446–453 (2008)
10. Chandrasekhar, V., Seah, W.K., Choo, Y.S., Ee, H.V.: Localization in underwater sensor networks: survey and challenges. In: WUWNet 2006: Proceedings of the 1st ACM international workshop on Underwater networks, pp. 33–40. ACM, New York (2006)
11. Erol, M., Vieira, L., Caruso, A., Paparella, F., Gerla, M., Oktug, S.: Multi stage underwater sensor localization using mobile beacons. In: Second International Conference on Sensor Technologies and Applications, SENSORCOMM 2008, August 2008, pp. 710–714 (2008)
12. Erol, M., Vieira, L.F.M., Gerla, M.: Auv-aided localization for underwater sensor networks. In: International Conference on Wireless Algorithms, Systems and Applications, WASA 2007, August 2007, pp. 44–54 (2007)

13. Enhanced Wireless 911 Services,
    http://www.fcc.gov/Bureaus/Wireless/News_Releases/1999/nrwl9040.html
14. Wylie, M.P., Holtzman, J.: The non-line of sight problem in mobile location estimation. In: 5th IEEE International Conference on Universal Personal Communications, 1996. Record, September-2 October, vol. 2, pp. 827–831 (1996)
15. Cong, L., Zhuang, W.: Non-line-of-sight error mitigation in tdoa mobile location. In: Global Telecommunications Conference, GLOBECOM 2001, vol. 1, pp. 680–684. IEEE, Los Alamitos (2001)
16. Chen, P.C.: A non-line-of-sight error mitigation algorithm in locationestimation. In: Wireless Communications and Networking Conference, WCNC 1999, pp. 316–320. IEEE, Los Alamitos (1999)
17. Venkatraman, S., Caffery Jr., J., You, H.R.: Location using LOS range estimation in NLOS environments. In: IEEE 55th Vehicular Technology Conference, VTC Spring 2002, vol. 2 (2002)
18. Borras, J., Hatrack, P., Mandayam, N.B.: Decision theoretic framework for nlos identification. In: 48th IEEE Vehicular Technology Conference, VTC 1998, May 1998, vol. 2, pp. 1583–1587 (1998)
19. Al-Jazzar, S., Caffery Jr., J.: New algorithms for nlos identification. In: Proceedings of the 14th IST Mobile and Wireless Communications Summit (2005)
20. Al-Jazzar, S., Caffery Jr., J., You, H.R.: A scattering model based approach to NLOS mitigation in TOA location systems. In: IEEE 55th Vehicular Technology Conference, VTC Spring 2002, vol. 2 (2002)
21. Chan, Y.-T., Tsui, W.-Y., So, H.-C., Ching, P.c.: Time-of-arrival based localization under nlos conditions. IEEE Transactions on Vehicular Technology 55(1), 17–24 (2006)
22. Smith, R.C., Cheeseman, P.: On the Representation and Estimation of Spatial Uncertainty. The International Journal of Robotics Research 5(4), 56–68 (1986)
23. Thrun, S.: Robotic mapping: a survey, pp. 1–35 (2003)
24. Elfes, A.: Sonar-based real-world mapping and navigation. IEEE Journal of Robotics and Automation 3(3), 249–265 (1987)
25. Moravec, H.: Sensor fusion in certainty grids for mobile robots. AI Magazine 9(2), 61–74 (1988)
26. Moravec, H.: Robot spatial perception by stereoscopic vision and 3d evidence grids. Technical Report CMU-RI-TR-96-34, Robotics Institute, Pittsburgh, PA (September 1996)
27. Yamauchi, B.: A frontier-based approach for autonomous exploration, July 1997, pp. 146–151 (1997)
28. Gerkey, B., Vaughan, R., Howard, A.: The Player/Stage Project: tools for multi-robot and distributed sensor systems. In: 11th International Conference on Advanced Robotics (ICAR 2003), Coimbra, Portugal (June 2003)
29. Gazebo, http://playerstage.sourceforge.net/index.php?src=gazebo
30. Smith, R.: Open dynamics engine, http://www.ode.org
31. Epic Games, http://www.epicgames.com
32. Karma physical engine, http://wiki.beyondunreal.com/wiki/Karma
33. Kaminka, G.A., Veloso, M.M., Schaffer, S., Sollitto, C., Adobbati, R., Marshall, A.N., Scholer, A., Tejada, S.: Gamebots: a flexible test bed for multiagent team research. Commun. ACM 45(1), 43–45 (2002)
34. Following the flow: An inside look at wastewater treatment,
    http://www.wef.org/AboutWater/ForThePublic/WastewaterTreatment
35. AUV Database, http://auvac.org/resources/browse/

36. Autonomous Ocean Sampling Network (AOSN) II,
    http://www.princeton.edu/~dcsl/aosn
37. Chappell, S.G., Komerska, R.J., Blidberg, D.R., Duarte, C.N., Martel, G.R., Crimmins, D.M., Beliard, M.A., Nitzel, R., Jalbert, J.C., Bartos, R.: Recent field experiences with multiple cooperating solar-powered vehicles. In: Fifteenth International Symposium on Unmanned Untethered Submersible Technology, Durham, NH (August 2007)
38. Pompili, D., Melodia, T., Akyildiz, I.F.: Three-dimensional and two-dimensional deployment analysis for underwater acoustic sensor networks. Ad Hoc Networks 7(4), 778–790 (2009)
39. Schill, F.: Distributed Communication in Swarms of Autonomous Underwater Vehicles. PhD thesis, The Australian National University (July 2007)
40. Kottege, N., Zimmer, U.R.: Acoustical methods for azimuth, range and heading estimation in underwater swarms. In: Acoustics 2008, Palais des Congrs, Paris (June 2008)
41. Kalantar, S., Zimmer, U.R.: IEEE/RSJ International Conference on Intelligent Robots and Systems, IROS 2008, September 2008, pp. 3146–3151 (2008)
42. Hu, H.: Biologically inspired design of autonomous robotic fish at Essex. In: IEEE SMC Chapter Conference on Advances in Cybernetic Systems, Sheffield, UK (September 2006)
43. Østergaard, E.H., Christensen, D.J., Eggenberger, P., Taylor, T., Ottery, P., Hautop Lund, H.: HYDRA: From cellular biology to shape-changing artefacts. In: Duch, W., Kacprzyk, J., Oja, E., Zadrożny, S. (eds.) ICANN 2005. LNCS, vol. 3696, pp. 275–281. Springer, Heidelberg (2005)

Evaluation of the Impact of the Topology and Hidden Nodes in the Performance of a ZigBee Network

Helena Fernández-López[1], Pedro Macedo[1], José A. Afonso[1], J.H. Correia[1], and Ricardo Simões[2,3]

[1] Industrial Electronics Engineering Department, University of Minho, Guimarães, Portugal
{hlopez,pmacedo,jose.afonso,higino.correia}@dei.uminho.pt
[2] Institute of Polymers and Composites, University of Minho, Guimarães, Portugal
rsimoes@dep.uminho.pt
[3] Polytechnic Institute of Cávado and Ave, Barcelos, Portugal

Abstract. Low power and small footprint IEEE 802.15.4/ZigBee based devices are a promising alternative to 802.11a/b/g and proprietary protocols for non-critical patient monitoring under important scenarios such as post-op and emergency rooms. However, their use in a healthcare facility to monitor several mobile patients poses several difficulties, mainly because these protocols were primarily designed to operate in low traffic load scenarios. This work presents simulation results used to evaluate the performance of an IEEE 802.15.4/ ZigBee based wireless sensors network (WSN) in a vital signs monitoring scenario, for both star and tree based network topologies. The scalability problem in non-beacon enabled networks is addressed to quantify the degradation in quality of service (QoS) markers when the number of sensor nodes increase. Additionally, the impact of hidden nodes is assessed for the star topology. Results indicate that, to achieve a delivery ratio (DR) higher than 99%, the number of electro-cardiogram (ECG) nodes in a star network must not exceed 35. However, considering a tree topology, the maximum number of nodes must be reduced to 18 to maintain the same DR. The network performance is severely impacted by hidden nodes. For instance, in the absence of hidden nodes, a star network consisting of 32 ECG nodes presents a DR higher than 99%; however, if the percentage of hidden nodes is increased to 5%, it drops to 94%. If the same percentage of hidden nodes is maintained, it is necessary to reduce the number of nodes to 13 to reestablish a 99% DR.

Keywords: ZigBee, wireless sensor networks, e-Health, remote vital signs monitoring.

1 Introduction

Non-critical patients can greatly benefit from continuous vital signs monitoring based on WSN technologies. WSNs are comprised of a large number of spatially distributed small devices with sensing, processing and radio communication capabilities [1]. Low power consumption, topology adaptation in response to changes in propagation conditions or node failures, and multi-hop routing, among other important features,

S. Hailes, S. Sicari, and G. Roussos (Eds.): S-Cube 2009, LNICST 24, pp. 256–271, 2009.
© Institute for Computer Sciences, Social-Informatics and Telecommunications Engineering 2009

make these networks attractive for pervasive healthcare applications. Despite of the evident benefits wireless communications can offer, some concerns prevent the spread use of WSNs for patient monitoring purposes. In a system designed to constantly monitor patients, large amounts of data have to be gathered and transmitted by the network, which is forced to operate in a high load scenario, non-typical for WSNs. A healthcare monitoring system should satisfy strict QoS requirements, such as sustainable throughput, small delay and high reliability; nevertheless, most of the research carried out in the field of WSNs does not address these issues.

In [2], we have proposed a wireless vital signs monitoring system for non-critical in-patients based on non-beacon enabled mode IEEE 802.15.4/ZigBee networks. Medical sensors were designed to be minimally obtrusive and modular. In this work, we present the performance analysis of an IEEE 802.15.4/ZigBee network in star and tree topologies and analyze the behavior of important QoS markers when the number of sensor nodes increases. We consider that each node generates traffic corresponding to one ECG signal. Only ECG sensors are considered because they are the most demanding ones, since they generate the largest amount of traffic. Although we examine the transmission of biomedical signals in this paper, results are also relevant for other WSN applications, especially for data-intensive scenarios.

This paper is organized as follows. In the next section, we present the related work and their conclusions. In Section 3, we briefly review the IEEE 802.15.4 and ZigBee protocols, focusing on the CSMA-CA algorithm. In Section 4, the star and tree network simulation scenarios and parameters are introduced, followed by the presentation and discussion of the results. The hidden node simulation scenario, including results and discussion, is also presented in this section. Finally, in Section 5, the conclusions and future work are presented.

2 Related Work

Several authors have assessed the performance of IEEE 802.15.4 based star networks used specifically for patient monitoring [3-5]; however, as far as we know, none have considered tree networks or the presence of hidden nodes. Most of the authors have also considered that each sensor node integrate a body area network (BAN) whose coordinator (usually, a PDA) also functions as a gateway, relaying traffic to a local area network (LAN). In the motivating application behind this work, sensor nodes from several patients share a common WSN infrastructure, which relays the data generated by all sensors to the coordinator, avoiding the need of several BAN coordinators.

In [6], the maximum data throughput and the delay of unslotted IEEE 802.15.4 is evaluated, in a simple one sender one receiver network, in different frequency bands and address structures. Due to the limited packet length of 127 bytes (maximum PHY service data unit size) and the relatively large overhead required, the maximum bandwidth efficiency under optimal circumstances (addressing field are omitted and no acknowledgment - ACK - is used) for the 2.4 GHz band is 64.9%. The maximum and minimum delays are also determined considering the use of the maximum data packet length. Although it is not referred, the packet delay varies as a function of the number of nodes and the network topology, among other factors. Therefore, in larger networks, packets can experience considerably higher delays.

In [7], the authors considered a non-beacon enabled star network consisting of IEEE 802.15.4 based ECG monitoring nodes as a case study to analyze the network performance as a function of the payload size variation. Considering a restricted scenario consisting of 10, 15 or 20 ECG nodes, where each ECG node generates 12 kbps of data, the authors observe that although the DR grows as the payload size increases, larger size packets may experience larger transmission delays due to the larger transmission times. So, in critical time medical applications, it is suggested that the trade-off between end-to-end latency and packet DR is considered.

In [8], the authors present simulation results used to evaluate the suitability of the IEEE 802.15.4 standard to a healthcare monitoring application. In a first experience, a star network consisting of up to 16 patient monitoring devices operating in the unslotted mode is considered. The most demanding sensor, a multiple-lead ECG, generates 1500 bytes every 250 ms. It is shown that using just three of such devices results in an overload of the network capacity. If packets are spaced out, rather than transmitted successively, the goodput is slightly improved, but the effects on packet loss and DR are not shown. Higher throughput and smaller delays are also achieved decreasing the maximum number of backoff periods or reducing the backoff exponent. Again, the impact of these changes in the DR is not analyzed. Unlike the monitoring device considered by the authors, our system uses three-lead one-channel ECG sensors, which generates much less data but are appropriate for continuous cardiac activity observation and arrhythmia detection.

No specific mechanism to avoid the hidden node problem is provided by the IEEE 802.15.4 protocol, which motivated some authors to consider specific scenarios and propose strategies to mitigate this problem. In [9], the author specifies, implements and evaluates H-NAMe, a new mechanism to solve the hidden node problem in synchronized multiple cluster tree IEEE 802.15.4/ZigBee networks. It is assumed that a synchronization service able to reach all nodes exists. Inside a cluster, time windows during the contention access period are assigned to groups consisting of fully connected nodes. As a result, these nodes can transmit without the risk of hidden-node collisions. The proposed mechanism is shown to improve the network performance by up to 100%. An alternative approach to mitigate the hidden node problem in IEEE 802.15.4 beacon enabled networks is proposed in [10]. Unlikely H-NAMe, this strategy requires that the network coordinator discover the hidden node situation before proceeding on a grouping strategy. Based on simulations, the authors demonstrate that, in the presence of hidden nodes, the proposed strategy guarantees the goodput achieved by the standard protocol in a hidden node free environment. Moreover, a considerable power saving is achieved. In [11], the authors propose TIme zone COordinated Sleep Scheduling (TICOSS), a mechanism that provides multi-hop support over IEEE 802.15.4 through the division of the network in time zones to mitigate packet collision due to hidden nodes belonging to nearby clusters. According to the time zone where a device is located; a time slot is allocated for it to transmit. Three timeslots types are allocated: upstream transmission, downstream transmission and local broadcast. Based on experiments and simulation, the authors conclude that TICOSS considerably extends nodes lifetime and provides more stable and deterministic performance in IEEE 802.15.4 networks. All the mechanisms presented consider beacon-enabled networks consisting of static nodes, which is not the scenario considered in this work. Rather than proposing a mechanism to solve the problem, the effect of hidden-nodes will be quantified, in order to contribute to further understanding of the problem.

3 IEEE 802.15.4 and ZigBee Protocols

The IEEE 802.15.4 standard [12] defines the physical (PHY) and medium access control (MAC) layers of the ZigBee network. The standard defines three operating frequency bands. The higher frequency band ranges from 2400 MHz to 2483.5 MHz and is divided into sixteen channels that operate at a rate of 250 kbps. The two other bands operate at lower data rates and will not be considered here. The MAC layer uses a contention based CSMA-CA scheme. An optional TDMA (Time Division Multiple Access) based scheme called guaranteed time slot (GTS) is also provided.

The unslotted CSMA-CA algorithm is represented in Fig. 1 [12]. Before accessing the channel, the device must wait for a random backoff interval defined in the interval from 0 to (2^{BE} − 1) backoff periods, where BE, the backoff exponent, initially takes the value *macMinBE* and one backoff period is equal to *aUnitBackoffPeriod* symbols. After that, if the clear channel assessment (CCA) function indicates that the channel is idle, the device starts its transmission after a turnaround time delay, which is the time necessary to for the radio transceiver to switch from receive to the transmit state. If the channel is busy, the device defers its transmission and increments NB, the number of transmission attempts for the current packet. BE is also incremented if it has not reached its maximum value, *aMaxBE*. If the maximum number of transmission attempts, *macMaxCSMAbackoffs*, was not reached, a new backoff interval is determined; otherwise, the algorithm declares a channel access failure. Unslotted CSMA-CA parameters are described in Table 1.

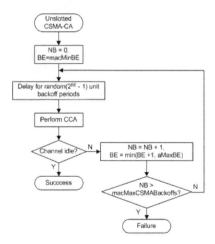

Fig. 1. Unslotted CSMA-CA algorithm

Table 1. Unslotted CSMA-CA parameters

Parameter	Description	Value
macMinBE	The minimum value of the backoff exponent	[0-3], default = 3
aUnitBackoffPeriod	The length of the backoff period, where the symbol period (SP) is 16 µs	20 SP
aMaxBE	The maximum value of the backoff exponent	5
macMaxCSMAbackoffs	The maximum number of backoff periods	[0-5], default = 4

The ZigBee protocol [13], developed by the ZigBee Alliance, stands on top of the IEEE 802.15.4 and defines the network and application layers. The network layer is responsible for routing frames to their intended destinations and provides functionalities such as network starting, newly associated devices address assignment, and mechanisms to join and leave the network. It also provides an interface to the application layer, which holds application objects and provides mechanisms for discovering and binding devices.

4   IEEE 802.15.4/ZigBee Performance Analysis

The performance of the IEEE 802.15.4 protocol was evaluated through simulations performed using OMNeT++ [14]. In all simulations, an increasing number of ECG sensors was considered. The unslotted mode is used because it presents the least overhead and complexity. It is assumed that the wireless channel is not affected by fading or external interferences, yet packets can be lost due to collisions or failure to access the channel, according to the CSMA-CA algorithm.

Every 250 ms, ECG sensors generate 108-byte messages. These messages are made up of 75 data bytes, 3 control bytes added by the application, 15 ZigBee overhead bytes, and 15 overhead bytes included by the IEEE 802.15.4 protocol. ACK packets consist of 5 bytes sent by the coordinator back to the sensor node. A retransmission is triggered in case of channel access failure or when a transmitted packet is not acknowledged. Sensors start to generate data at a random instant between the beginning of the simulation and 250 ms, so data generation from different sensors is not synchronized. Each simulation run ends when the network coordinator receives 100,000 messages.

In this paper, the terms message and packet are frequently used. A message represents a piece of information to be sent and a packet is an instance of a message that is transmitted in the channel. To send one message, a node may need to transmit more than one packet, depending on whether collisions occur.

4.1   Topology Analysis

The topologies considered in this section are exemplified in Fig. 2. Fig. 2 (a) shows a star network that consists of three end nodes, N1 to N3, which communicate directly to the network coordinator, C. A simple tree network is shown in Fig. 2 (b). In this case, all end nodes communicate to the coordinator through the router R.

Fig. 2. Star (a) and tree (b) network topologies

Two sets of simulations were done to compare the performance of a star and a tree network consisting of an increasing number of ECG nodes. This analysis assumed that each node could hear each other's transmissions. Four operation modes were considered:

a) no retransmissions (without ACK – 0 Ret);
b) up to one retransmission attempt per message (1 Ret);
c) up to three retransmission attempts (3 Ret); and
d) up to six retransmission attempts (6 Ret).

In the first case, the acknowledgment mechanism is not used. In the other cases, a retransmission is triggered each time a packet is not acknowledged or the channel access fails.

Collisions and failed transmission attempts. As the presence of hidden nodes is not considered in this section, collisions are only possible if, during a node's turnaround time, another node senses the idle channel and, consequently, starts to transmit after its own turnaround time. In this case, it is considered that both packets are lost. Fig. 3 presents the collided packets (a) and failed transmission attempts (b) curves for the star network, where it is possible to observe that, in general, when the number of nodes increases, the percentage of collided packets and failed transmission attempts also increases as a result of the crescent number of messages. It is also possible to verify that, for the same number of nodes, if more retransmissions are possible, the channel gets more congested and, consequently, more packets collide and more failed transmission attempts occur. Moreover, when a critical number of nodes is exceeded, the slopes of the curves increase quickly, which, depending on the number of allowed retransmissions, might cause an abrupt deterioration in the network performance if only a few more nodes are added.

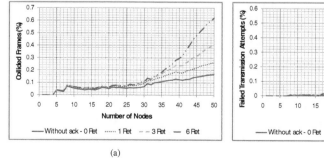
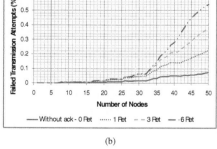

Fig. 3. Star network curves: (a) collided packets; and (b) failed transmission attempts

For the tree topology, it is considered that when packets from two ECG nodes collide, two collided packets are accounted for in the router domain. When a packet from an ECG node to the router collides with a packet transmitted by the router to the coordinator, one collided packet is accounted for in the router domain and another one in the coordinator domain. Fig. 4 shows the collided packets curves at the router (a) and at the coordinator (b).

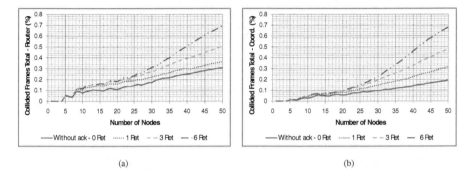

(a)   (b)

Fig. 4. Tree network packet collision curves: (a) at the router; and (b) at the coordinator

The nodes and the router contend for the channel in different conditions. Considering a network comprised of N nodes, during a 250 ms period, from the point of view of a node, it contends with N-1 nodes trying to send one packet each and a router trying to send N packets, while from the point of view of the router, it contends with N notes trying to send one packet each. It results in an asymmetry in terms of channel access, where the nodes' attempts to access the channel are more susceptible to failure than the router's, as shown in Fig. 5.

Similarly to the star topology, the percentage of packet collisions and failed transmission attempts in the tree network increases as the number of nodes increases and, in general, are more frequent if more retransmissions are allowed. It can also be observed that the percentage of collided packets at the router is significantly higher than at the star coordinator. It occurs because, for the same number of nodes, the number of messages being relayed by the router is twice the number of messages received by the star coordinator.

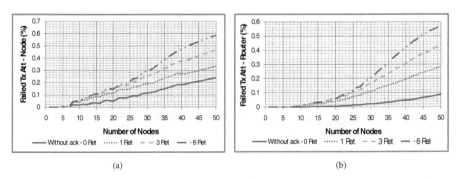

(a)   (b)

Fig. 5. Tree network failed transmission attempts curves: (a) ECG node; and (b) router

Throughput. The normalized throughput represents the ratio between the amount of traffic successfully received by the network coordinator and the network data rate. Fig. 6 presents the normalized throughput curves as a function of the number of ECG nodes for the star (a) and tree (b) topologies. The dark straight lines in both graphs represent the ideal throughput.

If up to six retransmissions are allowed, the star network can handle the traffic from 37 ECG nodes with a deviation from the ideal throughput smaller than 1%. It happens because despite the collided packets and failed transmission attempts, most of the messages are transmitted and reach the coordinator. Nevertheless, as collided packets and failed transmission attempts curves have a high slope when the number of nodes is high, a small increment in the number of nodes can cause the network to start collapsing. The performance of the tree network is worse. If up to six retransmissions are allowed, the network presents a deviation smaller than 1% from the ideal through-put for up to 18 ECG nodes; still, it starts to collapse if one node is added. It happens because messages transmitted by a node must be retransmitted by the router, resulting in a duplication of the network traffic load relatively to the star network.

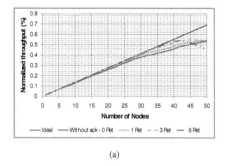   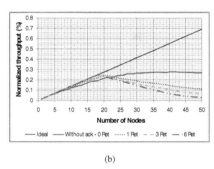

(a)   (b)

Fig. 6. Normalized throughput curves: (a) star network; and (b) tree network

Delivery Ratio. The DR curves for the star and tree networks are shown in Fig. 7. If retransmissions are allowed, high DR values can be achieved even when a relatively large quantity of nodes is active. The reduction in the DR for both networks when the number of nodes increases reflects the deviations from the ideal throughput shown in the graphs, and is ultimately caused by collisions and failed transmission attempts.

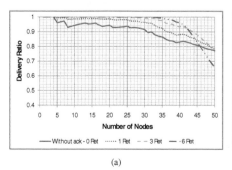   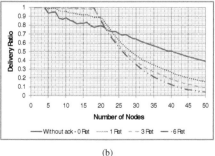

(a)   (b)

Fig. 7. DR curves: (a) star network; and (b) tree network

Delay. The delay a message experiences includes the queuing delay (time spent in the buffer of the node/router) and the access delay (time spent in the backoff process). Fig. 8 (a) and Fig. 8 (b) show the mean and maximum delay curves for the star network. It is possible to observe that the maximum delay is smaller than 150 ms for all cases. Since packets are generated with an interval of 250 ms, the buffer is always empty in this case.

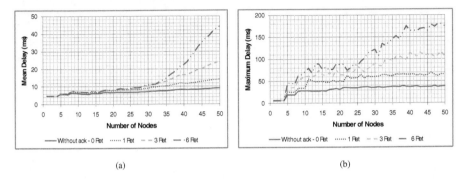

(a)   (b)

Fig. 8. Star network curves: (a) mean delay; and (b) maximum delay

Fig. 9 (a) and Fig. 9 (b) show the mean and maximum delay for tree network. For a small number of nodes, the maximum delay is small; however, when the number of nodes reaches 18 and up to six retransmissions are allowed, the maximum delay exceeds 250 ms. It was observed that message delays occur mainly due to the time they wait in the router's buffer to be transmitted, so the maximum number of nodes of the network and the router buffer size must be carefully considered depending on the delay bound requirements of the network.

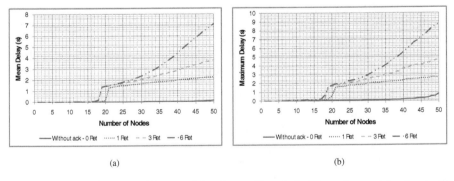

(a)   (b)

Fig. 9. Tree network curves: (a) mean delay (up to 50 nodes); (b) maximum delay (up to 50 nodes)

Energy Consumption. The average value of the energy spent by one node to deliver a message to the coordinator can be obtained as the ratio of the total energy spent by the node to deliver all messages, including packets retransmissions where applicable, to the number of messages sent by the node. For the energy consumption estimation, we have considered the voltage and current consumption values specified for JN5139 ZigBee modules [15], as we have based our sensors nodes on these devices. A voltage supply of 3 V was considered. When the microcontroller (CPU) of the module is on, the module consumption is 9.21 mA, as shown in Fig. 10. During sampling, the ADC is switched on, and the current increases to 9.79 mA. When the module switches the transceiver on during the backoff process, the current increases to 32 mA and, when the module starts transmitting, the current increases to 37 mA.

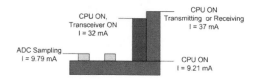

Fig. 10. JN5139 ZigBee module current consumption in distinct modes

Fig. 11 presents the curves of energy consumption per message, considering only the transceiver consumption. The total energy consumption of a node during one second interval is calculated as follows. For instance, for a star network consisting of 15 nodes that are allowed to make up to three retransmissions, the average energy spent by a node to transmit a message is equal to 0.607 mJ. Since during any one second interval the node transmits 4 messages, the consumption relative to the transceiver is 2.43 mJ. Additionally, the ADC is used to make 200 measurements, with each measurement taking 1 ms, which results in a consumption of 0.348 mJ [3 * 200 * (9.79 − 9.21) * 0.001]. The consumption of the microcontroller is 27.63 mJ (3 * 9.21 * 1), so the total energy consumption is equal to 30.41 mJ. If the module is powered by a +3V, 1200 mAh battery (12960 J), a lifetime of 118 hours of continuous operation can be achieved.

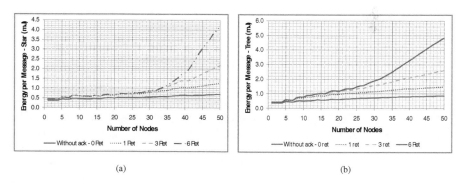

Fig. 11. Transceiver consumption per message curves: (a) star network; and (b) tree network

As can be observed from this analysis, the module consumption is dominated by the microcontroller consumption, which is constantly on as a consequence of the frequent ADC measurements required by the ECG signal. So, although the nodes from the star network spend less energy to transmit each message than the nodes from the tree network, the resulting lifetime of both sensors will not be much different.

Star and tree topologies comparison analysis. Table 2 summarizes the simulation results presented in this section. Three important QoS markers are considered: a throughput deviation from ideal smaller than 1%, a delivery rate greater than 99% and a maximum message delay smaller than 250 ms. The maximum number of nodes each network can have and still comply with the established requirements are shown in the unshaded cells. The % columns refer to the reduction in the number of ECG nodes supported by the tree network with relation to the star network. For instance, if up to 3 retransmissions are allowed, a star network with up to 35 ECG nodes presents a throughput deviation smaller than 1% from the ideal throughput. In the same operation mode, a tree network must contain no more than 18 ECG nodes to achieve a similar performance, which means a reduction of 47% in the number of ECG nodes.

Table 2. Star and tree topologies comparison summary

Operation mode	Throughput dev. < 1%			DR > 99%			Max. delay < 250 ms	
	Star	Tree	%	Star	Tree	%	Star	Tree
Without ACK – 0 Ret	16	7	56	4	4	0	> 50	42
1 Ret	25	11	56	7	7	0	> 50	19
3 Ret	34	18	47	32	12	62	> 50	18
6 Ret	37	18	51	35	18	49	> 50	17

It is possible to observe that an increase in the maximum number of allowed retransmissions contributes favorably to the performance of the networks, though an increase in the maximum delay is experienced and a small decrease in the lifetime of each ECG node is also expected. If up to three retransmissions are allowed, a star network must not exceed 32 ECG nodes to comply with the QoS requirements established, while in the case of a tree network, the maximum number of ECG nodes cannot exceed 12.

4.2 Hidden-Node Analysis

The performance of WSNs can be seriously degraded by collisions caused by hidden nodes. In a CSMA-based network, a node can only transmit if it senses the channel idle. The hidden-node problem occurs when the carrier sensing fails, so a node starts transmitting when other node has already occupied the channel. If both transmissions are within the reach of a receiver, a collision occurs. A generic hidden-node situation is illustrated in Fig. 12 (a), where the transmission range of nodes A and B are represented by circles drawn around the nodes. If B starts to transmit to D while A is transmitting to C, A's and B's packets collide at C. In this case, the transmission from A, which is hidden from B, is corrupted by the B's transmission. A more severe problem happens if C and D happen to be the same node, that is, if A and B transmit to a common receiver, C, as seen in Fig. 12 (b). In this case, if B starts to transmit while A is transmitting (or vice-versa), both packets are corrupted.

The hidden-node simulation runs were executed considering an increasing number of ECG sensors that send data directly to the coordinator, in a star topology. Five scenarios were simulated, considering that up to three retransmissions are allowed. Each scenario considered a different percentage of hidden nodes in the network, varying from 0% to 20%. The situation depicted in Fig. 12 (b) was simulated, since in the star topology all nodes transmit to the coordinator. In this case, if one node starts to transmit when a node that is hidden from it is already transmitting, both packets are lost and no acknowledgements are sent back by the network coordinator.

(a)   (b)

Fig. 12. The hidden-node problem schematics

Collisions and failed transmission attempts. Fig. 13 (a) shows the collided packets curves. It is possible to observe a pronounced increase in the number of collisions due to hidden-node collisions. Apart from collisions between packets, collisions between a node packet and an ACK transmitted by the network coordinator are also considered. This situation can occur if a node fails to detect a packet transmission but only starts transmitting just after the packet is received by the network coordinator. The packet-ACK collision curves are shown in Fig. 13 (b) and demonstrate that the

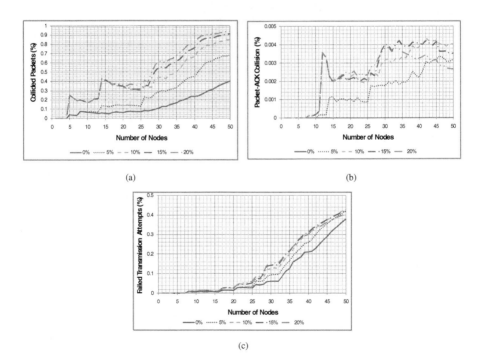

Fig. 13. Hidden-nodes analysis curves: (a) collided packets ratio; (b) packet-ACK collision ratio; and (c) failed transmission attempts ratio

occurrence of this type of collision is infrequent when compared to the collisions between packets. The failed transmission attempts ratio as a function of the number of nodes is presented in Fig. 13 (c). When the number of nodes increases, more collisions and, consequently, more retransmissions occur and the channel gets busier, increasing the failure ratio. Similarly, since collisions gets more frequent as the percentage of hidden nodes increases, the failure ratio also increases as the percentage of hidden nodes increases.

Throughput. Fig. 14 shows the normalized throughput curves as a function of the number of ECG nodes, considering a percentage of hidden nodes ranging from 0 to 20%. Additionally, the straight continuous line represents the ideal throughput. In the absence of hidden nodes, a deviation smaller than 1% from the ideal throughput can be achieved if the number of ECG nodes does not exceed 34 but, if the percentage of hidden nodes achieves 5%, the number of nodes must be reduced to 25 for the same deviation. If this percentage is increased to 20%, the number of nodes must not exceed 13.

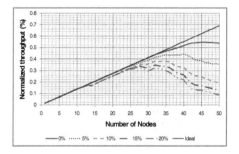

Fig. 14. Normalized throughput in presence of hidden nodes

Delivery Ratio. The DR variation as a function of the number of nodes and the percentage of hidden nodes is shown in Fig. 15. Due to the random selection of hidden-node combinations, the curves exhibit some fluctuations. Nevertheless, they correctly evidence the highly negative effect of hidden nodes in the network performance. In fact, if no hidden nodes are present, very high DR values are achieved with a relatively high

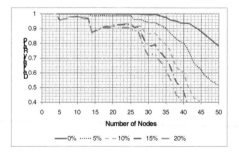

Fig. 15. DR variation in presence of hidden nodes

number of nodes, but if even a small amount of hidden nodes is present, the perform-ance of the network is seriously affected by the high amount of resulting packet colli-sions. For instance, more than 99% of the messages are delivered if the number of ECG nodes is equal to 32 but, if the percentage of hidden nodes is increased to 5% or 10%, the number of ECG nodes must be reduced to 13 or 4, respectively.

Delay. The maximum and mean message delay curves are shown in Fig. 16. It can be observed that the maximum delay is smaller than 150 ms for all cases. Additionally, it can be noticed that the mean delay is quite small, not exceeding 34 ms.

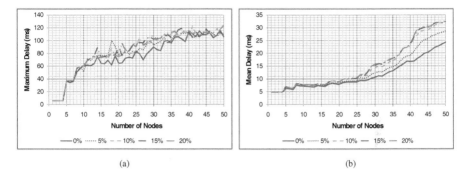

(a)   (b)

Fig. 16. Maximum (a) and mean (b) delay curves in presence of hidden nodes

Energy Consumption. The energy consumption curves shown in Fig. 17 were de-termined following the same procedure explained in Section 4.1, that is, they just consider the consumption from the transceiver. It is possible to notice that if the per-centage of hidden nodes increases, the energy consumption also increases. Despite of this, the reduction in nodes' lifetime is not high, since most of the energy consump-tion is due to the microcontroller. If we consider a network with 25 nodes, with no hidden nodes, the average energy spent by each node to transmit a message is equal to 0.718 mJ. In this case, the energy spent during one second is equal to 30.85 mJ, re-sulting in a lifetime equal to approximately 117 hours. On the other hand, if the per-centage of hidden nodes is 20%, each node spends an average of 1.22 mJ to transmit each message, resulting in an average consumption of 32.06 mJ during one second and a lifetime of approximately 112 hours, a small reduction of 4%.

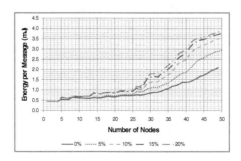

Fig. 17. Energy per message in the presence of hidden nodes

Hidden-node comparison analysis. Table 3 summarizes the simulation results presented in this section. The second column contains the maximum number of nodes a star network can have and still achieve a throughput that deviates less than 1% from the ideal. The third column presents the same information, but considering a delivery ratio greater than 99%. The maximum delay and the lifetime are not considered because the first is smaller than 250 ms in all cases and the second does not suffer a considerable variation. As can be observed, the effect of hidden nodes in the network throughput is significant, but the effect on the DR is quite severe. In fact, without hidden nodes a star network comprised of up to 32 ECG nodes is capable of achieving a minimum DR of 99%. To achieve this performance in the presence of 10% of hidden nodes, the maximum number of ECG nodes must be reduced to only 4.

Table 3. Hidden-node analysis summary

Percentage of hidden nodes (%)	Throughput dev. < 1%	DR > 99%
0	34	32
5	25	13
10	13	4
15	13	4
20	13	4

5 Conclusions and Future Work

In this work, the performance of an IEEE 802.15.4/ZigBee based WSN designed for continuous vital signs monitoring is evaluated in terms of scalability and topology. Additionally, different retransmission modes are considered. Assuming that the wireless channel is not affected by fading or external interferences, simulation results indicate that a star network, operating in the unslotted mode, can contain up to 34 ECG nodes and still comply with the performance criteria specified. Otherwise, if a tree topology, where are all sensor nodes are directly associated to a single router, is considered, the duplication of the network traffic load relatively to the star network causes a significant increase in the packet collisions and failed transmission attempts, resulting in a considerable deterioration of the DR. Moreover, the queuing delay suffered by messages in the router causes a significant increase in the maximum and mean delays. As a result, if the same performance relatively to the star network is to be achieved, it is necessary to reduce the number of sensor nodes, relatively to the star network, by half or even less.

The network achieves better throughput and DR if nodes are allowed to make several attempts to access the channel, which can be implemented at the application level. However, it was shown that the network collapses rapidly when the number of nodes grows, tightly constraining the maximum number of nodes. Additionally, an increase of the maximum delay is observed, which, in the case study presented, did not represent a constraint.

The impact of a variable percentage of hidden nodes is considered in the second part of this work. Simulation results indicate that in high traffic load scenarios the number of collisions due to hidden nodes increases substantially, seriously degrading the network performance, namely the throughput and the DR. This scenario is valid even for a small percentage of hidden nodes, as we have considered it ranging from 5% to 20%. For instance, in the absence of hidden nodes, a star network consisting of 32 ECG nodes presents a DR greater than 99%; however, if the percentage of hidden nodes is increased to 5%, it drops to 94%. Moreover, if the percentage of hidden nodes increases to 20%, it is necessary to further reduce the number of ECG nodes to only 4 to sustain the desired DR.

Our future work includes the study of techniques that could help alleviate the hidden-node problem in non-beacon enabled networks where nodes can be highly mobile.

Acknowledgments. This work has been supported by the Portuguese Foundation for Science and Technology and the POCTI and FEDER programs.

References

1. Ilyas, M., Mahgoub, I. (eds.): Handbook of Sensor Networks: Compact Wireless and Wired Sensing Systems. CRC Press, New York (2004)
2. Fernández-López, H., Afonso, J.A., Correia, J.H., Simões, R.: Extended Health Visibility in the Hospital Environment. In: BioDevices 2009, pp. 422–425 (2009)
3. Gao, T., Pesto, C., Selavo, L., Chen, Y., Ko, G., Lim, H., Terzis, A., Watt, A., Jeng, J., Chen, B., Lorincz, K., Welsh, M.: Wireless Medical Sensor Networks in Emergency Response: Implementation and Pilot Results. In: IEEE Conf. on Tech. for Homeland Security (2008)
4. Patel, S., Lorincz, K., Hughes, R., Huggins, N., Growdon, J.H., Welsh, M., Bonato, P.: Analysis of Feature Space for Monitoring Persons with Parkinson's Disease With Application to a Wireless Wearable Sensor System. In: 29th Annual International Conference of the Engineering in Medicine and Biology Society (2007)
5. Lorincz, K., Malan, D.J., Fulford-Jones, T.R.F., Nawoj, A., Clavel, A., Shnayder, V., Mainland, G., Welsh, M., Moulton, S.: Sensor networks for emergency response: challenges and opportunities. IEEE Pervasive Computing 3(4), 16–23 (2004)
6. Latre, B., Mil, P.D., Moerman, I., Dhoedt, B., Demeester, P., Dierdonck, N.V.: Throughput and Delay Analysis of Unslotted IEEE 802.15.4. J. Networks 1(1), 20–28 (2006)
7. Liang, X., Balasingham, I.: Performance Analysis of the IEEE 802.15.4 based ECG Monitoring Network. In: 7th IASTED, pp. 100–104 (2007)
8. Golmie, N., Cypher, D., Rebala, O.: Performance Analysis of Low Rate Wireless Technologies for Medical Applications. Computer Comm. (28), 1266–1275 (2005)
9. Severino, R.: On the use of the IEEE 802.15.4/ZigBee for Time-Sensitive Wireless Sensor Network Applications. Polytechnic Institute of Porto, MSc Thesis (2008)
10. Lain-Jinn, H., Lain-Jinn, H., Shiann-Tsong, S., Yun-Yen, S., Yen-Chieh, C.: Grouping strategy for solving hidden node problem in IEEE 802.15.4 LR-WPAN. In: First International Conference on Wireless Internet, pp. 26–32 (2005)
11. Ruzzelli, A.G., Tynan, R., O'Hare, G.M.P.: An energy-efficient and low-latency routing protocol for wireless sensor networks. Systems Communications, 449–454 (2005)
12. IEEE Std 802.15.4-2003—Part 15.4: Wireless LAN Medium Access Control (MAC) and Physical Layer (PHY) Specifications for Low-Rate Wireless Personal Area Networks (2003)
13. ZigBee Alliance, ZigBee Specification 053474r17, v. 1.0 r17 (2007)
14. OMNet++ Discrete Event Simulation System, http://www.omnet.org
15. Jennic Wireless Microcontrollers, http://www.jennic.com/

Coordinated Sleeping for Beaconless 802.15.4-Based Multihop Networks

A.G. Ruzzelli[1], A. Schoofs[1], G.M.P. O'Hare[1], M. Aoun[2], and P. van der Stok[2]

[1] CLARITY: Centre for Sensor Web Technologies, Dublin, Ireland
{ruzzelli,anthony.schoofs,gregory.ohare}@ucd.ie
[2] Philips Research Laboratories, Eindhoven, The Netherlands
{peter.van.der.stok,marc.aoun}@philips.com

Abstract. The last few years have seen a wide adoption of the IEEE 802.15.4 MAC/PHY standard for low-power communication between wireless sensor nodes. Within this work we study some fundamental drawbacks of the 802.15.4 specifications for multihop network deployments, which adversely affect efficient node energy consumption. These issues are rectified by investigating a timezone-based scheduling, V-Route, that builds on 802.15.4 beaconless mode to enable both a synchronized sleep scheduling and a bidirectional communication between nodes in the sensor network and the PAN coordinator. The contributions of V-Route are threefold: (1) mitigate collisions, (2) enable packet routing and (3) provide energy saving in a multihop context, while maintaining the full compliancy with the 802.15.4 standard. We present a performance evaluation on energy consumption and latency with real experiments on Philips AquisGrain sensor nodes. Enhancing 802.15.4-based multi-hop networks with V-Route yields energy reduction ranging from 27.3% to 85.3%.

Keywords: Sensor, network, wireless, routing, energy, 802.15.4.

1 Introduction

The advent of sensor-based wireless networks requires standard communication compliancy to allow interoperability among vendors in a multitude of applications. To this objective, IEEE defined in 2003 the 802.15.4-2003 standard [1] that specifies MAC and physical (PHY) layers to enable wireless communication between small battery-operated devices. In particular, the standard targets low data-rate communication in single-hop and multi-hop sensor networks. However, choosing a reliable, energy-efficient, and 802.15.4 compatible routing protocol that can relay packets from the Personal Area Network (PAN) coordinator to the sensor nodes and vice-versa is not part of the standard.

Energy-efficiency in low-power wireless PANs is fundamental, and related work has shown relevant drawbacks for both single-hop and multi-hop -enabled 802.15.4 communication [6,17,19,20]. This paper confirms such prior works and presents experiments on 802.15.4 single-hop and multi-hop networks that exhibited similar issues.

S. Hailes, S. Sicari, and G. Roussos (Eds.): S-Cube 2009, LNICST 24, pp. 272–287, 2009.
© Institute for Computer Sciences, Social-Informatics and Telecommunications Engineering 2009

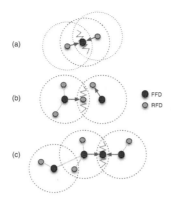

Fig. 1. (a) HTP in single-hop 802.15.4, (b) HTP with nearby independent star networks, and (c) HTP with aggregated star networks in multi-hop deployments

Figure 1 shows three issues with 802.15.4-based single-hop and multi-hop networks: (a) depicts the hidden terminal problem (HTP) in star networks when multiple out-of-range nodes assume a free channel and initiate time-overlapping packet transmissions, resulting in packet collision at the receiver node. The HTP is especially accentuated in the context of nearby independent star networks, as shown in (b); (c) is an example of an 802.15.4 multi-hop network as a form of aggregated star networks. Communication between stars is via Full Functional Devices (FFDs). FFDs carry full 802.15.4 functionality and all features of the standard. 802.15.4 provides no mechanisms for coordinated and energy efficient FFD-to-FFD packet transmission. Therefore, FFDs need to be kept powered on as communication is subsequently realized via CSMA-CA. This constraint reduces significantly the nodes' operative lifetime.

This work rectifies these issues by investigating a timezone-based scheduling that builds on top of 802.15.4 to enable energy-efficient bidirectional communication between nodes in the sensor network and the PAN coordinator. Our approach, named V-route, mitigates packet collisions due to hidden terminals and enables packet routing along with energy-efficient multi-hop communication. V-Route is inspired by and extends the MERLIN architecture which has been studied analytically and through simulations [14]. In contrast, V-Route, which utilizes a scheduling similar to that of MERLIN, is tested on real hardware and intends to experimentally validate the coordinated sleep scheduling and directed broadcast concepts on top of 802.15.4.

A major objective of V-route is 802.15.4 protocol compliancy. Therefore nodes that run our V-route scheduling can still communicate fully in single-hop with nodes that run a beaconless 802.15.4. We present a comprehensive description and empirical experiments of the multi-hop enabling scheduling along with three energy optimizations: transceiver sleep policy, reduced CSMA backoff, and MCU standby mode. Such optimizations yield energy reductions ranging from from 27.3% to 85.3%.

The remainder of this paper is organized as follows. Section 2 provides an overview of related work and compares our approach against existing architectures. Section 3.3 details the sleep scheduling and routing technique. Section 4 evaluates the proposed technique on Philips AquisGrain nodes. In Section 5 we propose some guidelines to decrease energy consumption for a multihop-enabled 802.15.4 network. Finally, we conclude the paper.

2   Related Work

Literature shows a great number of studies of the different issues intrinsic to the 802.15.4 standard. The problems of high energy cost for idle listening [15], collisions from hidden terminals due to the lack of RTS and CTS mechanisms [18,6], and the risk of frame collisions for nearby coordinators in a multi-hop deployment [19] have been investigated and demonstrated.

Some efforts in adapting energy-efficient mechanisms, such as Low Power Listening (LPL) [13] to 802.15.4, are presented in [10]. Since TI CC2420-like radios do not support long preambles similar to the ones implemented in BMAC, the long preamble is simulated by transmitting a **train of same packet**. However, the LPL/802.15.4 adaptation revealed serious reliability problems due to the interleave between such packet train as studied in [5]. Furthermore, enabling LPL on 802.15.4-based nodes prevents them from communicating with non-enabled LPL nodes, therefore reversing the 802.15.4 compliancy.

A more general approach to reducing energy consumption in the network is to provide a duty-cycle mechanism that regulates the activity of the nodes. However, there is a trade-off between energy efficiency and latency in packet delivery. Studies in [12] demonstrated that latency in packet delivery is heavily affected by the node duty-cycle. Some other experiments, for example in [14], confirmed that forwarding techniques for wireless networks such as [11,7] show a poor performance in delivery rate when deployed in a lossy environment [16] with unreliable nodes.

Besides, although the revised 802.15.4-2006 specifications [2] mention the cluster tree formation where most nodes are FFDs, the standard leaves the resolution of issues related to more complex topologies for higher layers. In particular, ZigBee [3] implements a version of the AODV [11] routing algorithm to automatically construct low-speed ad-hoc networks in the form of mesh or clusters. The current profiles derived from the ZigBee protocols support beaconless and beacon-enabled networks. In beaconless networks, CSMA/CA is used. In this type of network, ZigBee Routers typically have their receivers continuously active, requiring a more robust power supply and subsequently depreciating energy efficiency. In beacon-enabled networks, ZigBee Routers transmit beacons periodically to end-nodes that are able to sleep between beacon receptions, allowing for longer battery life. The usage of the beacon-enabled 802.15.4 is subject to the following issues: (1) ZigBee RFDs can communicate to only one parent FFD, the one responsible for both coordinating RFD sleeping intervals and routing packets from one star to another. However, there is no agreement for a distributed sleeping policy among FFD routers. Therefore, the *FFDs must stay awake the whole time* while only RFDs can go to sleep after transmission; (2) The uncoordinated activity of nearby stars especially affects *FFD beacons that are transmitted without checking the channel condition.* Beacons are prone to collide in presence of nearby stars activity. Such issues, confirmed by some of our initial experiments, prevented us from adopting the 802.15.4 beacon-enabled functionality in a multihop network. *Therefore, in the rest of this paper, we will concentrate on studying the 802.15.4 beaconless mode.*

3   Coordinated Sleeping Scheduling over 802.15.4

In order to mitigate packet collisions without affecting the 802.15.4 compliancy and to enable multihop communication we adopt the following 802.15.4 settings:

- **FFD functionality for all nodes:** It allows all nodes to communicate with each other in a peer-to-peer fashion by performing CSMA/CA before transmitting;
- **Beaconless configuration:** 802.15.4 reduces to a plain CSMA/CA with no handshake mechanism in place.

3.1   Traffic Patterns

The performance of a multihop routing algorithm and transmission scheduling can vary greatly according to the traffic patterns. In contrast to applications for mesh networks that might have any node exchanging packets with any other node, most sensor network applications requires many-to-one (towards the sink) or one-to-many (from the sink to the other nodes) multihop communication, referred to as *upstream* and *downstream* communication, respectively. There-fore, a cooperation between a routing algorithm and a sequential scheduling of transmission is advantageous. **In other words, it is beneficial if a packet retransmission is scheduled immediately after a node receives a packet traveling upstream or downstream.** Furthermore, theoretical studies in [8] demonstrate that an address-less forwarding policy merely based on directed broadcast towards nodes with higher or lower hop count relative to the sink node achieves greater energy saving and reliability than an address-based ap-proach. **V-route adopts this communication trend by *transmitting all the upstream or downstream packets without specifying a particular forwarder* with smaller or higher hop count respectively.** This minimal-ist communication approach is named **timezone-based directed broadcast** as nodes with different hop count are defined to be in a different timezone. This approach generates packet duplication which is appropriately reduced by allowing nodes to overhear packets being transmitted by neighbours and delete the ones successfully transmitted, in what amounts to a **packet overhearing mechanism.** Optimizing transmission allocation to forward packets consecu-tively to nodes with lower or higher hop count (i.e. to a lower or to a higher timezone) reduces the packet latency that can effectively be traded-off for en-ergy savings. Within this work we apply and demonstrate that directed broadcast

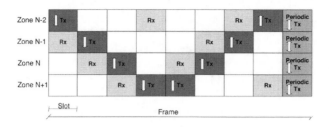

Fig. 2. The table of scheduling with periodic local broadcast

with overhearing is beneficial for 802.15.4 networks. In general, a certain number of consecutive upstream transmissions should also be followed by a number of downstream consecutive transmissions. This can be represented as an upstream/downstream V-shaped scheduling as shown in Figure 2. The next two sections highlight the division in zones of the 802.15.4 network and how the scheduling table of V-Route is implemented.

3.2 Setup and Maintenance Phases

802.15.4 beacons are used only during the association phase to form the network. Once completed, CSMA-CA is used for all communication. At the beginning of network formation, 802.15.4 nodes broadcast periodically a 802.15.4 Association Request (AR) in order to find a coordinator in the vicinity. When the PAN coordinator receives a AR, it starts associating neighboring nodes by an Association Response (AR) that contains the 802.15.4 PAN specifications. At this point the V-Route procedure begins. Following a subsequent Data Request from the node, the PAN coordinator issues a $2 - byte$ short address to the node together with timing information for synchronization. The node is now associated to the network. Using V-Route, the node can become a FFD in timezone 1 and therefore act as coordinator delegate for further nodes. Newly associated nodes will then be in timezone 2; the process is repeated recursively until all nodes are associated. *The timezone is provided in an extra byte field in each packet transmitted.* At the end of the association process the network is divided in timezones as shown in Figure 3. The timezone of a node is the minimum number of hops required for its packets to reach the PAN coordinator. For instance, the packets of nodes within the 3rd timezone need to be forwarded at least three times to get to the PAN coordinator. Nodes are now ready to adopt a coordinated sleeping policy provided by the scheduling table as described in Section 3.3.

In order to cope with network changes such as battery depletion, replacement and mobility, a node's timezone has a *preset expiration time*. A node's timezone expires if the node does not receive a zone update message, which all nodes send periodically, within a certain timeout period. In case of zone expiration due to a parent node failure or a link break, the node follows a zone re-establishment process. The node start broadcasting upstream and then downstream a Timezone

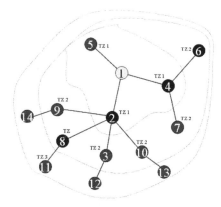

Fig. 3. The initial timezone setup by flooding and different path generation

Update Request (TUR). In case of no response, the node disregards the sleeping scheduling policy until it listens to any packet being transmitted to acquire the timezone and then restore the scheduling.

An important aspect of V-Route maintenance phase is the node synchronization. In order to synchronize the clocks of the AquisGrain sensor nodes in our testbed, we implemented an improved version of the FTSP protocol [9] enhanced with efficient linear regression and Kalman filtering as detailed in [4]. Network-wide time synchronization, relative to a unique time master node, is achieved. The adopted MAC-layer time-stamping, explained further on, effectively minimizes nondeterministic delay components that affect the time synchronization performance [9]. Clock drift rate estimation is used to estimate the difference in counting rate between nodes. It is used to decrease the sending rate of time synchronization messages and thus the energy consumption needed to achieve time synchronization, by estimating the time offset progress behavior in between synchronization instances.

3.3   V-Route Communication Scheduling

Following the setup phases described in section 3.2, the node can avail of the scheduling table shown in Figure 2 to regulate sleeping and activity periods of nodes. Although 802.15.4 does not support multicast, V-route can practically achieve it by broadcasting when either nodes with a lower or higher hop count are sleeping i.e. upstream or downstream broadcast. The V-Table is important as it regulates the cyclic sleeping of nodes within a frame so to reduce the chances of running into a HTP. We present the scheduling for 802.15.4 and its performance through experiments on real hardware. Following are the 3 types of transmissions supported by the V-table:

- **Upstream transmission** in which a node can transmit to nodes located 1 hop closer to PAN coordinator, i.e. to nodes in a lower timezone;

- **Downstream transmission** in which a node can transmit to nodes located 1 hop at a longer distance from the PAN coordinator, i.e. to nodes in a higher timezone;
- **Local broadcast** in which a node transmits simultaneously to all the neighboring nodes, i.e. those that are in the directly higher timezone, those from the directly lower timezone and those in the same timezone as the transmitting node.

While nodes within the same timezone contend the channel for transmission, the adjacent zone owns the slot for reception and nodes in further timezones are in sleep mode, to prevent possibilities of packet collisions due to HTPs. Packets traveling in each of the above directions are respectively enqueued separately in 3 small FIFO buffers. Packets are then dequeued according to the current slot time in the V-table. The total length of the V-table is equal to the length of a single frame while each small rectangle depicted in Figure 2 represents a time slot. It supports consecutive transmission of 4 timezones and therefore it consists of $4 \times 2 + 1$ timeslots: 4 timeslots for upstream transmission, 4 timeslots for downstream transmission, and 1 timeslot for local broadcast. Replicating the same table allows scheduling packet transmission for nodes located more than 4 hops away from the PAN coordinator. In general, the allocation of upstream, downstream, and local broadcast transmissions in a symmetric network of N zones requires $N \times 2 + 1$ timeslots per frame. We refer to [14] for more information about the V scheduling table, the optimal number of slots in a table an how to access it.

4   Optimization Techniques

This section describes three energy saving V-route based optimization techniques for beaconless 802.15.4. The techniques are presented in an incremental manner: *Each optimization uses the previous optimization in addition to a new energy saving technique.*

1. **Transceiver Sleep Policy:** This optimization regards the powering down of the transceiver at the transmitter and receiver sides. Recall that in V-route, packets of upstream, downstream and local broadcast communication are enqueued in 3 distinctive FIFO buffers. At the transmitter side, rather than waiting for the end of the allocated transmission slot before powering down the radio, we allow the transmitter's radio to be turned off right after the last packet transmission from the appropriate queue is acknowledged successfully. In addition, we provide each packet with a check-bit that is set to one if the packet being transmitted is the last in the sender buffer. This allows the receiver to turn off the radio immediately after the last packet in the queue is received correctly and the acknowledgment is sent. Enabling the transceiver sleep policy optmises the activity time both at transmitter and receiver sides according to the node data traffic.

2. **V-Route Short CSMA:** This optimization regards the 802.15.4 idle listening. With the CSMA-CA used by 802.15.4, a node with a packet to transmit

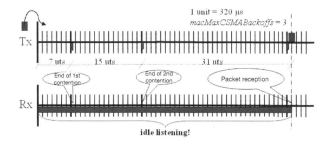

Fig. 4. Receiver idle listening of the CSMA period in 802.15.4

at time t picks up a time between t and $t + 2^{BE-1} units (1 unit = 320 \mu sec)$ where BE is the backoff exponent. The protocol provides a variable, namely $macMaxCSMABackoffs$, that regulates the number of packet retransmissions, which the standard 802.15.4 configuration sets to 3. This means that a transmitter can assess the channel 3 times consecutively after which it declares access failure and the packet is dropped. Although the backoff period is effectively used to increase the data rate in protocols such as IEEE 802.11, it is known to cause long period of idle listening at the receiver. On the other hand, decreasing the backoff period would adversely affect the reliability. To explain the CSMA idle listening of 802.15.4, Figure 4 shows how nodes in receiving zones would need to keep listening on the channel for at least 53.5 units (*53 units for CSMA and 1/2 units for CCA*), in order to catch a possibly late packet transmission and even if no packet is being transmitted.

Notifying V-route to re-schedule the packet in the next frame if a channel access failure occurs can solve this issue. Figure 5 shows how adding a function call, namely *V-Route Handle*, into the 802.15.4 code allows notifying V-Route of a channel access failure. Subsequently V-Route will be responsible for rescheduling the packet transmission in the next frame. This optimization allows the number of backoffs, $macMaxCSMABackoffs$, to be set to 0, hence reducing the receiver idle listening from 53 to 8 units of time (7 for CSMA and 1 for CCA). This translates in a reduction of receiver idle listening from $17.2ms$ to $2.56ms$. The number of packet retransmissions before transmission failure is now handled by V-route therefore allowing adaptation for example depending on the relevance of the packet itself.

3. **MCU Stand-by Mode:** This optimization regards putting the MCU in standby mode by availing of the V-Route zone activity coordination. As shown in Figure 7, some of our initial measurements at the oscilloscope of the beaconless 802.15.4 demonstrate that the current needed to power on the MCU can be greater than the current needed for the radio in transmitting mode. These measurements highlight the importance to implement coordinated duty-cycled activities also for the MCU, which is often overlooked when developing energy-efficient communication architectures.Using

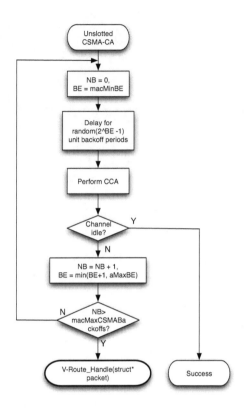

Fig. 5. The V-Route packet handling mechanism included in the unslotted CSMA of 802.15.4

CC2420 - Current consumption (mA)	
Listening	18.8
Transmit -25 dBm	8.5
Transmit -15 dBm	9.9
Transmit -10 dBm	11
Transmit -5 dBm	14
Transmit 0 dBm	17.4
Sleep mode 0	1
Sleep mode 1	0.02
Sleep mode 2	0.001
Data rate (Kbps)	250

ATMega 128 - Current consumption (mA)	
Normal	12
Stand-by	4.1
Power down	0.25

Fig. 6. The electrical node specifications measured at the oscilloscope

Low data rate: Energy per second (1 packet/m = 30 B/m)					
TxPower (dBm)	Etot (mJ/s)	Etx %	Elisten %	Eswitch %	Emmcu %
0	106.8393	0.0110	66.2767	0.0004	33.711
-10	106.8349	0.0070	66.2794	0.0004	33.7132
-25	106.8332	0.0054	66.2804	0.0004	33.7137
High data rate: Energy per second (10 packet/s = 300 B/s)					
TxPower (dBm)	Etot (mJ/s)	Etx %	Elisten %	Eswitch %	Emmcu %
0	107.5825	0.5890	65.9264	0.01738	33.4672
-10	107.3491	0.3732	66.0695	0.01742	33.5398
-25	107.2580	0.2886	66.1256	0.01744	33.5683

Fig. 7. Initial results of transmitter energy in single-hop 802.15.4

the scheduling of V-route, the MCU can go into stand-by mode in each time slot where the node is not scheduled to transmit or receive.

The next section highlights the performance evaluation of V-route along with the three energy optimization techniques for V-route-enhanced 802.15.4 presented in this section.

5   Performance Evaluation

This section presents the energy results obtained through experimentations on a network of Philips AquisGrain sensor nodes. Firstly, we specify the experiment configuration and related performance metrics. We then present the comprehensive results for V-route over 802.15.4 and plain 802.15.4 for both star network and multihop network environments.

5.1   Metrics and Setup

V-route is validated by the **node energy consumption per second** metric considering both CPU and transceiver consumptions. In order to include diverse application scenarios, we set 3 different data rates: (1) a low data rate of 1 *pkt per min*, (2) a medium data rate of 1 *pkt per sec*, and (3) a high data rate of 10 *pkt per sec*. Each packet transmission from zone to zone was acknowledged by the receiver. The length of the packet payload was fixed to 30 *bytes* while the length of each experiment was slightly more than 10 *minutes*. All the experiments were conducted in an office environment consisting of few rooms, corridors and people on their usual business activity.

The Philips AquisGrain sensor module includes a CC2420 radio transceiver (2400-2483 Mhz, 250 kbps, output power ranging from -25 to 0 dBm) and an ATMega128L microcontroller (4K RAM, 128K program memory). To improve the accuracy of the experiment we measured the node's consumption at the oscilloscope. The relevant electrical specifications are detailed in Figure 6. It is interesting to note that such values, which have been obtained by direct measurements at the oscilloscope in a Philips laboratory, differ slightly from the standard data sheet values though they do not affect the final energy consumption trend of the protocol.

The final energy was obtained by considering both transceiver and microprocessor consumption as they proved to be the two most consuming components on our nodes as shown in Figure 6. The energy calculation was achieved by timestamping each time the transceiver changed a state and then by incrementing 4 variables that held sleeping, receiving, transmitting and switching times. Such times were then periodically transmitted to the PAN coordinator, which was connected to a PC, that estimates the energy by using the values in Figure 6. Rather than calculating the energy directly at the sensor, this method proved to be largely more accurate due to difficulty of handling 64-bit variables at the node.

An important setup aspect is to calculate the minimum slot length to allow accommodating at least one packet transmission. In 802.15.4, the packet length varies depending on the data carried, with a payload that may vary from 0 to 127 *bytes*, always prefixed with 6 *bytes* of preamble and header. This makes a maximum packet length of 135 *bytes* which are transmitted in 4.256 *ms* at 250 *kbps* on 2400 *MHz* frequency band. Each packet is then transmitted with a prior CSMA-CA period of maximum 17.120 *ms* as described in section 6. This lead to a minimum possible V-route slot length of 21.376 *ms* plus a short time for packet ACK. In the experiments we tested 3 different slot times of 50 *ms*, 100 *ms* and 250 *ms* that allow transmitting 2, 4 and 6 packets respectively within the same slot.

5.2   802.15.4 Transmitter Measurements

The transmitter measurements are carried out in a single-hop environment consisting of a receiving node connected to the PC through serial port and 10 transmitter nodes. We set a high data rate scenario of *10 pkt per sec*. The experiment is repeated for 3 different transmission powers that correspond to the highest, the medium and the lowest possible transmitting power with a CC2420 chip. The goal is to identify the significant components that regulate the transmitter energy consumption in a high contention scenario. The results shown in Figure 7 are obtained by averaging the consumption of all the transmitters. The main interesting implications are summarized as follow:

- In contrast to common expectations, increasing the transmission power has an almost insignificant effect on the overall energy consumed by the 802.15.4 transmitter, as the percentage of time the transceiver is transmitting is very low. However, the transmission power to choose might be pondered taking into account that an excess of transmission power notably increases the chances of packet collisions and reduces the number of simultaneous transmissions in a multihop environment. This aspect may be a point for further studies.

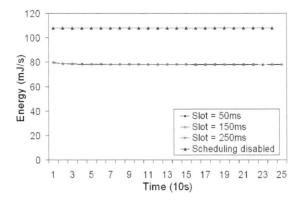

Fig. 8. Comparison between the energy consumption of a plain multihop-enabled 802.15.4 and 802.15.4 enhanced with V-route

- In spite of a high traffic condition per node, the transmission energy spent is almost insignificant with respect to the node's overall consumption. In fact the node spends a great amount of time in sensing the channel prior to transmission;
- Idle listening when no packets are sent and CPU energy consumption dominate the node energy utilizations. This confirms the 802.15.4 idle listening issue.

These transmitter measurements presented some relevant 802.15.4 drawbacks that will be addressed by V-Route and its optimization techniques, as detailed in the next section.

5.3   Energy Results

This section presents energy consumption results in a V-Route enhanced single-hop 802.15.4 network. These single-hop experiments compare a plain beaconless 802.15.4 to V-Route enhanced 802.15.4, providing us with energy gains achieved with the V-Table sleep scheduling. As shown in Figure 8, the node's energy consumption is reduced from an average of 108 mJ/s for a plain 802.15.4 to 78 mJ/s for a V-route-enhanced 802.15.4. This yields to about 27.3% energy savings.

In contrast to what we initially expected, figure 8 also shows that varying the slot time has no significant effect on the node's energy consumption. Clearly, by increasing the slot length we are in fact modifying both the active and sleeping slots and therefore the node duty cycle remains unchanged. Optimizations 1 rectifies this situation while Optimizations 2 and 3 focus on the 802.1.5.4 CSMA-CA backoff and microcontroller activity, respectively.

Figure 9 shows the improvements achieved with turning off the transceiver immediately after transmission of the last packet to a receiving zone (Transceiver

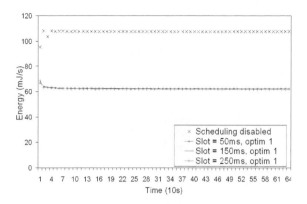

Fig. 9. Optimization 1: energy consumption results at transmitter side

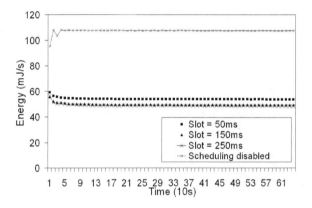

Fig. 10. Comparison of optimization 1 against beaconless 802.15.4

Sleep Policy at the transmitter side), as described in Section 4. The simple but effective optimization yields up to 42.9% energy consumption decrease with respect to having devices always on as shown in figure 9. This corresponds to additional energy saving of 15.6% with respect to the non-optimized V-route (when transceivers are kept on until the end of the allocated slot).

Figure 10 shows results of the Transceiver Sleep Policy at the receiver side, described in Section 4. The optimization allows 55.1% energy decrease with respect to having devices always on. This corresponds to an additional energy saving up to 12.2% for 250 ms slot time. It is interesting to note that by introducing the **Transceiver Sleep Policy**, we can now affect the node duty-cycle by varying the slot time. A longer slot time results in a smaller node's duty-cycle and therefore appreciable energy saving.

Figure 11 shows results from the second optimization, **V-Route Short CSMA** that reduced the 802.15.4 idle listening from $17.2ms$ to $2.56ms$. This

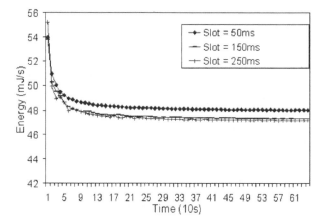

Fig. 11. Optimization 2 energy consumption results

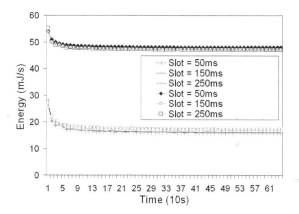

Fig. 12. Optimization 3 energy consumption results

allowed an significant increase of the 802.15.4 packet delivery rate. In contrast, the subsequent rescheduling of packets by V-Route generated an increase of packet overhearing. However, the optimization allowed further 1.3% energy reduction with respect to the previous optimization, therefore leading to 56.4% overall energy reduction.

Figure 12 shows results from the MCU Stand-by Mode optimization that allows coordinated **MCU stand-by mode**. The ATMega128 processor allows a 250 μA standby current that is restored to activity by clocking an external 32 KHz crystal. This optimization yields 15.9 mJ/s of energy which results to an extreme 85.3% overall energy saving. This is a further 28.9% energy saving with respect to the V-Route Short CSMA optimization.

6 Conclusion

802.15.4 intends to offer MAC and Phy layer capabilities for WPAN and wireless sensor networks. Therefore, it is key to understand the real performance of the protocol on typical multihop WSN scenarios. Furthermore, a major goal of this work is to build a routing architecture over 802.15.4 that preserves fully the protocol compliance. Initially this paper highlighted some key issues of 802.15.4 beacon-enabled mode for multihop networks. This imposes the usage of beaconless mode and a subsequent implementation of activity coordination among nodes. The paper proposes V-route as an 802.15.4 compliant packet scheduling and routing policy to enable energy-efficiency and high reliability in both single-hop and multihop environments. V-Route is allows enhancing the 802.15.4 with three energy optimization techniques. Experimentations of V-route yielded high data delivery rate and energy reduction ranging from 27.3% to 85.3% against a beaconless 802.15.4.

Acknowledgments

This work is supported by Science Foundation Ireland under grant 07/CE/I1147.

References

1. IEEE standard for information technology - information exchange between systems - local and metropolitan area networks specific requirements part 15.4: wireless medium access control (mac) and physical layer (phy) specifications for low-rate wireless personal area networks (lr-wpans), IEEE Std 802.15.4-2003, 1–670 (2003)
2. IEEE standard for information technology - information exchange between systems- local and metropolitan area networks- specific requirements part 15.4: Wireless medium access control (mac) and physical layer (phy) specifications for low-rate wireless personal area networks (wpans), IEEE Std 802.15.4-2006 (Revision of IEEE Std 802.15.4-2003), 1–305 (2006)
3. Zigbee Alliance, Zigbee working group web page for rf-lite (2002)
4. Aoun, M., Schoofs, A., van der Stok, P.: Efficient time synchronization for wireless sensor networks in an industrial setting, pp. 419–420 (2008)
5. Benson, J., O'Donovan, T., Roedig, U., Sreenan, C.J.: Opportunistic aggregation over duty cycled communications in wireless sensor networks. In: In Proc. of ACM/IEEE Symposium on Information Processing in Sensor Networks (IPSN), April 2008, pp. 307–318 (2008)
6. Harthikote-Matha, M., Banka, T., Jayasumana, A.P.: Performance degradation of ieee 802.15.4 slotted csma/ca due to hidden nodes, pp. 264–266 (2007)
7. Johnson, D.B., Maltz, D.A.: Dinamic source routing in ad hoc wireless networks. Mobile Computing 353, 153–181 (1996)
8. Jurdak, R., Ruzzelli, A.G., O'Hare, G.M.P., Higgs, R.: Directed broadcast with overhearing for sensor networks. To appear on Transactions for Sensor Networks 2, 1443–1448 (2009)
9. Maróti, M., Kusy, B., Simon, G., Lédeczi, Á.: The flooding time synchronization protocol. In: Proc. of Sensys 2004 the 2nd Conference on Embedded networked sensor systems, pp. 39–49 (2004)

10. Moon, S., Kim, T., Cha, H.: Enabling low power listening on ieee 802.15.4-based sensor nodes. In: Proc. of WCNC 2007, Wireless Communications and Networking Conference, March 11-15, pp. 2305–2310 (2007)
11. Perkins, C.E., Royer, E.M.: Ad-hoc on-demand distance vector routing. In: Proc. of WMCSA the Second IEEE Workshop on Mobile Computer Systems and Applications, p. 90 (1999)
12. Petrova, M., Riihijarvi, J., Mahonen, P., Labella, S.: Performance study of ieee 802.15.4 using measurements and simulations. In: Proc. of WCNC 2006, Wireless Communications and Networking Conference, vol. 1, pp. 487–492 (2006)
13. Polastre, J., Hill, J., Culler, D.: Versatile low power media access for wireless sensor networks. In: Proc. of Sensys 2004, the 4th Conference on Embedded networked sensor systems, pp. 95–107 (2004)
14. Ruzzelli, A.G., O'Hare, G.M.P., O'Grady, M.J., Jurdak, R.: Merlin: Cross-layer integration mac and routing for low duty-cycle sensor networks. Elsevier Journal Ad Hoc Networks Special Issue on Energy efficient design in wireless ad hoc and sensor networks 5(8) (2008)
15. Suh, C., Ko, Y.-B., Lee, C.-H., Kim, H.-J.: Numerical analysis of the idle listening problem in ieee 802.15.4 beacon-enable mode, pp. 1–5 (2006)
16. Vyas, A.K., Tobagi, F.A.: Impact of interference on the throughput of a multihop path in a wireless network. In: Proc. of Conference on Broadband Communications, Networks and Systems, pp. 39–49 (2006)
17. Woon, W.T.H., Wan, T.-C.: Performance evaluation of ieee 802.15.4 wireless multihop networks: Simulation and testbed approach. Int. J. Ad Hoc Ubiquitous Comput. 3(1), 57–66 (2008)
18. Woon, W.T.H., Wan, T.C.: Performance evaluation of ieee 802.15.4 ad hoc wireless sensor networks: Simulation approach. In: IEEE International Conference on Systems, Man and Cybernetics, SMC 2006, vol. 2, pp. 1443–1448 (2006)
19. You-min, Z., Mao-heng, S., Peng, R.: An enhanced scheme for the ieee 802.15.4 multi-hop network. In: Wireless Communications, Networking and Mobile Computing, WiCOM 2006, pp. 1–4 (2006)
20. Zheng, J., Lee, M.J.: A comprehensive performance study of ieee 802.15.4, 218237 (2006)

Author Index